"*Winning Marriage* is a deeply reported and deeply felt insider's account of the marriage equality movement. Astute, committed, and fair-minded, Solomon's story chronicles the political sea change on marriage equality. Solomon is an authoritative voice, observer, and participant. This is an important history about how America is changing."—Bob Woodward

"*Winning Marriage* may well stand as the definitive political history of marriage equality. It's certainly the book that leaders of the movement deserve, and that latecomers to the movement need to read. After each new pro-equality court ruling, Americans seem to look around in wonder and ask, *How did we get here*? With this riveting, passionate book, Solomon has provided the answer."—*Slate*

"Solomon's deep knowledge and passion for the cause is clear . . . [This] narrative serves as a tribute to those who made gay marriage happen and as a manual for how to craft a successful political movement in the future."
—*Publishers Weekly*

"A great read for political junkies, giving the full blow-by-blow of the underdog effort."—*The Atlantic*

"Brisk, readable, and often exhilarating . . . [*Winning Marriage*] makes clear that parentage rights for this success belong to many."—*Huffington Post*

"[A] stirring movement memoir."—*Politico Magazine*

"Every now and then a book about current events reads like a high-wire suspense story. Marc Solomon's *Winning Marriage* provides an insider's view of one of the most urgent questions of justice and social policy of our time. Gripping, concise, clear-eyed, Solomon's work isn't only a welcome history, *Winning Marriage* is a stimulant to the continuing pursuit of civil rights."
—Gregory Maguire, author of *Wicked* and *Egg and Spoon*

"Marc Solomon's book is one of the most valuable I've read about the fight for legal equality for LGBT people. It is by far the best, and most accurate, of the accounts to legalize same-sex marriage. [Solomon's] narration demonstrates the crucial role that the intelligent, dis--------------------------------------ro-cess played in the successes we have w_____
—Barney Frank, former U.S. congress___

"*Winning Marriage* offers a front-row seat to the historic progress we have seen across our country. Marc Solomon captures a very important chapter in our movement for marriage equality and tells the inspiring story of more and more Americans deciding that they want to leave to the next generation a country that is more equal, not less."—Senator Tammy Baldwin (D-WI)

"It's hard to imagine a more thorough, lively account of the fight for marriage equality coming from someone who labored on the front lines for over a decade. Marc traces in careful detail the emergence of the first major social movement of this century in a way that will inspire activists on the side of justice and equality for decades to come."
—Chris Hughes, publisher and editor-in-chief of *New Republic*
and co-founder of Facebook

"This movement was years in the making, yet the speed and manner in which opinion on the topic has changed is breathtaking. Marc's ringside narrative of this achievement is inspiring and historic."—Chris Anderson, curator of TED

"Even though I knew where each chapter would end, I was drawn into Marc's detailed, carefully researched, and deeply personal account—and it left me wiping my eyes and pumping my fist."
—Dee Dee Myers, former White House press secretary to Bill Clinton
and contributing editor to *Vanity Fair*

"The recent and unprecedented victories we've seen in the battle to secure marriage equality would not have been possible without Marc Solomon. In *Winning Marriage*, he delivers a compelling and moving inside story."
—Eric Garcetti, mayor of Los Angeles

"Solomon's powerful account of this enormously successful civil rights battle is both an inspiration and a hugely important guide for strategists, organizers, and everyone else who seeks to take on the system and create what my grandfather called 'a revolution of the mind and heart.'"
—Christine Chavez, former political director of United Farm Workers
and granddaughter of Cesar Chavez

WINNING MARRIAGE

WINNING

MARRIAGE

THE INSIDE STORY OF

HOW SAME-SEX COUPLES

TOOK ON THE POLITICIANS

AND PUNDITS—AND WON

MARC SOLOMON

WITH A NEW AFTERWORD ON

THE FINAL SUPREME COURT DECISION

ForeEdge

ForeEdge
An imprint of University Press of New England
www.upne.com
Afterword © 2015 Marc Solomon
© 2014 Marc Solomon

First paperback edition published in 2015
Manufactured in the United States of America
Designed by April Leidig
Typeset in Garamond Premier Pro
by Copperline Book Services, Inc.

Paperback ISBN: 978-1-61168-899-3
Ebook ISBN: 978-1-61168-919-8
Library of Congress Control Number: 2014936578

5 4 3 2

For Mary Bonauto and Evan Wolfson
Tireless fighters both

The greatest weapon in the hand of the oppressor
is the mind of the oppressed.—**Steve Biko**

I know that you cannot live on hope alone, but without it,
life is not worth living. And you . . . And you . . . And you . . .
Gotta give 'em hope.—**Harvey Milk**

Power concedes nothing without a demand.
It never did and it never will.—**Frederick Douglass**

If you will it, it is no dream.—**Theodor Herzl**

Love recognizes no barriers. It jumps hurdles, leaps
fences, penetrates walls to arrive at its destination full
of hope.—**Maya Angelou**

CONTENTS

Illustrations follow page 220.

Today across America, you can marry whomever you love.

In countless speeches as governor of Massachusetts, I recounted with pride Massachusetts's role as the first state where that was so. It often got a sustained response because that truth, divine in its simplicity, was burdened with a past that was anything but simple.

Twelve years ago, the Massachusetts Supreme Judicial Court ruled that under the state's constitution, a marriage license could not be denied to same-sex couples. The whole country gasped, and pundits and pollsters held forth on the political hazards. What happened next was wonderfully unremarkable. The sky did not fall. The earth did not open and swallow us up. Thousands of good, contributing members of our society made free decisions about whom to marry. Most have been joyful and lasting. Some have failed. People just kept on being people, choosing their life partners by the same old mysteries. It turns out that gays and lesbians, like blacks and whites a generation ago, wanted nothing more than to be ordinary.

In fact, our court simply affirmed an ancient and even ordinary principle—citizens come before their government as equals.

It seemed anything but ordinary in the immediate aftermath of the court's decision. I was in the midst of my first campaign for governor then, and the question of marriage equality was hotly debated. The "smart" politics vacillated between condemning the ruling and being lukewarm about it, essentially urging that the decision be left to popular referendum. Most candidates—Democrats and Republicans alike—stayed within that narrow philosophical band. Because I believe deeply in the principle of equality before the law, I supported the ruling openly and unequivocally. Because I practiced civil rights law and am familiar with its history, I knew how constitutionally suspect it was to let a majority decide which civil rights a minority should have. And because I knew gay and lesbian people as friends, I knew how deep the yearning went to be treated like everyone else.

It was during this time that I first met Marc Solomon. A ridiculously tall, gangly fellow with a boyish face and anxious eyes that squint slightly as he listens, Marc led the effort to save marriage equality in the wake of the court's decision and efforts to undo it. Long before the national attitudes began to soften and other states followed Massachusetts's example, Marc, his small team of strategists, and his legions of grassroots activists showed how the politics of conviction, rather than of convenience, could make a new and better reality in Massachusetts. Then he took the campaign on the road to other states, and then nationally, to do the same. This is that story. And there is no one better to tell it than Marc.

Through these stories of challenges, setbacks, and triumphs—in Massachusetts, in other states across the country, and ultimately in the US Supreme Court—America has written a new chapter in its long struggle for social justice. That's why this is an important book. Just as these heroes take their inspiration from earlier struggles, ones that also seemed impossible at the time, the struggle for marriage equality provides a source of courage and conviction for future strivers trying to advance the cause of civil and human rights. As it did with marriage equality, this progress will depend on keeping faith with a simple and more profound principle—in America, all citizens come before their government as equals.

Deval Patrick
Former Governor of Massachusetts

In this book, I give the reader a seat at the strategy-setting and decision-making tables in the campaign to win and protect the freedom to marry in America. I begin with the battle to win and protect marriage in the first marriage equality state, Massachusetts, in 2003, and continue into early 2014, by which time we had won seventeen states and the District of Columbia, grown public support to nearly 60 percent, and seen the Supreme Court strike down the so-called Defense of Marriage Act. I tell the story of how we did battle with some extraordinarily powerful forces—the Catholic hierarchy, the Mormon Church, the religious right, and opportunistic political operatives on the right like Karl Rove—and how we've tipped the balance of power our way and won. We've endured plenty of setbacks along the way, and I talk of them too, while illuminating the pathway forward to finishing the job.

I tell this story by re-creating the most compelling parts of different campaigns across the country—how we've organized; made our case to legislators and governors; defeated lawmakers who have stood against us and reelected those who have stood with us; enlisted powerful and unexpected allies to the cause; mobilized same-sex couples, family members, friends, and allies of every stripe to step out of their comfort zone and speak their truth about why the freedom of same-sex couples to marry is important and right; and won the support of millions of Americans. The stories in this book reveal our movement's approaches to building power and achieving victories.

During my thirteen years of work on this battle, I've been actively engaged in most of the campaigns I describe in this book—first in Massachusetts as executive director of the statewide equality group MassEquality and most recently as national campaign director for Freedom to Marry, the campaign to win marriage nationwide. Others I'm recounting based on in-depth conversations with fellow marriage campaign leaders and advocates. I am also very mindful of the fact that I joined a movement that was years in the making, beginning in earnest with court victories in Hawaii in the 1990s. The efforts I describe in this book rest firmly on the foundations set then, as well as on all the hard work of coming out, sharing stories of our lives, fighting for our lives and those of our loved ones, and winning legislative and legal victories in the era following the 1969 Stonewall Riots.

The first two sections tell stories of legislative victories. The first section is about Massachusetts, the first marriage equality state in the country, where we won in court and then had to fight for three and a half years to hold onto the decision, while anti-gay forces from all over the country tried to take our victory away. The second is about New York, where we lost, our community strategically and relentlessly engaged in legislative elections to demonstrate our resolve, and then worked with a powerful governor, Andrew Cuomo, to move a bill through a Republican-led State Senate.

The third section tells the story of winning at the ballot. I begin with the painful story of Proposition 8, which took away the freedom to marry in California, and then depict how our movement came back; figured out the best ways to explain to voters why they should support marriage for gay and lesbian couples; rebutted our opponents' attacks; and won at the ballot four times in 2012.

The fourth section tells the story of President Barack Obama's evolution from reluctant opponent to powerful champion and the role that advocates played in helping speed up his journey.

The final section discusses our work during the period in which the Supreme Court considered challenges to California's Proposition 8 and the so-called Defense of Marriage Act. The focus is not on legal strategies but on advocacy strategies to demonstrate that America was ready for freedom to marry rulings.

Because I've chosen to break the book out into discrete campaigns, it's generally but not perfectly chronological. As a result, I include a chronology of state wins to help the reader keep track.

Perhaps the most difficult challenge with a book like this is that there are so many important stories I cannot tell. In Massachusetts alone, there are dozens of lawmakers—including some of our most committed allies—who don't appear in the book. And there are entire state battles, such as those in Iowa, New Hampshire, and Vermont, that I barely mention. Rather than writing an exhaustive account, I've instead chosen to highlight—in depth and with texture—some of the stories that truly capture our struggle.

My most fervent hope for this book is that it is helpful to those who seek to build and grow movements for social change in America and around the world. There are lessons to be learned from our fight—both in where we got things right and in where we didn't. Every battle is different, and every group and cause has different strengths, opportunities, and challenges. Yet I do believe others can adapt and utilize our most successful approaches to organizing, mobilizing, politicking, and communicating to build power and win.

To give additional perspectives to scenes and stories I was a part of, as well as to re-create efforts I wasn't a part of, I've turned to trusted partners in this movement. Over the past four years, I've conducted dozens of formal interviews with colleagues in the fight—campaign managers and strategists, elected officials, key staffers to electeds, lobbyists, attorneys, field organizers, donors, and couples who got involved in the campaign. These are people with whom I've been through battle, and I feel very lucky that they've entrusted me with their unvarnished accounts of events.

I use quotation marks in accounts where either the speaker or someone who was part of the conversation recounts the line as a quote. I also use quotation marks if a comment is from a transcript, tape, or direct notes. If there is dialogue without quotation marks, it means that it is a paraphrase.

Any mistakes are mine and mine alone.

Early on the morning of Tuesday, November 5, 2013, I boarded a flight from New York to Chicago where I'd catch a connection to Springfield, Illinois. It looked to be another big day, a winning vote in the Illinois House of Representatives, which would secure the freedom to marry in the Land of Lincoln, the state nicknamed for its most famous resident.

For the past thirteen years, I'd been volunteering and then working full time as a strategist and campaigner to win and defend the freedom of same-sex couples to marry, first in Massachusetts, then elsewhere in New England, then in California, and for the last three years, nationwide as national campaign director for Freedom to Marry, the organization founded and run by the architect of the marriage movement, Evan Wolfson.

This first Tuesday in November was a relatively quiet Election Day, with gubernatorial races in New Jersey and Virginia leading the news cycle. As I walked through the airport and glanced at newspaper headlines about the elections, I couldn't help but think about Election Day one year before and everything that had happened since.

Last Election Day, not only had the country reelected the first president who had stood for marriage equality, but we'd also won ballot fights on marriage in four states after losing thirty-three times straight. Then, in a two-week stretch in May, we'd driven bills through state legislatures in Rhode Island, Delaware, and Minnesota, and each one was signed into law by a supportive governor. In June, the US Supreme Court issued its monumental ruling gutting the discriminatory Defense of Marriage Act (DOMA), which made legally married same-sex couples strangers in the eyes of the federal government. The justices also allowed a district court decision invalidating California's Proposition 8 to stand, restoring the freedom to marry to America's largest state and sending the odious constitutional amendment—which had taken marriage away—to the dustbin of history where it belonged.

As I headed to Illinois, Evan—my boss and partner in the work—was readying to travel to Hawaii for the signing of freedom to marry legislation in the Aloha State. It was coming full circle for Evan. Twenty years before, he had served as co-counsel in Hawaii with a straight lawyer there, Dan Foley, in the case that launched the ongoing global freedom to marry movement. Evan and Dan had won the first-ever full-fledged trial in favor of the freedom to marry, only to see it overturned by Hawaii voters through constitutional amendment. That court case and subsequent loss at the ballot set Evan on a course, beginning in the 1990s, of criss-crossing the country advancing, to whomever would listen, a vision of marriage for same-sex couples and a strategy for how to win nationwide—some called him "the Paul Revere of gay marriage" for traveling the country saying "marriage is coming"—while also making the case for a well-funded public education campaign to grow support to the point where we'd be able to hold onto victories and build momentum. Having driven the cause nationally ever since the Hawaii breakthrough two decades before, it would be a sweet return for the Hawaii bill signing, particularly after Freedom to Marry had played a key role guiding the bill through the legislature.

Just two weeks before, at 12:01 a.m. on October 21, 2013, I stood in Newark City Hall as Mayor and US Senator-elect Cory Booker officiated at the marriages of the first same-sex couples in New Jersey, the result of a court order that superseded Governor Chris Christie's veto of marriage legislation. So in sum, in the last 365 days, there were a total of four ballot wins, eight new freedom to marry states with Hawaii and hopefully Illinois coming soon, and the DOMA law struck down to boot. It had been an unbelievably historic year.

For me, Illinois felt especially crucial. I was born and raised in Missouri, had worked for my home-state senator for a number of years, and had gotten to know the rural farming communities and small cities there that mirrored those in Illinois. The idea that gay couples living in those small cities would be able to marry in front of family and friends meant viscerally to me that we'd reached a turning point from which there was no going back. In addition, Illinois was one of the most important states in the country—the fifth most populous, with America's "Second City" as its hub. With a victory there, we'd have three of the five most populous states in the country and almost 40 percent of the nation living in a freedom to marry state, up from only 11 percent one year before, getting us much closer to a point where the Supreme Court would finish the job and rule for marriage nationwide.

The politics in Illinois were especially challenging, which made pulling off a win there all the more intriguing and rewarding. In the state where former Governor Rod Blagojevich had no compunction trying to sell off Barack Obama's US Senate seat to the highest bidder, and where four out of the previous seven governors had gone to jail, I shouldn't have been surprised that lawmakers from both parties were brazen in asking for money—and yet I was. It was never put as a quid pro quo for a vote, but Springfield wasn't known for subtlety either. It reminded me a lot of Albany, which was known by those who spent a lot of time there as a "transactional" state capital. Except in Springfield, the city Abe Lincoln had called home, the transactions were watched over by Honest Abe artifacts of every kind on every corner of the city.

I got off the plane in Springfield and deposited my bags at my hotel, the President Abraham Lincoln Springfield. The vote was to take place that day, but I'd packed for the week, remembering two years before when I'd gone to Albany for what was supposed to be a one-day trip, only to return home thirteen days later. Fortunately, I came back with a marker of the victory in hand—a pen given to me by Governor Andrew Cuomo that he used to ink the marriage bill into law.

I hustled over to the ornate capitol building, whose dome—taller than the one atop the US Capitol—towered over the city. I headed up to the gallery, where I ran into many of the advocates, lobbyists, and consultants with whom I'd been working closely. After handshakes and hugs, I took my seat just as the debate was beginning.

Illinois had been an especially tough fight. As recently as the night before, the lead sponsor of the bill had advocates huddling in his office discussing what to do if we were still a vote or two shy of the sixty "yes" votes we needed to pass the bill. And this was after we'd already pulled out all the stops, bringing together multiple groups into a campaign we called Illinois Unites for Marriage, employing a top campaign manager and teams of lobbyists, and building a massive field effort with dozens of field organizers mobilizing thousands of couples, family members, and LGBT people. We even had David Axelrod's old communications shop leading the media efforts. Gay Chicago philanthropist and leading Democratic donor Fred Eychaner had played a crucial role in funding and building the effort, and Laura Ricketts, the lesbian co-owner of the Chicago Cubs, contributed significant dollars and raised more. Even President Obama had waded in, urging his former colleagues in Springfield to pass the bill. All of this on top of years of organizing and public education.

However, there was one—and only one—person who could make things move: Mike Madigan, the seventy-one-year-old speaker of the Illinois House of Representatives, whose iron-fisted rule had stretched to twenty-nine years. Advocates could only get things so far without the speaker's help. Many members owed their seats to Madigan and waited for a signal or an "ask" from him before committing their support.

Finally, after many frustrating months of using every lever at our side's disposal to get Madigan engaged, we'd learned a couple of weeks before the vote that he had activated his lieutenants to count votes and had begun making the case to undecided members. As of late the previous night, the Illinois campaign's lead strategist told me Madigan had locked in fifty-nine votes with nine undecided. By the next morning, he'd secured sixty-one. With the votes in hand and Madigan moving quickly to the bill, it was a done deal. There was no better vote counter in the country.

I sat down in the gallery above the floor of the House of Representatives and looked down at the lawmakers who had begun debating the marriage bill. I turned to my left, and there at the end of the row was Marty Rouse, the Human Rights Campaign's national field director. Marty was my first boss in the movement, a veteran organizer and strategist who'd come to Massachusetts nearly ten years earlier to run MassEquality, the campaign to protect the marriage ruling in the nation's first marriage equality state. Marty had been an important mentor to me when I worked as his political director before taking the helm when he departed. As I looked to my right, in Speaker Madigan's section of the gallery, there was Patrick Guerriero, another one of my mentors from the earliest days of the Massachusetts fight. A former Republican legislator and mayor in Massachusetts before heading up gay philanthropist Tim Gill's political advocacy shop, Guerriero—one of the most talented strategists I knew—was now advising philanthropist Fred Eychaner's team on finishing the job in Illinois.

With the Illinois debate going on in front of me, two of my mentors and longtime partners in the work sitting on either side, and Evan—with whom I was emailing back and forth—prepping for a triumphant return to Hawaii, I thought about how far we'd come over the last decade. From zero states to what would soon be seventeen. From 37 percent support nationwide to what was now a solid majority. From national politicians running and ducking from the issue to a president embracing the cause and employing it to appeal to young voters. And from so many pundits thinking nationwide victory was improbable to so many declaring the battle already over (a bit too early for my taste—we were winning but hadn't yet won).

"Did u ever think 10 years ago we'd be here together for state #16?!" I texted Marty.

He just turned to me, gave me a big smile, and shook his head.

STATE VICTORIES, 2003–2015

2003	Massachusetts	Judicial
2008	California	Judicial*
	Connecticut	Judicial
2009	Iowa	Judicial
	Vermont	Legislative
	New Hampshire	Legislative
	District of Columbia	Legislative
2011	New York	Legislative
2012	Washington	Legislative, ballot
	Maryland	Legislative, ballot
	Maine	Ballot
2013	Rhode Island	Legislative
	Delaware	Legislative
	Minnesota	Legislative
	California	Judicial
	New Jersey	Judicial
	Hawaii	Legislative
	Illinois	Legislative
	New Mexico	Judicial

*Voter-approved constitutional amendment repealed the freedom to marry in November 2008.

2014	Oregon	Judicial
	Pennsylvania	Judicial
	Colorado	Judicial
	Indiana	Judicial
	Oklahoma	Judicial
	Utah	Judicial
	Virginia	Judicial
	Wisconsin	Judicial
	Nevada	Judicial
	West Virginia	Judicial
	North Carolina	Judicial
	Idaho	Judicial
	Alaska	Judicial
	Arizona	Judicial
	Wyoming	Judicial
	Kansas	Judicial
	South Carolina	Judicial
	Montana	Judicial
2015	Florida	Judicial
	Alabama	Judicial
	Arkansas	Judicial
	Georgia	Judicial
	Kentucky	Judicial
	Louisiana	Judicial
	Michigan	Judicial
	Missouri	Judicial
	Mississippi	Judicial
	Nebraska	Judicial
	North Dakota	Judicial
	Ohio	Judicial
	South Dakota	Judicial
	Tennessee	Judicial
	Texas	Judicial

MASSACHUSETTS

THE DECISION HEARD
'ROUND THE WORLD

November 18, 2003. Mary Bonauto, the forty-two-year-old civil rights project director at the New England legal defense organization Gay & Lesbian Advocates & Defenders (GLAD), left her home in Portland, Maine, at 6:00 a.m. It was a cold, clear morning as she got in her maroon Chevy Prism for the 201-mile drive to Hartford, where she was scheduled to testify on a proposed law before a committee of the Connecticut Legislature.

More than eight months earlier, on March 4, Mary had argued a marriage case before the Massachusetts Supreme Judicial Court, a case that she had painstakingly assembled along with her colleagues at Boston-based GLAD. So many had been waiting with great anticipation for the ruling, which ordinarily came within 130 days of the oral arguments. With this one, however, the normal rules didn't apply.

At 8:00 a.m., Mary had just reached Boston when her phone rang. It was Evan Wolfson, the longtime marriage advocate with whom Mary had worked for many years making the case for marriage equality, at first to a skeptical gay community and later to judges and the American people. Earlier that year, Evan had established Freedom to Marry, a non-profit organization driving a strategy to achieve marriage for same-sex couples nationwide.

"It's on the website," Evan said.

"What's on the website?" Mary asked him.

"The decision's coming out," Evan said.

Today was the day.

Mary, whose smarts, discipline, and relentless drive to win were packed into a slight, five-foot frame, had been GLAD's first civil rights lawyer beginning in 1990. For years, Mary had heard firsthand the heartbreaking stories of same-sex couples, some together for decades, who had to deal with indignities such as having blood relatives who had been out of touch for years swoop in after a death to claim property that the couple had shared for their entire lives, or needing blood relatives to rush across the country to make medical decisions because the life partner was not permitted to do so. She knew marriage would fix all of this, as well as serve as a marker of the full citizenship of gay and lesbian people for whom the denial of marriage was a powerful injustice. But Mary held off on filing a marriage lawsuit for years, believing the courts weren't yet ready.

After the victory in the Hawaii trial court in 1996, Mary knew the time was right. She wasn't deterred by the fact that Hawaii voters in 1998 approved a constitutional amendment undoing the decision and giving the Legislature the power to restrict gay couples from marrying. The Hawaii ruling also triggered Congress to pass the so-called Defense of Marriage Act in 1996, by the overwhelming margins of 342 to 67 in the House of Representatives and 85 to 14 in the Senate. It was signed into law immediately by President Bill Clinton. That law established that the federal government would not respect the marriages of same-sex couples performed in a state where it was legal.

Ever the meticulous lawyer, Mary's assessment was that of the six New England states she worked on, Vermont made the most sense to go first, due to a combination of the political legwork that had already been done and the relative difficulty to amend the state Constitution to undo a ruling. So she worked with two Vermont attorneys to identify three same-sex couples to apply for marriage licenses in 1997. When they were denied, the attorneys filed a suit on their behalf. Two years later, the Vermont Supreme Court ruled unanimously that the state's prohibition on marriage for same-sex couples violated the Vermont Constitution. It ordered the Vermont Legislature to either extend marriage laws or create a separate status that provided all of the state benefits and protections.

The outcry in Vermont from our opponents was powerful. Lawmakers quickly took marriage off the table and instead settled on a new status called "civil union," which offered benefits and protections to gay couples but not the status of marriage. In the following elections, what became known as the "Take Back Vermont" movement organized campaigns against lawmakers who voted for the civil union law and defeated sixteen. This defeat gave the GOP control of the state's House of Representatives for the first time in sixteen years.

Following the Vermont ruling, Mary Bonauto went right to work on a marriage case in Massachusetts. By April 2001, she was ready. Seven carefully vetted same-sex couples went to their town clerks to apply for marriage licenses. Each was denied. And on their behalf, Mary filed *Goodridge et al. v. Department of Public Health*, named for the lead plaintiffs, Julie and Hillary Goodridge. In oral argument, Mary explicitly repudiated civil unions, stating, "One of the most important protections of marriage is the word because the word is what conveys the status that everyone understands is the ultimate expression of love and commitment."

=

After receiving Evan's call, Mary pulled off the highway, told those expecting her in Hartford that she wouldn't be able to make it, and instead headed to GLAD's office in downtown Boston. Shortly before ten, Mary walked along Boston's famous Freedom Trail to the historic John Adams Courthouse, named for the author of the Massachusetts Constitution, to pick up a copy of the opinion. Although opinions posted instantaneously to the court's website at ten, Mary didn't want to stand around a computer with a bunch of others and scroll through it. She wanted to have a hard copy of the opinion handed to her in the way she was accustomed to, and wanted her own private moment looking at it.

By the time she arrived, the opinions were already being handed out. She took one and opened to the middle, to where she thought the ruling would be, and began reading. Her heart sank. It looked like a loss. But then she realized she was reading a dissenting opinion. She skipped to an earlier page, found the majority opinion, and realized that it was a full win by a 4–3 decision. It took her breath away.

=

That morning, New England Cable News (NECN) called me and asked if I'd provide live commentary as the decision came in. For the past three years, I had been an active volunteer and, during one intensive period, a paid lobbyist, for the Massachusetts Freedom to Marry Coalition, a grassroots group advocating for marriage for same-sex couples. I was thirty-seven years old, living in Boston, and finishing up a mid-career master's degree at Harvard's Kennedy School. I had made my way to school early that morning to complete an assignment and was wearing a flannel, black-checked shirt. I wanted to go home to change, but there wasn't time, so flannel it would be. I got into a taxi in Harvard Square for the ten-mile ride to their Newton studio. As my taxi pulled up right at ten o'clock, I called Gavi Wolfe, GLAD's public education staffer, to find out what the ruling was.

Hold on, he told me. Mary Bonauto was flipping through the decision at the courthouse, and they were waiting.

I waited, butterflies fluttering in my stomach.

It's a win, Gavi said excitedly.

What's that mean? I asked. A full win?

A full win. Same-sex couples would be able to marry in Massachusetts.

I walked into the NECN headquarters and was whisked into the studio, wired up, and then directed to join the anchors who were reporting live on the decision. They were confused about what it meant. Did it mean marriage, or could Vermont-style civil unions suffice? I said that, while I hadn't read the opinion, I understood it to be full marriage for same-sex couples, for the first time ever in American history.

Statements from political leaders across the spectrum began pouring into the newsroom. The anchors literally pulled them off the fax or wire and asked me to comment. I knew that opposition would be fervent, though the rapidity of response from some of the most powerful forces in the country was jarring. The White House immediately released a statement from President George W. Bush, who was gearing up for his reelection campaign: "Marriage is a sacred institution between a man and a woman. Today's decision of the Massachusetts Supreme Judicial Court violates this important principle. I will work with congressional leaders and others to do what is legally necessary to defend the sanctity of marriage."

Massachusetts Governor Mitt Romney responded with similar resolve. "I agree with 3,000 years of recorded history," he said. "I disagree with the Supreme Judicial Court of Massachusetts. Marriage is an institution between a man and a woman. Our Constitution and laws should reflect that," said the governor, who by the day was tacking to the right as he geared up for a possible presidential run.

Religious right groups jumped into the fray, predicting apocalyptic consequences. Dr. James Dobson, who headed up Focus on the Family, the largest religious right organization in the country with a $130 million annual budget, said in a statement, "The dire ramifications of what is happening in the United States and other Western nations cannot be overstated." The Catholic hierarchy, which until the recent sex scandal had near veto power over legislation in Massachusetts—the second most Catholic state in the country after Rhode Island—was apoplectic. Former Boston mayor and US ambassador to the Vatican Raymond Flynn, who served an informal mouthpiece for the church in Massachusetts, called the issue "a ticking time bomb in America for the last several months that has exploded in Massachusetts."

What was especially painful was that from those who were normally sympathetic to gay rights on the national level, we heard mostly silence or tortured attempts to rationalize their opposition. Dick Gephardt, the former Speaker of the House of Representatives from Missouri and then a long-shot candidate for president, spoke out in opposition to the ruling, in spite of the fact that he had a lesbian daughter. Our own senator, John Kerry, who was locked in battle with Howard Dean for the Democratic presidential nomination, reiterated his opposition even while trying to sound positive: "I have long believed that gay men and lesbians should be assured equal protection and the same benefits—from health to survivor benefits to hospital visitation—that all families deserve. While I continue to oppose gay marriage, I believe that today's decision calls on the Massachusetts State Legislature to take action to ensure equal protection for gay couples."

The only statement the anchors read to me from an elected official that was 100 percent supportive was from openly gay Massachusetts

Congressman Barney Frank. The decision, said Frank, "will enhance the lives of probably thousands, maybe tens of thousands, of Massachusetts citizens, and will have no negative effects on anyone else."

=

That night, the Freedom to Marry Coalition, GLAD, and numerous other groups in support of the freedom to marry that had formed a loose coalition called MassEquality held a huge rally at Boston's Old South Meeting House, the historic Quaker house of worship where in 1773 the Boston Tea Party was organized. It had served as a hub of rebellion for many years, from abolitionism to pro-Union organizing during the Civil War.

We reveled in the decision.

"The day in Massachusetts when same-sex couples could be excluded from the institution of civil marriage is over," proclaimed GLAD's executive director Gary Buseck to an enormous roar. Couples were singing, "Going to the State House and we're going to get married." The building was electric, the joy palpable, and the cheers raucous; a new freedom movement was gaining strength.

=

My path to becoming an activist for the freedom to marry was anything but a direct one.

I grew up in an activist liberal political household in Kansas City, Missouri, going door to door as a child with my mother on behalf of her favorite, usually female, candidates. Nixon was terrible, Reagan was very bad, Carter was okay, Ted Kennedy was better, and JFK was great.

Around adolescence, I started developing my own political identity, and it was to the right, away from my parents, to their horror. By 1984, I was seventeen years old and driving my grandmother's old 1972 Oldsmobile Cutlass to Reagan campaign headquarters to volunteer, with a sticker affixed to the back that said, "Another Student for Reagan-Bush '84." I parked the car in front of our house, which had a large "Mondale-Ferraro" sign in the front yard. Our house was like the television show *Family Ties*, with me in the role of Alex Keaton, played by Michael J. Fox.

In retrospect, it was no coincidence that I turned to the right. In addition to being an adolescent rebellion against my parents' political views, I think my shift had to do with my recognition that I was gay and desperately didn't want to be. I was casting about for anything I could come up with to prove to myself that I wasn't really gay. If I were a Republican, so my thinking went, that was a sign I was tough, not weak, and straight, not gay. Horseback-riding, Russia-hating Ronald Reagan was the embodiment of the strength and toughness that I thought would provide an antidote to what I was hoping beyond hope wasn't actually my sexual orientation.

I have a pretty stubborn and determined make-up, and so I stuck to my guns, both my Republicanism and unwillingness to accept that I was gay. My junior year at Yale, I teamed up with two college friends to form "Connecticut Students for Dole," organizing college students from throughout Connecticut to travel to New Hampshire and stump for the Kansas senator, who was running for the 1988 Republican presidential nomination. Even though Dole lost to Reagan's vice president, George H. W. Bush, I was rewarded with an internship in Dole's leadership office in the US Capitol the summer after my junior year. It was exhilarating being in one of DC's epicenters of power, watching the senators I read about coming in and out for strategy meetings. I was also asked to serve as an alternate delegate from Connecticut to the Republican National Convention in New Orleans, where I cheered as Vice President Bush said, "Read my lips, no new taxes," and as President Ronald Reagan gave his farewell address to adoring fans, of whom I was one.

Following college, I returned to Capitol Hill in 1989 and went to work as a policy adviser, this time for my home state senator, Republican Jack Danforth of Missouri. When Clinton took the White House in 1992, I began to recognize that I was more in sync with him ideologically than I was with Danforth and other Republicans on the Hill. That said, I liked Danforth a great deal, especially his willingness to think things through for himself and let the chips fall where they may, rather than following a rigorous party line.

In DC, I attempted other ways to repress or change my sexuality—dating women, engaging in Freudian psychoanalysis (many analysts who were classically trained at places like Harvard and Yale still offered up hope that analysis could change one's orientation), and trying observant Judaism. But none of it made any difference at all, and the agony of denying—actually trying to crush—an essential part of myself became too much to bear and, I had come to know, pointless. So at the age of thirty, I decided it was time to accept and begin to embrace my sexuality. I began dating men and telling the important people in my life that I was gay.

I left DC and moved to St. Louis to rejoin Danforth, who had retired from the Senate, to help him launch a region-wide civic revitalization venture called St. Louis 2004. It was during that time that I had an experience that more than anything propelled me into marriage equality advocacy work and helped shift my politics leftward back to my family's roots. I was selected to participate in a fellowship called Next Generation Leadership, or NGL for short, sponsored by the Rockefeller Foundation. It brought cohorts of advocates together a half dozen times over the course of two years to probe different challenges facing democracy. We went to Mississippi for four days to discuss inequality and race, to Los Angeles to focus on immigration, and to South Africa to explore a newly emerging democracy with its profoundly difficult history and its struggles with the AIDS epidemic.

In my cohort were advocates in policy areas such as immigration reform, gun safety, economic inequality, youth empowerment, labor rights, indigenous people's rights, and more. This group of people supported me, as friends and allies, as I came out as a gay man and challenged me to think hard about how the discrimination I endured as a gay man and the path I'd put myself on to try to deny who I was, was similar to the discrimination and oppression that other groups of people endure. It sunk in, and I recognized that my fight was against oppression—both my own and others'.

I moved to Boston to go to graduate school and spent some time figuring out how to integrate my sexuality and now transformed political ideology into my life. I read about an all-volunteer group called the Freedom to Marry Coalition of Massachusetts and began going to their meetings. It was one of the many grassroots groups that had been inspired by the Hawaii ruling and by Evan Wolfson's call to action to build support for marriage equality. They had speakers bureaus to make the case in houses of worship and community centers, attended pride celebrations around the state to build support within the LGBT community, and most interestingly to me advocated for marriage equality to legislators, something from which most established gay groups shied far away.

By the time GLAD filed the *Goodridge* suit in April 2001, I was hooked. Culturally, marriage was a rite of passage in our society. Not everyone needed to marry, but to be denied the opportunity meant that your fundamental humanity was being disrespected. If we could get the government to respect the inherent dignity and equality of gay people as expressed through how the government treats our committed relationships, we'd be fundamentally bettering the lives of LGBT people—both today's couples and LGBT young people who would have a vision of what their own future could be that offered up more possibilities and hope than my own did.

My political work to date had been middle-of-the-road to moderately conservative ideologically. It was frightening to take on a cause that felt edgy. Marriage for gay people was something that hadn't hit the mainstream at all, even within the gay community. But I knew, at a deep place, how right it was. And if there was one thing I learned from my fellow activists in the Rockefeller fellowship, it was to be willing to accept fear and plunge ahead anyway. So that's what I did, stretching myself far beyond my comfort zone, and ready to employ the political strategies, organizing techniques, and a relentless determination to win culled over many years to drive this cause forward.

The *Goodridge* ruling gave the Legislature and agencies 180 days to prepare, specifying that marriages would begin on May 17, 2004. There were limited options available to our opponents to try to stop them. Leading Massachusetts Democrats, including the Senate president and the attorney general, argued that the opinion was similar to the Vermont decision and the Legislature could approve a civil union law instead of marriage. Mary Bonauto scrutinized the opinion, and she was positive that wasn't the case. It was clear to her that marriage, and only marriage, would suffice. So Mary didn't view that as a threat.

To Mary, there were only two ways that marriages could be stopped from ever happening. First was a lawsuit that would overturn the decision or delay its implementation. Since the opinion came from the Massachusetts high court, a state court intervention seemed implausible. The only case that could have a fighting chance was a federal challenge. The other option that Mary could imagine was Governor Romney simply refusing to allow clerks to issue marriage licenses. That, too, seemed implausible, but she had to be ready for anything.

In my realm—political as opposed to legal—there were two other ways to undo the decision: to amend either the Massachusetts or the federal Constitution. Without question, the former was much more likely, though groups like Focus on the Family were pushing hard for the latter as well. The good news for us was that amending the Massachusetts Constitution was a multistep process that would take several years. That process could not be complete until November 2006 at the earliest, more than two years after gay couples would begin marrying.

However, even if the process were drawn out, it wasn't especially difficult. There were two ways to go about it. First, an amendment could originate in the Legislature. If it passed the Legislature by majority vote twice—in two consecutive legislative sessions—it would go to the people for a vote. With a majority vote of the public, it would be added to the Constitution. The other way was through a citizen-initiative process. If our opponents collected a sufficient number of signatures—approximately 65,000—the amendment would be referred to the Legislature. It still had to be voted on in two consecutive sessions, but this time it would need only 25 percent support from the Legislature to advance to the ballot.

We knew we had a huge mountain to climb to prevent either type of amendment. At the time of the ruling, as we assessed the Legislature, we could count on about fifty out of two hundred lawmakers who were solid supporters of marriage equality. The rest were somewhere between skittish and virulently opposed. Getting a majority, let alone 75 percent, would be extremely difficult if not impossible.

And there was no time to waste. Ever since the filing of the *Goodridge* case in 2001, our opponents had sought to advance a constitutional amendment to preempt a favorable ruling. In my first foray into professional lobbying on the cause in 2002, I'd helped beat back such an amendment. Now that the result our opponents feared was real, there would be tremendous momentum. The amendment was scheduled to come to the floor of the Legislature for a vote in February 2004, just three months from now.

Our strongest opposition was the Catholic Church. Even though the church was in the midst of the horrific sex scandal that was centered in Boston, we knew that on this issue it would stop at nothing. The preceding year, the Vatican had declared that "there are absolutely no grounds for considering homosexual unions to be in any way similar or even remotely analogous to God's plan for marriage and family." It excoriated lawmakers who supported marriage for same-sex couples, stating that "to vote in favor of a law so harmful to the common good is gravely immoral." It was clear that the Catholic hierarchy in Massachusetts would be under strict orders from Rome to do everything in its power to try to undermine this ruling.

The week of Thanksgiving, the Massachusetts Catholic bishops struck back hard, instructing every priest in the state to read a letter from the pulpit on November 30 that blasted the ruling, calling it "a national tragedy."

Over the next month, the religious right—never a strong presence in Massachusetts—sent national reinforcements and began converging on the state. Focus on the Family organized five pastor-only gatherings throughout the state and invited thousands of conservative clergy members. By mid-December, we at the Freedom to Marry Coalition started getting phone calls from our members letting us know that they had gotten automated calls asking if they supported traditional marriage and telling them to push the 1 key if they did. Our opponents were apparently identifying their supporters around the state to get ready to activate them.

On Thursday, December 12, Senate President Robert Travaglini, the man who would preside over the constitutional convention—the joint session of the Legislature in which the proposed amendment to undo the decision would be considered—moved a civil union bill through the Senate while also asking for an advisory opinion from the Supreme Judicial Court as to whether that would suffice to meet the court order.

To Mary Bonauto, the meaning of the opinion was crystal clear. However, having the most powerful leaders in the state—the governor, attorney general, Senate president, House speaker, and even Senator Kerry—all strongly questioning the court's ruling was certainly an invitation to the court to change its position. She didn't think the court would accept that invitation based on how they'd written the opinion, but it was nerve-racking nonetheless.

Mary's nervousness grew when she read an article in the *Boston Herald* in which the famous liberal constitutional law scholar, Harvard's Laurence Tribe, speculated that the court might backtrack. "It wouldn't shock me," Tribe said, about whether the court would go along with civil unions in its advisory opinion. "It would disappoint me in terms of the question of whether the court has the courage of its convictions, but it wouldn't be the first time that a court has injected a dose of political realism into its determinations."

Mary knew how influential Tribe was. She immediately dialed him up. "What do you mean by this?" she asked.

"I do feel like I was misquoted," he told Mary. "And I do want to set the record straight." He volunteered to write a brief on the advisory opinion and enlist other constitutional law scholars to sign on.

On the political front, our opposition continued to organize. Focus on the Family's affiliated state group, the Massachusetts Family Institute, announced that it was launching a political action committee to funnel dollars to candidates who supported a constitutional amendment to undo the ruling, with the thinly veiled threat of promising to try to knock out those in opposition. And three days before Christmas, the Massachusetts Catholic Conference—the public policy arm of the Catholic hierarchy—announced it was joining forces with the religious right in a unified campaign called the "Coalition for Marriage."

This was unusual, as the Catholic brand of Christianity was far different from the fundamentalism practiced by the religious right. With Ron Crews, the head of the Massachusetts Family Institute, serving as spokesperson, they promised an all-out grassroots and media campaign in support of the constitutional amendment.

While our opponents appeared strong and organized, the group of organizations working on the political front to protect the decision was not. Several on our side, including my group the Freedom to Marry Coalition, had been meeting under a loose confederation called Mass-Equality for several years. However, between our groups, there was only a handful of full-time staff members focused on protecting the decision. Even more concerning, there were ideological and turf conflicts that led to a real lack of trust among the organizations and an inability to agree on a course of action. When I first began attending MassEquality meetings, I was shocked at the level of acrimony between leaders who were all ostensibly working for the same thing.

We were like a small country watching, almost paralyzed, as an American-style military was surrounding it, getting ready to pounce. I put in writing a plea to the leaders of the groups that made up Mass-Equality that we would have to strengthen the entity and turn it into a real campaign organization if we were to have any hope of combatting our opponents. Thankfully, others agreed. So the MassEquality coalition decided to hire a political operative to build and manage a campaign to defend the marriage decision from constitutional amendment.

MassEquality settled on Marty Rouse, a gay man and seasoned campaign operative who had most recently been working for the Democrats in Vermont to clean up the electoral wreckage after civil unions had passed. Marty's strength was in grassroots field campaigns and electoral strategy. He hit the ground running, in what I soon learned was his trademark frenzied mode. How many names do you have? How many e-mail addresses? How many per district? He asked lots of questions like these in his rapid-fire style. He clearly had a sense of the overwhelming force that was about to come after us in the Legislature at the February constitutional convention and was trying to untangle what the different organizations on the ground on our side could produce.

In January 2004, I finished up my program at the Kennedy School and took a full-time job as legislative director of the Freedom to Marry Coalition. Since the decision in November, I'd been doing the work as a volunteer for more than forty hours a week. Now I could dedicate myself to the battle full time. I offered to help Marty in every way possible, knowing that the groups that made up MassEquality had to work together as seamlessly as possible if we were to have a chance of stopping a constitutional amendment.

On January 8, the second day of the new legislative session, MassEquality organized a noon rally at the Massachusetts State House. We held it in the beautifully ornate Nurses' Hall under the gold rotunda of the State House, and we made sure to pack the building. One of our great advantages was that, unlike most states, the Massachusetts capitol was in the heart of our largest city, with a large concentration of LGBT people and progressive allies. We knew plenty of them could cut away for a lunchtime rally, so we scheduled it for noon. More than 1,000 people showed up, far outnumbering a previous day's rally held by our opponents.

It was an impressive debut. Phil Johnston, the Massachusetts Democratic Party chairman and longtime friend of the Kennedy family, promised to help lobby what was the most Democratic Legislature in the country against the amendment. The Reverend George Wells, a straight Episcopal priest from Brockton and a founder of the Religious Coalition for the Freedom to Marry, gave a galvanizing speech, proclaiming in his booming voice, "Let freedom ring!"

The largest round of applause was reserved for the two women whose names would be forever affixed to the cause, Hillary and Julie Goodridge, the lead plaintiffs. Hillary expressed the optimistic view, which I felt as well, that the freedom to marry would prevail in Massachusetts. Why?

"Because love always prevails," she said.

Our worst-case scenario, one that was realistic, was that a constitutional amendment would pass overwhelmingly during that legislative session; that our opponents would defeat some of the lawmakers who voted our way in the 2004 elections, as they had in Vermont; and that the Legislature would approve the amendment a second time in 2005, setting up a referendum in November 2006 on whether or not to undo the marriage decision. And if it got to the ballot, who knew what would happen? Our track record on LGBT matters at the ballot wasn't especially good, and our opponents knew how to sow doubts about gay people in voters' minds. If they followed through on the ruthless campaign they'd promised, I feared it could put a serious damper on our movement nationwide. The narrative of liberal Massachusetts rejecting marriage for gay people—with legislative supporters getting defeated at the polls—would be difficult to overcome.

Our MassEquality team of lobbyists, led by Arline Isaacson—the co-chair of the Massachusetts Gay and Lesbian Political Caucus and a fixture in the State House advocating for our community for many years—provided a target list of lawmakers who they believed would be the most likely to come our way. We at the Freedom to Marry Coalition were focused on getting the membership of all the MassEquality coalition partners to contact their legislators. Not surprisingly, most of them lived in progressive parts of the state where lawmakers were already supportive. In many outlying legislative districts, our groups together had only a handful of supporters or none at all. Marty Rouse contracted with a phone vendor that called hundreds of thousands of voters in these target districts. If they supported the freedom to marry, they were asked to express that support by calling their representatives. For those who agreed to call, MassEquality followed up with direct-mail pieces reminding them to do it.

Yet even with all of this activity, we knew that once the Catholic Church turned up the heat, we'd never be able to match their reach. On Friday, January 16, the church fired on all cylinders. For the first time since the death penalty debates in 1999, the four Massachusetts bishops held a joint press conference, explaining that they were undertaking an unprecedented effort to mobilize the state's three million Catholics and would mail an appeal to one million households. "This historic endeavor reflects the seriousness with which we take the need for the Legislature to give initial approval to the marriage amendment on February 11," said Boston Archbishop Sean Patrick O'Malley. "Will our efforts inspire more people to talk to their legislators, which in turn may encourage legislators to do the right thing? We hope so. The stakes are too high, and we will have to answer to God for anything we fail to do."

I was extremely demoralized. The church's lobbyists had deep relationships in the State House, and I'd heard that one of their lead lobbyists had already met with more than 100 lawmakers. Lawmakers told us that the bishops were calling them directly, putting the squeeze on and telling them that their faith demanded that they vote for the amendment. Other lawmakers reported being targeted from the pulpit in their home churches. And with one million letters asking people to take action with their lawmakers, how could we compete?

=

On Tuesday, January 20, President Bush jumped back into the fray, addressing the subject in his State of the Union address: "Activist judges . . . have begun redefining marriage by court order, without regard for the will of the people and their elected representatives. On an issue of such great consequence, the people's voices must be heard." The president continued, "Our nation must defend the sanctity of marriage."

=

The Coalition for Marriage began running radio ads that I found especially repugnant. One in particular outraged me to my core. A voice-over compared the silence of religious conservatives in the face of the "threat" to marriage to the complicity of those who didn't stand up to the Nazis. In the background a voice repeated, over and over, a butchered version of Pastor Martin Niemöller's famous quote about the passivity of German intellectuals in Nazi Germany: "First they came for the Trade Unionists, but I wasn't a trade unionist so I did not speak out. Then they came for the Jews, but I was not a Jew so I did not speak out. And they came for me." As a Jew and a gay man, this was infuriating to me on so many levels. But I knew I couldn't dwell on it. We had too much work to do.

=

In Boston, we could turn people out. But the state was full of working-class, industrial communities inhabited by Irish, Italian, and Portuguese Catholics and anchored by Catholic churches. That's where we were at a serious disadvantage. A new, more rabid group, Mass Voices for Traditional Marriage, began organizing rallies for January 25 in the socially conservative strongholds of Fall River and Springfield, as well as in Massachusetts's second-largest city of Worcester—all places where our presence was weak.

They circulated angry, vitriolic fliers: "Last November the Massachusetts Supreme Judicial Court ripped aside 2,000 years of tradition, common sense, the well-being of children, and they called us bigots if we disagree," said one. "The court ruled that two men having anal intercourse are just the same as a husband and wife raising children together. Two women are just the same as a mother and father. Only irrational or hate-filled people, they implied, could disagree."

In spite of our concerns about a fight breaking out, we organized a counterpresence at all three rallies to ensure the press would cover our side as well. And while we were vastly outnumbered—our opponents turned out about 2,000 people compared to our 300—we did get modest coverage.

A few days later, on February 5, just a week before the constitutional convention would convene, MassEquality held a lobby day in the State House, where we asked as many constituents as possible to join us and lobby their representatives. I joined our lobbyists in training hundreds of attendees on how to make their case and then sent them off to see their lawmakers, along with a form for each of them to fill out letting us know where their lawmaker stood.

One group, from the Boston suburbs of Medford and Somerville, went to meet with their representative, Vinny Ciampa, a conservative Democratic member of the House leadership who looked to be against us. Among the visitors was Carl Sciortino, a twenty-five-year-old openly gay public health worker who had announced a couple of weeks before that he'd be challenging Ciampa in the Democratic primary.

Ciampa hadn't noticed Carl was part of the group until they began taking seats in his office. He said, in his severe Boston accent, "Carl, is this your committee?" sarcastically asking if he were meeting with his challenger's campaign committee.

"No, Vinny," Carl responded. "These are your constituents."

The group went around and introduced themselves to Ciampa, told him what part of the district they lived in, and talked about why they were there. Some talked about how long they'd been in a relationship with their partner. One lesbian mom took out a photo. "This is my son David," she said. She told Ciampa how her partner and she had struggled to take care of his special educational needs. The fact that they couldn't marry, they explained, made it much more difficult and costly for the two of them to take care of him.

"Well, why don't you move to Vermont?" Ciampa asked.

Others in the group couldn't believe what they'd heard. He'd just told this family to leave Massachusetts because they were gay. They were appalled. Several people stood up and were about to storm out, until others prevailed upon them to finish the meeting. In the hallway after they left, Carl said, "Just so you all know, I'm running for office." Several people signed up for his campaign right there.

After the lobby training, I stationed myself in the cafeteria on the second floor of the State House and waited for the citizen lobbyists to stop by with their completed lobbying forms. The reports we were getting showed our opponents' tactics were having an impact. One couple met with Rep. Doug Petersen, a progressive lawmaker from the wealthy North Shore city of Marblehead, who said he thought a civil union "compromise" might be the way to go. If we couldn't hold Petersen firm on marriage, we were in real trouble.

=

That same day, the Supreme Judicial Court issued its advisory opinion on civil unions. In its 4–3 opinion, it stated clearly that marriage, and only marriage, was permissible. Civil unions would establish "an unconstitutional, inferior, and discriminatory status for same-sex couples," the opinion read. "Separate is seldom, if ever, equal."

Now it was clear to lawmakers that they had two choices: either back marriage for gay couples or back a constitutional amendment to take that right away. The ruling meant one other thing as well: given the lengthy process for advancing a constitutional amendment, barring a successful lawsuit, lawful marriages for same-sex couples would begin on May 17 for the first time in American history.

President Bush immediately released a statement threatening a federal constitutional amendment: "Today's ruling of the Massachusetts Supreme Judicial Court is deeply troubling. Marriage is a sacred institution between a man and a woman. If activist judges insist on re-defining marriage by court order, the only alternative will be the constitutional process. We must do what is legally necessary to defend the sanctity of marriage."

Even more harmful for our fight in Massachusetts was the response of Senator Kerry, who was now in the driver's seat for the Democratic presidential nomination. "I believe the right answer is civil unions," he said. "I oppose gay marriage and disagree with the Massachusetts court's decision."

=

The next day, the *Wall Street Journal* ran an op-ed penned by Governor Romney entitled "One Man, One Woman: A Citizen's Guide to Protecting Marriage." What happened in Massachusetts "cannot happen again," he wrote. "It is imperative that we proceed with the legitimate process of amending our state Constitution." Romney made reference to President Abraham Lincoln's speech opposing the infamous *Dred Scott* decision. "President Lincoln faced a judicial decision that he believed was terribly wrong and badly misinterpreted the U.S. Constitution. By its decision, the Supreme Judicial Court of Massachusetts circumvented the Legislature and its executive and assumed to itself the power of legislating. That's wrong."

I was absolutely floored. Comparing the *Goodridge* marriage decision to one of the most vicious US Supreme Court decisions ever, one that denied the citizenship of black Americans, was beyond the pale.

GLAD's communications guru, Mary Breslauer, had the same reaction. We could not let Romney publish this outrageous op-ed unchallenged. The plaintiffs had made multiple requests for a meeting with the governor but to no avail. Now they would go to the governor's office to deliver a message, with the press listening in, whether or not he was there to hear it in person.

The next day, seven of the fourteen plaintiffs, along with Mary Bonauto, showed up at Romney's office in the State House to ask for a meeting. Breslauer had given the State House press corps the heads-up that they were coming.

Romney's communications director, Eric Fehrnstrom, told the group that the governor wasn't available. So they began a quasi-news conference, and Mary Bonauto launched right in.

We're here because this is an important issue, she said.

It's important to us, to the plaintiffs in this case. And clearly the governor thinks it's really important, because he's writing about it and appearing on national television about it. He's talking about it all the time.

I think *Dred Scott* cuts the other way, Mary continued, referring to the *Wall Street Journal* piece. The court failed to see the humanity of a person, and that's the real lesson of that case.

As the plaintiffs proceeded to read their prepared statements, more and more press came over to listen. Suddenly, Beth Myers, Romney's chief of staff, interrupted them. The governor has had an unexpected change in plans, she told them. He will see you now.

The plaintiffs left the media in the hallway and filed into the governor's office, where after about five minutes of waiting in the foyer, they were ushered into a private conference room, with a long, thin conference table. Romney, dressed for the day's snowy weather, stood at the head of the table. Several support staff members joined. After requisite handshakes, they took their seats and Mary gave brief introductory remarks.

Governor Romney, with a stony expression on his face, said nothing and offered no eye contact.

Ever the optimist, Julie Goodridge had confidence that she could make some headway. Over the past few years, she'd been telling the story of her partnership with Hillary, their joy in raising their daughter

Annie, the challenges because they were legal strangers, and how marriage was so important to their family. Surely this family man, who with his wife had raised five sons, would be able to relate.

Now that we've gone through the court case, Julie said, we've told our eight-year-old daughter Annie that we won. It means so much to her and to us that we are finally going to be a legal family in the eyes of the state. Annie cannot understand why anyone would want to get in the way of that.

I didn't know you had a daughter, Romney responded.

Everyone in the room was floored. The details of their historic case had saturated international media and upended the political conversation in Massachusetts. Again and again, Massachusetts press had covered the story of how Hillary, not being considered next of kin, had not been granted access to Annie or Julie, the birth mother, when Julie struggled with complications at birth. How could the top elected official in the state, regardless of his position on the issue, not know this?

Despite his unfamiliarity, the governor showed zero interest in learning more. He asked no questions. Julie thought the governor treated her just as if she'd been a gnat: annoying but insignificant. She recalled meeting James Dobson, the rabidly antigay leader of Focus on the Family. Even he came across as more human.

Hillary thought provocation might get Romney to engage.

Why do you think your family is more deserving of protections than my own? Hillary asked.

Instead of responding directly, he talked about his sister, who was a single mother. It struck Hillary as an awkward attempt to show he understood that families come in many configurations.

The stone-cold, emotionless reception from Romney was enraging to the plaintiffs, but months of experience with politicians and a not-always-sympathetic press corps had trained them to always maintain composure. One by one, they politely but forcefully talked to the governor about their families.

Richard Linnell talked about his daughter Paige, whom he and his husband Gary Chalmers had adopted as an infant. It matters a great deal to Paige for her dads to be married, he told Romney.

David Wilson and Rob Compton talked about their blended, inter-racial family of five adult children and grandchildren.

I believe children should have a mother and a father, Romney said, again and again. To David, Romney was cold as ice, not anything like the politicians he'd dealt with who seemed to have a sixth sense of empathy and could find common ground even as they disagreed. David felt invalidated and dismissed.

David's partner Rob, a dentist, thought of the ads that Ted Kennedy had run against Romney in their 1994 contest for the Senate, highlighting Romney's history as a ruthless venture capitalist. Now he felt he could understand how a venture capitalist could just go in and fire all the employees of a company and not feel anything about it.

Mary knew this meeting had to come to an end. Julie Goodridge was crying, several of the other plaintiffs were teary eyed, and from her vantage point, Romney had swatted David down particularly harshly. Thankfully, the chief of staff announced the meeting was over. The governor had another appointment scheduled.

As they walked back into the foyer to exit, an exasperated Julie Goodridge turned toward Romney, looked him in the eye, and made one final appeal, parent to parent. "Governor Romney, tell me, what would you suggest I say to my eight-year-old daughter about why her mommy and her ma can't get married because you, the governor of her state, are going to block our marriage?"

"I don't really care what you tell your adopted daughter," he replied, once again ignorant of the fact that Julie was the birth mom. Looking toward her but avoiding eye contact, he said, "Why don't you just tell her what you've been telling her for the last eight years?"

Julie burst into tears. Never in her life had she stood in front of someone who appeared to have no capacity for empathy. It was kind of terrifying to her to be so vulnerable and share these personal stories with somebody who showed no warmth at all.

The plaintiffs were barraged by waiting reporters upon their exit, but it wasn't long before Romney called the media into his office. He explained that he had met with the plaintiffs in the spirit of cooperation.

=

One of the most painful elements of the battle for me was the fact that African American clergy were so strongly aligned against us. I believed that our fight was a civil rights struggle—very different from the African American fight for equality to be sure but a civil rights struggle nonetheless. Unfortunately, the most outspoken leaders of African American churches in Massachusetts didn't see our fight that way.

On Saturday, February 7, the three largest groupings of African American clergy in Massachusetts, the Black Ministerial Alliance of Greater Boston, the Boston Ten Point Coalition, and the Cambridge Black Pastors' Conference, issued a joint statement supporting a constitutional amendment. Rev. Wesley A. Roberts, president of the Black Ministerial Alliance, wrote, "I don't see this as a civil rights issue, because to equate what is happening now to the civil rights struggle which blacks had to go through would be to belittle what we had gone through as a people."

Bishop Gilbert A. Thompson Sr., pastor of the huge New Covenant Christian Church located in Mattapan, a nearly all–African American section of Boston, was much harsher: "To say there is such a thing as a gay Christian is saying there's an honest thief. Today, we look back with scorn at those who twisted the law to make marriage serve a racist agenda, and I believe our descendants will look back the same way at us if we yield to the same kind of pressure a radical sexual agenda is placing on us today. Just as it's distorting the equation of marriage if you press race into it, it's also distorting if you subtract gender."

In the State House, on the other hand, our strongest, most powerful voices in favor of the freedom to marry were those of African American legislators. Rep. Byron Rushing of Boston, who had formerly headed Boston's Museum of Afro-American History, was more than willing to take on the African American clergy. Responding to the clergy's joint statement, Rushing said, "Martin Luther King is rolling over in his grave at a statement like this. They are not acknowledging the responsibility that any people have who have been able to struggle and gain civil rights, which is that you have to then support others who are seeking civil rights."

One of the most outspoken of the African American clergy, Rev. Eugene Rivers, alleged that we were "pimping" the civil rights movement. I was asked to debate Rivers on the radio and asked Rushing for guidance about what to say. "You shouldn't say anything," he said. "Let me take this one on." His was a courageous, powerful voice.

=

The Sunday before the constitutional convention, the "Coalition for Marriage"—the alliance of the Catholic hierarchy and the religious right—gathered for a huge rally on the Boston Common in the late morning. Bishop O'Malley, the Family Research Council, Concerned Women for America, the Massachusetts Family Institute, and many other groups—along with thousands of people—joined forces at the rally. About 350 of our supporters gathered across Tremont Street at St. Paul's Cathedral, the home of the Episcopal Archdiocese of Massachusetts. Boston has a tremendous concentration of gay and lesbian Catholics and ex-Catholics, a good number of whom had attended Catholic school from kindergarten through high school. Many were outraged to see the Catholic hierarchy in bed with the virulently antigay religious right organizations, willing to put down differences in theology and unite in their homophobia. We urged our people to remain calm and stay away from the Common, but this was too much. Friends of mine crossed the street and screamed at O'Malley. My friend Ed Maclean, who had entered a seminary before coming out as gay, was outraged as O'Malley stood on the podium in silence as a religious right leader implied that AIDS was God's response to homosexuality. As O'Malley exited, Ed got in his face and said, "Hey O'Malley, you stay out of my bedroom and I'll stay out of your church." Another friend, Michael DiPalo, carried a sign in and out of the crowd that said, "Catholic by Birth, Homophobic by Choice." An old woman tried to rip it out of his hands and tear it apart, but he held onto it.

One man I didn't know held a sign about the sex scandal, attacking O'Malley for promoting pedophilia. Predictably, the news cameras honed in on it. I asked him to put it away, knowing that our primary audience was 200 lawmakers, the vast majority of whom were Catholic. He did so, grumbling. But when he took it out again and I asked him again, the guy railed at me: "Why's our side acting like a bunch of Nazis?" Tensions were high, to say the least.

Sundays were never going to be our day, so we prepared to have a final rally on Tuesday, February 10, the day before the Legislature met. The day started well, as the *Boston Globe* ran an editorial entitled "No to Discrimination" opposing the amendment. It concluded, "Same-sex marriages pose no threat to anyone but rather affirm a commitment of love, an emotion that is universal. . . . We hope legislators vote to affirm progress, bolster individual rights, and uphold the sanctity of a Constitution by and for all the people of the state."

We had once again booked Nurses' Hall in the State House for a noontime rally. We had been so busy getting people to weigh in with their legislators that our only publicity was via e-mail, and we had no idea how many people would show. But the turnout was amazing. When we hit about 3,000, the police stopped letting people in the building. Another 1,500 rallied outside.

Representative Byron Rushing fired up the crowd: "The drafters of the Constitution of Massachusetts in the 1780s did not know that you would be here today. Of course they did not. The drafters of the United States Constitution didn't think I was going to be here today," he said, to thunderous applause. Rev. Peter Gomes, the famous African American minister at Harvard's Memorial Church who had performed the benediction at the inauguration of President Ronald Reagan and who had come out as openly gay, gave a rousing, rhetorically powerful talk about expanding civil rights. We were on "the eve of an historic opportunity to do good or mischief," he said. "In this constitutional process, our legacy and our futures are at stake."

That day, we learned that Senate President Robert Travaglini and Senate Republican Leader Brian Lees were going to offer what they were calling a "compromise" amendment. It would define marriage as being between a man and a woman and create Vermont-style civil unions. They argued to us that we were most certainly going to end up with a constitutional amendment on the ballot and that it would be better to ensure that if an amendment were to pass, it would guarantee gay couples civil unions rather than leaving them with nothing.

We were getting pressure from many in our community to accept a civil union compromise. I questioned myself whether it was right to go for broke if that could mean ending up with no protections in the end. For me, single and reasonably secure, it didn't seem like a big gamble. But for couples struggling to get by and needing access to their partner's health insurance, it was a different story. Why would we fight for a word? I was asked this over and over. If our opponents were so fired up about marriage and willing to fight so hard to keep us from it, why not let them have it, as long as we received all the benefits and protections? I dialed up one of the people I trusted the most, my close friend Eric Garcetti, the now mayor of Los Angeles who was then a city councilperson. I'd gotten to know Eric through the Rockefeller Foundation fellowship we'd done together. Eric listened carefully and understood the pressure we were under. But his advice was simple. Civil unions are a legal status, a piece of paper. Marriage is about love.

"Fight for love," Eric told me.

That struck a chord deep within me. As a gay man who had struggled for a long time with my sexuality, fighting for my own authentic love was a fight to which I had come late, but that I knew was so crucial. From then on, no matter what political strategy or tactic was suggested, my position was clear. I was fighting for love, and that meant the freedom to marry.

That night, we held a candlelight vigil outside the State House as we prepared for the debate of our lifetimes. Thousands of people gathered, and the light shone as far as the eye could see.

=

Wednesday, February 11. The day of the constitutional convention had arrived, and the raw emotion could not have been more intense. We had asked our people to arrive early in the morning, before the State House opened at 8:00 a.m. and many hours in advance of the 2:00 p.m. convention so that we could stake out the areas where lawmakers would be able to see and hear us. Our opponents would be busing in their supporters from all over the state, and we figured they wouldn't arrive too early. But they were streaming in by 8:00 a.m. Before long, a capacity crowd of 5,000 flooded the building and security shut the doors, leaving the rest to hold signs and chant outside on this chilly winter day.

For as long as I live, I will never forget what it was like walking around the State House that morning. The building was packed, people on both sides of the issue jammed together, occasionally pushing and shoving. Small groups of fundamentalist Christians were sitting together, holding hands, kneeling, and praying, some with eyes closed and hands to the sky making noise, speaking in tongues. Some were loudly praying for us, putting their hands over our heads. As Mary Bonauto walked through the corridors, some followed her around, chanting at her in an eerie tone, "eeeevil, eeeevil."

While most were the older white folks who normally rallied against us, there were also many people of color—Latinos, Asians, and African Americans—who had come in groups. It was clear their churches had organized buses to the State House. Our opponents were wearing yellow stickers, while we'd branded ourselves in all-American red, white, and blue. There was back-and-forth chanting.

"One man, one woman. Let the people vote," said their side.

"No discrimination in the Constitution," said ours.

"Let the people vote."

"Let the people marry."

Security was trying to keep a pathway in the center of the corridors open, but they were having a hard time with the pandemonium in the building.

As loud and wildly intense as it was inside, outside it was even more vitriolic. The religious right from all over America had descended on Boston. One man was carrying a massive cross back and forth in front of the State House. Others were holding wildly offensive homemade signs. One said, "Sodomy: It's to die for." Another sign, this one held by a girl, said, "No sex is better than same sex," and a sign held by a young boy said, "It just isn't natural."

On our side, throngs of same-sex couples and young LGBT people for whom the prospect of marriage was now a reality were standing outside, chanting and holding signs. Many used the printed signs MassEquality had made—"No Discrimination in the Constitution"—while many others had homemade signs, with lots of rainbow flags in the mix.

That morning, Carl Sciortino—the gay public health worker who was running for the Legislature in Medford and Somerville—took the T (Boston's version of the subway) to the Park Street station in the Boston Common. He'd taken the day off of work to watch the debate live. As he climbed Beacon Hill toward the State House, a woman walked right up next to him and screamed "Sodomite!"

Carl picked up the pace and kept walking, but the woman continued screaming. "Sodomite! You are a Sodomite!" Over and over. Carl wasn't wearing anything to identify himself, and it wasn't even clear where he was going. Shocked and flustered, he told the woman to stop and continued up the hill to the State House. This was going to be intense.

Mary Bonauto began her day in a meeting with freshman Representative Barbara L'Italien and several other women lawmakers, making the case on marriage. L'Italien, a Democrat who hailed from the northern Massachusetts city of Andover, represented one of the most Republican-leaning districts in the state. She'd always thought that supporting civil unions was the progressive place to be, but with the court ruling, she knew she needed to support marriage. She'd gotten vicious phone calls, including a death threat at her home, and she was worried about how combustible the day might be. The mother of four young kids, L'Italien was especially concerned about the safety of her young staff person Megan, and so she brought in a cooler packed with food so Megan wouldn't have to leave her office. Mary and the lawmakers met in the ornate Senate Reading Room on the second floor of the State House, where they had a clear view of the front of the State House. Mary explained what the ruling meant and why marriage was so important—what the word conveyed.

For L'Italien, it was hard to concentrate with the roar of the crowd inside the building and wave after wave of people from the church-sponsored buses unloading in front of the State House on the outside.

"Yeah, I'm gonna be with you," L'Italien said, as Mary finished her explanation. "It may cost me my seat, but I'm gonna be with you."

The halls were completely packed, and the area outside the House chamber, where debate would take place, served as ground zero for the warring sides. After a couple hours of back-and-forth chanting, our side began singing patriotic songs, knowing that would put our opponents on the defensive. Would they join in? Would they drown them out? We sang "God Bless America," "The Star-Spangled Banner," and "This Land Is Your Land." We also sang civil rights songs, especially "We Shall Not Be Moved," for hours on end, substituting verses most applicable to our fight. "Go Massachusetts, We shall not be moved / Defend don't amend, We shall not be moved / Do the right thing, We shall not be moved / Let the people marry, We shall not be moved." That song will always be seared into my memory, reminding me of the power of our resolve.

Finally, it was 2:00 p.m. The Senate sergeant at arms, marching with top hat and cane, led the senators past the screaming crowds, their pathway cordoned off by rope, into the House chambers. The scene harkened back to the days of John Adams, who wrote the Massachusetts Constitution in 1779. Senate President Robert Travaglini marched immediately behind the sergeant at arms, and the thirty-nine other senators followed him.

What would happen next was unclear. We believed we had about fifty legislators who were full allies, opposing any kind of amendment. On the other side, there were certainly more than 100 lawmakers who opposed the marriage ruling and would vote for an amendment. But they would have two choices: an amendment that banned marriage for same-sex couples and replaced it with nothing and the "compromise," supported by Travaglini and Republican Leader Brian Lees, which took away marriage and replaced it with civil unions. There were a good number of lawmakers who followed the Catholic Church line and would not vote for a bill that included civil unions. And there were others who opposed marriage but supported legal protections for same-sex couples and would only vote for a measure that included civil unions. Our best-case scenario: no proposal would get a majority of 101 votes. In that event, the debate would end in a stalemate. The status quo was very good for us.

But that was not at all a likely outcome. It was clear, going in, that a solid majority of the Legislature supported at least some kind of amendment that would keep same-sex couples on the outside looking in.

First up was Senate President Robert Travaglini who presided over the convention and was preparing for a debate on the "compromise." As a courtesy, he recognized House Speaker Tom Finneran, the most powerful lawmaker in the building and a devout Catholic who was a virulent opponent of marriage for gay couples. The wily speaker shocked the Senate president by pulling an amendment out of his pocket and introducing it. It would ban the freedom to marry and replace it with nothing. Some on our side objected mightily, but the speaker hadn't broken any rules and so debate ensued.

Carl Sciortino had met up in the State House with a couple of his colleagues from work. They were down on the first floor, in the enormous Great Hall, where giant television sets were streaming the debate. The room was packed wall to wall with people, pro and con, sitting on the marble floor, watching and listening. They watched as Dianne Wilkerson, the only African American member of the Senate, was recognized. "I was born in my grandmother's house in a shotgun shack in a little town called Pine Bluff, Arkansas, having to do so because the public hospital did not allow blacks to deliver children at that time." The crowd in the Great Hall was silent, rapt, and focused completely on Wilkerson. She paused, tears coming to her eyes and, filled with emotion, she continued. "To this day, I carry the name of that dark and ugly history resulting from being almost equal. You see, Mr. President, it was the common practice of that day for the slaves to be given the surnames of their slavemasters." She explained that Wilkerson, like Johnson and Jackson, was probably derived from the name of an ancestor's slave owner. "I know the pain of being less than equal and I cannot and will not impose that status on anyone else." A smile came to her face. "My grandmother who is almost 100 years old and lives in a nursing home in Pine Bluff, Arkansas today would never forgive me."

Carl had tears streaming down his face. After the pain of hearing African American clergy proclaim that marriage equality was anything but a civil right, here Senator Wilkerson was challenging that notion powerfully and emotionally.

With the lawmakers in session and debating, there wasn't too much

organizing that could be done, so I'd been leading some of the singing for a while, keeping the crowd focused on patriotic songs. Later I
moved into the office of openly gay Senator Jarrett Barrios and watched
the debate on television with Mary Bonauto, Marty Rouse, and other
members of our coalition.

At 4:55 p.m., the vote was called on the Finneran amendment.

Barbara L'Italien knew that now it was real. She had no question how
she was going to vote, but as she pushed the "No" button and saw the
red light pop up by her name, she figured the vote would probably cost
her her job.

Travaglini took the rostrum to announce the result: "By a roll call of
98–100, the Finneran Amendment is rejected."

Holy shit. We'd survived. Just barely. But we'd survived.

Now Senator Lees, the moderate Republican leader of the Senate,
took the floor and offered the "compromise" civil union amendment on
behalf of himself and Travaglini. The debate continued.

Outside the chamber, the singing from our community grew louder
and more emotional. It felt like the singing was the only thing in our
control. I joined back in, and we kept going. As evening fell, our opponents began leaving the building, filling up their buses to return home
as scheduled. Many of them lived in Boston's exurbs and in smaller cities
and rural communities. So we now outnumbered them in a big way.

By the end of the day, not only had the Finneran Amendment gone
down, but the Travaglini-Lees Amendment had failed as well, by a vote
of 94 to 104. There continued to be a solid majority against marriage,
but with the dueling approaches of Finneran on the one hand pushing for the Catholic Church's position—an amendment without civil
unions—and Travaglini and Lees supporting an amendment that included civil unions, it was unclear if our opponents would be able to rally
around a unified approach. That was what we wanted—disagreement
where no amendment could secure a majority vote.

From our vantage point, we had survived. We would live to see another day.

Thursday, February 12. Neither we nor our opponents had planned
for a multiday convention. But with so many supporters based in Bos-

ton, we were able to far outnumber our opponents. The singing, which felt as if it had worked magic the previous day, began immediately.

On this day, the convention restarted at noon and turned to another amendment like Finneran's, which eradicated marriage and replaced it with nothing.

Sean Kelly, a thirty-nine-year-old, quiet, conservative Republican from the Berkshire Mountains, took the floor.

"Liz, this is for you," Kelly began, referring to his colleague, openly lesbian Liz Malia, who'd been with her partner Rita for thirty years. "Is she eight-tenths of a citizen? Nine-tenths? Ninety-nine-point-nine out of a hundred? Anything less demeans the spirit of Massachusetts it seems to me. If you believe that the love that Liz has for her partner is less than the love you have for your spouse, I would suggest that you're wrong. I think that this is really what this is about, is the judgment of love and the importance of it." The whole chamber was dead silent, and the only sounds were Kelly's voice and the singing outside. Malia was shocked and overcome with emotion. Tears streamed down her face. She knew Kelly a little bit; she sat a couple rows away from him and they used to visit and tell jokes, but they weren't especially close.

To the shock of most everyone, Kelly moved to adjourn the convention. And while that vote failed overwhelmingly, Liz Malia knew that the debate had been transformed. Her colleagues had talked about gay people in their lives, but no one had made it personal to someone whom they all knew. Liz gave Kelly a giant hug while others wept at the poignancy of Kelly's remarks.

Jarrett Barrios, the only openly gay senator, addressed the convention. He recounted a story with which he thought many of his colleagues who were parents would be able to identify. Barrios and his partner Doug had recently adopted two children, and the younger one had gotten very sick. "His fever grew worse and worse," Barrios said, his lip quivering with emotion. "I am a new parent. I did what my mom used to do. Sweat the fever out. Put a blanket on him. It kept getting higher. It was 104.5 when I called the hospital. I was very upset. My seven-year-old was screaming. I reached a nurse and started going into the symptoms. She said, 'Are you the parent?' The parent they had listed was Doug. She said, 'You are not listed. Are you married?' What ensued seemed like an eternity when my child with a 104.5 fever, I thought he could die on my watch, while I was fighting with a nurse over whether I was his parent or not." Barrios pointed out that most of his colleagues would never have to bear such indignities or go through such challenges.

On the other side, Phil Travis, the author of this amendment, reminded his colleagues of the danger he alleged they were in: "I will not let you get off the hook on the question of marriage. . . . You will not escape the wrath of the public who are calling you, who are writing you. They know the facts."

Vote for an amendment or lose at the ballot box, he was arguing.

Apparently, his colleagues weren't as worried, as this amendment failed by a vote of 94 to 103. We still held on, and we kept singing.

As day turned to night, many of those who had been singing on our side since the morning trickled out, and we needed reinforcements. I called over to the most popular gay bar in Boston, Club Café, and told the manager we needed more people. By 9:00 p.m., they came, steadily, and the singing was as loud and strong at 11:00 p.m. as it had been in the midafternoon.

Our legislative allies had gone into filibuster mode, knowing that if they could run the clock to midnight, the 200 legislators would need to agree unanimously to continue debate, something our allies would never do.

The clock finally struck midnight, and the convention recessed, this time for several weeks. For a second consecutive day, we'd held on. Our people were still singing, hundreds strong. Some of them had unfurled an enormous American flag and had been holding it over their heads for hours. As our allies came out of the chambers, our supporters offered thunderous applause and chanted, "Thank you, thank you." Many of the lawmakers walked through the crowd ebulliently, right under the American flag. It was an exceptionally moving scene. I gave Cory Atkins, a representative from Concord, a huge hug. Some of the legislators, such as Rep. Mike Festa, one of our leaders, kept saying, "No. Thank you." They clearly had been buoyed by the singing and the crowds.

The numbers were still weighted strongly against us. Of the 199 legislators (one seat was open), 137 had voted for one of the two approaches to overturn the *Goodridge* decision. However, there had now been two votes on each of the dueling options, and neither the straight-up ban nor the ban with the civil union replacement could get a majority. Could we emerge with no amendment? It still seemed unlikely but more possible now, two days in.

=

Around the nation, the goings on in Massachusetts were unleashing pent-up energy on both sides. The morning of the second day of the convention, February 12, San Francisco mayor Gavin Newsom announced San Francisco would begin marrying gay couples that day, in contravention of a state law prohibiting the marriages. At 11:06 a.m. in City Hall, pioneering lesbian activists Phyllis Lyon and Del Martin, ages seventy-nine and eighty-three and together for fifty-one years, were married. By the end of the day, eighty-seven couples were wed.

There was real debate about whether these marriages in San Francisco were a good idea. It was one thing to duke it out in Massachusetts through the courts and Legislature, but it was quite another to have a mayor essentially performing acts of civil disobedience. I thought it was helpful to open up a second front in the marriage fight, taking a bit of the antigay wrath off of us in Massachusetts and showing that the demand for marriage was omnipresent. But others, like Barney Frank, disagreed strongly and called it an unhelpful, feel-good measure.

A total of 3,700 couples married in San Francisco before the courts ordered their cessation on March 11. Local officials in other municipalities followed suit: Sandoval County, New Mexico; New Paltz, New York; and Multnomah County, Oregon.

=

Back in Massachusetts, the Catholic hierarchy was up in arms at the fact that they hadn't prevailed. So they turned up the pressure on individual lawmakers, some from the pulpit in front of their family and fellow parishioners.

The Sunday after the convention, Barbara L'Italien and her husband took their four children, aged twelve, ten, eight, and five, along with L'Italien's seventy-nine-year-old mom, to St. Augustine's Catholic Church in Andover, as they did pretty much every Sunday. L'Italien was very active in the church. It was the church she grew up in, and she helped lead the children's and adult's choir and was also a cantor. This Sunday, L'Italien would be cantoring and sharing the altar with the priest for the entire Mass. The priest took the opportunity to tackle head on the need to protect "traditional" marriage and referred to the failure of the Legislature to do so. He didn't call out L'Italien by name, but this was her hometown, her church, and lots of the congregants knew what was going on. It was extremely awkward.

L'Italien would never respond directly or create any kind of scene; that just wasn't her style. But neither would she back down from her votes and her position, which were in keeping with what, for her, the best of Catholicism stood for. So in her cantor role, she broke into her favorite song, "Come to the Table of Plenty," her alto voice loud and clear for everyone to hear: "God will provide for all that we need / here at the table of plenty."

To L'Italien, there was room for everyone at the table.

As the days went by, L'Italien saw the vitriol grow. She was getting furious calls at home and rude messages on her personal voice mail. And her kids, especially her eight-year-old, were hearing it at school from friends whose parents were upset with their mother's vote.

That especially bothered L'Italien, to have her eight-year-old taunted about her mom's votes. She and Kevin, her husband, sat the kids down and did their best to explain what was going on.

"Guys, Mom is there to do the right thing," she told them. "This really is the civil rights movement of the new millennium, and Mommy has the awesome opportunity to be in the right place at the right time and make a difference."

She tried to reassure them that it was all worth it.

"You guys are gonna read about this in a couple of years in history books. Isn't it cool that Mom gets to be a part of this?"

The next time it was L'Italien's turn to cantor, the priest was even more outspoken. He talked of the special obligations of Catholics who hold office and the profound disappointment in all the lawmakers representing Andover—Senator Sue Tucker and Representatives Barry Feingold and Barbara L'Italien, all of whom were voting to undermine the "traditional" family.

Tucker was Unitarian and Feingold was Jewish, so it was pretty clear that his focus was on the woman on the other side of the altar.

Like before, L'Italien was quiet until it was her turn to sing: "Come to the feast of heaven and earth! / Come to the table of plenty!"

L'Italien would cede ground to no one.

L'Italien's seventy-nine-year-old mom, a devout Catholic who lived with the family, at first had been completely opposed to gay people marrying. She simply couldn't understand it. By now, she'd evolved to a place where she could live with civil unions. Yet as the nasty calls came in to their home, she couldn't believe how many people were saying, "I'm a Catholic" and then spewing hateful, distasteful things in the name of their faith. She got into "mom" mode, protective of her daughter and grandchildren and just disgusted. Her eyes really started opening to what she saw was the hate that was behind the calls.

"Those people are wrong and they're hateful," she finally told L'Italien. "You know, you're right. This is the right thing to do. I'm so proud of you."

By L'Italien's way of thinking, her mother had had a bit of a baptism by fire, but if the woman who watched Mother Angelica's show on Catholic television and prayed the rosary every day could come full circle in just a few months, then anyone could.

=

On Saturday, February 21, the *Boston Globe* released a poll that had been done the week after the constitutional convention. Support for the freedom to marry was down significantly. In this poll, just 35 percent supported legalizing gay marriage and 53 percent were opposed. Right after the *Goodridge* decision, it was 48 percent in support and 43 percent opposed. I wasn't shocked, given the intensity of the protests at the State House. But it was a real blow. For it to appear to lawmakers that the public had moved against us didn't bode well for our ability to keep holding off amendments.

Even more jarring, on Tuesday, February 24, President Bush endorsed a federal constitutional ban.

Speaking from the Roosevelt Room at the White House, President Bush said, "Today, I call upon the Congress to promptly pass and to send to the states for ratification an amendment to our Constitution defining and protecting marriage as a union of a man and woman as husband and wife."

The president referred to "activist judges and local officials" in Massachusetts, San Francisco, and New Mexico who are undermining "more than two centuries of American jurisprudence and millennia of human experience." The president warned that "activist courts" could ensure that "every state would be forced to recognize any relationship that judges in Boston or officials in San Francisco choose to call a marriage." That wasn't the case; states weren't obliged to recognize marriages performed in other states. But no matter, it was an effective scare tactic.

So while we in Massachusetts remained completely focused on holding on to our victory, national gay rights organizations had to shift their focus to stopping a federal amendment.

We had another setback as well. While Senator Kerry spoke out against the president's call for a federal constitutional amendment, for the first time he embraced the call for one on the state level. "If the Massachusetts Legislature crafts an appropriate amendment that provides for partnership and civil unions, then I would support it, and it would advance the goal of equal protection. I think you need to have civil union. That's my position."

Kerry was clearly sensitive to the fact that Bush and his strategist Karl Rove were gearing up to use marriage as a wedge issue in the November elections. State legislatures around the country were preparing to put anti-marriage constitutional amendments on the November ballot, which guaranteed this would be a topic for debate. Having this debate centered in Kerry's home state made it especially easy to caricature him as a wild-eyed Massachusetts liberal. So Kerry sought to head off this line of attack by supporting the Massachusetts constitutional amendment that replaced marriage with civil unions.

While I understood what Kerry was doing, I sure didn't like it. If Kerry was behind the scenes making the case that passing the amendment was important to his presidential chances, he was making it much harder for us. And even if he wasn't going that far, his position gave State House Democrats cover to back the amendment.

During the several weeks before the constitutional convention reconvened, we went to work nonstop to persuade legislators to vote our way. We were hearing from too many that they had heard far more from our opponents than from our side. March 2 was the Massachusetts presidential primary, and we knew there'd be a large turnout to vote for Kerry. So we organized hundreds of people to stand outside nearly 100 polling places in important legislative districts throughout the state, asking voters to sign postcards to their lawmakers. I ran the effort, which was a logistical nightmare, but we collected 10,000 postcards to deliver. And we had the added benefit of running into members of the Legislature and their staffs and family members at the polls. We showed them that we had strong supporters living in communities all over Massachusetts and that we'd be relentless until this battle was won.

We also went on television with a nearly $300,000 ad buy making the case against civil unions and in support of marriage. We featured committed same-sex couples along with their kids. "If the Legislature amends our Constitution to take away marriage rights for committed gay and lesbian couples," the voice-over said, "they'll be made second-class citizens—permanently. Tell your legislator. Civil unions are not equal. Don't put discrimination in our Constitution."

The weekend before the constitutional convention reconvened for a final time, the Catholic hierarchy did a final push, delivering a video to be played in every church. It alleged among other things that marriage for same-sex couples could cause crucial benefits to be diverted away from the poor and elderly. That was without one scintilla of truth.

The *Pilot*, the archdiocesan newspaper, talked of the Massachusetts Catholic Conference beginning its first statewide voter registration drive. It would take place through parishes, with a strong focus on racial and ethnic minorities. "Legislators who decide to vote to harm the institution of marriage—either by allowing same-sex marriage to stand unchallenged or by creating civil unions—will feel a backlash in November."

By the time the constitutional convention convened on March 29 for the last time, one of the two amendments—the one with civil unions— had momentum behind it and the more draconian amendment had been shelved, the result of some smart strategic maneuvering by our legislative allies and lobby team. Our most vitriolic opponents—those who followed the Catholic hierarchy or Governor Romney—would have to vote to advance it or else no amendment would move forward. Our long-shot hope was that enough of the most conservative legislators couldn't bring themselves to vote for an amendment with civil unions. I was huddled up in Barrios's office with Mary Bonauto, Marty Rouse, and a handful of others watching on a small television and hoping that the amendment would fail. In the end, though, Romney urged Republicans to back the pending amendment and it was approved by a vote of 105 to 92. This meant it would go before a second constitutional convention during the next legislative session and, if it passed again, would go to the public for a vote in November 2006. Of the ninety-two who voted against it, about eighty-three were now with us on marriage, with another nine or so voting no because they couldn't bring themselves to vote for something that included civil unions.

Even though we'd lost, as we walked down to Nurses' Hall for a rally, I was feeling buoyed. We'd beaten back the most powerful lawmaker in the building, the House speaker, as well as the Catholic hierarchy, in their efforts to pass the harsher amendment. We'd shown that we had staying power far beyond what anyone anticipated. The vast majority of those who spoke, spoke up on our side and brought to the debate the best of themselves, speaking about the love and commitment of the gay couples they knew and the role of the Massachusetts Constitution in guaranteeing freedom and equality for everyone. Over the course of the debate that spanned a month and a half, we'd boosted our ranks of supporters by about thirty lawmakers, who had heard from their constituents and their colleagues about why they should oppose the amendment, had searched their conscience, and had voted to stand with us.

At the rally, we gave shout-outs to the legislators who voted our way. Over the course of the last two months, I'd gotten to know a number of them well. Barbara L'Italien, who had become one of my favorites, pulled me aside. "Marc, I think I might really lose my election over this vote. But if I do, I want you to know what an honor it has been to take these votes and to serve during this time." L'Italien's primary motivation for running was to improve services for children like her son who were autistic. Yet here she was, fighting for a cause that she hadn't anticipated, accepting that her electoral fate might have been determined. I committed to myself that we would not, could not, let her lose.

After the rally, I asked Senator Barrios if he would come outside with me to address the crowd that had chanted and held signs all day. He and I walked down the stairs together. "Marc, I am so sad," Barrios said, as he tightened his lips holding back tears. It had been a draining, emotional time for him, the only openly gay man in the 200-person Legislature and the only openly gay senator, having the very difficult challenge of making the case for his full humanity to his colleagues and yet watching a number of them still vote against it.

Outside, Barrios took the megaphone and set aside his usually measured demeanor. "No governor, no religious bigots, no speaker of the House, no Senate president will be able to take away our right on May 17."

Not that they wouldn't try.

Governor Romney tried to get the Massachusetts Supreme Judicial Court to delay marriages until after final action on the constitutional amendment had been taken. That would be either during the next legislative session or, if it advanced to the ballot, in November 2006. However, the attorney general refused to represent the governor in court or appoint an attorney to do so. Romney's last effort was to file emergency legislation that would allow him to make an appeal directly to the court, but the Senate president dismissed the legislation immediately.

A week later, Romney announced that he'd "mitigate" the effect of the ruling. He promised to dust off an unenforced law passed in 1913—known as the "1913 Law"—that barred couples from marrying in Massachusetts if it were illegal for them to marry in their home states. That would, in practice, keep nearly all same-sex couples who lived in other states from marrying in Massachusetts. The law had ugly, racist roots: the Legislature approved it at the height of Jim Crow to ensure that interracial couples wouldn't leave their home states where it was illegal for them to marry in order to marry in Massachusetts. "Massachusetts should not become the Las Vegas of same-sex marriage," Romney proclaimed with derision.

There were now five lawsuits pending by different groups to stop marriages from beginning on May 17. Mary Bonauto and the GLAD team were stretched to the limit. They were working furiously to respond to all the legal challenges while putting together a proactive challenge to the enforcement of the 1913 law. The suit that concerned Mary the most was a federal suit filed by Rev. Jerry Falwell's Liberty Counsel. Federal action seemed like a long shot since marriage had always been the province of state law, but to Mary it was the only realistic scenario for mischief given the stance of the Massachusetts high court. She was especially troubled when the federal district court judge wouldn't let GLAD intervene, leaving her to rely on the attorney general, who had opposed marriage, to defend the *Goodridge* decision.

Adding to Mary's nervousness, communications consultant Mary Breslauer had insisted that all of the plaintiff couples marry on May 17. The national and international media would be descending on Massachusetts, and they wanted to cover weddings. "Feed the beast," was a mantra of Breslauer's. So she'd worked with the plaintiffs to space the weddings out over the day. Mary had given a thumbs-up to the plan, but what if something went wrong—if one of the courts granted a stay and postponed the beginning date for marriages? Some of the plaintiff couples had said to her that they knew something could happen and for her not to worry. But Mary was determined that nothing go wrong. This was a court ruling, she was their lawyer, and the couples were going to marry in Massachusetts on May 17. If somehow things didn't work out, she'd feel responsible for having given them bad advice. The idea of family members coming to town and expensive bills for celebrations piling up with no marriages was even more pressure to ensure things went off without a hitch.

GLAD swatted down lawsuit after lawsuit until all that remained was the federal suit. Falwell's group wanted the federal court to issue an injunction to stop marriages until their claim could be considered. The district and appellate courts refused, so the group asked for immediate Supreme Court review. The justice assigned to the case, David Souter, referred the question to the full court.

On Friday evening, May 14, Mary got the call she'd been waiting for. The US Supreme Court had refused to step in. Marriages would begin on Monday morning, May 17.

With the immediate political challenges having subsided for now, the international media turned to the first legal marriages of same-sex couples in American history. From our dingy Freedom to Marry Coalition office just off the Boston Common with the exhaust from the Burger King below blowing through the window, our staff of three—Advocacy Director Josh Friedes, Field Organizer Robyn Maguire, and I—began fielding calls from media outlets from all over the world. The press was desperate to cover first-day weddings, so they reached out to us because we had a strong database of same-sex couples in Massachusetts. They especially wanted big, traditional weddings, with hundreds of people, cakes, bouquets, tuxes, and bridesmaids' dresses. And while they had the seven weddings of plaintiff couples to choose from, many were looking for an "exclusive"—a wedding that only they were covering.

There were a few problems with that scenario. First, the wedding licensure in Massachusetts was designed to be a multiday process. After applying for their wedding license, a couple had to wait for three days before they could get legally married. The waiting period could be waived by a judge if there were good reasons, and we expected most to be pretty lenient, but weddings actually taking place on May 17 were going to be few and far between. Second, most of the couples who wanted to marry immediately had been together for years, with many already having had religious marriage ceremonies or commitment ceremonies. Just because the state was finally catching up didn't mean that these couples were going to hold 300-person events.

The press was in a frenzy. We were chasing down couples for demanding crews from the BBC, the *Washington Post*, media outlets from China and Japan, and more. My favorite was one outlet that wanted to cover a wedding of a gay father and his gay son both marrying on the same day. I could only laugh, shake my head, and roll my eyes.

We, on the other hand, were focused on ensuring the press would capture images that showed our dignified couples taking their marriages seriously. Guided by media consultant Mary Breslauer, we wanted to project images worldwide that depicted the sincerity and solemnity with which the vast majority of same-sex couples approached marriage, having lived through discrimination and being denied marriage for so long. The cameras, on the other hand, were often looking for scenes that viewers would find outrageous or provocative.

Yet we persevered because we knew that projecting positive images throughout the world was so important to the future of our movement. If the pictures wrongly conveyed to the straight world that our community was simply trying to make a political statement and didn't take marriage seriously, it would hurt our cause badly. So it was important that we consciously put forth images that represented what was actually taking place.

GLAD had vetted the seven plaintiff couples carefully. They were the ones we wanted to show the world. Breslauer knew the media would be focused on Boston, and so she worked closely with our staunch ally, Boston Mayor Tom Menino, his staff, and the three couples who would be marrying in Boston. The city could whisk the Boston couples through the multistep licensing process beginning Monday morning, and their weddings would be the first shown to the world. Or so she thought.

The city of Cambridge decided that it wanted to be first and would begin issuing marriage licenses at 12:01 a.m. on May 17. Breslauer worried this would be a chaotic shit show and we'd be leaving the publicity of the first marriages to chance. Sue Hyde, a MassEquality board member who was also a longtime activist from the National Gay and Lesbian Task Force and Cambridge denizen, took this one on. She made the case to Cambridge City Manager Robert Healy that it would be wise if the city selected the first couple to marry.

He was aghast. Oh no, he told Sue. That wouldn't be fair. It had to be first come, first served. This was uber-progressive Cambridge, after all.

That didn't deter Sue. She would identify the first couple; they'd just have to get in line first.

Sue got home and called Jean McGuire, a fellow Cambridge resident and former director of the state HIV/AIDS bureau. She left a message explaining the situation and asked Jean if she could think of a couple from Cambridge whom everyone would feel really proud of, a couple straight people could really relate to. Jean called back a few minutes later.

"I have the couple," she said. "Marcia Hams and Susan Shepherd. They've been together twenty-seven years, are very grounded, and have a son who is a college hockey star." Perfect. Sue knew them but not well. She dialed them up and Marcia answered. Sue told her that she was helping organize the first day of marriages in Cambridge.

"Oh, Susan and I are planning to apply for our license that day," she said.

"There's that," Sue said. "And then there's something else. I want you and Susan to be the first couple in line to take your intentions to get your marriage license."

"Why do you want us to do that?" Marcia replied.

Sue explained that the world's media focus would be on the first couple and that their family would be perfect. "I want it to be you and Susan and Peter," Sue said.

Marcia had a family caucus and then called Sue back. "We're in."

On May 16 at midnight—twenty-four hours before Cambridge would begin issuing marriage licenses—Sue, Marcia, and Susan unfolded beach chairs right in front of the Cambridge City Hall front door. They opened up a bottle of red wine, ate chocolate, and chitchatted all night long. Marcia and Susan's son Peter came by and brought them coffee and food. No one else showed up to wait in line until midafternoon. At about 6:00 p.m., the city began handing out numbers. Marcia and Susan got number one, and Sue—who would be marrying her longtime partner Jade—got number two. Mission accomplished!

That evening, I was a mile away at a special interfaith service at Christ Church Cambridge in Harvard Square sponsored by the Religious Coalition for the Freedom to Marry. The dean of the Cambridge-based Episcopal Divinity School who was leading the service asked all the same-sex couples who were about to be married to rise. The couples stood, and the many clergy in attendance divided up and offered each couple a benediction. It was beautiful and extraordinarily meaningful to see so many couples standing before their God as equals as they prepared to stand before their state as equals as well.

After the service, I went over to Jarrett Barrios's home and, with his partner Doug Hattaway, Freedom to Marry Coalition Advocacy Director Josh Friedes, and a few other of Barrios's friends, toasted the history that was about to be made. I then walked over to Cambridge City Hall. When I arrived, I couldn't believe what I was seeing. There were thousands of people approaching from all directions. It was as though they were drawn by magnetic force to this overwhelming scene of happiness. Many were holding signs expressing the joy they felt. I remember one sign that captured the moment so beautifully. It simply said, "YAY."

Mary Bonauto had been invited to say a few words at a reception at Cambridge City Hall late that night, just before they'd begin to issue licenses. She pulled into Cambridge completely exhausted after her last few days spent swatting down last-ditch lawsuits designed to stop the marriages from taking place. When she saw the hundreds of people in line to apply for a license, and the thousands more who were there to celebrate, her jaw dropped. Over the past few months, she'd dealt with all the conflict: questions about whether the decision really meant marriage, lawsuit after lawsuit, political maneuvering in the State House, and more. Yet here there were so many happy people. For Mary, it was the couples and families in line who moved her the most. They were about to experience the security, the protections, the piece of mind, and the basic dignity that came only with marriage. Through her work over the past decade and a half, Mary had come to know what a crucial badge of citizenship marriage was. If you are barred from marrying, she'd come to believe, you're being denied your full humanity. These couples would soon be able to say to their children, yes, your moms are married. Yes, your dads are married. She knew what enormous peace of mind it would give those kids. She also knew all too well the concrete protections that these families had been denied and would finally be able to access. That night, there was so much basic human equality and dignity coming together.

Just before midnight, Mary took the microphone inside City Hall. She quoted Dr. Martin Luther King's famous line, "the arc of the moral universe is long but bends toward justice." "In a few minutes," said Mary, "it's going to take a sharp turn." They then broke out a three-tier wedding cake and waited for the clock to strike midnight.

=

Across the Charles River in Boston, Ralph Hodgdon and Paul McMahon, aged sixty-nine and seventy-one respectively, sat on the green couch that doubled as a fold-out bed in their cramped apartment, which was filled beyond capacity with objects that told the story of their lives. They were watching the eleven o'clock news and saw the massive outpouring at Cambridge City Hall. Though they hadn't planned to attend the revelries that night, they decided they wanted to be there.

I'd first met Ralph and Paul at a Boston Pride celebration, where they were marching with their simple yet profound sign: "Together 47 Years." On the back of the sign, Ralph had pasted photos to show the evidence across five decades. We asked them if they'd mind if we used their image in a Freedom to Marry Coalition poster, and they obliged. Since then, the two of them had become willing symbols of our cause. They were proud to show the world that same-sex relationships embody love and deep commitment and can endure for a lifetime, even through years of hardship imposed by society, along with the ups and downs that every relationship has.

They grabbed their sign, which now read "Together 48 Years," hurried across Tremont Street to the Park Street T station for the short ride on the Red Line to Central Square station, and walked up the street to Cambridge City Hall.

When they arrived just moments before midnight, it seemed as if the entire media world had descended on the city north of Boston for the countdown. As was usually the case, their sign attracted attention. A young woman approached the couple and handed them a full bouquet of lilies of the valley, which happened to be Paul's favorite flower. He saw the gift as an omen.

Caught up in the emotions, Ralph and Paul decided to apply for a marriage license that night. They wouldn't use it until May 29—they had already decided to get married on their forty-ninth anniversary. But the history being made here was profound to the two of them and they wanted to be a part of it. They got in line and received number 249. They'd have to wait for hours until they got their chance. But that was nothing compared to the forty-eight years they'd already waited.

=

Ralph and Paul met in Central Park on May 29, 1955. Paul, wearing a bright green shirt and on his way to a social gathering, stopped to talk with Ralph, who was sitting on a rock, sketching. Their love affair almost never happened because Ralph initially said very little. He grew chatty just in time to stop Paul from leaving. Paul never made it to his other event that day. Instead, he convinced Ralph to take a walk and then go to the movies to see *Wuthering Heights*.

The two courted assiduously. Within weeks, Paul had purchased two gold rings because he wanted them to function like a married couple, even if neither man dared to dream of actually marrying. Though homophobia made it difficult for them to find a place to live together, even in New York City, the two eventually found an apartment.

In 1960, the two moved to Boston. In the neighborhood of Bay Village where many gay men lived, they found community but endured harassment by gangs of thugs from South Boston who would periodically come to wreck trees and smash window boxes. They'd been attacked once when leaving the Punch Bowl, a gay bar in the neighborhood. Ralph ran to a nearby police cruiser screaming that a guy had just punched Paul in the head. The officer did nothing but warn Ralph to tone down his language or risk arrest. Back then, the police were more likely to threaten or dismiss gay people than protect them.

The two became activists, joining up in Boston's early Pride parades in the 1970s, marching alongside teachers who wore paper bags over their heads because they could be fired for being gay, and enduring jeers and avoiding thrown tomatoes on the route that police refused to protect.

That night, things couldn't have been more different. When they emerged from City Hall around 5:00 a.m., there was still a crowd of well-wishers applauding them. *Good Morning America* grabbed them for an interview. They were beaming.

Mary Bonauto stayed in Cambridge for the night and tried to get some rest, but she barely slept at all. Her day began with a 6:00 a.m. television interview. She did a few more morning shows and then wanted to check in on her seven client couples, each of whom would be applying for a marriage license that day. She was in touch with the non-Boston couples by phone and headed over to Boston City Hall to meet up with the three Boston couples. All three would be going through the entire process that day—license, waiver, and marriage.

What was kept quiet were the elaborate security arrangements that the Boston Police Department had put into place. With the religious right predicting Armageddon, it wasn't beyond imagination that some crazed individuals would try to take matters into their own hands by using weapons to try to stop gays from marrying. At the Freedom to Marry Coalition office, we'd received one quasi-death threat that focused on clergy who were on our side. We reported it to the police who recommended that we install a much tighter security system at our office. That day, May 17, sharpshooters were positioned on Boston rooftops, plainclothes police officers mixed in with the people celebrating on City Hall Plaza, and dozens of uniformed officers were assigned to protect Mary and the plaintiffs.

As she walked onto City Hall Plaza, Mary saw the line of ecstatic couples waiting to apply for licenses. They kept stopping her to say thank you, and many wanted a picture with her. As on the night before, Mary could feel the meaning of the day through their joy.

Mary met up with the three Boston couples—Julie and Hillary Goodridge, David Wilson and Rob Compton, and Ed Balmelli and

Mike Horgan—in Mayor Menino's Situation Room at 9:00 a.m. The mayor had done everything he could to make sure things went smoothly. There was juice, coffee, and water for them. Menino came down to greet everyone, chatting with the Goodridges' eight-year-old daughter Annie. Mary explained the process: First they would fill out their applications for marriage licenses at City Hall, then they'd go to probate court to get a waiver of the three-day waiting period, and then they'd return to City Hall to complete and pick up their license. Finally, there would be the wedding ceremonies.

Shortly after nine, the three couples walked with Mary to the window at City Hall to fill out and submit their applications. It was a media circus. Hundreds of photographers clicked photos as the three couples signed their applications for a license. Then the couples left the building surrounded by police to walk the four blocks to the Suffolk County Probate and Family Court to secure their waivers of the waiting period. Even with police escorts, they were swarmed by the press and had to move in a line, holding each other's hands, to make sure no one got left behind in the crush of media and supporters.

After entering the courthouse, the three couples filled out more paperwork and then went to see the judge. Julie and Hillary Goodridge were first.

Judge Nancy Gould asked, Why are you seeking to marry without delay?

Mary responded on their behalf: "They've waited seventeen years," she said. "They'd like not to have to wait an additional three days." The judge granted the waiver to the Goodridges and the other two couples. The couples returned to Boston City Hall to file the waivers and get their licenses.

The Freedom to Marry Coalition erected a tent on City Hall Plaza and served wedding cake to couples as they emerged after having applied for their licenses. I stationed myself on the plaza to watch for any trouble between advocates and protesters. We wanted the images of the day to reflect joy-filled couples, not dueling protesters. By and large, our opponents behaved themselves, and most stayed away. That left me to simply watch and share in the joy as couples emerged from City Hall, holding up their licenses with giant grins on their faces while onlookers clapped and shouted.

The first wedding was that of David Wilson and Rob Compton at Arlington Street Church, the prominent Unitarian Universalist Church in Back Bay abutting the Boston Public Garden. Mary hitched a ride to the church with a documentary film crew that was in town to shoot the first weddings. Finally after all of the running around, she sat down in one of the first pews in between Jarrett Barrios and Rob's mother. Mary caught her breath, listened to the organ music filling the church, and watched the guests who came to join in the joyous yet solemn occasion.

At that moment, it dawned on Mary that it was finally real. These two people who really loved each other would soon be saying, "I do." They'd already made a pledge to one another in their hearts. Now they could do so under the law. It was such a powerful feeling she burst into tears. She thought about the hundreds, if not thousands, of people over the past fourteen years whom she'd spoken with at GLAD, people who had wanted this opportunity but couldn't have it, people whose lives would have been enhanced in so many ways and whose painful experiences would have been alleviated if they'd been able to marry. She had a hard time getting herself under control, and the wedding hadn't even begun.

It was a beautiful, elegant wedding. Mary felt so moved by David and Rob who, along with the other six couples, had stuck their necks out for everyone. They had all been warned of the risks: public criticism, attacks on their families, and potential repercussions at work. David and Rob, an interracial couple with five children and seven grandchildren between them, took a chance to be vulnerable, to tell a story to the world about their lives and why marriage mattered to them and their families. And people heard it and responded.

When Rev. Kim Crawford Harvie, who was performing the ceremony, got to the line, "By the power vested in me by the Commonwealth of Massachusetts," the crowd erupted in cheers. David looked Rob in the eyes and shook his head as though he could hardly believe what was happening.

Mary's partner Jenny, who had come down from Maine for the day, met up with Mary at the wedding. As David, Rob, and everyone else streamed out of the church, the two of them just sat at the end of one of the pews and cried together.

Mary and Jenny went to three other weddings that day: Julie and Hillary's, which took place at the headquarters of the Unitarian Universalist Association, where Hillary worked; Ellen Wade and Maureen Brodoff's, which took place at Newton City Hall; and that evening, the reception of Gary Chalmers and Richard Linnell, near Worcester.

While religious right opponents recognized that their protests would be ill mannered and counterproductive that day, the White House couldn't restrain itself. President Bush issued a statement calling again for a constitutional amendment barring same-sex couples from marrying. "The sacred institution of marriage should not be redefined by a few activist judges," said Bush.

That night, I went to the wedding of my friends Mike Horgan and Ed Balmelli, another of the plaintiff couples, who lived in the Jamaica Plain section of Boston and had been together for ten years. About 100 people gathered at the Boston Marriot Copley Place. In many ways, it felt like any other wedding. There were drinks, food stations, and jazz music. But as I listened to the Rev. Kenneth Orth of the United Church of Christ's Old South Church perform the ceremony, I realized how different this one was. I thought of the other weddings I'd been to of my straight friends and how I'd always had a feeling of wistfulness that our society—epitomized by the state—recognized and celebrated their love but not mine. For once, this felt perfect. Two committed men declaring their love for one another and having it given the dignity of any other marriage, recognized as the ultimate relationship by the state.

At the end of the ceremony, the couple kissed to great applause. Then, with giant grins on their faces, they turned to the assembled crowd and waved. My Freedom to Marry Coalition colleague Josh Friedes, who was very close friends with the two of them, offered a toast: "I guess the question that everybody is wondering is, how can you make the perfect day even more perfect?" said Friedes. "And for me it's being at my best friends' wedding on the day in which, for people like me, they achieved full civil rights for people like all of us."

Ed and Mike then stepped to the dance floor for their first dance, "Where My Heart Will Take Me," from the sci-fi movie *Enterprise*, Mike mouthing the words to Ed.

In the end, Cambridge accepted marriage license applications from 268 couples on May 17. And over the first two days, Boston granted licenses to 213 same-sex couples.

Mary and her partner stayed over that Monday night in Cambridge and then headed back to Maine on Tuesday. As they rode on a city bus to catch their bus back to Maine, Mary noticed many people reading the *Boston Globe* and *Herald*, both of which had giant headlines about the prior day's proceedings. What are they thinking? she wondered. Are they about to explode? This was something that had never happened in this country before. From the looks on their faces, it seemed to be a big yawn to most of them. But still she wondered.

A week and a half later, on May 29, Ralph and Paul held their wedding in the Boston Public Garden, on the forty-ninth anniversary of their meeting in Central Park. A justice of the peace married the men, who wore matching tuxedos with lilies of the valley boutonnieres. They were joined by a small group of friends. After the ceremony, they celebrated with a festive meal at the Ritz Carlton, which provided them with complimentary champagne and bathrobes for their wedding night.

Two weeks later, I had the great privilege of marching with them in a boisterously joyous Boston Pride parade. They were our guests of honor, riding high up in the back of a hot red Volkswagen Beetle convertible. They sat on the trunk with their feet resting on the back seat, big smiles on their faces, and holding their sign high—"49 Years Together! Just Married!" The crowds lining the streets went crazy with cheers.

O nce May 17 was behind us, we turned our attention completely to the 2004 elections for the Massachusetts Legislature, where all 200 seats would be up for grabs. The constitutional amendment that had passed in March would be voted on again after the elections, and if it passed for a second time, it would be placed on the ballot in November 2006. Were it to pass, it would mean the end of marriages for same-sex couples in Massachusetts.

The stakes in these elections couldn't be higher. We knew that if we were to have any hope of defeating the amendment in the Legislature, we had to demonstrate to legislators that voting our way wasn't a serious electoral liability. That meant reelecting them. Lawmakers like Barbara L'Italien who were willing to put their seats on the line for our cause—or any cause—were few and far between. Above all else, most lawmakers prioritized continuing to be a lawmaker. But if we could reelect those who'd vote our way, we'd show others who were a bit less courageous but who agreed with us that casting a vote for marriage equality wasn't a risk. Conversely, if supportive incumbents lost, we'd be dead. And it didn't much matter why an incumbent lost. With the Catholic hierarchy and the religious right gunning for us, we knew they would claim any loss of an ally to be the result of their marriage vote, and that would frighten our potential allies.

The conventional wisdom was that we'd lose badly. Just four years earlier in Vermont, sixteen pro-equality lawmakers were knocked out, and the Vermont House of Representatives shifted to Republican control for the first time in sixteen years. And those deposed legislators had only voted for civil unions, not marriage.

Our opponents had promised to engage electorally. The Massachusetts Family Institute, the local affiliate of the behemoth religious right group Focus on the Family, had formed a political action committee

(PAC), and the Catholic hierarchy had announced an aggressive voter registration effort and promised "a backlash in November."

Most ominously, Mitt Romney was launching an all-out electoral blitz. Massachusetts had one of the least Republican legislatures in the country, with only twenty-two Republicans out of one hundred and sixty members in the House of Representatives and seven out of forty in the Senate. Romney's priority was to capture one-third or more of at least one branch to have a better chance of sustaining his vetoes, which were routinely overridden.

On Tuesday, May 25, at Boston's ornate Park Plaza hotel, Romney unveiled the campaign. "Let me introduce you to the reform team of Massachusetts," Romney announced to a crowd of supporters and the press. The curtains dropped, revealing through falling confetti more than 100 of the 131 Republican candidates who'd be running for the Legislature. After the rock-and-roll music stopped, Romney said, "I've been looking forward to this day for a long, long time." Romney and team promised to invest $3 million dollars in electing the candidates, far more than the Democrats traditionally raised and spent. "We're a party that's going to fight hard," Romney continued. "We're going to fight back. We're not going to be intimidated."

As we learned more, it became clear that Romney and his political team had set up a Bain & Company–style incentive system for its candidates, holding campaign boot camps and training sessions and promising campaign staff, direct mail, and dollars to those who hit benchmarks of doors knocked and dollars raised. The Massachusetts Democratic Party, not used to organized challenges such as this, wasn't at all prepared to counter.

Romney didn't describe the initiative as an effort to line up more votes for the marriage amendment, and I don't believe that was his primary goal. It was a more general effort to break the overwhelming Democratic control of the Legislature, one that threatened most of Romney's policy initiatives and left him largely impotent to stop the priorities of the Democratic Legislature. Nevertheless, it was a potentially crippling development. Sixty-one of the GOP challengers were taking on Democratic lawmakers who had voted our way, and nearly all of them opposed the freedom to marry. This combination of the GOP effort along with the threats of the Catholic hierarchy and the religious right looked like a perfect storm of opposition that would be very difficult to counter.

MassEquality's campaign head Marty Rouse had had several stints leading state-level electoral battles. In his last role, he had run the Vermont Democratic Party's coordinated campaign, where he'd been tasked with winning back Democratic seats in the Legislature after the civil union battle and had multiple successes. I was now working, de facto, as Marty's right-hand guy on the political front and would soon officially become political director of MassEquality. I was eager to learn from him. I'd long been a political junkie and played an active role in federal races, but local races were completely different beasts, and I didn't have much experience at all.

With the general elections nearly six months away, we turned first to the September 14 primaries. Wouldn't it be amazing, Marty would say over and over in his hyper, high-adrenaline style, if we could knock out a couple of Democratic legislators who had voted against marriage equality in the primary and for it to be clear that it was the result of their marriage vote? *That* would start changing the power dynamic in the Legislature. Many were skeptical it could be done. Incumbents were almost always reelected in Massachusetts, and primary defeats were especially rare. What's more, we'd be judged largely on whether we protected those who voted with us, not on whether we knocked out those who opposed us. Marty made the case that primaries offered a much better opportunity for us to make an impact. Turnout was notoriously low, which meant we could focus on making the case to a small universe of voters—those who voted in nearly every election—and bombard them with direct mail, door knocks, and phone calls. In contrast, November turnout would be at least eight times greater, with Massachusetts' favorite son, John Kerry, on the ballot for president. It would be much harder and more expensive to have a real impact on those elections.

We were starting late though. Marty was used to recruiting candidates whom he'd vetted. This time, we had to take the hand we were dealt.

The first candidate he met with was Carl Sciortino, the openly gay twenty-five-year-old from Somerville. Carl already had the backing of a couple of progressive organizations, and he presumed MassEquality would jump to his aid.

He sat down and Marty went right at him. Why do you think you can win? What's your message? Which voters are you targeting? What's your fundraising plan? How many pieces of mail are you going to send? Where are you getting volunteers from? Have you done polling?

Carl was shocked at the interrogation. Here he was, an openly gay man taking on a known homophobe, Vinny Ciampa, and he wasn't being shown any appreciation or given the benefit of the doubt. He'd expected the approach to be, How can we help you win? Instead, it was, We'll decide if we're going to help you if we like what you're doing. What's more, Carl's political consultant, Dan Cohen, had told him he should run an under-the-radar campaign. If Ciampa knew Carl was a serious threat, he could pull in resources from House Speaker Tom Finneran and organized labor that would make it next to impossible for Carl. However, if Ciampa thought he was simply a gay kid who was running a campaign just to make a point, Carl could capitalize on Ciampa's overconfidence. So when Marty began drilling him, he clamped up. Carl had a plan, but he didn't want to share it with Marty, whom he barely knew.

The meeting ended extremely awkwardly. For Marty, his fears were confirmed that Carl was a lightweight who had no idea how to run a serious campaign. For his part, Carl was upset he'd been caught off guard. He called his consultant Dan to vent, and they set up a second meeting for two days later.

This time, Carl let Dan do the talking. Dan was a wiry thirty-something-year-old guy who ate next to nothing and lived on coffee, beer, and cigarettes. He stayed up all night so was impossible to reach until at least noon and yet was an extremely talented strategist. Dan had been a progressive activist but thought progressives were doomed unless they figured out how to run smart, strategic campaigns. So he'd gone back to school and studied polling and electoral analysis.

Carl can win this race, Dan told Marty. He took out a poll and showed Marty the numbers. Carl was, of course, completely unknown. However, Ciampa wasn't as well known as he should have been, given that he'd served for sixteen years. More importantly, only 32 percent of

Democratic primary voters thought Ciampa deserved to be reelected, with 33 percent saying someone else should be given a chance and the rest undecided. These were terrible numbers for someone who had served as long as Ciampa. When they tested issues, they found that Ciampa's conservative positions—on choice, education spending, taxes, and marriage—were less popular than Carl's positions.

Dan laid out Carl's campaign plan, which was in fact very strategic. He was about to go part time at his job so that he could spend his afternoons raising money and his evenings knocking on doors. They planned for the campaign to raise a minimum of $25,000 and to identify 3,000 likely voters who were supporters. With low turnout expected on primary day, that would be enough.

Marty heard what he needed. MassEquality was in. What's more, in Dan he'd met a kindred spirit—someone who was committed to a data-driven, relentless pursuit to electoral wins. Marty was determined to vet all the primary challengers to our opponents in this way to see if they were with us on marriage and then if they were running a serious campaign.

MassEquality had some real assets we could bring to the table. We had a large number of highly motivated volunteers who would go door to door, make phone calls, and do whatever it took to get our allies elected. We had donors, both local and national, who were ready to contribute up to the $500 maximum to multiple candidates. Perhaps most importantly, with Marty we had real knowledge about how to win state legislative races, in most cases much more than the candidates themselves. And we were relentless in reaching that end. That was what Marty taught me more than anything; it wasn't enough to endorse a candidate, write a PAC check, and e-mail members. If you wanted to make an impact, you had to go all in: find a pathway to victory for the candidate and ensure that the plan was being executed. In every case, that meant supplementing what the candidate was doing. And in some cases, it meant running our own shadow campaign because the candidate wasn't equipped to do it.

From the Portuguese South Coast near New Bedford, we found Steve Canessa, a twenty-two-year-old school board member from Lakeville who was running against a freshman who'd consistently voted against us. Marty picked up the phone late one night, reached Canessa, and asked him about the amendment. Canessa said that he'd never vote for it. So Marty told him we wanted to meet with him. In a late-night get-together, Marty offered the prospect of fundraising and volunteer support if he'd promise to do more door knocking and talking to voters.

Senator Jarrett Barrios called me about yet another candidate he thought had a decent shot: Steve "Stat" Smith, who was running against longtime incumbent Ed Connolly in the notoriously corrupt, working-class community of Everett. Smith was the only candidate on the Everett City Council who had endorsed Barrios in his Senate race.

Smith had no idea how to deal with our community. At one event, he brought his wife over to meet me. "See, honey, he's the one I told you about. He doesn't seem gay at all, does he?" Oh my God, I thought. But he was from a very working-class community, he meant well, and he was with us, I reasoned. So I responded, "Stat, come outside with me. I can throw a football twenty yards further than you, too." We all laughed.

I went to Everett to check out his campaign. After accompanying him on some door knocking and then to an event at a senior center, I saw that he was serious and driven, he was talking to likely primary voters using the voter file from the Massachusetts Democratic Party, and people in the community seemed to really like him. We polled independently, and though it was an uphill climb, his campaign was so strong that we decided to get in.

Even as we vetted every candidate and decided to back several, the one race that had become a symbol of the marriage fight was the Carl Sciortino race. A young, openly gay candidate was running a smart, methodical campaign against an incumbent who'd been nasty to his gay constituents, had voted against our equality, and was part of the terribly antigay House speaker's leadership team. That was compelling.

There was much pent-up energy from the gay community after the loss on the constitutional amendment vote, and Carl's campaign took advantage of it. They put out the call for volunteers and would get a handful of people in the office volunteering night after night. At first, people came by even though they thought Carl would lose. It was a nice thing to do, to help the gay guy who was challenging this bad incumbent. It was a good way to vent. But when volunteers saw how serious the campaign was, over the course of the summer people started to believe. They'd go out to knock on doors and come back and say, I talked to thirty people and fifteen of them said they're voting for you. That kind of positive response turned others on to the campaign, and soon, Carl had a solid cadre of volunteers—ten to fifteen every day, mainly gay and motivated by the marriage fights—who believed he could win.

Other less positive developments reminded us this was no ordinary campaign. One day, as Carl was walking up to his door, he heard his cat meowing as though it were crying. As he approached it, he saw that it was lying on the front porch with a noose tied around its neck. The cat was okay, but it scared the shit out of Carl. Carl and his staff also noticed Ciampa's cronies driving by the office and peering into the windows, trying to gauge what was going on. From then on, Carl would only go door to door with a volunteer, never alone. And each night, Carl's campaign manager took all the campaign materials and confidential voter information home.

One day in early August, the campaign hit a key milestone: of the voters whose doors they'd knocked on, the number of supporters now surpassed the number who said they were either undecided or opposed. Oh my God, thought Carl. We might actually be able to pull this off.

At the MassEquality offices, Marty and I turned to our direct-mail program. Our plan was to hit every likely voter in one of our target races with a minimum of four mail pieces, large postcards with the candidate's picture on the front and some of their key accomplishments on the back. Marty believed that people selected their state legislators based on whether they liked them more than on their policy positions. So we found good pictures of them with their families and in their communities, and highlighted their local roots and community involvement. We almost never talked about marriage unless polling showed it was an advantage. Instead, we'd talk about issues that polling showed were important to voters: education, health care, jobs, and the like, always tying back to their biographies and local accomplishments. We also knew that it could be problematic if the lawmakers we were trying to defeat could publicize that an outside, gay marriage group was bombarding voters with mail. So in many cases, we contributed money to other groups—multi-issue groups like the Commonwealth Coalition and Neighbor to Neighbor—who supported the same candidate and would do the mailings themselves.

While working on the direct mail, Marty and I really bonded. Together, the two of us pulled several all-nighters, writing literally dozens of mail pieces. We were punchy, giddy, going to the 7-Eleven at midnight to load up on snacks to carry us into the morning.

By the first week of September, Carl Sciortino's jig was up as far as operating under the radar was concerned. The fundraising report he had to file with the state showed that through August 27, he had far surpassed the initial $25,000 he'd budgeted. He had raised $52,000 and spent $30,000 of it, and his plan was to spend the rest before the primary election. When Ciampa and Speaker Finneran saw those numbers, they were shocked. Ciampa had only spent $23,000 and had $45,000 sitting in the bank—far more than he could put to use effectively in the last week-plus. For Finneran, losing Ciampa meant a demonstration of weakness that he would not tolerate, particularly if he lost to a gay kid who was running on gay marriage. Finneran worked the phones, getting the AFL–CIO to pressure any group associated with organized labor to stop helping Carl Sciortino. Carl's volunteers began seeing Ciampa frantically knocking on doors around the district.

Meanwhile, the Sciortino mail pieces we paid for began hitting right after Labor Day, one nearly every other day for two weeks, five pieces in total for Carl.

On Saturday, September 11, the weekend before the election, our MassEquality office looked like campaign central, filled with volunteers making phone calls to voters in our priority districts. We also had volunteers across the state working directly with priority campaigns—door knocking and making phone calls. MassEquality volunteers made up as many as half the volunteers for several of our priority races. In addition, we began prepping for a big election night party for supporters. We wanted to continue to get them deeply invested in the elections and highlight the fruit of our labor with some wins.

On Primary Day, Tuesday, September 14, I nervously checked in with campaigns around the state and prepped for our event that evening. In the midafternoon, I got a panicked call from Carl Sciortino's campaign consultant Dan Cohen who was managing Carl's Election Day efforts. They were carefully tracking who had voted during the day, matching it to the list of the 3,000-plus who had committed to voting for Carl. Turnout was much higher than expected, and far too many of Carl's identified supporters hadn't yet voted. This combination spelled trouble.

We need MassEquality to send out emergency e-mails to its metro Boston lists right away, Dan told me. We need lots more people at campaign headquarters by 5:30 p.m.

If they were going to win, they'd have to drag out every last identified Sciortino supporter from their home, and that would take manpower that they just didn't have. We blasted out an e-mail right away.

At 5:30, Carl headed back to the campaign office. Wearing his one dark green suit that he'd bought for the campaign, Carl had been greeting voters at the polls all day and wanted to take a break. What he saw moved him deeply. People from all different directions—from the bus stop, the T, their cars, and the neighborhood—were converging on the campaign office, and there was a line outside the door, winding down the block. Volunteers had responded to the plea and were arriving to help this improbable candidate who wouldn't relent.

Volunteers were each given the names of a handful of voters located in close proximity to one another who had committed to supporting Carl. They were told to camp out at their doors and make sure they went to vote. Volunteers would nab people as they were pulling into their driveway after work, reminding them—insisting—that they go to vote for Carl before the polls closed at 8:00 p.m.

When the polls closed, Marty and I gathered in a "war room" that we'd set up in the office of event planner Bryan Rafanelli, upstairs from Boston's largest gay bar, Club Café, where the election night party would take place. We had multiple phone numbers for every campaign, and by 8:15 p.m., we started calling around to see how our pro-equality slate of candidates had done.

The early news we got was good: all of our incumbents who had voted with us and had drawn primary challengers had won handily. We then started getting calls from some of our challengers, and that news was not as good. Several we'd written off, yet a few of the races where we thought we had a shot turned against us. In Everett, the votes were all tallied, and Steve "Stat" Smith had lost by forty votes.

We were desperate for something positive to show we'd made an impact. Finally, our first piece of good news came: Steve Canessa, the twenty-two-year-old from southeastern Massachusetts, knocked out the incumbent backed by Finneran by ten percentage points. We were the only statewide group that had endorsed him; it would be a sign of our clout.

But the one we were all waiting for was Carl's race.

I nervously dialed Carl's campaign. "Too close to call," his staffer told me.

"I'm dying over here," I responded.

At the Sciortino headquarters, Dan Cohen and crew were tallying the results that were coming in from their volunteer poll captains. They'd gotten results from nine of eleven precincts, and Carl was up by 300. But the two remaining were among Carl's weakest. They didn't know if they'd hold on or not. Finally, the numbers came in from those final two. They'd lost them by 183 votes, but that meant they'd held a victory by a margin of 117, which was later reversed downward to a margin of 93 votes.

Dan called and told us the great news. I was ecstatic. We could finally go downstairs and tell all the volunteers and donors who'd put so much into these elections that their hard work had paid off.

Sue Hyde, the longtime activist with the National Gay and Lesbian Task Force, was acting as MC. "Okay, folks, the war room folks are back. Marc and Marty, our heroes, the inimitable duo from the war room. They have some results."

Sue handed over the microphone to Marty.

"As we began this evening," Marty said, "our goal was to end up with a net gain of two seats." He continued, "We informed you all about how it's extremely difficult to knock out incumbents. And as you have seen from the results so far tonight, that is indeed true. It's very, very difficult to knock out incumbents."

Marty talked about the races where we'd endorsed challengers and lost, going through them one by one. We'd made ballot-like cards with the names of the candidates that we'd passed out to all attendees so they could check off the winners. You could feel the tension in the room as everyone wondered if we'd defeated any incumbents at all.

"In the city of Everett, challenger Steve Smith, a supporter of ours, ran a very good campaign but came up short this evening. Now, Representative Ed Connolly has won this race by forty votes."

Someone screamed, "Recount!"

Marty replied, "There will be a recount, but Ed Connolly has won by forty votes."

He told the crowd that a write-in campaign we were involved in was still too close to call.

Then Marty changed his tone. "There are two other races that are remaining that we can call. In New Bedford, Representative Howland, who was an opponent of ours, has been defeated by supporter Steve Canessa. I spoke to Steve Canessa's campaign manager as we were walking down the stairs. They are so thrilled and so excited that we supported them wholeheartedly."

The crowd cheered enthusiastically, but they were holding back for the Sciortino race.

Then Marty said, "The other race that I can announce as well is Vinny Ciampa down in Somerville can pack his bags because . . ."

Marty was drowned out in screams. People were ecstatic, screaming, crying, hugging one another, and jumping up and down. Carl Sciortino was the heart of our electoral work. He represented the hope that was lit in us at the constitutional conventions, as the lawmakers kept debating and we kept surviving. If Carl could win against what seemed like insurmountable odds, well, we could too. He represented the indomitable spirit of the movement for the freedom to marry. Carl believed in the issues he campaigned on: education, health care, and fairer taxes. But the soul of his campaign was marriage. Harris Gruman, a veteran progressive operative who spent a lot of time on Carl's race, liked to share that he'd gone door to door with this amazing guy who talked about the intricacies of the tax code and the need to make it more progressive.

Gruman asked him if that's what inspired him to get involved. He responded, "No, I'm engaged to my partner and I want to make sure we can get married."

Carl joined us at Club Café later on, to tremendous cheers and many tears. We hailed him as the new representative—there was no Republican running in the general election, so he'd be running unopposed.

A few days later, a union lobbyist that I knew told me he'd been in the men's room in the State House and he overheard two conservative representatives talking to one another. "Did you hear what the gays did to Vinny?" one said to the other. Music to my ears!

=

Days after the primary, Governor Mitt Romney was the featured guest at the home of North Andover Selectman Jim Xenakis at a fundraiser for Maria Marasco, the Republican running against Rep. Barbara L'Italien.

Romney's campaign effort viewed L'Italien as one of the most vulnerable incumbents and was doing everything it could to defeat her. Marasco, who had worked for two GOP governors and had run for office two times before, was getting the royal treatment from Romney's operation: a trained campaign manager, tens of thousands of dollars in contributions, polling, messaging support and training, and six pieces of direct mail from the state Republican Party to all likely voters.

Romney told the crowd of 100 who'd contributed at least $150 per person, "I need help at the State House. I need people like Maria to help me reform state government." He called out the Democrats for wanting "to give illegal aliens in-state tuition rates." Romney didn't raise the marriage vote, but Marasco did. "In matters of such monumental social importance," she said, "the voters have the sole right to decide. They should be able to vote up or down as provided by our state constitution." [Tom Duggan, "Romney Endorses Marasco," *Valley Patriot* 1, no. 9 (November 2004).]

Though Romney's "reform team" included more than 100 challengers, they were now focused on about twenty-five priority races. The districts were geographically concentrated in a ring to the north and west of Boston along the exurban I-495 corridor, as well as on Cape Cod, which in spite of its lore as the Kennedy homestead, was a GOP stronghold. In addition to L'Italien, we were very concerned about Matt Patrick, a supporter of ours who had won by only seventeen votes in his Cape Cod district two years before and was facing the same challenger in a rematch. The big issue in his district wasn't marriage but a wind farm off the coast of the Cape. Patrick supported it, but many locals, including the Kennedy clan, opposed it out of concern for the views from their homes along Nantucket Sound. We knew that would be much more influential in the race than the marriage vote, but we also knew our opponents would hold any loss against us as proof of the perils of the marriage vote.

The State Senate looked to pose bigger problems. Two of our stalwart supporters, Sue Fargo and Pam Resor, were being challenged by extremely wealthy Republican men who could self-finance their campaigns. Rob O'Leary, the first Democrat ever to represent the outer part of Cape Cod, was being targeted as well. As we evaluated the races, we could see that Resor was off to a good start raising money and driving an aggressive effort forward, and O'Leary was doing okay. However, Fargo was very disorganized and had not raised much in the way of funds; we were really worried. We weren't the only ones either. I met up with the Senate president's campaign consultants, who were leading a coordinated campaign for Senate Democrats. Fargo is a lost cause, they told me.

We didn't accept the conventional wisdom, however. The Republicans were clearly targeting conservative-leaning districts, and that made sense. But it still wasn't clear whether or not they had actually conducted polling to evaluate the vulnerability of the incumbents they were seeking to take out. In a high-turnout general election, it would be extraordinarily hard to knock off incumbents that were popular with their constituents.

We had Dan Cohen poll in each of the Romney priority races that we thought might be competitive, and what we found was extremely encouraging. The vast majority of the Romney targets who had voted our way were extremely popular. While Sue Fargo's numbers weren't as good as most, when voters heard about the positions she was running on and those her opponent was emphasizing, they preferred her by a margin of 62 to 30 percent. This was the case on down the line, with just a few exceptions. Dan's polling analysis showed that the only incumbents who were truly vulnerable were Barbara L'Italien and Matt Patrick, the wind farm guy. That meant we could hone in on those two races and then seek to play aggressively in open seats where retiring members were being replaced. We could even go on the offensive against Republican incumbents who'd voted against us and who polling showed were vulnerable. I was shocked that Romney's team hadn't done this same kind of analysis before setting such high expectations for the elections. I assumed they had a trick up their sleeve to knock out popular incumbent Democrats and pull out some victories. But it was hard to imagine what that could be.

That promising news was offset by some bad news. On Tuesday, October 12, Vinny Ciampa announced he would run a write-in campaign against Carl Sciortino in the general election. He ripped Carl, calling him a "one-issue candidate." "He thinks government is about self service," Ciampa told the *Boston Globe*. "It's all about gay marriage."

I was worried. In the primary, Carl had focused on only a small number of Democratic voters whom his campaign expected to go to the polls. Now, with everyone voting in a presidential election, Carl had to introduce himself to many more voters—voters who knew Ciampa much better.

And while homophobia was in the background during the primary, this time it leapt to the forefront. An extreme antigay group called Article 8 Alliance, named for the article in the Massachusetts Constitution that allowed for the impeachment of judges and that wanted to utilize this article to oust judges who ruled in favor of marriage, sent the most vitriolic mail piece I'd ever seen to every voter in the district.

"The Homosexual Lobby," it said, is running "a secret campaign to install a homosexual, anti-Catholic extremist in the state legislature." The group had somehow gotten its hands on a picture of Carl with his then boyfriend standing up and turning his back on the altar at a Catholic mass to protest the church's position on marriage. The piece called

Carl a "militant homosexual activist" and spoke in graphic terms of programs sponsored by the LGBT rights group at Tufts University that Carl had led when he was in college. They'd done their research.

Ciampa claimed he knew nothing about the piece, yet it included a picture of Ciampa and his family that hadn't been seen in public before.

With no Republican running in the race, Carl had dismantled his campaign. He quickly pulled his team back together to run an all-out general election campaign. For us, this election immediately moved to the top of the list. For Carl to lose because of his stance on marriage would be hugely damaging. The primary win would be perceived as nothing more than a fluke, and the marriage issue would appear to be volatile electorally.

In the district, there was plenty of backlash from the antigay mail piece. Constituents called Carl's office outraged, asking how they could help. Yet others asked, "Is it true you only care about gay marriage?" And for every one who asked, there had to be dozens more who were wondering the same thing.

The next Saturday night, I walked Carl around the annual Boston gala of the Human Rights Campaign, the national gay rights organization, introducing him to as many potential donors as I could and handing out the homophobic mail piece along with a contribution envelope.

Around the state, the GOP began a relentless direct-mail attack on Democratic incumbents. Voters' mailboxes were flooded with pieces attacking Democrats on in-state tuition for illegal immigrants, bilingual education, taxes, and even for "voting to protect the identities of sexual predators over the safety of our children." That one was especially over the top. It had a picture of a boy with a tear running down his cheek and a male predator standing behind him. The mail pieces were cookie-cutter, with the name of whichever incumbent Democratic lawmaker they were targeting inserted in the appropriate spots.

At MassEquality, we once again turned our office into campaign central. We had volunteers calling voters in our target races. We asked our major donors to write $500 checks—the maximum allowed by law—to our priority candidates. And once again we did a massive mail program. In contrast to the GOP effort, our mail was nearly all positive, highlighting our candidates' positions on education, health care, job creation, and other issues important to voters. And they were individualized, using photos of the candidate, usually with their family, and describing their local roots and accomplishments.

In L'Italien's district, Team Romney was doubling down. The governor made a second appearance in the district with Marasco. The GOP did their full battery of negative mail against L'Italien, even criticizing her for votes that took place before she became a representative. We conducted our most robust program as well: five mail pieces to every likely voter and thousands of dollars raised directly for the campaign. We enlisted Barney Frank to host a fundraiser in the district, and I got my friend Bob Cahill, one of the best and most dependable campaigners I knew, to be our eyes and ears on what was happening on the ground. On multiple weekends, he'd round up volunteers, including his mother, and drive up to Andover so he could keep up on how things were looking.

By the last weekend of October, Barbara L'Italien was feeling positive. First, there was an omen. The Boston Red Sox won the World Series for the first time since 1918, and that gave L'Italien—a huge fan—hope for her own underdog run. More tangibly, and just as astonishingly, she received the endorsement of the *Lawrence Eagle-Tribune*, her local paper with the most conservative editorial page in the state. She was upbeat. But like a good Red Sox fan, she knew never to get confident until the final out.

MassEquality did a round of tracking polls in October to gauge the impact of the Republican attacks and found they had little effect. L'Italien was now leading 45 to 23 percent, Matt Patrick was ahead 47 to 33 percent, Sue Fargo maintained a thirty-point lead, and on down the list.

Because things were going so well, we went all in for upsets in two Cape Cod races. Our polling showed Republican Rep. Susan Gifford was vulnerable to her opponent, Joel Malloy, a twenty-seven-year-old political neophyte who owned a small painting company. We did all we could for Malloy: I prepped him for debates, and we organized a powerful direct-mail program. We made sure to highlight his background as the son of a local fisherman who understood the district better than Gifford, who was a transplant from Michigan. The other race was for an open seat in the central Cape, in a district that had never been represented by a Democrat. Cleon Turner, an attorney and former cop, was running against a local Republican. We sent one of our top organizers, Chris Mason, to the Cape to help Turner's campaign get organized, and we did multiple pieces of mail with pictures of Turner decked out in his police garb looking tough.

In Somerville and Medford, Ciampa's vicious campaigning had alienated him from the entire Democratic establishment. Labor unions and Democratic officials that had supported Ciampa in the primary had endorsed Carl as the Democratic nominee. But we still didn't know how Ciampa's targeting of Carl as a single-issue, radical homosexual would play out with voters. We knew Ciampa had pissed off a lot of people, but would he motivate even more?

On Election Day, we sent volunteers out across the state, but Carl Sciortino was our top priority. Ciampa had to get his supporters to write in his name or affix a sticker with his name on the ballot. With so many voters going to the polls, it would be very difficult to get stickers in all their hands on Election Day. However, it quickly became clear that Ciampa's campaign had done a good job of mailing the stickers to voters in advance because a large number of people had them.

This time around, Carl knew the election would be a street fight. Carl even told his mother not to come up from Connecticut to help out. On the day of the primary election in September, she'd gotten into an argument with Ciampa's wife outside a polling location. With homophobia so blatant in this election, who knew how bad it would get this time?

Carl stopped by campaign headquarters early in the morning before heading out to vote and introduce himself to voters at polling stations. At one station, an Asian woman came up to Carl and asked, "So you're gay?"

"Yeah."

She looked flummoxed. "But your face is too nice to be gay."

"Well, the campaign's not really about that. It's really about all the issues we've been campaigning for."

Carl tried to deflect, but she was having none of it. "But you know, the girls. You don't like the girls?"

"Well, the campaign is not about that. That's about my family and me privately."

"Is your family gay?" she asked.

"No, just me."

She then pointed to a volunteer standing next to Carl. "Well, is he gay?"

"Well, ask him," Carl responded.

The volunteer held up his hand that had his wedding ring on it, and she responded, "Oh, good boy." He didn't tell her about his husband!

"Well, I'll vote for you anyway," she concluded and walked inside to vote.

That was an amusing high point of the day. It went downhill and got ugly, fast. At a polling site at a fire station in Somerville, Ciampa's volunteers were pointing to Carl's picture on his signs and calling him a faggot, over and over again. Carl's volunteers called headquarters, and Carl went over to the precinct to introduce himself. If they're going to call me a faggot, he thought, they should at least know who they're talking about and have met me. He introduced himself, and as he suspected, they quieted down and were pleasant once he got there.

Carl's treasurer, a slender guy named Zachary Newton who was only one year out of college, got it even worse. A Ciampa volunteer at the polling place at the Kennedy School in Medford was telling voters there had been a mistake on the ballot and that's why Ciampa's name was left off. Zachary heard him and immediately walked over to correct him, but the volunteer elbowed Zachary out of the way. After the voters walked away, the Ciampa volunteer said to Zachary threateningly, "Faggot, don't get in my face when I talk." Zachary wouldn't back down. "Get lost, faggot," the volunteer said. Zachary refused. He shoved Zachary, and a crowd gathered around them. Zachary reported all this back to campaign headquarters.

Carl headed over to the precinct to try to defuse the situation. He approached the guy who was threatening Zachary. "How's things going? Are we getting along okay? Are my guys treating you okay?" He wouldn't even look at Carl or shake his hand. So Carl walked up to a police officer to complain about the abusiveness.

The officer told Carl matter-of-factly, "Oh, that's Vinny fucking Piro. There's nothing I can do." Carl was stunned. Piro had been state representative from the district in the early 1980s until he was indicted for taking bribes.

At another polling place, Ciampa volunteers actually entered the voting area and were shouting to people to vote by sticker. Carl's volunteers reported it to the police, who kicked the Ciampa volunteers out. But then outside, the Ciampa people started screaming insults at Carl's volunteers and loitering in the parking lot, to the point where Carl's volunteers were afraid to leave. "Can't you clear these people out of here?" Carl's precinct captain asked of the police. But they wouldn't.

At yet another station, a Ciampa volunteer got up into Carl's face. "Your guy keeps following me over the line," he said.

"Over what line?" Carl asked.

The volunteer pointed to the chalk line that Carl's precinct captain had drawn delineating the 150 feet from the polling place. By law, campaign volunteers had to stay at least 150 feet away. "Yeah, I'm just going to hand them stickers and he follows me."

Carl was dumbfounded. "You want me to pull my volunteer back from following you breaking the law? Sorry, can't really talk to him."

The Ciampa volunteer proceeded to yell at Carl, who was starting to feel as if he was going to vomit. "If you'd like to talk, I'm happy to talk. But don't scream in my face." The man kept screaming, so Carl walked away.

I was on call for Carl's campaign, and they asked me to go to one of the toughest precincts in Medford, where thuggish guys were giving our volunteers a tough time. At six feet five, I was one of our side's "big guys." No one was going to push me around. When I arrived, there was Vinny Ciampa himself, handing out stickers and talking to voters outside the polling station. At that point, I was furious about what I'd been hearing about the goings-on that day, as well as his bigoted actions over the past month. So as soon as he'd finish making his appeal to a voter, I'd immediately say, "And if you want to vote for the Democratic nominee in this race, vote for Carl Sciortino." Or, "You don't need those [stickers] if you want to vote for the Democrat in the race." Every time I'd say that, I could see the smoke emerging from Ciampa's head. Finally, he couldn't take it anymore and gave me a shove. My instant reflex was to shove back, but with cops across the street, I thought better of it and walked away.

Based on what I was seeing, I was really nervous. It seemed as though the majority of voters had stickers or were taking them from Ciampa's volunteers. Granted, this polling site was heavy Ciampa territory. But when I spoke with Marty Rouse, he told me he was having a similar experience at another polling place.

A bit later, I got a call from a twenty-three-year-old organizer named Chris Mason, a young guy to whom I'd become a mentor. "Marc, they're taunting us," he told me. "How?" I asked. "They keep asking me if Carl's ever fucked me up the ass." Just endless taunting. I said I'd be right over to the polling place where he was volunteering. I got in my car and picked up Chris and another volunteer, but before I left, I rolled down the window and shouted at the Ciampa volunteers: "You should be ashamed of yourselves, picking on twenty-three-year-old kids. Pathetic." They screamed back and gestured as though they'd charge the car, but I drove away.

I headed to Club Café where we again hosted an election night party to watch the returns come in. This time, people were interested in the legislative races, but all eyes were glued to the television to see how John Kerry was going to do in the presidential race. Kerry's national election night party was literally three blocks away in Copley Square, with headliners from Jon Bon Jovi to the Black Eyed Peas performing. Marty and I were back in our war room upstairs. We knew we'd have a wait for Carl's race because it was a write-in and they'd have to hand count the ballots. But the others came in quickly. Barbara L'Italien's campaign consultant called me at 8:30. It was a blowout! L'Italien had won in every precinct and defeated Marasco 58 to 42 percent. "Yeah!" I shouted and pumped my arm in the air.

In the western suburbs of Boston, Senator Sue Fargo won overwhelmingly, securing 60 percent of the vote, just as the polling had predicted. Republican Cape Cod produced great results as well. Senator Rob O'Leary, the first Democratic senator representing the Outer Cape, won with 59 percent of the vote. Rep. Matt Patrick, who had won by only seventeen votes last time, this time got 53 percent. In the central Cape, where we'd put in a lot of resources, the former cop Cleon Turner defeated his opponent by 434 votes, securing the first Democratic win ever in that district. Joel Malloy, the painter and son of the fisherman, lost but by less than five percentage points. That race was on no one's radar screen except for ours, and people were shocked at how close it was.

It was a great night for us so far, but we were still waiting for the votes to be counted in Medford and Somerville. Once the results finally began coming in, it was immediately clear that this time it wouldn't even be close. Carl was winning by a 2–1 margin, sweeping Ciampa even in the parts of the district where Ciampa had bested Carl in the primary.

At Club Café, I introduced Carl. This time, I said, there is absolutely no doubt that Carl will be sworn in as the new legislator representing Medford and Somerville. Carl gave an emotional speech, thanking the LGBT community for standing by his side through all of the homophobic attacks.

In the end, we couldn't have asked for a better night. We defeated every single one of Romney's candidates who challenged a pro-equality Democratic incumbent, all sixty-one of them. This happened in spite of millions invested, hundreds of thousands of pieces of direct mail and donated campaign consultants and managers. Romney's effort was an epic failure, with a net result of two fewer Republican seats than when he began. Some argued that having Kerry at the top of the ticket was the reason Romney had done so poorly. But with the exception of the Matt Patrick race on the Cape, not one of Romney's challengers came within ten points of defeating a Democratic incumbent who had voted our way. The Kerry effect was just an excuse for a poorly conceived, poorly executed effort. The two closest races of challengers were pro-equality Democrats challenging anti-equality Republicans, both of whom lost by less than five points.

We'd accomplished our mission in a powerful way. We'd knocked out two incumbents in the primaries, held all of our pro-equality lawmakers through the primaries and generals, and won many more open seats than we lost, in spite of the most serious Republican electoral challenges in Massachusetts in many years. The Catholic hierarchy and religious right had much more bark than bite; we barely saw any evidence of their involvement. Lawmakers who had heard the horror stories of Vermont saw that, if there was any electoral impact of a vote on marriage, it was in our favor, not our opponents.

In total, MassEquality supplied hundreds of volunteers to about twenty priority races, spent $700,000 and raised more, conducted dozens of individual polls, and sent more than half a million pieces of mail—far more I suspect than any group other than the Republican Party.

Even though I was a political junkie and cared deeply about what was happening on the national stage, over the course of this year I simply hadn't had the time to focus beyond Massachusetts. As our victories took hold on election night, though, I gazed out at what was happening in the rest of the country and saw that our freedom to marry movement was getting pounded. Bush's electoral guru Karl Rove and the Republican National Committee thought that putting constitutional amendments banning gays from marrying on the ballot would boost turnout among social conservatives. So they supported the efforts of local officials to advance ballot measures in eleven states, from Ohio to Georgia. As expected, every single one of them passed, most overwhelmingly. Oregon offered our best hope, yet our side lost by a vote of 43 to 57 percent. Those defeats provided fodder for our opponents' talking point that the only way there would be gay marriage is if "activist judges" ruled that way. The American people, they argued, stood strongly against it.

Around the corner from our election night party at Kerry's headquarters, things weren't looking good either. Reports earlier in the day said that exit polls showed a Kerry sweep, but they were wrong. The election had come down to just one state, Ohio, and the numbers weren't promising.

As our party died down at 1:00 a.m., some friends and I walked from Club Café to Copley Square, where thousands of Kerry supporters were still gathered. At about 2:30 a.m., Kerry's running mate, Senator John Edwards, addressed what had become a forlorn crowd: "It's been a long night, but we've waited four years for this victory, so we can wait one more night." By the time I woke up the next morning, Kerry was conceding defeat. We'd have four more years of a president who had no compunction about using national and state constitutional bans on marriage to score points with the religious right and try to turn out voters.

Immediately that day, pundits focused on the marriage battles and blamed them for being a major factor in Kerry's loss. "If Issue 1 [the marriage referendum] had not been on the ballot, John Kerry would have won Ohio," said Ohio Democratic strategist Greg Haas in a *USA Today* article entitled "Presidential Election May Have Hinged on One Issue: Issue 1." The national press honed in on exit polling that showed that 22 percent of Americans chose "moral values" as the reason they picked one presidential candidate over another, the most of any of the choices. They ignored the fact that, according to *Los Angeles Times* exit polling, "moral values" was the highest vote-getter in 1996 and 2000 as well. And they ignored that Kerry came closer to winning Ohio than Al Gore had in 2000, even as Kerry ran several points behind Gore nationwide.*

In a close election, you can blame virtually any factor for causing the win or loss. One top Kerry adviser told me he thought the marriage issue did have a negative impact, but nowhere close to the impact of Kerry's verbal flub that he was "for it before he was against it," which enabled Bush to characterize him as a flip-flopper. Unfortunately, gays made for an easy scapegoat for politicians and a sensational one for the media. And so the national narrative that gay marriage is a dangerous electoral issue stuck, which hurt our cause nationwide. But the narrative we created in Massachusetts helped us tremendously in our statewide battle.

---

*Several analyses performed after the election showed that the marriage ballot fight had no impact on Kerry in Ohio. See Matthew Dowd, "The Facts: Gay Marriage Didn't Tilt 2004 Election," ABC News, May 9, 2012, http://abcnews.go.com; Paul Freedman, "The Gay Marriage Myth: Terrorism, Not Values, Drove Bush's Re-election," Slate, November 5, 2004, http://www.slate.com; and Stephen Ansolabehere and Charles Stewart III, "Truth in Numbers: Moral Values and the Gay-Marriage Backlash Did Not Help Bush," Boston Review, February 25, 2005, https://www.bostonreview.net.

On a late December day in 2004, Amy Mello, MassEquality's field coordinator, headed to a windowless, bureaucratic office with bright fluorescent lighting in South Boston that housed the Massachusetts Department of Vital Statistics.

Most people went to that office to get an official copy of their birth certificate, marriage license, or family member's death certificate. Not Amy. She was there to record every marriage license of a same-sex couple that had taken place in Massachusetts in 2004; 6,500 was our best estimate.

Now that state lawmakers knew they wouldn't lose their seat for voting our way, we needed to make our best affirmative case to get more of them to want to vote with us. The gay couples who had married in Massachusetts were our most powerful assets in making that case. The Legislature would vote one more time in 2005 on a constitutional amendment to ban marriage and replace it with civil unions. If it passed, it would go to the ballot in November 2006.

Our opponents tried to terrify lawmakers by describing what they alleged were the unforeseen consequences of allowing gay couples to marry. They said it would harm kids, degrade families, and lead us down a slippery slope to polygamy, incest, bestiality, and more.

We knew that the one thing that could break through the fear was allowing lawmakers to get to know married couples and their families. When they did, they would understand viscerally that these families were not much different from their own and that they should treat gay families as they'd want their own family to be treated. We already had many married couples who were actively volunteering with us, but we knew there were thousands more who were not. These were regular folks who weren't politically active, so it would take some prodding to get them to engage.

Geographically, we needed much more diversity among our advocates. We had many couples from the parts of Massachusetts one would expect: Boston and its progressive suburbs and the progressive western Massachusetts cities of Northampton and Amherst. Not coincidentally, those were areas that were represented by liberal lawmakers who were already voting with us. A good portion of the state was "no-man's-land" for us. We were especially weak in the shrinking, ethnic, working-class communities throughout the state: the Portuguese South Coast cities of New Bedford and Fall River; the northern industrial cities of Lowell, Lawrence, Methuen, and Haverhill; the "Twin Cities" of Fitchburg and Leominster; and what we began calling our Bermuda Triangle, the area south of Boston from Quincy to Brockton and Plymouth. More than anywhere else, the struggling western Massachusetts city of Springfield—the third-largest city in the state—was where we were completely outgunned by our opponents.

Based on our conversations, we knew that a number of lawmakers didn't know any married same-sex couples from their own districts. They'd seen the reports of marriages on television, but those were mostly in "other" places. And even if they'd read in their local paper that a few gay couples had gotten a license at the town clerk's office, they hadn't had real interactions with them. So we were on a mission to find these gay couples and convince them to share their stories.

Amy Mello discovered that the process of examining the marriage licenses at the Department of Vital Statistics was a royal pain in the ass. First, she was told that she and her team of volunteers would have to check each one out one at a time, but she managed to persuade the bureaucrats to let them check the documents out in small batches. They were required to go and look at the licenses in an adjacent room, and they weren't allowed to photocopy the documents. So Amy and her team manually entered the names and addresses of couples who sounded as though they were same-sex couples into a spreadsheet. Once they got through a batch, they had to go to the end of the line to return the documents and check out another small batch. Amy understood that the department was being strict because these were the only permanent copies of the licenses. On each daylong visit, Amy and her team would get the names of about sixty-five couples.

By the end of the winter, they'd found 4,500 same-sex couples from every part of the state. We loaded all the names into our database, coded them by legislative district, and sent a letter to every couple. We told them their uniquely critical role in the campaign and asked them to fill out a form providing us with details about themselves and their marriage: how long they had been together, if they have children, if they know their legislators, and so forth. For those from crucial legislative districts—places where we didn't have many supporters and where the lawmaker seemed open to switching their position—we had volunteers, often married couples themselves, look up their phone numbers and call to ask them to get involved.

We did have one unfortunate incident: We got an irate phone call from a guy from New Bedford who told us we'd "outed" him to his parents. He'd apparently used his parents' address on his marriage license but hadn't told them he had gotten married—or that he was gay for that matter. We apologized profusely. On the whole, though, the effort was extremely successful. Many of those we mailed or called were very willing to help out and impressed we'd tracked them down.

The path ahead was challenging. After the elections, we could count on eighty-six reliable votes, so we needed to move a minimum of fourteen lawmakers our way. We also knew that lawmakers generally hated changing their position for fear of being attacked as flip-floppers. As we looked at the list of lawmakers with lead lobbyist Arline Isaacson and her team, we identified about forty who seemed "gettable." About twenty of those seemed particularly ripe for change. We didn't know precisely when the next constitutional convention would be. So we had to move quickly to activate our base around the state.

On Monday, December 20, I rented a car and drove in frigid, single-digit, snowy weather to Holyoke Community College for our first post-election gathering of our Springfield/western Massachusetts affiliate. Joe McCoy, the leader of the group, greeted me as I walked into the room in the early evening. There were about fifteen people there.

Joe, a veterinarian who worked in a lab in Springfield, had met his husband Stan on an online dating site three years before. They married the first Saturday it was legal at the Unitarian Universalist Church in Northampton. When Joe thought about how far he'd come as a political activist, he was amazed. Before the marriage fight, he was an infrequent voter. That changed when some of his friends invited the couple to drive to Boston for one of the constitutional conventions. The moment Joe got to the State House and witnessed the intensity of the fight, he was hooked. He'd spent the fall volunteering for a state representative candidate in far western Massachusetts, trekking an hour-plus each way on multiple occasions. Now he was looking to us for the next steps.

I stood in front of the room and gave my pitch. "These elections showed that lawmakers can feel free to vote with us without any fear of repercussion from their constituents. And to the extent there's any repercussion to their vote, it's in voting against us."

But we still had a big job in front of us. Getting a minimum of fourteen lawmakers to change their votes was no easy task. "We showed them there's no danger in voting our way. Now we need to make our strongest case about why they should vote our way."

How would we do it? Organizing. Constituent contacts. My mantra was quality and quantity contacts. A quality contact, I explained, was one of three things: (1) Someone prominent in the community whom the lawmaker needed to listen to—a business or labor leader, a clergy person, an elected official, or the like; (2) Someone who is personally influential to the elected—a family friend or a longtime campaign supporter; or (3) A married same-sex couple from their district, or a family member of the couple, who could speak personally about how marriage had changed their lives and how the love and commitment of same-sex couples was no different from that of straight couples. These were all powerful contacts that would be most likely to get lawmakers to rethink their positions.

Quantity of contacts, I explained, demonstrated to lawmakers that their constituents supported marriage. For the most part, lawmakers are an extremely risk-averse group. In making the case to a lawmaker, I could point to all their colleagues who'd voted our way and won re-election and say that there was nothing to be worried about, but the response I'd get more often than not was, "Well, I don't want to be the first" or, "They don't have to run in my district." We had to do our best to prove to any lawmaker whose vote we wanted that voting our way was what their constituents wanted and wouldn't harm their bid for reelection. This meant postcards, phone calls, e-mails, and letters—as many as we could get—from their constituents. We knew our opponents had a built-in advantage: the Catholic Church, which could activate its hierarchical network at any time. So we had to be creative.

I then laid out the priority lawmakers in the region. There were several in Springfield, none more important than Senate Republican Leader Brian Lees, one of the two authors of the "compromise" amendment supporting civil unions. Lees was a moderate Republican who was proud of his generally pro-gay voting record. If we could convince him to vote against his own amendment—not an easy task to be sure—others would no doubt follow.

I turned the podium over to Amy Mello, our field leader. Her favorite saying was, "If you can't measure it, it didn't happen." As usual, she'd preplanned several actions to get people's feet wet with the kind of work we needed to do: standing outside grocery stores, going to progressive churches and collecting signatures on postcards for their lawmakers. How many people will join me on this date, at this location, to collect postcards? Amy asked. And she'd wait until a good number would raise their hands and then sign them up on a flip chart. "How many newly married couples are here tonight?" Many people raised their hands. "How many would be willing to meet with their legislator?" A smaller number raised their hands. "And how many would be willing to host a meeting at your home and call the legislator's office to request it?" An even smaller number. But we had takers for every task.

Over the course of the next few months, we did similar meetings with affiliates throughout the state.

=

On Tuesday, March 1, 2005, MassEquality held a volunteer kickoff party event at Dido, a gay bar in Boston. There, I met Alex Hivoltze-Jimenez, a thirty-year-old theology master's student at Boston University. He had an amazing spark to him, was hilariously irreverent, and extremely handsome. We hit it off immediately and made a plan to meet up soon after the volunteer event.

Of German and Spanish-Mexican descent, Alex was on his own journey of finding an authentic pathway for himself. Raised a conservative Christian, he had been a dedicated youth leader for a church group; he had then run a very successful business in his twenties, owning a web consulting firm and then working in corporate intelligence. But he was closeted, wasn't passionate about the work he was doing, and realized he wanted a course adjustment. So he delved into academic work to figure out ways to reconcile his religious upbringing with his sexuality, working in both theology and queer theory, a newer academic field challenging societal norms from the perspective of a nonnormative sexuality.

A romantic relationship between us didn't work out, but "best friends" doesn't do justice to what we became to one another either. We were more like soul mates. We saw each other all the time, talked several times a day, and texted and instant messaged even more. When our leases were up, we rented a place together and were inseparable. We helped one another out in our professional lives too. Alex was brutally honest— sometime so honest it got him into trouble. I helped him become more strategic and "political" to help him get what he wanted without making too many waves. In turn, he pushed me to be more assertive and less political. "Stop talking about what makes sense," he'd say. "What do you want?" And he'd help me figure it out. As someone who'd fought my own urges and inclinations for a long time, I definitely needed the help. And figuring it out with Alex made everything so much better. My relationship with Alex was a pillar from which I drew great strength for the rest of my time working on marriage in Massachusetts.

=

New England is famous for its town meeting, an annual event in the spring when citizens in small cities and towns get together to discuss and vote on matters important to their community. As spring approached, we launched an initiative to be at more than 100 town meetings in target legislative districts, with local volunteers wearing MassEquality shirts and asking people to sign postcards. We knew the town meeting would attract the most active citizens, including many local electeds, and it was a perfect way for our advocates to demonstrate their resolve and collect signatures from the active citizens that lawmakers were most likely to know—as well as have conversations with lawmakers themselves. Though challenging to organize, this effort had the intended effect of showing we were upbeat, relentless, and everywhere.

=

We knew our opponents—the Catholic hierarchy, the religious right, and Governor Mitt Romney—hated the pending constitutional amendment nearly as much as we did. While we couldn't stand the fact that it took away marriage, they disdained the idea that it guaranteed civil unions. We'd long been hearing rumors that they would pull support from it in favor of one of their choosing, and on Thursday, June 16, they did just that.

"Asking citizens to vote on the pending amendment," the head of the Massachusetts Family Institute Kris Mineau said, "is like asking them to vote for John Kerry and George Bush on the same ticket." He announced that they would now oppose the amendment, call on their supporters to do the same, and instead launch a "citizen initiative" to collect signatures on an amendment that would get rid of marriage and replace it with nothing.

For our opponents, there was a serious trade-off in pulling their support for the pending amendment. By starting the constitutional amendment process over, their amendment couldn't make it to voters until November 2008, more than four years after same-sex couples had begun marrying. The upside for them was that according to the Constitution, a citizen-initiated petition only needed the support of 25 percent of the Legislature in two consecutive sessions, in contrast to the majority vote required for an amendment initiated by legislators. Keeping them under 25 percent seemed an impossible hurdle for us.

That day, Governor Romney held a press conference announcing his support for the more draconian amendment. I ducked in, even though it was closed to advocates—at least those on our side.

"We have a high degree of respect and tolerance for people whose lifestyle and choices and orientation is as they may choose. And therefore it's important that as we discuss matters of this nature that we always do so in a way that is respectful of other people's opinions."

I couldn't believe his language. Lifestyle? Choices? He really couldn't sound tolerant even if he tried.

When asked about whether there'd been any evidence gay marriage had undercut the institution of marriage, Romney responded that "the implications of same-sex marriage will only be measured over generations, not over years or months."

With our opponents now working against the pending amendment too, there was no question it would fail. But we stayed the course, seeking to build a solid majority of lawmakers who would vote it down for the "right" reasons and lining up votes for our tougher fight against the amendment to come. Throughout that summer, married couples met with legislators; volunteers collected postcards at fairs, festivals, and parades; and paid canvassers went door to door asking voters to sign postcards and make phone calls. We always took the high road, always sought to persuade, and appealed to lawmakers' better angels.

=

In the rural town of Charlton in southern Worcester County, Deb Grzyb and Sharon Murphy were pondering what to do about the Mass-Equality organizer who was asking them to meet with their senator, Steve Brewer. Charlton was only fifty-three miles from Boston, but culturally, it couldn't have been more different. It was the country: pick-up trucks with gun racks cruising over the narrow roads that wound through the wooded terrain and American flags everywhere, including on Deb and Sharon's small but beautifully adorned home.

The two were the most unlikely activists. They'd just celebrated their twenty-fifth anniversary together, but until they'd married the year before, they'd told next to no one they were lesbians or a couple. In fact, a few days after they applied for their wedding license, they each raced around the state coming out to family members—including Sharon to her mom and siblings—because they learned the local paper was going to print the names of all those who had applied. They were glad there were activists who fought for equality for gay people. But that just wasn't who they were.

The MassEquality organizer was persistent, explaining how crucial it was for lawmakers to hear from married couples who were their own constituents. Their rural district was one where we had next to no advocates, so they were especially critical. They finally relented and agreed to set up a meeting with their senator when he was in their community.

It turned out Deb and Sharon would be meeting with a staff person rather than the senator himself, but they were still extremely nervous and intimidated, both sweating as they headed over. As they sat down with the staffer, they explained that they got married after already being together for twenty-four years. They said that their marriage was so important to them and that they wanted State Senator Steve Brewer to vote against the constitutional amendment.

The staffer listened carefully and was extraordinarily nice but didn't give any signal of how the senator would vote.

"I'll let the senator know," he told them.

They left very relieved. It wasn't nearly as bad as they thought it would be.

Not long after, they received another call from the MassEquality organizer, thanking them for visiting with the staffer and asking if now they'd set up a meeting with Senator Brewer himself.

Oh boy. They sure didn't want to do that. But when the organizer told them how badly we needed them, they relented. He helped prepare them for the meeting, explaining that they didn't need to be experts on the amendment or the legislative process; they only had to describe why marriage mattered so much to them.

On a warm Wednesday in July, Deb and Sharon took the forty-minute drive through rural Worcester County to Senator Brewer's district office in Barre. They were terrified.

The middle-aged senator welcomed them into his office. He'd served in the Senate for sixteen years, representing his hometown of Barre as well as the rest of the district that stretched the length of the state, from New Hampshire on the north to Connecticut on the south.

Sharon took the lead. She told the senator that the two of them were regular people who lived in Charlton, both working for one employer, Commerce Insurance, for nearly their whole careers. They'd met in Boston twenty-five years before; it was love at first sight, and two months later Sharon had moved in with Deb at her home in Dudley, near where they lived today.

In a million years, they never expected to be able to get married. But now that they were married, Sharon explained, they recognized how important marriage was for their relationship.

They asked Senator Brewer to vote down the constitutional amendment.

He listened carefully to their story, interjecting at times. He told them he'd been to a wedding of a lesbian couple in Barre, a personal friend of his whom he liked tremendously.

I'm the type of politician who plays my hand close to the vest, Brewer explained. But I want you to know that I'm going to vote against the amendment. He told them that they were the first to know and asked them not to share the information with anybody. They thanked him profusely and told him his secret was safe with them.

"One of the best things I can tell you to do," he advised, "is to become more visible in your community. Be part of your community and become involved in your community." That was the best way they could get more support, especially in their neck of the woods, where most people didn't know married gay couples.

Driving back to Charlton, they were ecstatic. They really liked him. And he committed his vote. That was huge!

—

In late summer, we asked dozens of other married couples who'd had meetings with their lawmakers to follow up and try to get commitments. And as Labor Day approached, they started securing them. Senator Michael Knapik, a Republican from western Massachusetts, told couples that had met with him that it was a no-brainer; he was voting no because he believed in their right to marry. Rep. Eric Turkington told a group of his constituents on Martha's Vineyard that he'd vote against the amendment, though he was concerned there would be a ballot fight on the new amendment and our side would lose everything. Senator Jim Timilty phoned a woman who had hosted a meeting with him back in May to tell her that he'd vote against this amendment as well as the new, more draconian one that was coming. For him, it was meeting the children of a few gay couples that did it. They were no different from his own, so how could he ever vote to treat their family any differently? A newlywed couple met with their representative, Hank Naughton, in his local office in Clinton. The lawmaker told them how shocked he'd been at the viciousness of some of the hate groups arrayed against our side and that he'd be voting our way. And on it went, many couples learning that sharing their stories had paid off and that they really did have the power to influence their legislators' votes. That was extremely gratifying and empowering.

On September 14, 2005, at 1:04 p.m., Senate President Robert Travaglini gaveled the constitutional convention into session. Today was the day they'd vote on the amendment that eliminated marriage and created civil unions. Because our opponents were urging a no vote as well, we knew this amendment would go down in flames, but for us a victory meant a clear majority who voted our way because they believed in the freedom to marry. We knew they'd stand with us for the rest of this fight.

Senator Brian Lees, the Republican leader of the Senate and coauthor of the amendment, spoke first. "I've received over 7,000 letters, e-mails, and phone calls from people," he said. "The majority of people asked me to vote against this proposal."

Joe McCoy, the head of the western Massachusetts affiliate who was watching on the big-screen television in the Great Hall with his husband Stan, was pinching himself. Their group had gone to event after event, festival after festival, and door to door collecting postcards for Senator Lees. Now here he was talking about their work.

"Gay marriage has begun and life has not changed for the citizens of the commonwealth with the exception of those who can marry who could not before. That is why I would vote no today on this amendment."

The crowd of several hundred people gathered in the Great Hall were ecstatic, hugging and cheering. And when Senator Lees came in to greet everyone soon after his speech, people greeted him as if he were a rock star. I went over to thank him and shake his hand. He seemed nervous, and a bit overwhelmed, but relieved and very gratified at how happy everyone was. From then on, he'd be a staunch ally.

After a couple more speeches, Carl Sciortino took the floor and gave his first floor speech about marriage. "I can tell you that myself, and all the members that are here from the GLBT community and around the commonwealth that are watching today, no matter what happens on this vote, or next year's vote, we're not going away. We will be here fighting for our rights until we are recognized as fully equal under the law."

"Trust me," he continued, "I know what it's like to campaign and have this issue thrown on me through no choice of my own. But I wear that badge proudly. I am proud to stand here today as an open member of the GLBT community and to ask you to look into your hearts and truly consider whether you would vote to take away the right of your own mother, father, son, daughter, sister, or brother to marry the one that they love."

I was standing in the Great Hall watching, and my eyes were filled with tears. Carl had become one of my very close friends, and I couldn't have been more proud of the voice he'd given to our struggle.

Nearly as soon as it began, the vote was called. The tally was 39 in favor, 157 opposed.

Our opponents claimed victory and promised to immediately begin collecting signatures on their new amendment. But it was clear to me we'd more than accomplished our goal. Based on my quick count, we now had 120 lawmakers who voted against the amendment for the "right" reasons, a gain of twenty-six votes from the last time around. We had our solid working majority.

There was no question that between paid signature collectors and the Catholic Church network, our opponents would be able to reach the number of signatures they needed easily. The church engaged aggressively, even sending Catholic school kids in Fall River home with petitions for their parents to sign. By December, the secretary of state had certified 123,356 signatures as legitimate, nearly double what was required.

With the clock having started over, we went right back to work. But there was one big difference: Marty Rouse had left MassEquality to join the Human Rights Campaign, and the board had chosen me to replace him and run MassEquality. The pressure was on, and yet I couldn't have been more excited to drive our campaign, using every tool, strategy, and trick in our arsenal to propel us to the finish line.

=

While things were moving in the right direction in Massachusetts, around the country the losses at the ballot and the blame that came our community's way for Kerry's loss led some in the national LGBT equality movement to raise the question of whether the marriage fight was worth it, or whether it should be seriously deprioritized. A spokesman for HRC—which had become a top funder of MassEquality—said, "This election may have shown us that the change agents for gay marriage are looking too much like a noisy red Ferrari speeding down quiet Main Street." I was horrified at the prospect that we'd retreat in any way. Thankfully, the national freedom to marry movement was being driven by Evan Wolfson, and he'd faced down much more significant pushback in his more than two decades of leading on the cause.

=

Evan was one of the truly rare people who—after recognizing he was gay as a young man in the 1970s—didn't turn inward and wonder what was wrong with himself. He turned outward and wondered what was wrong with everyone else for discriminating against people whose natural attraction was toward the same gender. In reading Yale historian John Boswell's 1980 work *Christianity, Social Tolerance, and Homosexuality: Gay People in Western Europe from the Beginning of the Christian Era to the Fourteenth Century*, Evan learned that there was a period in European history—during the eleventh and twelfth centuries—when same-sex couples formed unions that were respected by the church and society. That opened Evan to a deep exploration of what a different modern-day world could look like for gay people, culminating in a 1983 law school thesis entitled "Same-Sex Marriage and Morality: The Human Rights Vision of the Constitution."

"Ours is a sexualist society," Evan began. "In particular, we have come to believe in constraints on the love which can exist between women and women, and men and men. Unlike other cultures and other times, we have made the gender of our beloved, and not the quality of the love, the overriding issue. This sexualism is pervasive and insidious."

In his thesis, he laid out a vision for marriage for same-sex couples and the beginnings of a roadmap for how to achieve it.

Marriage hadn't been beyond the imagination of others in the post-Stonewall era. In 1970, Richard Baker and James Michael McConnell, two University of Minnesota students, applied for a marriage license, were denied, and filed suit. However, the nascent equality movement wasn't close to being at a point where their claim was taken seriously. It was during the AIDS crisis that many Americans first learned of the loving, committed relationships of same-sex couples, as the images of sick and dying gay men being cared for by their partners made their way over the airwaves into people's homes.

In 1983, after graduating from law school, Evan went to work in the Brooklyn district attorney's office, but his passion was the pro bono work he began doing for Lambda Legal, the first legal advocacy organization focused on challenging discrimination based on sexual orientation. Evan took on constitutional matters, writing the brief in the unsuccessful 1986 Supreme Court challenge to state sodomy laws, while advocating for marriage. He encountered stiff resistance in the gay community, both from those who thought marriage was too assimilationist an aspiration for gay people, as well as from those who thought it would be too difficult to achieve. He was joined in advocacy by gay *New Republic* editor Andrew Sullivan, who penned a cover story, "Here Comes the Groom," making the conversative case for freedom to marry.

Evan joined Lambda full-time in 1989 and began pushing hard for the organization to take up the cause. It became an urgent and real question when three Hawaii couples reached out to Evan, who was already known as the lead advocate for the freedom to marry, to represent them in a lawsuit against the state. When Lambda, like all the other small band of gay organizations, decided they wouldn't take the case on, Evan pushed back hard, and things grew so heated that Lambda fired Evan. Under pressure from the board and community, Lambda's leaders rescinded the firing, and with Lambda's permission, Evan went to work on the case behind the scenes, helping out Dan Foley, the straight local Hawaii attorney who now represented the couples. After leadership changes at Lambda, Evan was allowed to draft a friend of the court brief to the Hawaii Supreme Court in 1992, and the following year, the state high court handed down its groundbreaking ruling ordering a trial and requiring the state—for the first time ever—to prove that gay couples' exclusion from marriage was justified. Foley invited Evan to join the case in a more formal role, and this time Lambda assented and Evan served as co-counsel. After three full years, voluminous briefing, and a two-week full-on trial with experts testifying on various aspects of gay relationships, the well-being of children, and the meaning of marriage, the judge ruled that the Hawaii constitution guarantees gay couples the freedom to marry.

Evan used his status as one of the lawyers who prevailed in Hawaii to make the case throughout the country that marriage for gay couples was a real possibility shimmering on the horizon, and to summon people to the cause in order to hasten the day when we'd win, first in one state and ultimately nationwide. He spoke to hundreds of groups, at law schools, community centers, and to churches, wherever he could get a few people together, as well as in the media. In my work today, I frequently run into people who tell me they heard Evan speak at their law school or somewhere else in the 1990s. Sometimes they tell me they thought he was dreaming or off his rocker, but more often than not they tell me that's when they first recognized that this vision was worth fighting for. In multiple cities, advocates inspired by Evan came together and formed grassroots groups to advance the work and build support. He, along with GLAD's Mary Bonauto, inspired the formation of the Massachusetts Freedom to Marry Coalition, the group I first got involved in.

Evan fought against resistance to the Hawaii victory from all quarters. In 1996, Congress rushed through the so-called Defense of Marriage Act that barred the federal government from respecting the marriages of legally married same-sex couples. In Hawaii, voters approved a constitutional amendment that gave the legislature the right to bar same-sex couples from marrying, which snatched Evan and Dan's legal victory away. And in state after state, legislatures enacted laws that barred the state from respecting the marriage of a same-sex couple performed in a different state.

And yet, Evan was undeterred, continuing in his role as Lambda's Marriage Project Director to speak out proactively. "It's a mistake to define the work of our current civil rights movement by what seems currently realistic or attainable," Evan would say. "Our job is not to make it easy for politicians or judges to do what they want. It's to make it easier for politicians to do what we want—to do justice. We should not dumb down our demand for equality, for possibilities open up not in some linear, tidy way but in spurts of creeping and leaping."

And he would always finish his talks by reminding those assembled of the profound vision and opportunity. "Shimmering within our reach is a legal structure of respect, inclusion, equality, and enlarged possibilities, including the freedom to marry. Let us build the new approach, partnership, tools, and entities that can reach the middle and bring it all home."

If the resistance and counter-attack following the Hawaii court victory weren't enough to deter Evan, then certainly the onslaught after Massachusetts wasn't. After all, actual couples were marrying. And Evan knew that actual win and ensuing marriages would show straight people that there was no threat whatsoever, and it would imbue gay people throughout the country with hope and determination to continue the fight.

And yet he knew that it was important to fight back hard against

efforts to curtail the marriage movement. If the movement's lead organizations and funders took their foot off the accelerator—or put it on
the brake—winning marriage nationwide could take a very long time.

===

Evan joined with the ACLU's Matt Coles to shore up movement buy-in
to move the marriage fight forward aggressively and nip the calls for
slowing down or ending it in the bud. With the support of the Gill
Foundation, Evan, Matt, Mary Bonauto, and other leaders met up in
Jersey City to draft a strategy document called "Winning Marriage:
What We Need to Do."

Evan encouraged Matt to be the primary drafter, and together they
hammered out a document that laid out anew the strategy Evan had
long pushed for how we were going to win nationwide. He'd studied
carefully other civil rights battles, and particularly the battle to dismantle bans on interracial marriage. The way to a national win was to
get one of the two national actors—either Congress or the US Supreme
Court—to act. However, history showed clearly that neither would
act until there was a critical mass of states and a critical mass of public
support.

"Historically," the strategy document argued, "Congress and the Supreme Court have [been] much more willing to insist that 'hold out'
states abide by widely accepted social norms than they have been willing
to set norms for the nation generally."

For a period of time, the paper said, it would be a patchwork struggle
with wins and losses, and in the beginning there would be more losses
than wins. So there would be progress in Hawaii, then resistance and re-
versals. Then progress in Vermont, and establishment of civil unions—
not what we wanted, but for the first time, a significant set of benefits
for gay couples. Then progress in Massachusetts, but statewide constitutional amendments to follow. Ultimately, as we grew support through
massive amounts of public education, millions of conversations, and
smart political and electoral engagement, we would achieved victories in
courtrooms and in legislatures and get the critical mass that we needed.

In their hotel in Jersey City, Evan, Matt, Mary, and the rest engaged in an exercise to exemplify how this strategy for staying the course would bring us to national victory. By 2020, they wrote, we could win marriage in ten states—for example, California, Connecticut, Maryland, Massachusetts, New Jersey, New York, Oregon, Rhode Island, Vermont, and Washington. We could win civil union or "all but marriage" status in another ten, secure limited protections in another ten, and grow support in the final twenty (This became known as the "10-10-10-20" program; Evan called it the "20/20 vision."). With that kind of momentum, they concluded, we'd have the critical mass to turn to one of the national actors—either Congress or more likely the US Supreme Court—to finish the job and decide in favor of the freedom to marry nationwide. But, they cautioned, transformation of this magnitude, including a national Supreme Court win, would require much greater investment in public education, organizing, and electoral work, as well as the development of a national marriage campaign to lead and guide the efforts.

This "10-10-10-20" strategy paper was signed by all the major LGBT groups, and conversations within the movement about curtailing the march toward marriage eased.

=

When I took the helm of MassEquality, it had been more than two years since our court victory in Massachusetts. My most fervent hope was that we'd win another state. We'd been the singular target for our opponents for a long time now, and it was exhausting having a bull's eye on our back. In California advocates had gotten close: the Legislature had passed marriage legislation in 2005, but Governor Arnold Schwarzenegger had vetoed it. Movement leaders expected that 2006 would be the year. Legal challenges had worked their way to the highest courts in New York, Washington, and New Jersey, and those in the know predicted a favorable ruling in at least one and potentially all three.

Yet it wasn't to be. The New York high court ruled first, on July 6, 2006, 4–2 against a state constitutional right for same-sex couples to marry. Two and a half weeks later, the Washington State Supreme Court ruled 5–4 to uphold a state ban on marriage for gay couples, reversing two lower court rulings. And on October 25 in New Jersey, that state's high court ruled unanimously that the state couldn't deny equal benefits and protections to gay couples. However, by a 4–3 vote, it ruled that the Legislature could determine whether or not to call the relationship marriage. Democratic Governor Jon Corzine said right away that he'd drive to civil unions, leaving Massachusetts as the only state with marriage for the foreseeable future.

═

November 7, 2006, Election Day in Massachusetts. This time, instead of holding our own election night party, I headed to Boston's Hynes Convention Center to join Deval Patrick, the Democratic nominee for governor, at his party. Patrick was a newcomer to Massachusetts politics, an African American attorney with a powerful story of overcoming grinding poverty in Chicago, attending Harvard for undergrad and law school, and then serving as assistant attorney general for civil rights in the Clinton administration. Patrick's vision for civil rights prominently included equality for the LGBT community, including the freedom to marry. With his powerful oratorical skills, he'd built a movement of followers unseen in recent years in a Massachusetts gubernatorial election. Running against Romney's lieutenant governor Kerry Healey, it looked as if he'd win overwhelmingly.

While most others were schmoozing, I had my computer set up and was monitoring state legislative elections, checking in with our team that was scattered around the state working with campaigns. With 120 legislative allies, I knew it would be very difficult to maintain our undefeated streak that we'd begun in the 2004 election cycle. And yet I wanted to, badly, as it was a simple, clear, and powerful talking point—that no lawmaker who had voted with us on marriage had ever lost. Once again, we'd invested a tremendous amount in direct mail and polling: one million dollars this time, prioritizing races the polling told us gave us the best opportunities.

The results were great. We held our streak together: every incumbent who'd voted our way and run for reelection won, two more anti-equality incumbents were defeated, and we'd filled the majority of open seats with pro-equality candidates, netting a total of four pro-equality seats. We'd burnished our reputation again as an aggressive, strategic, and relentless electoral player. In total, over these two electoral cycles, we'd had pro-equality incumbents run for reelection 195 times, and they had won every single race.

I joined Deval Patrick's party as the results in the governor's race were announced. Patrick had prevailed by a margin of 56 to 35 percent. I was truly elated. Romney would soon be on his way out, and we'd have a champion for our cause in the corner office of the State House.

"You are every black man, woman, and child in Massachusetts and America," Patrick said in his victory speech that night. "And every other striver of every other race and kind who is reminded tonight that the American dream is for you, too."

What a change this would be.

Our celebration lasted for just that night, however, as we prepped for a constitutional convention days away, on November 9, on the new amendment. The Constitution said that amendments initiated through citizen petition required only 25 percent of the vote of the Legislature to advance. In practice, though, the Legislature had for many years effectively killed such petitions by using a simple majority to either recess or adjourn the constitutional conventions. Since MassEquality didn't have 75 percent of the Legislature on our side, we worked closely with the new House speaker, our staunch ally Sal DiMasi, to use a majority vote on November 9 to recess the convention until 2:00 p.m. on January 2, the final day of the legislative session. The motion to recess was approved by a vote of 109 to 87. We didn't have our full 120 supporters voting with us because some objected to this strategy of recessing and adjourning; they wanted to follow the process by the book and have an "up-or-down" vote on the amendment itself. But that was a vote we knew we would lose. After the vote, we declared victory and celebrated. All we'd have to do was to use our majority and adjourn on January 2, and the amendment would die.

But it wasn't to be.

The day after Thanksgiving, November 24, Governor Romney, who was still in office until January 3, along with his religious right allies, filed

what seemed like a last-ditch, Hail Mary lawsuit to order the amendment placed on the ballot if the Legislature refused to have an up-or-
down vote on January 2.

On December 27, the Supreme Judicial Court issued its ruling, and it
was devastating. While it conceded that there was no way it could force
the Legislature to act, it stated clearly that the Constitution required the
Legislature to have an up-or-down vote on the amendment. It said that
by not holding a vote on the amendment, lawmakers were "avoid[ing]
their lawful obligations" and condemned "the Legislature's indifference
to, or defiance of, its constitutional duties."

We tried to hold our majority in the Legislature together and finish the job. After all, lawmakers had stopped proposed amendments in
this way many times before, as recently as this year. Over the next two
days and through the New Year's weekend, our team of lobbyists and I
divided up the list of supportive lawmakers and called them. Our fears
were confirmed: the vote was slipping away.

On Monday, New Year's Day, I was in my office, exhausted, calling
through my lists of lawmakers and pulling them out of New Year celebrations to plead with them to stick with us. There was a lot of equiv-
ocating on the calls, and given that we could only afford to lose nine
votes, it looked bad. I received a call on my cell and picked it up, hoping
it was a lawmaker returning my call.

"Marc, it's Deval," said the voice on the other end. It was the governor-
elect, and he was calling from Logan Airport after a postelection R & R
trip to South Africa. "I'm sorry I haven't been around. Tell me how I
can help."

I told him that we really needed a strong statement from him urging
the Legislature to put an end to this debate tomorrow. And we needed
him to get on the phone and make calls to legislators.

"Done," he said. He asked me to send him a draft of a statement
that he could review. "And tomorrow, can you meet me in the transition office in the State House at nine and we'll start calling through
legislators?"

That was the best news I'd heard in awhile. I didn't yet know Deval
well. He had said all the right things during the campaign, but that was

a campaign. It would have been so much easier for him to stay on the sidelines until he was governor, or to offer to help by making a couple of calls. At that moment, electeds were running from us, not to us. This demonstrated to me that he was truly a champion, willing to expend political capital for our cause.

At 9:00 a.m. the next morning, the day of the vote, I met Deval at his small transition office in the State House, in the executive wing of the building. I gave him a list of people I thought it would be most helpful for him to call. He gave the list a scan and said he wanted to start with Steve Panagiotakos, a state senator from Lowell who wasn't on the list. I told him that he was hopeless; he was observant Greek Orthodox and had voted against us every time. "I think I can talk to him," Deval said. So he called and got him, and I sat there as they chatted. Patrick explained why he was calling and then listened for what seemed to be a long time. Patrick finally said, Well, I guess we're going to have to disagree on this one. I smiled on the inside; he was a bit of a rookie at this. But he was working it, and that was a lot more than most. After a little longer, I left to meet with legislative allies, and he stayed with the list and promised to keep making calls.

As I gathered with our allies for a strategy meeting at the Boston Bar Association across the street from the State House, it was clear what a mess things were. Many of our allies were skittish about voting against what the court had said was their duty. Others believed the court was stepping on their prerogative as lawmakers and couldn't believe that their colleagues wouldn't finish the job. None held that position more strongly than Boston State Representative Marty Walsh, who was elected mayor of Boston in 2013. I will never forget Walsh, infuriated at his liberal colleagues, pleading red-faced with them in his heavy Boston accent, and accusing them of snatching defeat from the jaws of victory.

Worst of all, House Speaker Sal DiMasi and Senate President Robert Travaglini, both old-school pols who hailed from Boston's North End and who had an icy and competitive relationship, weren't speaking to one another.

I walked back to the State House and huddled with our close legislative allies near Speaker DiMasi's office. We couldn't come up with a plan that would work. The Senate president wasn't an ally, and without him or a majority we were in trouble. After a couple of hours of chaos on the floor of the Legislature, Travaglini moved to a vote on the actual amendment. The vote was 62 in favor to 134 against, far exceeding the fifty votes our opponents needed to move it into the next legislative session for its second vote.

I was in great pain and anguish. We were only a few hours away from running out the clock, killing this amendment and protecting marriage in Massachusetts. What's more, we'd declared the amendment dead. Could I rally our troops one more time? We had one more shot next session. We'd netted four seats in the elections, so as of the next day, the first day of the new session, our opponents would be down to fifty-eight votes. And yet, pulling this off would be the most challenging thing I'd ever taken on in my professional life.

On Thursday, January 25, 2007, I picked up a Zipcar and drove thirty miles north in the frigid cold to the old textile manufacturing city of Lowell, Massachusetts's fourth-largest city. I pulled into downtown and entered a progressive coffee shop, Brew'd Awakenings, for an evening meeting of the Greater Lowell Equality Alliance, our MassEquality affiliate.

Judging from the e-mails and calls I'd gotten, I knew our advocates were shocked and in mourning after the January 2 vote at the constitutional convention. I needed to fire them up once again for the stretch run. We scheduled nine meetings with our affiliates in every part of the state between January 16 and 29.

I first thanked them profusely for all they'd done to get us to this point. I then talked them through a short PowerPoint presentation. I wanted to show them graphically how far we'd come and how close to the finish line we were—from 50 supporters in the Legislature in November 2003 to 142 supporters. Through persuasion and elections, we'd turned ninety-two seats from anti-equality to pro-equality in just over three years. I reminded them that the activists in this room knew how to do it; they'd persuaded two of the three representatives from Lowell to switch positions. We had nine to go statewide. We could get there, no question, by June 14, the scheduled date of the final constitutional convention. We knew how. We just needed to reach deep and call on the strength of our desire to protect the freedom to marry, and on our know-how that we'd accumulated over the last three years. It had gotten us this far and would propel us to victory.

We got to specifics, talking through the importance of finding people who had personal connections with lawmakers and could make the most persuasive case, as well as how crucial married couples would once again be. And we spoke of some of the targets they could work on.

As I moved around the state, I found the same dynamic at play: lots of raw emotion, some tears, but strong attendance and great resolve and rededication to sharing their own stories, collecting postcards, and identifying people who were close to lawmakers and asking them to reach out—whatever it took. By now, these were sophisticated advocates who knew how to leverage power in their communities. For me, even though I was exhausted, seeing these activists—many of whom were married—so dedicated to the fight energized me at a deep level. They were in. And they were looking to me to lead them.

One of my biggest concerns after the loss was whether our lead funders would stick by us. One major funder emailed me angrily asking, "what the f happened?" Thankfully, we had one donor, Tim Gill, who was in for the long haul, knew that losses were part of any social movement, and had cultivated a community of donors who invested in LGBT equality and looked to Tim for leadership. Gill, a Denver-based tech entrepreneur, had dedicated much of his time to the cause of equality after Colorado voters passed a horribly anti-gay statewide constitutional amendment in 1992. He sold his company and took a substantial portion of its profits—$250 million—to establish the Gill Foundation to invest in organizations working for LGBT equality. After the multiple losses at the ballot in 2004, he turned his attention to political giving, establishing the Gill Action Fund to back advocacy campaigns and candidates advancing our agenda and—as he like to put it—to "punish the wicked." He'd hired Patrick Guerriero, the gay former legislator and mayor from Massachusetts who had most recently run Log Cabin Republicans, to head up Gill Action.

Patrick, who had been helping us in Massachusetts for some time and who had become a trusted friend and mentor, called me very early on after the loss to tell me he and Tim Gill had my back and they were ready to help. We came up with a plan: Patrick would reach out to the advisers to several of the largest gay donors in the country—Jon Stryker, David Bohnett, Jim Hormel and others—and get them to Boston to listen to my pitch. And I would come up with a detailed plan and budget, get a few Massachusetts political leaders to meet with the assembled group, and pull together an event with MassEquality's major donors. I arranged for Governor Patrick to come to our office for a meeting, and he did a great job of explaining his commitment to the fight and support for MassEquality's strategy to win. At the Massachusetts donor event, Patrick Guerriero spoke of Tim Gill's and his unflinching commitment to my leadership and to the fight in Massachusetts and asked them to redouble their investments.

The visit was a home run—Patrick told me immediately after that Tim Gill was in for $200,000, and a number of the other major national and local donors let me know of their commitments soon after.

The campaign plan I'd put together had to focus on changing the minds of a minimum of nine lawmakers—and ideally a few more so we had a bit of a cushion. You never knew who would get a call from their priest or mother on their way to the vote, and change. We needed to make the case inside the State House and leverage every ounce of power from prominent business, labor, and political leaders, but these votes would be votes of conscience and they would be won or lost in lawmakers' districts. The list of lawmakers we had to work on was a difficult one. Most of those left were in one of two categories: religious Catholic Democrats who were primarily pro-life and living in working-class communities or neighborhoods, or conservative-leaning Republicans who had stood with Governor Mitt Romney through all of the votes.

I developed a very targeted field program, with one organizer focused on no more than two target lawmakers. We needed to figure out everything we could about our target legislators: who they listened to, what made them tick, who were the gay people—or parents, friends, or siblings of gay people—in their lives who could make the case. That required serious detective work and relentless execution, and it would be taking place mainly in conservative districts where we had a small membership base. It could only come through smart organizing work.

Guerriero had suggested to me that we hire an opposition researcher to create "dossiers" of each of our twenty-six targets. It wasn't to dig up dirt or illegal activities but rather to research everything we could about our targets to help us find who and what arguments would be most persuasive to them. I loved the idea. I asked around about who was best, and everyone pointed to the guy who had led ops work for Deval Patrick and John Kerry, among others. I hired him immediately.

=

On Sunday evening, January 31, Deb Grzyb and Sharon Murphy—the couple from rural Worcester County who had worked to persuade Senator Steve Brewer—joined Pastor John White and eight others from their church, First Congregational Church of Dudley, for a meeting with the local state representative, Paul Kujawski. Mark Stefanik, a congregant who had played college baseball with Kujawski, had arranged the meeting and was hosting it at the request of Pastor John who was working closely with our local organizer.

For Kujawski—known to most as Kujo, from the Stephen King novel of the same name (though spelled Cujo) about a rabid dog—there was no question in his mind that his vote for the constitutional amendment was the right one. The pro-life, pro-gun Democrat grew up in a home above his family's meat market in Webster, where immigrants worked in the city's brick factory buildings making shoes and textiles. He regularly went to Mass at one of the Catholic churches in town. With one exception, the block he grew up on was 100 percent Polish, and life revolved around the Polish American Citizen's Club, which hosted polka dancing every Sunday. Kujawski thought life was supposed to be pretty straightforward: you go to Catholic school, find a girlfriend, get married, have children, and lead a traditional family life as it is supposed to exist. He barely knew anyone who was gay, let alone a married gay couple.

Kujawski listened as the speakers talked about marriage. Much of the conversation was around the importance of legal equality, the benefits that came from marriage, and how civil unions didn't provide the same number of benefits. To Deb and Sharon, it was all logical but a little cold.

Kujawski mentioned that the court decision was a 4–3 split. Shouldn't people vote on something so controversial, something that was decided by only one vote? He wondered about what it would mean for kids and talked about how stubborn people were on the definition of marriage, on both sides. Wouldn't it be better if it went to a vote, rather than having legislators make the decision?

He also spoke to the politics. This is Dudley and Webster, not exactly Cambridge. His constituents wouldn't go for this.

When it came to same-sex relationships, he observed, people seemed not to mind if two women got married, but they had a real problem if two men got married.

"Well, isn't it every man's fantasy to see two women together?" replied Sarah, the pastor's wife, to a stunned Paul Kujawski.

"What church do you belong to?" he joked. "I want to join it now."

As the meeting reached the two-hour mark, Kujawski became curious to know about the lesbian couple in the room. He'd been told there was one married couple in the group. "Well, who is the gay couple here?" he asked. Sharon and Deb each said, "Me." Pointing, Kujawski said, "Oh, I thought *you* two were together." Deb was sitting next to a straight woman, not next to Sharon.

"So are you married?" Kujawski asked.

"Yes, we are," Sharon said.

"Well, when did you get married?"

"July 12, 2004," she responded.

"Where did you get married?"

"Oh, we got married in the headlands in Rockport."

Kujawski was doing his best to engage them, but they were reticent. Pastor John gave Sharon a gentle pat on her arm and said, "Tell him your story."

Sharon proceeded to talk for ten minutes about how she and Deb met twenty-seven years ago in Boston. They knew they were in love and moved in together in Dudley soon after. Growing up as a child, she said, you always think that some day you'll get married. And then when you realize who you are and the way that the world is, you realize that, well, that might never be an option for me.

She talked about how she and Deb lived quietly, first in Dudley and then up the road eight miles in Charlton, and created a life together but that something was missing.

She told Kujawski about their wedding day, about how they took their vows overlooking the Atlantic Ocean in Rockport, and how much that day, and their marriage, mattered to them. For the first time, they were legally related to one another.

All we want is what everyone else has, she said. We don't want anything more. But we don't want anything less, either.

Everyone was listening with rapt attention, and Deb had tears streaming down her face.

Paul Kujawski just sat there listening, staring, appearing a bit dumbfounded. This was a lot different from what he'd expected to hear. The people he knew of who were gay seemed like loners. He'd never seen them with anybody, and he never thought of it as a way of life.

Kujawski was captivated by the experience of two women from backgrounds like his own. Deb had grown up in a Polish family in Dudley, the neighboring city to his hometown of Webster. He was impressed by Sharon's strength and was sure of their love for one another, after twenty-seven years together. All of a sudden, what had seemed like a black-and-white decision on the marriage question turned stark gray. His heart felt heavy.

"Wow. Why didn't you say that sooner?" Kujawski asked.

One of the last to leave the meeting, Kujawski told Sharon and Deb that he'd like to speak to them again at some point. As he left the home and walked to his car, his friend Mark, who had hosted the meeting, thought it looked as if the weight of the world was on his shoulders. Deb and Sharon sent Kujawski a follow-up letter the next day to thank him. They said they would be happy to have more conversations with him.

=

By March, we were fully staffed up, our dossiers were mainly done, and we were now hard at work organizing in each of our twenty-six target districts. We'd restarted our paid door-to-door canvass as well. Between canvassers and full-time organizers, we had about forty people total on our field team.

I had raised enough money from national and local donors to be able to focus on getting to know each of our targeted lawmakers personally.

I wanted to make my own best case and make sure no stone was left unturned.

I began with the freshman lawmakers, those who hadn't yet cast a vote but who had run on a platform of "letting the people vote." I figured we'd have the best shot with them, first because they'd want to court favor with their new speaker, staunch ally Sal DiMasi, and second, because they hadn't already voted the other way. There were three on the list.

=

The "let the people vote" argument was a strong one for our opponents. Most artfully put, people would argue that irrespective of whether or not you are for gay marriage, the people should be able to decide, not unelected judges. It sounded benign and democratic. Polling showed that the vast majority of voters wanted to have the chance to vote on marriage—and on any matter of importance for that matter. Even a majority of our supporters wanted to be able to vote, as they wanted to cast their ballot our way. We had to educate those who supported marriage equality that public referendums weren't an appropriate way to settle matters of civil rights for minority groups. If that's how we did it, how long would it have taken African Americans, religious minorities, and others to progress? Communications expert Doug Hattaway helped us simplify this argument into a media campaign that we called "It's wrong to vote on rights."

For lawmakers, I made the case that the Massachusetts Constitution gave them an important role in deciding what belonged on the ballot. It required them to vote on these measures not once but twice. Putting the rights of a small minority group on the ballot, with all of the ugliness that would ensue in a campaign, was precisely the kind of thing they had the responsibility to stop.

=

I stopped by the office of freshman Rep. Angelo Puppolo, a young Springfield attorney who had served as Springfield City Council president. During the election, he said publicly that he supported the people having the right to vote. Our only electoral hope was to back a write-in candidate who was with us, but the candidate ran a nearly nonexistent campaign and Puppolo won big.

I'd never met Puppolo in person, but from the moment I stepped into his office, it was clear the brash new representative was going to give me a hard time for endorsing his opponent. "MassEquality," he said with some incredulity. How can I work with you after you endorsed my opponent? I told him that he'd taken a position against us. Our endorsement criteria were clear. But that didn't seem to make a difference to him.

What do you want me to do? Support you now?

I could tell he was pissed. But his focus wasn't on the issue itself. It was on our endorsement of his opponent. That gave me hope. I figured he felt an obligation to give me a hard time; then hopefully we'd be able to get down to business.

I don't really have a problem with gay marriage, he told me. But I told people they'd be able to vote on it in the campaign.

I listened with as much earnestness as I could muster. Can we begin anew? I asked.

Anew? After what you did to me? But it seemed as though there was some tongue in cheek going on, even through the genuine annoyance. After we'd talked for some time and I laid out my best arguments for switching his position, he said he just didn't know. I promised I'd be back to see him.

As I left, I had a bit of a kick in my step. He didn't oppose us. He was up for some back-and-forth. I could tell he wanted to give me a hard time, and I let him indulge. I'd stay in close touch with him, and we'd go at him hard in our field program.

My own approach to making the case to lawmakers was to figure out ways to connect. I always came to meetings knowing as much as I could about them, and when waiting for a meeting I'd scan the plaques and photos in their reception area to find things we had in common. If they were Republicans, I'd talk about my work as a Republican staffer on

Capitol Hill. I could usually chat them up about Boston sports, and always about local politics. My goal was to build a relationship with them that allowed me to stay engaged. Sometimes I'd stop by to talk about the issue, and other times I'd just chitchat about politics over a beer at a fundraiser. As long as we were talking, I always felt I had a chance.

—

A few days later, I left a meeting on the fourth floor of the State House and ran into Paul Kujawski, whom I'd never met before. I introduced myself.

Glad to know you, he said to me with a friendly smile.

"I'd love to have the chance to sit down with you and talk to you about the marriage issue," I told him. "Could we schedule something?"

"How about right now?" he asked me.

I followed him past his reception area and into his office. There was baseball memorabilia everywhere. Right across from his desk was a big, signed picture of Tony LaRussa, the St. Louis Cardinals manager. I asked him if he was a Cardinals fan, and he said no but that a friend of his worked in public relations for General Motors. LaRussa was their spokesperson, so he'd introduced Kujawski to LaRussa when he'd come to Boston. I told him I was a huge Kansas City Royals fan.

The Royals were great in their day, he said. George Brett, he was something.

Brett, I told him, was my favorite player, my hero growing up.

We talked baseball for a while. I had played some baseball in high school, still played in a competitive softball league, and was a huge fan. Kujawski played through college and had coached as an adult. It was something we could connect on, and I wanted that connection before I jumped into the issue before us.

Sitting behind his desk, he told me that he was really thinking hard about the marriage issue. He talked about how he was in a more reflective place and maybe a little less judgmental than he'd been. He spoke about changes he'd been through over the past few years, a lot of which were the result of his having been arrested for driving drunk, to which he'd pled guilty. He told me he had stopped drinking cold and that since that public humiliation, which he'd brought on himself, he'd changed. He spent more time at home with family, less time in Boston after hours.

More and more, I'm thinking about how people should just be able to live their lives, he told me.

He told me how great he thought Deval Patrick was, which was surprising coming from someone so conservative. He's such a bright guy, easy to get to know, easy to like, he told me. A really charming and wonderful guy. He said he knew he'd be speaking to Deval about this at some point and looked forward to that.

Then he talked about this couple he'd met in his district at a meeting, a couple named Deb and Sharon. What a wonderful couple. They have a powerful story, and they are great spokespeople for your cause. He told me about some other couple who, conversely, had been sending him nasty e-mails since his last vote. That's not going to be terribly effective with me, he told me.

I'd filed in my mind that I needed to have Deval reach out to Kujawski. But I'd never remember the name of these two women, so I took out my pen and, when he wasn't looking, wrote their names on my hand.

I was surprised at how open he was with me. What I'd heard about him was primarily from progressives, who spoke of him with derision. He could tell that I was all ears, and he wanted to share his own journey with me and think this through with me.

After more than an hour, we said goodbye. I really liked him—we had a great rapport. I asked him if I could come back sometime, and he said anytime.

And you can call me Kujo, he said as I left.

Once in the hallway, I took out my Blackberry and e-mailed Amy Mello. We need to have this couple—Deb and Sharon—stay close to Kujo, every step of the way until there's a vote.

We're on it, she told me.

=

By the end of March, our field team had been at full speed for a month and was producing impressive results. They'd arranged for thirteen meetings of married couples and family members with target legislators, as well as forty-five meetings between lawmakers and "grasstops" leaders—influentials such as presidents of rotary clubs, superintendents of schools, mayors, and selectmen.

Even with all the great work taking place, it was time to open up a new front in this battle. I noticed on Governor Patrick's public schedule that he was heading to DC for a meeting of the Massachusetts congressional delegation. We needed to activate our twelve-person delegation and get them more engaged in the fight. In prior years, we'd asked individual members of the congressional delegation to help. But this time, I wanted to have a very coordinated approach. I asked Doug Rubin, Patrick's chief of staff, if he could ensure it was an agenda item. Separately, I called Barney Frank and asked if he'd prioritize the marriage vote at the delegation meeting. Frank agreed. After the meeting, Rubin reported back that all twelve said they would help.

On April 17, our political director Matt McTighe and I followed up with our own trip to DC to meet with members of the congressional delegation to talk specifics. We gave each member an individualized list of state lawmakers for them to contact. I wanted to be sure they knew what they were supposed to do and which people they needed to contact. It was a great visit. Senator Ted Kennedy, the dean of the delegation and the most influential of all, was completely on board, and his staff promised that he'd engage at the right time. And every other member or staffer agreed to do the same.

I also met with Brian Bond, a senior staffer at the Democratic National Committee (DNC) who had headed up the Gay and Lesbian Victory Fund, a political action committee focused on electing openly gay candidates. The idea that having marriage on the ballot was a loser for Democrats continued to hold sway, so I figured we might as well use it to our advantage. I asked Brian if DNC Chair Howard Dean would make the political case that it would be bad for the Democratic presidential candidate to have a marriage referendum on the ballot in Massachusetts in November 2008; it would once again draw attention to the issue while boosting Mitt Romney's presidential candidacy by demonstrating his effectiveness in getting it to the ballot. Brian was in; he asked us to write up a detailed memo to Dean.

On Friday, April 27, Matt McTighe and I drove to Barney Frank's district office in Newton. He hadn't been available when we were in DC, and he was key to our efforts to activate our delegation. By now, I'd worked with Frank for five years on this issue and was used to how he dealt with people. He had absolutely zero time for small talk and would make mincemeat out of you if he thought your request was foolish. Once, I tried making small talk over the phone with Frank, and he said, "Marc, you're wasting my time. What do you want?" On another occasion, when I wasn't sure he understood what I'd asked for and repeated the question, Frank responded, "Is there something the matter with you?"

But it was all worth it, because Frank was the most effective and responsive elected with whom I'd ever worked. He never bullshitted you, would tell you if he thought something was a bad idea, and always did what he said he'd do. I learned never to ask Frank to record an automated call for a candidate because I'd get a lecture about how useless they were before he'd say no. But he was enthusiastic about headlining fundraisers for pro-equality Democratic candidates for the Legislature. For several years, I'd been calling him and running through lists of target lawmakers to whom I wanted him to reach out. He'd tell me the people he knew and didn't know, whom he could make an impact on and whom he couldn't. And he'd always call and report back, quickly, on how his calls went.

Matt and I sat down with Frank, and we made our "asks." First, we gave him a master list of the congressional delegation—the ten members of the US House of Representatives and two members of the US Senate—with the list of state lawmakers we'd asked each member to call. The number of names on each list varied, depending on how engaged on our cause the member of Congress was and how strong his relationships with members of the Legislature were. The request was for Frank to oversee the effort, checking in with his colleagues to ensure they were following through and making the contacts.

Yes, he'd do it.

Second, our lobbyists recommended that we have House Speaker Nancy Pelosi reach out to the brand-new Senate president, Therese

Murray—the first woman to occupy the top leadership position in the Massachusetts Senate or House—to congratulate her and let her know how important it was for Democrats to keep the marriage amendment off the ballot in November 2008. We also wanted Pelosi to call Speaker DiMasi as well.

Frank was part of Pelosi's inner circle. Yes, he'd make that happen.

Frank also offered to reach out to Bill Clinton to see if he'd make some calls.

Twenty minutes later the meeting was over, and I was back in the car for the drive back to Boston. We'd gotten what we asked for, and I knew it would be done.

=

By April, Deb and Sharon were getting antsy that they hadn't heard back from Rep. Kujawski. It had been more than two months since they first met with him, and they knew the clock was ticking toward the final vote in the State Legislature on June 14. So they sent another letter, this time inviting him to their home for coffee or lunch.

Kujo, though, hadn't been sitting still. While he didn't think he'd met many gay people in his district before, now he was hearing from them pretty consistently, thanks largely to David Kent, MassEquality's field organizer assigned to the district. At Bartlett High School, Kujo's alma mater, he'd met two women who had moved to Douglas from Colorado because their families out west did not accept them.

There was the friend who lived in Dudley whose father, an archconservative, had represented Worcester in the State Legislature in the sixties and seventies. She reached out to Kujo because her daughter was a lesbian and the two had some very deep conversations.

We also enlisted two of Kujo's openly gay former colleagues, Susan Tracy, a partnered lesbian, and Patrick Guerriero, the adviser to philanthropist Tim Gill, to meet with him. Patrick had occupied the office adjacent to Kujo's and knew what a huge baseball fan he was. Patrick and Susan had strategized in advance, so at the meeting Susan passed around a photo of her son in his Little League uniform. Later, Kujo told me that seeing the picture of Susan's son had really gotten him in the gut.

The most challenging arguments on the other side came from his parish priest in Webster, Father Michael Roy. Roy had stuck by Kujo when things were at their worst, after his arrest for drunk driving. He had become a real confidant. On this issue, Roy was firm—marriage was between a man and a woman. He lobbied Kujo exhaustively.

Yet three other Catholic priests from the area reached out and asked Kujo to vote against the amendment. They were very secretive about their efforts, knowing how perilous it would have been had they been public. One of them lobbied Kujo constantly; he called him and stopped him on the street to ask for his support. He explained that his interpretation of the scriptures was that there is a good and loving God and that everyone is born in his likeness and ought to be treated with respect. That made a lot of sense to Kujo.

Kujo was also aware that he represented more than just Catholics. What about his responsibility to serve the others? And although he'd never before given the issue of homosexuality much thought, he had begun to conduct his own research since his first meeting with Deb and Sharon. Most people were probably born gay, he learned. They definitely didn't choose to be gay. What role in society did the Catholic Church propose to offer them? It was as if church doctrine eliminated an entire group of people. That just didn't jibe with the religious values he was taught.

Kujo finally called Deb and Sharon on April 23. I'm giving lots of thought to the issue, he told them, in no small part because of you.

His number one concern, he explained, was how changing his position would affect him and his family. What would people say about them in the community? What would happen when his wife ran into someone at the store? Webster and Dudley were conservative communities anchored around the Catholic Church. Also, Kujo had run as a stalwart opponent of gay marriage. Some of his constituents would feel that he'd betrayed them by telling them he would vote a certain way and then voting a different way. And in some ways they'd be right. He promised to be back in touch.

=

One of the two Republican lawmakers on our target list was a gentle and gregarious representative in his early fifties named Richard Ross. He was the only lawmaker in the Legislature who'd voted our way and then reversed and voted against us. He'd confided in me that his wife was extremely religious—a Southern Baptist who'd gone to Jerry Falwell's Liberty University—so voting our way had made things extremely difficult in his domestic life. But I also knew that, unlike most lawmakers in either party, Ross made it a practice to seek out different opinions and draw his own conclusions, even if that meant bucking his party or discovering new information that might lead him to change his mind. So we'd put an organizer on him.

Ross owned a funeral home in the heart of Wrentham, one of the more Republican parts of the state thirty-two miles southwest of Boston. Soon after the January vote, he'd gone over to the Parish of St. Mary, the Catholic church across the street that provided most of the funeral home business, to meet with the local branch of the Catholic fraternal organization the Knights of Columbus and talk about gay marriage. "Now that they're getting married," Ross asked the group of about thirty-five, "what's changed?" Nobody could point to anything concrete. The best they could do was to argue about where this was all going, and they'd make what to Ross were outrageous claims about polygamy and bestiality.

Our organizer made sure that Ross would have access to opposing views, so he arranged for same-sex couples and families from the district to meet with him, and they had their intended effect. He was especially moved by a veterinarian and her wife from Medfield, as well as a lesbian couple and their children living in Plainville who had invited Ross over to their home. He also met some kids with gay parents who attended King Philip Middle School with his own kids.

At home, he'd share his experiences and his thought process with his family, particularly his wife and his high school–age daughter Maeghan. "This is a much deeper issue than I've had any idea about. I'm having trouble reconciling this in my mind."

His wife couldn't believe it. "How can you do this as a Christian?" she'd ask, as he thought out loud about voting against the amendment. Or, "You'll never get reelected." The arguments raged around the dinner table.

On May 17, less than a month out from the final vote, MassEquality hosted a three-year anniversary fundraiser at a swanky nightclub in downtown Boston. We honored Ralph Hodgdon and Paul McMahon, the senior couple famous for carrying their sign, which on this night said, "Together 51 Years! Married 2!" Deval Patrick gave a rousing talk to huge applause.

It was a joyful night, but I was preoccupied—worrying about money. I'd been all set to make a final television buy for a powerful ad we were running, one that combatted head-on the "let the people vote" argument with "it's wrong to vote on rights." But at the last minute, a donor on whom I'd been counting for $200,000 didn't come through. The ad couldn't make an impact without that money.

At the event, a young guy in his mid-twenties came over to me and introduced himself. He said his name was Andrew and that he had been an organizer with the Gay, Lesbian, and Straight Education Network as well as the National Gay and Lesbian Task Force. He and his boyfriend Corey had volunteered and organized a phone bank for MassEquality at Harvard, where both were graduate students.

"We really like what you guys are doing and want to help," Andrew told me.

I thanked him and told him I'd be happy to introduce him to Amy Mello, our field director.

"No, we really want to help," Andrew said. He asked if he could call me at the office.

I had no idea what he had in mind, but the next day he called.

"How much more money do you guys still need for the campaign?" he asked.

I told him that we'd just lost a key donor and I was $200,000 short for a TV buy.

"I think we should be able to do that," he said.

I couldn't have been more floored.

It turned out that he was Andrew Singer, the son of Paul Singer, the billionaire New York hedge fund titan. Andrew and Corey didn't want any recognition for the gift, and the contribution needed to be completely anonymous because Andrew's father—one of the most important Republican donors in the country—was a leader in Rudy Giuliani's presidential campaign. Though Paul Singer was personally supportive of the cause, his advisers didn't want to stir anything up for the Giuliani campaign about his making a six-figure contribution for gay marriage.

I promised Andrew it would be 100 percent anonymous. Only our finance director knew the name; to everyone else at MassEquality, on staff and board, the donor was known as Anon Anon.

After the call, I immediately reached out to our media firm. Get ready to move with the TV buy, I told them.

=

In the dossier we'd had compiled about freshman Rep. Angelo Puppolo, we'd discovered a potential hook: he was a passionate fan of Broadway musicals. One of MassEquality's strong supporters was Gregory Maguire, the author of the novel *Wicked* on which the Broadway show was based. Gregory lived in Concord with his husband and three children.

I asked Gregory if he'd reach out to Puppolo, which he did on May 21 via e-mail.

He invited Puppolo to his home "to meet my husband and three kids, talk about the marriage question, and in the interim show you bits and pieces of WICKED-iana such as have come my way."

=

On May 23, I dropped by to see Puppolo. Since the last time I'd visited, we'd arranged to have local couples meet with him, and the reports back were that he'd come a good way our direction. He was no longer comfortable with the position he'd run on. He told me he had no problem with gay marriage but was still concerned about going back on what he'd said in his campaign. He was really conflicted.

He told me with a smile that he'd heard from Gregory Maguire and assumed that we'd made it happen. How did we know he loved musicals? he asked.

We have our ways, I said with a broad grin.

=

That evening, Brian Bond from the DNC sent me an e-mail telling me that Howard Dean had spoken with Senate President Therese Murray, and had left a long message for Speaker DiMasi. Dean offered to be helpful in any way possible, both because of the political significance and because he thought it was the right thing to do to keep marriage off the ballot.

=

Gregory received an e-mail back from Puppolo. "First, as I have yet to tell you—that I am a huge fan of theater and I have seen *Wicked* twice on tour and it was excellent—while I haven't read the book—the play was wonderful."

Puppolo told Gregory that he'd love to meet but that it would be difficult. He told Gregory he was meeting with many families in his district on the issue.

"Please understand that I do NOT have a problem with the gay marriage issue—but have during the past campaign discussed the people's right to vote."

Puppolo encouraged Gregory to e-mail his thoughts in case they couldn't get together before the vote on June 14.

Gregory responded right away:

As you suggested above, I will write a few thoughts here in case we don't have a chance to meet before the 14th.

You can tell from WICKED the play that my heart is very much with the underdog. The green-skinned Elphaba, passionate and devoted to the abused citizens of Oz, is a victim herself of snap judgments and slurs and prejudices. I don't claim her intelligence (nor her voice). However, her warmth of concern for those considered unworthy of dignity is mine, from experience.

When I heard the argument "Let the people vote" I was quite swayed myself, at first. Why not, I thought. I have trust in the citizens of Massachusetts, and if it has to come to that, I hope they will do the right thing—what I think of as the right thing, anyway. But what if they don't? What if mob rule, the tyranny of the majority, and the inflated rhetoric of the religious right (and I speak as a practicing Catholic) blow a civic discussion up into a bloody battlefield?

It took some time before I could see what might happen—let's say in November 2008—if this divisive matter is put to a public referendum. My oldest son will be ten. His dads will have been legally married for four and a half years. What will the buzz in the schools be, around him, as the voters weigh in on the legitimacy of his dads' marriage, of his family structure? Yes, the Maguire Newmans as a legitimate marriage would be grandfathered in, but that will be cold comfort to him if kids around him are razzing him for being part of a historic fluke, an aberration of history in addition to being part of a minority population.

We are mostly concerned with the justice of the case. We have become convinced that it is not in the tradition of Massachusetts legislation that the rights of a minority should be determined by a vote of the majority. (E. M. Forster once titled a book "Two Cheers for Democracy"—meaning that the democrative vote, the strict majority-rule vote of the public, worthy though it often is, has the capacity of installing a preferential treatment favoring majorities and disenfranchising minorities.)

So it's not just our family we care about—though we care about our three kids and what they might go through next year, if the ugly, overheated battle is allowed to be joined. We're concerned about the larger issue of justice for minorities. Especially as seen through the faces of our own kids, and how they are treated on the soccer pitches, the school bus rides, the birthday parties in our town. We don't want them to feel any more of what Elphaba felt [than] they possibly have to.

Thank you so much for taking this matter so seriously. I do hope we have a chance to meet, even briefly. And I hope we can defy gravity on this one!

Cheers,
Gregory Maguire

The next morning, Puppolo responded via e-mail:

> Thank you so much. I wanted to let you know that I have read your thoughts and do appreciate the analogy—it was very well taken—and right to the point.
>
> Please know that I am still struggling over this issue in my mind—and it is the only thing I am focused on right now.
>
> Sincerely,
Angelo J. Puppolo, Jr.

Paul Kujawski walked over to what was known as the corner office in the State House, the office occupied by the governor. Deval Patrick had invited him over to talk about the marriage issue. The two sat in the governor's stately office, on two chairs angled toward each other.

"This issue has happened," Patrick said. "It's over. Let's not bring it back."

He talked about what a huge distraction it would be for everything else they wanted to accomplish if they had a big referendum fight on marriage.

We don't need to go back and create something that would be more of a problem, Patrick said. We're beyond this.

Kujo knew this issue was really important to Patrick but could tell the governor wasn't doing the heavy-duty sale. Instead, the governor seemed to be making a case that would work better with him and he appreciated that.

Patrick listened carefully as Kujo talked about what he thought the consequences were going to be in his own life, both political and personal, and how this would affect his family, who would have to endure comments and confrontation at the grocery store and in church. He also talked about the stories of couples that had a real impact, Deb and Sharon in particular.

Patrick could see this was a struggle for Kujo; his body language made it clear. He leaned forward in conversation. He sweated a little bit. That's the kind of struggle this issue deserved, Patrick thought, at least for those who weren't automatically drawn to the civil rights arguments. He admired Kujo for challenging himself and his assumptions, thinking really hard about what the right thing to do was and how he'd get there. Patrick didn't think this should be a political call; he wanted the lawmakers to struggle and get to the right place because they were making a vote of conscience.

Patrick told the conservative Kujawski that, for those who believe in limited government, why would we ever want to tell people whom they can marry? This isn't about telling a church or a synagogue what they have to do inside a sanctuary, whether they sanction or conduct a marriage. It's really about who gets a license—that's the government's role in this. Why would we want the government to get into people's lives by telling consenting adults which person is acceptable for them to marry?

He also talked about "the facts on the ground." We'd now had three years of marriages. The sky hadn't fallen. The ground hadn't opened up and swallowed us all away. People who celebrated gay marriages, celebrated them. And those who weren't on board didn't accept the invite or didn't get invited. It just hadn't been disruptive, as some opponents had predicted.

Kujo listened carefully. Even though Patrick was much more liberal than he was, he genuinely liked the governor. He was a charming guy and had such a positive way about him.

"There are no other states that have this," Kujo said. "We're the pioneer. Why can't we be the pioneer on other things as well?"

Governor Patrick offered himself up as a resource to help in any way he could, including visiting the district.

Kujo chuckled and said to him, "You don't have to come out. I don't really like you there." The liberal governor wouldn't be a help to him on this issue in his conservative district.

As Kujawski left, Patrick believed he would vote against the amendment. But Kujo still hadn't made up his mind.

—

On Wednesday, May 30, three weeks before the vote, Kujo called Deb and Sharon and said he wanted to come by their place. They'd invited him several times but had assumed that since he hadn't responded, he might not feel comfortable. They set a date for five days later, late afternoon on Monday, June 4.

Kujo came by around 4:00 p.m. after playing in a golf tournament. They sat in an enclosed porch at the back of the house that looked out at the woods. It was a beautiful, serene setting, with hummingbirds congregating around the bird feeder.

Kujo was honest with them. He told them that he continued to be concerned about how his voting against the amendment would affect him in the community. What if it cost him his job and hurt the well-being of his family? He commiserated with Deb about what it's like being a Polish Catholic in Webster and said he'd been talking to his priest. He mentioned someone in his family who was dating outside the faith and what a big deal that was for his family. And that was nothing compared to this.

Sharon wanted to shift the conversation back to questions of fundamental fairness. In a gentle way, she asked, What if one of your sons was gay? How would you feel if he wanted to get married someday? Kujo was thinking about how his vote would affect his family, so Sharon wanted to encourage him to think about his family in another way.

Kujo said that when he met with supporters of the amendment, he would tell them that maybe it isn't right to vote on the rights of people. He said he'd gotten to know and respect the people at MassEquality.

Deb and Sharon showed Kujo their wedding album and family photos, gave him a tour of their home and gardens, and served him homemade oatmeal and chocolate chip cookies. It was the first time he had been welcomed into a gay couple's home, and it felt just like visiting any other family. He stayed for a couple of hours.

As Deb and Sharon reflected on the meeting after he left, they thought he was looking for a way to vote no, but he wasn't sure of the path yet. Once again, they followed up with a thank-you letter and reported on the meeting to the MassEquality field organizer. They still didn't know where he'd come down.

=

The one voice we hadn't yet heard from, one I knew would be influential, was that of our senior senator, Ted Kennedy. Not only was he the Lion of the Senate, but also he was the conscience of Massachusetts. To state representatives thinking about their place in history, a call from Kennedy could make a real difference. Kennedy's staff had agreed to help, but we were getting close to the vote, and he hadn't done anything yet. I reached out to Kennedy's close friend, former Massachusetts Democratic Party Chair Phil Johnston, one of our earliest supporters. Could he push to get the calls to begin? He told me that he was in touch with Kennedy's people and he was confident Kennedy would help at the right time. Soon after, I heard from a senior Kennedy staffer. He asked for the most up-to-date list of legislators we were working on. And he made me promise that our conversation was completely off the record. He told me that advocates would often start talking about the fact that Ted Kennedy was making phone calls on an issue—and that would create a story, sometimes even before Kennedy had picked up the phone. That always backfired.

Of course, I said.

Soon after that call, as I made my rounds in the State House, I began hearing a buzz. You'll never believe who called me about gay marriage. Ted Kennedy. It was having the effect we'd hoped.

Senate President Murray, House Speaker DiMasi, and Governor Patrick met weekly, and as the vote approached, it became the priority topic on their agenda. Their senior staffers were in constant communication with one another. I stayed in close touch with each of them and with their senior staff, and was back and forth all the time trading intelligence with Doug Rubin, Patrick's chief of staff.

Heading into the final weekend before the vote, we had three solid commitments in place, with six to go to hit our magic number.

On Tuesday morning, June 12, two days out from the vote, Republican State Senator Richard Ross, the one with the Southern Baptist wife, headed over to St. Mary's Church across the street from his funeral home for the final Mass of the local priest and to present the priest with a proclamation for his years of service. Afterward, Ross went to the rectory for coffee and cookies, and some of the parishioners gathered around to talk to him about the marriage vote.

"I'm not the guy you have to worry about," Ross told them. "Call all the other guys in there. They're the ones that probably aren't going to vote the way you want them to."

Even though he could still feel some wrestling going on inside, he'd settled on his position and knew being consistent with his last vote was a comfortable place to be for many reasons.

After things wrapped up at the church, Ross headed to the State House for some meetings, including a get-together with Patrick Guerriero.

Patrick, the gay former Republican state representative from Massachusetts, had over the past few years been meeting with a number of his former colleagues, as well as newer Republicans in the Legislature like Ross. This afternoon was Patrick's final meeting with Ross to try to get him over whatever obstacles stood in the way of voting no.

Patrick listened carefully to Ross and recognized he was still conflicted about the issue. "I have watched you go through this process and be so thoughtful," Patrick told him. "I know where you need to end up, and not for us, but for you."

But Ross seemed to have his mind made up. After a good amount more back and forth, Patrick still didn't see the path to getting Ross to a no vote. As he got up to leave, he inquired about the kind of clients Ross served in his funeral home business.

The question triggered something deep inside Ross, who had a flashback about something that happened more than thirty years prior. He remembered the summer day in 1976 just a few weeks before his father passed away from heart disease. Once he realized how sick his father was, Ross, who'd been studying at American University to become a diplomat, dropped out and came home to help his father with the funeral home. Soon, Ross would be taking over the family business, and his father wanted to impart some advice.

"I want to tell you certain things about people, son, that will make your life a whole lot easier," Ross's father said. "Folks from all walks of life are going to ring that doorbell. Do yourself a favor. When you open that door, don't look them up and down and judge them by what you think you see. You look them in the eye and you find one thing about their character or their makeup that you like about them, and you build a relationship around that. And I promise you this: nobody will ever leave your life as an adversary."

Ross started to sob uncontrollably at the memory. Patrick asked what was wrong. Through the tears, Ross could barely get the story out. He'd told that story many times before, but it had always been an intellectual exercise. Today, though, his heart was raw. "I can't believe I'm about to treat people in one day job differently than I treat them in another day job," he responded.

"This is the real deal, isn't it?" Patrick asked.

"Yes it is," said Ross. "I'm realizing my heart and head are not reconciled. You're on one side of an issue. There's a whole lot of other people talking to me in a variety of ways on this issue as well. I need everybody to disappear for the next ten or twelve hours. Because until my head and heart agree, I'm not going to be where I need to be on this."

After Patrick left, Ross packed up his belongings and headed back to Wrentham.

That day, two more representatives confirmed they would vote our way, one to the governor and another in a media interview. That meant we had five commitments. Four more to go.

=

In Wrentham, Richard Ross had retreated to what he called his "man cave," the first floor of his funeral home. He didn't feel free at his house, with his socially conservative wife, to ponder this question. He'd grown up at the funeral home, an enormous and beautiful historic house right in the center of town. It was where his father had proffered that advice just weeks before he died.

Ross felt a great spiritual connection to his parents, both of whom were deceased: his father, a first-generation Scotch Irish Catholic Democrat, and his mother, a twelfth-generation Yankee Protestant Republican. The funeral home, which he maintained beautifully, could have doubled as a museum, with hundreds of town histories and genealogies of Wrentham and his mother's family dating back to before the Revolutionary War.

Ross entered the parlor room where portraits of his parents hung prominently on the wall. In good times and in dark times, he found their presence comforting. He sat in just the right place, in front of his father's portrait, where the natural light shone off it and it took on a different tone. It felt as if the image of his Dad lifted right off the canvass and he was still standing right there.

After awhile, he turned and looked at the photo portrait of his three children on the wall behind him—his daughters Maeghan and Chandler and his son Chase. As he sat and reflected in that room, it became clear that he needed to vote against the amendment, no matter what, even if it cost him his job, which he thought it would. He was a Republican from one of the most conservative parts of the state. He knew he'd be letting down some of his constituents, those who had entrusted him to carry their message. They'd feel betrayed, especially those he spoke to that morning at the church gathering. But he knew what he needed to do.

=

In Boston that evening, I was working at my desk when my phone rang. It was Rep. Paul Loscocco, an iconoclastic Republican from suburban

Holliston. Over the years, he'd given multiple long-winded speeches about marriage and the *Goodridge* decision, and I could never figure out exactly what he was getting at. What I knew was that he'd voted against us every time, and he wasn't on our radar screen at all.

He went into a spiel about how the *Goodridge* decision was wrongly decided. I was exhausted and trying to follow what he was saying. I certainly wasn't in the mood to have an argument about the legal justification for *Goodridge*, but it was clear he was calling at this eleventh hour because he wasn't comfortable voting for the amendment. He made the case that if we could get behind a bill that would ensure no houses of worship or other religious entities would have to marry same-sex couples, he'd be much more inclined to vote our way.

I asked if he'd be willing to meet with the attorneys from GLAD in the morning to talk this through. He told me he'd already reached out to them, and he had a 10:00 a.m. meeting. We'd agreed to talk afterward, and I wrote a quick e-mail to Mary Bonauto and Gary Buseck at GLAD about my conversation.

The next day, one day before the vote, I was at my desk making calls when some shocking news came across the wire. The headline was "Verga Falls, Removed on Stretcher." Holy shit.

I felt sad for the senior Democrat from Gloucester, a devout Catholic and chair of the Committee on Veterans and Federal Affairs on whom we'd been aggressively working to persuade. We'd sent in every single gay veteran we could find to make the case.

I kept reading:

> Rep. Anthony Verga fell on the stairway outside the House chamber around 3:30 pm and was taken out of the building on a stretcher, after being tended to by park rangers and two colleagues who are nurses. Verga, a 72-year-old Gloucester Democrat, slipped on the top step and banged his head, said business development undersecretary Robert Coughlin, who said he had shaken hands with Verga seconds earlier. "I went by, shook his hand, and he went down on the first

step." Coughlin said, "It was a thud. I was standing right there. He took a fall."

A later State House News story said that, instead of being carried out of the building on a stretcher, "he was wheeled out of the building after about 20 minutes."

The *Boston Globe* reported that "the 72-year-old Verga was conscious but it was not clear whether he would be able to attend Thursday's constitutional convention."

Something didn't seem right about this story. I thought back to my meeting with Verga; he'd told me several weeks before that if he had his way he'd miss the vote and even talked of scheduling a hernia operation for that day. Just a few days before, he'd been very coy with a gay veteran we'd asked to meet with him, saying only that he hoped the veteran would be pleased. And his wife had told one of our canvassers who was knocking on doors in Gloucester that we wouldn't have to worry about her husband's vote.

It dawned on me what was up. For us, a no-show was as good as a vote our way. Our opponents needed to get fifty votes out of the two-hundred-member Legislature. If Verga wasn't there, he couldn't be one of the fifty.

It seemed like a lot of drama to get out of taking a vote, but it meant one more down, this time literally, with three more to go.

=

That evening, our team of door-to-door canvassers completed their work, having surpassed their goals for the year. We'd had a paid door-to-door canvass program for three years, and we'd gotten really good. We'd collected hundreds of thousands of postcards and gotten people to make thousands upon thousands of phone calls right from their door to their lawmakers. As the canvassers debriefed about their work that day and for this final stretch, I came in and thanked everyone. They'd been chased by dogs and by homophobes, made it through rainstorms and the brutal summer heat, been questioned by police, and—for the LGBT ones—had their identity challenged in profound ways. And yet they kept at it every day, working to beat their performance from the day before and guided by the cause.

I'm sure it's hard for you to remember it on a day-to-day basis, I told them, but you've been a crucial part of making history. You spoke to many people who had never had a serious conversation about marriage equality or about gay people for that matter. And you brought those conversations to their door, in some of the most conservative parts of the state.

I thanked them for their courage and tenacity, and they gave themselves a huge round of applause.

=

That night in Webster, Paul Kujawski gathered his two sons and wife. He'd made up his mind and wanted to talk to them about the next day's vote. In the end, he saw clearly that the people who were urging him to vote yes were doing so because of their beliefs, but it wouldn't affect their lives. For most of those who had talked to him about voting no, the vote would affect their lives in really important ways. He needed to vote no and make their lives better.

His wife and two sons supported his decision strongly. They'd already been there. It meant so much to him to have his family by his side regardless of the reaction in the community.

=

I headed home late Wednesday night. Even though we hadn't gotten enough commitments yet to put us over the finish line, I felt a sense of calm for the first time in many months. Part of the reason was I felt there was not one stone we'd left unturned in trying to line up the votes. It was also because I thought we were going to win. We needed three more votes, and it seemed as though we'd certainly get Kujo, Angelo Puppolo, and a third, Rep. Geraldo Alicea from the district right next to Kujo's. There were four others, including Ross, the funeral director, and Loscocco, who had met with GLAD lawyers that morning. I also had tremendous confidence in the Senate president, who would preside.

She was a no-bullshit, rigorous, and sharp leader. Not only that, but the three leaders were very much in sync. Still, it was hard to sleep; there were lots of ways things could go wrong.

I lay in bed, responded to some e-mails on my Blackberry in the middle of the night, and finally got up at 6:00 a.m. I put on a gray pinstriped suit, blue shirt, and red tie and hailed a cab to my office.

After reviewing drafts of two press releases—one for a win and another for a loss—I headed over to St. Paul's Cathedral, the main Episcopal Church in Boston. There, Bishop Tom Shaw hosted a 7:30 a.m. prayer service for people of faith on our side. The Religious Coalition for the Freedom to Marry had organized this event, and they had enlisted twenty-three denominations to join together for prayer and then to march across the Boston Common to the area in front of the State House where hundreds of supporters were gathering.

The bishop—who had repeatedly spoken out on our side, serving as a powerful counterweight to the Catholic cardinal—offered strong words about what we were fighting for and told us that God was on our side. I wasn't terribly comfortable with the idea that God was choosing sides, but I knew that if there were a God taking an active interest, he would certainly not be on the side of our opponents. I went to the service not to speak but instead to gain inspiration and grounding for the day ahead, which I knew would be long, grueling, and emotional.

After the service, those in attendance lined up by denomination behind signs that they'd made: Methodists Support Marriage Equality; Reform Jews Support Marriage Equality; Lutherans Support Marriage Equality; Unitarian Universalists Support Marriage Equality; and so on. Liberal pastors who hadn't worn their collars all year were decked out in collar and cross. We marched out of the church and crossed Tremont Street into the 366-year-old Boston Common. This public space at the heart of Boston had served as a Revolutionary War staging ground, the site of a rousing Martin Luther King Jr. speech during the civil rights movement, and the epicenter of this fight. Many of the marchers broke out into the South African religious freedom song "Siyahamba," repeating over and over, "We are marching in the light of God."

The music warmed my soul. The sight of the clergy and lay people—gay and straight—marching for freedom for LGBT people as an imperative of their faith was unspeakably moving that morning.

As we approached Beacon Street, which separated the Common from the State House, we saw our opponents with their green VoteOnMarriage T-shirts and "Let the People Vote" signs. When they heard the singing, many turned to see what was happening. It seemed to me they thought that all these clergy and religious people were their reinforcements. But instead of joining them, this group of hundreds of people of faith crossed the street to join our people—the people with the rainbow flags and the equality signs. It was another powerful moment that I will never forget. Our supporters who had already gathered on our side of the street reacted with elation, cheering the demonstration of support from people of faith—a demonstration that many had craved from their own faiths for much of their lives.

Nothing buoyed me more than the activists on our side who had rallied for the cause outside the State House over the past three years, holding signs and chanting. As I walked down Beacon Street toward our MassEquality offices, I hugged some of the stalwarts who had been there year after year and then entered my office for what could be, for all practical purposes, the last day of our campaign.

Representative Carl Sciortino took the T from his home in Somerville to Park Street and headed up the hill through the Common toward the State House. He too loved the activists who'd gathered outside for every one of these constitutional conventions. It had been only three years since he'd been one of them. He had a pang of sadness that this was it; this was the end. Before people noticed him, he pulled out his phone and snapped some pictures. He then greeted some of the activists, who cheered as soon as they saw him. For so many, he was a powerful symbol of the perseverance of our community in this fight. After a few hugs, Carl hustled toward his office. He didn't want everyone to see that he was crying.

=

Early that morning, Kujo saw himself on the front page of the *Boston Globe*, to which he'd given an interview about his own thought process: "A Legislator Finds Himself Tugged in Two Directions." It talked about his meetings with his priest, the governor, and the speaker. It said that "Kujawski appeared to be heading toward a change of heart" and mentioned Sharon Murphy and Deb Grzyb "who endured so many struggles and are now so happy together." It quoted him as saying, "Am I going to . . . take that away?"

Before he left Webster that morning, Kujo knew there was one conversation left to have. He swung by Sacred Heart rectory, where Father Michael Roy lived. He wasn't there to debate but to give him the courtesy of telling him how he'd be voting. Just before 9:00 a.m., he knocked on the door, and a deacon answered. He told Kujo that Father Roy was out of town at a retreat. "It's important that I talk to him," Kujo said, explaining it was about the gay marriage vote.

"Well, I'll try to contact him and let him know," the deacon said.

God's with me today, thought a relieved Kujo, as he got back into his car and headed into Boston. That was a tough conversation he'd rather not have.

Heading north and then east for the fifty-six-mile drive, Kujo was resolute that he was doing the right thing. If I were gay, he thought, how would I want to be treated? And how could I vote to treat anyone else differently from that? It was the real-life stories that he'd heard, especially that of Sharon and Deb, that made him understand. He figured no one had approached him in the past because of his reputation as a conservative. But no matter, now he got it.

=

First thing that morning, Richard Ross headed over to King Philip Middle School in Norfolk, the next town over, for the eighth-grade graduation of one of his kids. As he walked across the lawn, he ran into Dan Winslow, the former chief counsel to Governor Mitt Romney whose daughter was also graduating.

"Big vote today," Winslow said.

"I know," Ross responded. "And you won't believe what I'm about to do."

"What?"

"Dan, I'm changing my vote."

"Oh, thank God," Winslow said.

Ross was shocked. "What do you mean, thank God? You were Romney's point man on the legal stuff."

"I was on the bench for a number of years," Winslow responded, referring to his years as presiding justice of the Wrentham District Court. "There are certain things you never put on the ballot and allow people to vote on. This is one of those gut-wrenching things that has too much to do with faith and a whole lot of other things. People need to have you make the decision."

That gave Ross an extra boost of confidence.

At a little after nine, Ross got back in his car, a black 1997 Corvette, for the drive into Boston. He continued to feel, at his very core, that his parents were with him as he grappled with his decision that morning. What came to mind now was a quote that his mother loved: "To thine own self be true." He thought it was Shakespeare but wanted to know for sure and from which play it came. As he approached the State House, he hit traffic so he called his staffer Angela and asked her to look up the quote.

She told him it was from *Hamlet*, Polonius's last piece of advice to his son Laertes:

This above all: to thine own self be true,
And it must follow, as the night the day,
Thou canst not then be false to any man.
Farewell, my blessing season this in thee!

Ross knew what he had to do.

＝

In the Boston suburb of Milton, Governor Deval Patrick got into his car for the ride up to the State House. For the first time, he was joined by his daughter Katherine, who had just graduated from a boarding school in Delaware. Because she'd been away, she hadn't ever seen her father in action as governor. Since this day looked as if it would be historic, she wanted to be there.

I was back in my office, on the lookout for last-minute problems. With this many legislators and the stakes so high, there was no way there wouldn't be any. Sure enough, I got a phone call and learned that a few archrivals of House Speaker Sal DiMasi, led by conservative Democratic Rep. John Quinn of Dartmouth, were threatening to vote to advance the constitutional amendment even though they'd voted the other way before. It was clearly an effort to embarrass the speaker, for whom defeating this amendment was a top priority. Pettiness was nothing new in the State House. One small faction flips and we have no chance of having the votes. I called Barney Frank, who had worked on Quinn and had gotten his commitment last go-around, and asked if he'd make another call. He told me he would.

In Charlton, Deb and Sharon had turned on their computer to get the live stream setup for the 1:00 p.m. vote. But there was something wrong with the live stream. Sharon then looked at her e-mails and saw ones from MassEquality and GLAD encouraging everyone to come to the State House.

"Do you want to go to Boston?" Sharon asked Deb.

The two talked about it, and coincidentally Pastor John White, who had organized the very first meeting with Kujo, gave them a ring to see how they were doing. Before they knew it, the two of them, Pastor John and his wife, and two other friends were in a van heading to the State House.

=

We had scheduled an 11:30 lunch with our close legislative allies at St. Paul's Cathedral to go over any last-minute items. Before heading over, I received a phone call from Angelo Puppolo's aide. Angelo wants to meet up with you, the aide told me. Can you meet up near the State House at 11:30? The two were driving in from Springfield for the vote.

We met outside the Capitol Coffee House across Bowdoin Street from the State House.

I just want you to know that I'm going to vote your way, Puppolo told me.

Thank you so much, I said.

I know I'll be attacked by my opponents and will draw a challenger, so I'm going to need your help, he said.

I told him that MassEquality had always been there to support our friends. No legislator who had voted with us had lost their reelection. I promised we'd do everything within our power to make sure that continued to be the case. He thanked me and told me he was going into the building to tell the speaker but wanted me to know first.

I walked over to the lunch at St. Paul's. There were twenty or so legislators there, both senators and representatives, mainly our core supporters. I asked Senate President Tempore Stan Rosenberg, the Democrat from Amherst who had been one of our stalwart leaders, to update us on how we were doing in the Senate and Rep. Byron Rushing, the second assistant majority leader from Boston, to update us on anything new in the House. There really wasn't anything new to report, they told the group. Everything was in the hands of the big three right now, the governor, the Senate president, and the speaker of the House. The speaker's whip system was in place, Rushing told us, and doing its work. We'd learned by then that Rep. Quinn was back in the fold.

There was a cautious sense of optimism but still uncertainty and lots of nervous energy. At this point, it was out of our control.

This core group, most of whom had been working together since the *Goodridge* decision three and a half years before, took comfort in being with one another. There was great solidarity. There were newer members, such as Barbara L'Italien, who'd survived tough election fights. And there were others, such as Alice Wolf from Cambridge and Byron Rushing, who'd been fighting for gay rights for decades and who'd signed up for the cause when it looked like just a pipedream. But now it looked as if we really might win. The feeling that this was a history-making day was palpable.

I left lunch at about 12:30 p.m. and walked back over to the State House, to the second-floor area right outside the House chambers, which was cordoned off with a rope barricade and reserved for lobbyists from both sides. As I walked down the corridor, I ran into Rep. Paul Loscocco who looked out of sorts. He pulled me aside.

Marc, he said, I was up until 4:00 a.m. this morning reading through case history. I've decided I'm voting against the amendment.

I thanked him profusely.

When it comes down to it, Paul told me, I simply can't vote to take away people's rights.

Everything was falling into place.

I walked over to assume my position outside the House chamber, where the Legislature would meet shortly to decide our fate. House members walked in, many offering greetings, a smile, or a thumbs up. Some of these legislators had become close friends. I felt as if we had the kind of lifelong friendships forged in battle. Lobbyists Arline Isaacson and Norma Shapiro of the ACLU, MassEquality Political Director Matt McTighe, and Gill Action's Patrick Guerriero were standing right by me.

One of our opponents, Kris Mineau, the executive director of the Massachusetts Family Institute, was just a few steps away. I wondered if he had any idea how much work we'd done in the months since the last vote. His all-out focus had been to get the Legislature to hold a vote rather than put it off, and it seemed as though he was confident he was going to win.

Mineau saw Loscocco walk past the lobbyist area in front of the House chamber and gave him the thumbs up. I hope we can count on your vote, Mineau said. Loscocco didn't respond or make eye contact. He hurriedly walked past the barrier and into the House chamber.

At 1:01 p.m., it was the moment of truth. The Senate sergeant at arms led the senators into the House chambers, marching with top hat and cane. Senate President Therese Murray marched behind him, and the other members followed her. As they entered, House members offered ceremonial applause, as they served as hosts to the senators. I stood against the ropes that separated the senators from us, trying to make eye contact with some of them as they walked into the chamber and hoping that my presence would remind them of all the gay and lesbian couples who had shared their stories and opened their lives to them. Throngs of media shouted questions and took photographs. Inside the chambers on the rostrum, House Speaker DiMasi stood with Senate President Murray, the outgoing DiMasi joking around with other lawmakers and slapping them on the back.

At 1:08, Murray gaveled the joint session to order. The lawmakers recited the Pledge of Allegiance and then proceeded immediately to the amendment.

"When recognizing marriages entered into after the adoption of this amendment by the people," read the clerk, "the Commonwealth and its political subdivisions shall define marriage only as the union of one man and one woman."

This time, there was nothing left to debate. Everything had been said. The only question was, who had the votes?

By custom, the Senate voted first. The clerk went through the names in alphabetical order. We knew we'd do well in the Senate; thirty-two out of forty had already voted our way, and only three were targets.

Antonioni
No
Augustus
No
And on down the list it went.
Brown
Yes

It was no surprise that State Senator Scott Brown, who would go on to be elected to the US Senate, would be the first yes. He'd once called it "unnatural" for a fellow lawmaker, openly lesbian State Senator Cheryl Jacques, to have a child. He was never a serious target.

Candaras

This was the first change in vote we were counting on. Gale Candaras, the new state senator from Springfield, had voted against us every time while she served in the House of Representatives. Now a senator, we had delivered more than 6,000 postcards from constituents and organized as many meetings as she'd take. Most importantly, the Senate president had worked to secure her vote.

No
Yes! One down.

Hedlund

This was the only Senate Republican on our target list. We'd pulled out every stop with him. He had seemingly gone back and forth, but based on conversations over the last few days, we thought we had him.

Yes

Fuck.

No more suspense until we got to the *M*'s, when Senator Mike Morrissey of Quincy would cast his vote. Our Quincy group had done amazing work on him, even enlisting several of the harbormasters from area yacht clubs to speak with Morrissey, whose passion was sailing.

Morrissey

No

Yes! I clenched my fist.

Matt McTighe had his gaze right on Kris Mineau, and he could see Mineau's jaw tighten and his posture slump as Morrissey voted. Matt was sure Mineau knew, right then, that he was going to lose the whole thing.

The final Senate tally was five yes, thirty-four no.

Next was the House. Of the 160 House members, we needed to hold our opponents below forty-five votes. Forty-five votes in the House combined with the five in the Senate would get our opponents to fifty, the 25 percent threshold they needed. Unlike the Senate, House members vote electronically. In the front of the House chamber is a big board with a lightbulb next to each of the 160 names. A green light means yes, a red light stands for no. At 1:13 p.m., the House vote began.

For some time now, Richard Ross had been discussing the vote with Paul Loscocco. The two Republicans had both been really conflicted about the issue, but they approached it from such different perspectives. For Ross, it was all about heart and emotion, while for Loscocco, it was all about process and the legal perspective. The two were talking in the back of the chamber as the vote began. Loscocco wanted final confirmation that Ross was going to vote against the amendment. "I'm not doing this alone," Loscocco told him. Ross confirmed his no vote once again. The clerk was shouting out, "You gotta vote, you gotta vote," so they rushed to their seats to cast their votes.

I was crowded in front of a small television that was part of a camera crew setup, trying to see which lights were lighting up next to which legislators. I was gripping ACLU lobbyist Norma Shapiro's hand.

Carl Sciortino was on the floor, watching the board closely. Carl had been tasked by our legislative leaders to pay close attention to the vote and contact a member of leadership if he saw that someone voted "off"—meaning they voted yes instead of the no we expected.

Richard Ross pushed the red button. He felt as if his was the deciding vote and knew he was doing the right thing. He also was sure that this would mark the end of his career. He immediately burst into tears. Rep. Alice Wolf, the longtime gay rights champion from Cambridge, was right next to Ross. She embraced him, as did Barbara L'Italien.

Carl watched carefully as the board filled quickly: 40 yes, 116 no. We'd won! Carl couldn't hold back the tears that began streaming down his face. The Senate president immediately announced the final, combined vote: 45 to 151, in the negative. "The amendment fails," she said.

Outside the chamber, I jumped for joy, shouted, pumped my fist in the air, and hugged our lobbyists and others who were gathered around the television. We'd done it! Deb and Sharon were a floor above, looking down at our scrum of lobbyists, and as soon as they saw me pump my fist in the air, they knew. Huge cheers broke out all over the State House, including the House floor, and there was hugging, kissing, cheering, and crying everywhere.

Carl looked up at the board again and saw that Paul Loscocco had a red light next to his name. He gazed across the floor and saw Paul, and when they made eye contact, Carl could see Paul looked as if he was about to break down in tears.

Carl approached him and asked what happened.

I couldn't live with myself if I didn't do the right thing, Paul told Carl. Carl hugged Paul in a firm embrace.

Carl then saw his freshman classmate, Richard Ross. He had talked at length with Ross, and he knew that Ross's wife was a religious conservative and a vocal opponent. Carl knew what the personal ramifications of this vote could be, and he was deeply moved. He walked up to Ross, who was surrounded by others, and gave him a big hug. They were all weeping.

Ross's phone immediately rang. It was Scott Brown, calling from the other side of the chamber. Scott was a very close friend as well as the state senator covering the House district Ross represented.

"Richard," he said.

"Yes, Scott."

"What the fuck are you doing?"

"What do you mean?" Richard asked.

"Why did you take that vote?"

"Because I realized the one we took was the wrong one," he said, referring to the vote they had both taken in January in favor of the amendment.

"All you had to do was vote the same way."

"I couldn't," Richard told him. "It was the wrong vote."

Brown told Richard he was sure it was going to cost him his career.

Deval Patrick was in his office watching the vote on television with Chief of Staff Doug Rubin and a couple other top aides. He'd gotten his daughter Katherine a seat in the gallery, where she could watch the proceedings live.

As the governor watched the Senate president announce the vote, he felt the enormity of what had just happened. He wanted to sit there and just absorb it. But his staff told him he needed to join the legislative leaders at a press conference on the grand staircase in the center of the State House. It didn't feel right to get in front of a camera at this transcendent and historic moment, but that's what the job expected of him, so he dutifully went along.

Downstairs in Gardner Auditorium, where the room was full of supporters and opponents watching on a large screen, our opponents began cheering when they first heard the House vote total, somehow thinking they'd won. But when the Senate president announced the final vote total, our side erupted for a good ninety seconds. It seemed to go on forever: hugging, crying, and complete elation. There was disbelief that the dozens of visits to the State House, the organizing in their home towns, and their sharing of truly personal stories about their own families and the families of friends and loved ones all paid off. The Massachusetts Legislature did the right thing, and for the first time in American history, we'd secured the freedom to marry once and for all.

After taking his vote, Kujo left the floor and walked into the members' lounge. There, he saw a colleague, Representative Brian Wallace, on the phone with tears running down his face. Wallace, who represented the heavily Irish Catholic neighborhood of South Boston, was another swing vote who had cast his vote against the amendment. Kujo could tell Wallace was getting screamed at for his vote.

"Come on, let's go," Kujo said. "Let's walk upstairs." Wallace got off the phone, and Kujo hugged him and held him. Kujo then walked with his arm around Wallace.

I can't believe how mean and nasty some people are, Wallace said.

"What we've done, we're going to be very proud of," Kujo responded. "History's going to show that we've done the right thing." They headed toward Wallace's office. But as they turned the corner, Kujo saw Deb and Sharon. He left Wallace and walked toward them.

Deb and Sharon saw Kujo walking down the corridor toward them with a giant grin on his face. Sharon hugged and kissed him, and through the tears thanked him for everything. Kujo gave Deb a giant bear hug. The tears were flowing, and they were all so happy.

You made the difference for me, Kujo told them.

After more tears and embraces, they got an onlooker to snap a few pictures of them all together.

A few minutes later, Deb and Sharon looked downstairs, saw their senator, Steve Brewer, and called out to him. He saw them, broke into a great big smile, waved, patted his heart, and pointed to them. He climbed the stairs, crossed through the roped-off area, and reached out to hug them.

"Who said two people couldn't make a difference?" he told them.

After a short news conference, we all went outside for one final rally. By now, I had become the unofficial MC of these rallies. This time, thousands of our supporters were gathered around holding signs, celebrating, and chanting, while our opponents were across the street chanting and promising that the fight wasn't over.

I looked into the crowd and saw so many people I'd come to know over the past six years since I'd started volunteering. I could see my best friend and soul mate Alex Hivoltze-Jimenez looking at me with great pride. We'd all been through a battle together, and it felt so good to see how profoundly happy everyone was.

I took the megaphone for one last time, my neck kinked sideways, knotted up from all the stress. Governor Patrick and Speaker DiMasi stood behind me, and their colleagues streamed in as well.

"We did it!" I said, pumping my fist in the air.

People were shouting, absolutely ecstatic, some chanting, "Thank you, thank you."

"You, all of you, are the reason we won," I told them. "Thank you!"

"You shared your stories, opened your homes to your lawmakers, collected postcards, got involved in elections, came back after setbacks, and showed the kind of relentlessness that demonstrated to lawmakers how important marriage is and how we wouldn't give up until it was protected in the Commonwealth of Massachusetts. That's why we won."

"For the past six months," I said, "we've had a governor who has shown he's the real deal. He's fought, he's persuaded, and he's been with us every step of the way every day he's been in office, and even before."

Then I introduced Governor Deval Patrick. The crowd went wild.

Deval looked out at the crowd and saw so many people holding each other and weeping. He knew they were thinking they'd never see this day and couldn't believe it was over. And it wasn't just the LGBT community that felt that way. He himself, and so many of the other straight allies who were there, knew that what had just transpired affirmed the best of who we were, both as people and as a country.

After speaking about what a monumental achievement this was, Deval reminded everyone of the humanity of those who did not agree with us. "The folks on the other side of the street," he said about those who were jeering and chanting, "are your brothers and sisters too. And we must reknit our community if we are going to move on to all of the issues important to all of us."

Deval's daughter Katherine had joined the thousands outside the State House. She'd been seated in the gallery watching the vote, and when the result was announced, she joined in the elation, the hugging, crying, and cheering. She'd followed everyone else outside and was watching her father with intense pride.

One thing Katherine hadn't yet told her father was that she was just about positive she was a lesbian. Over the past few years, she'd had strong feelings toward women, and now that she'd graduated from high school, she was getting ready to come out publicly. In the crowd, she felt as if she shared something with so many of those around her, the community she was about to become a part of. And she felt tremendous joy.

She always knew her parents to be great with gay people. They'd always had lots of gay friends around, and her father never shied away from saying where he stood on LGBT issues. But it was one thing to hear him talk about it at home, as her dad. It was another hearing him speaking to thousands, and through the media to the entire country, as governor of Massachusetts. She could see so clearly that equality for gays and lesbians was something he really stood for, at his core. He'd worked his hardest and put it all on the line to fight for her rights without even knowing that it would affect her. That felt incredible. At that moment, she knew that when the time came for her to tell her dad she was a lesbian, he'd be there for her with arms open.

After the rally, Katherine walked over to Old South Church, just across from Copley Square in Back Bay. That summer, she'd been going there a lot to reflect on what her life would be like living openly as a lesbian. Three weeks later, at their country home in the Berkshires, Katherine did come out to her parents. And her dad did his typical thing. He cried a little bit and then gave her one of his giant hugs. All was good.

After the governor finished speaking, he handed me back the megaphone. I said, "From Boston's North End, our hero, our tireless fighter, House Speaker Sal DiMasi."

Another eruption followed. The speaker talked about how proud he was of this day and of our community that had been so persuasive, simply by living our lives as we were, respectfully and with dignity.

I had been looking around for the Senate president and finally saw her ascending the steps to join us. But then, just as quickly, she stopped and turned the other way. I knew that this scene—big crowds, speeches, and acknowledgments—was not at all her thing. And yet she, as much as anyone, deserved the thanks. She had set a date for the vote and stuck to it even in the face of enormous pressure to postpone, knowing that if she gave any hint of moving it, legislators would avoid making up their minds. She worked hard to move legislators our way. She drove the process, and we won. So as she turned around, I acknowledged her determined, steely leadership and thanked her. Once again, the crowd erupted.

The rally over, the crowd adjourned to celebrate at Club Café, the popular gay bar that served as our de facto community center in the South End, the center of Boston's gay scene. I had some press calls to return and e-mails to send before I headed over, so when I got there it was full, even though it was late afternoon. People were cheering, hugging, and watching the news segment of the vote repeating over and over on TV. I finally saw Alex, who'd been a great adviser and source of love and strength for the last two and a half years. He pulled me into his arms. "You did it," he said. Over and over. I broke into tears, sobbing into his shoulder. "You did it. You did it. You did it." Finally, I could let go.

After celebrating for a couple of hours, I returned to my office to check e-mails and voice mails. There were so many congratulatory e-mails.

"Mazel tov and THANK YOU!!!!" wrote Evan Wolfson.

"Congratulations!!!!! What a victory! You did it!!!! I am so proud of you," wrote my mom.

The ones that moved me to my core were from ordinary LGBT people around the state and their family members.

I haven't stopped crying since the second ALL of us in the basement of the State House heard the news we have been WAITING FOR! THANK YOU, MASSEQUALITY for working so hard in this effort. WE. DID. IT!

Marc, This is the happiest news I've received in a long time. All your hard work has paid off. On behalf of my daughter, her partner and my 5 month old grandson, my heartfelt thanks to everyone whose passion and persistence has achieved this victory.

I am sitting at my desk at work and believe it or not, I burst into tears. I had no idea how deep this issue had gotten into my heart and soul. You are an amazing group of organizers. I am honored to be living in this state at this time in history and grateful that you all worked so hard to ensure that civil rights [remain] civil!

Marc Solomon! We LOVE YOU! You must be beaming with pride at all the work you've done. Ellie continues to have a legally protected two-Daddy family. Now get some sleep, man!

My heart was filled with joy. I plugged in my cell phone, which had run out of juice, and checked my voice mails. One was extraordinarily moving:

Marc, Ted Kennedy calling from Washington, DC. Congratulations on what you did today. What you accomplished for the people of Massachusetts is tremendous. Good work, my friend.

Kennedy was my hero. Nothing could be better than that.

The Massachusetts Family Institute put out a statement saying that they were considering all their options. But it was over. Not long after, they issued another statement: until the composition of the Legislature changed, they could not win.

The freedom for gay couples to marry was secure in the United States, at least in our beachhead of Massachusetts.

NEW YORK

December 2, 2009. Things weren't supposed to turn out this way in New York. At the recommendation of his political advisers, gay entrepreneur and philanthropist Tim Gill, along with the network of donors he'd organized, had poured more than $1 million into New York during 2008, which helped flip the State Senate to Democratic control for the first time in forty years. The Assembly—the lower branch, equivalent to the House of Representatives in Massachusetts—had been approving freedom to marry legislation since 2007. However, the Republican-controlled Senate had always refused to consider it. Now, with the upset victory, the primary obstacle to a freedom to marry victory in the Empire State was gone. The Senate Democratic leader, Malcolm Smith, had promised repeatedly to get the job done, and Governor David Paterson, an outspoken supporter, would sign the bill into law.

Yet on that cloudy December day in Albany, with the eyes of the country upon them, the marriage advocates were mired in defeat. That afternoon, in its first appearance on the New York State Senate floor, the marriage bill suffered a wrenching loss, going down by a lopsided vote of 38–24. Eight Democratic senators, including one whose campaign had relied on gay dollars and volunteers and another who had committed his vote, had voted no. The Democratic leadership that had promised to get the bill passed when asking for money had broken that promise when it came to delivering the votes.

===

The prior two years had been a real roller coaster on the marriage equality front. And they'd been a tremendous roller coaster for me personally and professionally as well.

Following the June 2007 final vote in Massachusetts, I'd turned my attention to winning marriage in other states. I had MassEquality join up with GLAD on a partnership to win each of the other five New England states by the end of 2012, an effort that GLAD named "Six by Twelve." The states that showed the most short-term promise were Connecticut and Vermont, and so with GLAD's Executive Director Lee Swislow, I hit the road. I made several trips to Hartford consulting with Anne Stanback, who ran the Connecticut freedom to marry organization Love Makes a Family, and I deployed Amy Mello, our MassEquality field director, to guide field strategy in Connecticut. I also supported Vermont Freedom to Marry's Beth Robinson in making the case to legislative leaders in the Vermont Senate and House about moving the first civil union state to full marriage.

—

In September 2007, I drove to Chicago with my best friend and soul mate, Alex Hivoltze-Jimenez. Alex was moving there to begin a PhD program in theology at the University of Chicago. Over the subsequent months, even though we weren't able to see each other nearly as frequently, we were still just as close. He was the first person I'd talk to in the morning and the last I'd talk to before I went to bed. We both expected that, no matter where our lives took us, we'd be soul mates forever.

Alex was in Washington, DC, on his birthday, Friday, May 2, 2008, doing some consulting work he'd taken on to make some extra money. When we talked on Sunday morning, he told me he'd come down with a fever and had barely slept. He flew back to Chicago that afternoon and called me from the taxi from the airport into the city. He said he hadn't felt that sick in a long time. Yet he wasn't so sick not to be annoyed that he'd be missing Madonna Rama, a theme party at a gay bar that night, where he was going to meet up with some friends to celebrate his birthday.

I texted him before I went to sleep telling him to call me if he needed to talk during the night, but I didn't hear from him. The next morning, I called and texted. When I heard nothing, I kept calling over and over. By the afternoon, I was panicking. I eventually tracked down a friend of his on Facebook, a fellow grad student who went over to Alex's place. When no one answered the door, he got a police officer to open the door and they went in together.

They found Alex dead, at the age of thirty-four, of blood poisoning from a terribly lethal kind of bacteria.

I was in utter shock and completely devastated.

I headed to Chicago first thing the next morning to do the exceptionally painful things you need to do when a loved one dies: identify the body, help make arrangements, and pack up a lifetime of belongings. I met up with Alex's mother and two sisters, and with his older sister, stayed for a week packing up his apartment. I spent evenings with his stunned friends from the university, where Alex had been a spark, the life of the party, the center of debate, and a magnetic presence just as he had been in Boston. Alex's family followed me back to Boston for a memorial service I'd put together.

Alex and I loved each other deeply, and yet it was hard to find the right word to describe what we were to one another. We weren't lovers, we weren't married, and yet "friends"—even "best friends"—didn't convey the level of emotional connection we had. So in addition to grieving, it was extra painful to try to explain to those who didn't know us well what his loss meant to me. Among other things, it gave me a deeper understanding of what it was like for same-sex couples over the years who'd had to struggle to explain the depth of their relationship, to have it taken seriously, and to have it be respected and acknowledged for what it was when it wasn't legally respected and marriage was denied.

On May 15, the day before the memorial service, the California Supreme Court ruled 4–3 in favor of marriage for gay couples, in a case argued by the National Center for Lesbian Rights and the City of San Francisco, with marriages to begin in one month. It had now been four and a half years since the *Goodridge* decision, and that was news for which I'd been waiting for so long. But on this day, I didn't want to have my mind drawn into the marriage fight. I simply wanted to remember Alex.

After Alex's memorial service and the celebration of his life at the gay bar Club Café that evening, I felt the need to dive back into work to distract myself. The next week, I called Governor Patrick and asked him if he'd work with me on repealing the so-called 1913 law that barred out-of-state same-sex couples from marrying in Massachusetts. He agreed and then raised it the next Monday with House Speaker DiMasi and Senate President Murray. They were in as well, and we went to work. On July 31, 2008, Patrick signed the bill into law.

In the meantime in California, our opponents qualified a ballot measure, Proposition 8, for the ballot that would take away the freedom to marry. Unlike in Massachusetts, in California a measure goes right to the ballot if it has sufficient signatures, with no role for the Legislature. And in November of 2008, the freedom to marry came to an abrupt end in California with the devastating passage of Proposition 8 (I talk more about the Prop 8 battle in the "Winning at the Ballot" section).

Like so many in our community, I was devastated by the loss of marriage at the ballot in California. I knew there would be a pall over the LGBT community throughout the country until Prop 8 was lifted and the freedom to marry restored. I was also buoyed by the newfound activism among so many young people in our community, in both California and around the country, to win marriage back and fight for our equality. Also after Alex's death, I was ready for a change of scenery. He and I had talked about moving to California, Alex's home state, and working together to stop a constitutional amendment there. We'd even talked about his taking leave from school to do it. All that together led me to decide to resign from MassEquality and move to Los Angeles to join Equality California to head up the marriage work and eventually put together a ballot campaign to restore the freedom to marry.

=

Around the time of Prop 8's passage, the marriage movement put together a string of victories. Just before it passed in October, GLAD secured a marriage win in court in Connecticut. Then, on April 3, 2009, the Iowa high court ruled unanimously for the freedom to marry in a case brought by Lambda Legal. Four days later, for the first time, a state approved marriage equality through legislative action: the Vermont House and Senate each delivered the two-thirds vote required to override Republican Governor Jim Douglas's veto. On May 6, Maine followed suit, with Governor John Baldacci signing marriage legislation into law. And on June 3, after several fits and starts, New Hampshire Governor John Lynch signed a freedom to marry bill into law, adding to the progress in New England. And while voters reversed the marriage law in Maine in November by referendum, New York was on track to be the next legislative victory. Beyond the tens of thousands of New Yorkers whose lives would be made better, the symbolic value of a win in America's third-largest state and financial and cultural center could not be overstated.

===

In New York, with a slim 32–30 Democratic majority in the Senate, the advocates on the ground knew that we'd need at least a few GOP votes if we were to prevail, as there were a handful of certain Democratic no votes. Log Cabin Republicans of New York engaged a top-notch team of Republican lobbyists: Mike Avella, the straight former counsel to the Senate Republicans, along with openly gay GOP strategist and lobbyist Jeff Cook. The thinking was that if the Senate Democrats lined up twenty-eight out of their thirty-two members, the GOP team would find four to get them to the magic number of thirty-two.

The session quickly turned into a mess. As the advocates appeared to be getting close to a vote on the Senate floor in June, two Democrats defected from their party and joined up with the Republicans, ostensibly returning control to the GOP in what became known as "the coup." However, Democratic leaders retaliated by literally locking the doors to the chamber to shut business down and try to stop the Republican coup. Then one of the defectors changed his mind, resulting in a deadlocked Senate. Finally, the second defector reverted to the Democrats. There were rumors that the Democrats agreed to kill a vote on the marriage bill in exchange for regaining their majority. Whether or not true, the dysfunction paralyzed the Legislature, meaning that the marriage bill and other legislation were held up.

By October 2009, frustration within the gay community was boiling over. Alan van Capelle, the brash executive director of the Empire State Pride Agenda, the statewide LGBT equality organization, knew playing the usual Albany inside game wasn't going to shake the bill loose. At the fall dinner of the Pride Agenda, van Capelle called out the Senate's Democratic Conference chairman, John Sampson, and Tom Duane, the Senate's first openly gay member and chief sponsor of the marriage bill. "Senator John Sampson, you are the leader of the State Senate," said van Capelle in front of 1,000 guests at the Sheraton Hotel in Midtown Manhattan. "Senator Tom Duane, you have told us on multiple occasions you have the votes to pass this bill. Give us the dignity, the rights and respect we deserve. Bring this bill to the floor for a debate and a vote."

Finally, in late November it looked as if there was an opening to move the bill forward. The Pride Agenda enlisted the help of three powerful lesbian Democratic insiders to support the lobbying and vote-counting efforts: Emily Giske, a powerhouse Democratic lobbyist; Amy Rutkin, chief of staff to Congressman Jerrold Nadler; and New York City Council Speaker Christine Quinn. As they began making the rounds and talking to Democratic lawmakers they knew, they could see the bill was in trouble. Giske, a legendary vote counter, couldn't see a path to thirty-two votes.

Early in the afternoon of December 2, the day the vote was supposed to take place, Senator Sampson called a meeting in his conference room with Duane, Quinn, and Giske. Alan van Capelle was called in after the group had already been talking. "We've been discussing it, and we don't think we have the votes to pass the bill," said Sampson. "It's really your decision now," Sampson said to Alan. "We could not take the vote today and leave the session with no vote, or we could take the vote right now and whatever happens, happens."

Taking a vote you were likely to lose went squarely against the culture in Albany, where lawmakers only liked to vote on measures they knew would pass. Democratic leaders definitely didn't want to hold a vote and fail after they'd promised a win and raised huge dollars from LGBT donors.

"We don't have the votes. The vote will lose," affirmed Duane.

Quinn said, "Alan, this is a really big decision for you. It's yours to make, as a community leader and as an individual, and you will be judged on this decision."

The insiders seemed to be counting on Alan to say no to a vote. Why would he want the blame that was sure to come his way with a defeated bill?

But Alan didn't want to offer the Democratic lawmakers an out. Without a vote, people would continue to believe that senators who were not there on the issue were supportive. The gay community would be a cash machine for the Senate Democrats for another election, with no accountability. He thought that gay New Yorkers deserved to hear their lives debated on the Senate floor and that the Democrats needed to be put on record. Too many people had sacrificed huge amounts of time, energy, and dollars into the effort for it to end without a vote.

"I want a vote," said Alan. Duane and Quinn looked shocked.

"Are you sure?" asked Quinn. Giske chimed in, "Alan, the vote's going to lose. Tom's saying it's going to lose."

Alan said, "I don't know how we go into the next election cycle in 2010 without a work plan, and the only work plan I can think of is targeting the people who voted no."

The meeting lasted around twenty minutes.

The senators gathered in the Senate chambers in their assigned seats, and the marriage bill was called. When they got to the vote, the clerk called the roll, starting with the beginning of the alphabet. Joe Addabbo, the Queens Democrat who had received extensive gay support in 2008 during his bid to unseat a virulently antigay Republican, was called first. Addabbo had told leaders including Alan that he would vote yes, but the first-term lawmaker developed cold feet when the prospect became real. That prompted a last-minute scramble to nail down his vote.

"No," said Addabbo.

They didn't get to Addabbo, thought Republican Jim Alesi of Rochester, who was next up. This is going to go down worse than anybody imagined. Alesi wanted to vote in favor badly; he had had a gay cousin who died of AIDS, and they had been very close. He knew it was the right thing to do. But in a meeting of all the Republican senators just before the vote, they had committed to voting no as a bloc, sure that the Democrats hadn't gotten close enough so that a few yes votes from Republicans would put them over the top. Why would they expose a handful of members to primary challenges for voting yes on a bill that would fail?

For one of the first times in his life, the chatty Alesi felt inarticulate and frozen, holding his head in his hands, as if time were standing still. His heart was torn, and he was struggling to get the words out of his mouth. With his eyes closed, he said, "No."

In the end, eight Democrats joined all thirty Republicans in defeating the bill.

Jeff Cook, the lobbyist for the Log Cabin Republicans, could not hold back the tears. As he sat in the gallery above watching the bill go down in flames, he locked eyes with some of the Republicans he'd spent much of the last year lobbying, several of whom he was sure knew what the right thing to do was. Their facial expressions showed a mix of terror and shame.

Bill Smith, the deputy executive director of the Gill Action Fund—Tim Gill's advocacy and political giving shop—was disgusted and furious. To the Alabama-born operative who learned the art of campaign warfare under Karl Rove before coming out as gay, it was perhaps the most visceral and painful blow in his fifteen years in politics.

He instinctively reached into his pocket to check his phone, and there was a short, simple e-mail from Tim Gill: "That was sad. What's next?" Bill felt truly lucky that he worked for a guy who was undeterred by setbacks. Gill liked to say that if you won them all, it meant you weren't taking on difficult enough challenges. Bill knew he'd need to come up with a new strategy to put before Gill.

=

Following the stinging defeat in the Senate, the LGBT community across the state, particularly in New York City, went to a place of raw anger. A rally in Times Square the evening after the vote drew hundreds of protesters. A forlorn remake of the classic I Love New York logo, with a rainbow heart in broken halves, became ubiquitous on Facebook.

=

The murky, transactional world of Albany had thrown the national gay funders for a loop. While donors had succeeded in showing lawmakers a carrot—campaign money—Bill Smith saw that the culture of the State Capitol required a stick as well. Democratic lawmakers felt certain they'd be backed by the gay community no matter what, because there was no alternative if the community wanted to see a marriage bill move. Consequently, there had been no fear on the part of the Senate Democratic leadership or individual lawmakers about doing the wrong thing. In fact, there was incentive to keep the donors hanging—and investing—as long as they could before they passed a bill and national gay donors put their attention elsewhere. It was time to engage in bare-knuckle politics, with the single-minded purpose of getting thirty-two senators to vote for the marriage equality bill. With the solid pro-equality majority in the Assembly, and a friend in the governor's office, that would get the job done.

"Nothing matters but the path to thirty-two," said Bill. "We'll cut the path through whoever's backyard we've got to go through."

The idea of punishing lawmakers who double-crossed the community had been percolating even before the disastrous New York Senate vote. Now, with a scorecard to show where senators actually stood, it was finally possible to create an outlet for the free-floating anger and frustration. People were out for political blood, and Bill—with Tim Gill's blessing—was ready to provide a strategic way to channel it.

=

In January, Bill met up with lesbian Democratic operative Emily Giske at Governor David Paterson's state of the state address in Albany, the annual see-and-be-seen event for political insiders in New York. The Karl Rove–trained operative from Alabama and the liberal Jewish lesbian from Bayside, Queens, couldn't have come from more opposite backgrounds, yet they became fast friends—so much so that Bill would join Emily for Shabbat dinner with Emily's partner and other lesbian friends. That same day, Bill met Val Berlin, a high-powered lesbian political consultant. Together, he, Emily, and Val formed the core of the PAC they called Fight Back New York.

The group knew their effort would need to be something completely fresh. This was not about building relationships for the long haul but about being purposefully disruptive in the short term. The campaign would come from out of nowhere and use its own edgy voice for maximum impact. Using a bold strategy, hunting targets with surgical precision, and being relentless with tactics to punish the bad guys would be the order of the day. Targets would not know what hit them until it was too late. The days of relying on a party in power to pass marriage legislation were over. To Bill, this was gay people going after bad people who screwed over gay people. And the infamous coup and dysfunction in Albany provided perfect fodder for challenging incumbents of both parties.

A situation unfolding in Queens would offer their first test case. Democrat Hiram Monserrate had been elected to the Senate from Queens in 2008 with the endorsement of the Empire State Pride Agenda. He completed a questionnaire that said he supported marriage equality, and then one year later, he voted against the bill. He represented the popular gay neighborhood of Jackson Heights, where he had marched in the borough's annual Pride parade.

One of the lawmakers who defected during the leadership coup, Monserrate was convicted in October 2009 of misdemeanor assault for slashing the face of his girlfriend with broken glass and then dragging her down the hallway of his Queens apartment building. The episode had been captured on a security camera, which provided an endless loop of gut-wrenching evidence. His fellow senators voted 53–8 to expel him in February 2010.

The Democratic establishment coalesced around Jose Peralta, an assemblyman who had voted yes on marriage, to replace Monserrate in a special election called for March 16. But Monserrate, a former Marine and police officer, refused to go quietly and launched a bid for reelection. Fight Back New York jumped into its first contest with less than a month left. They pursued a two-part strategy of courting donors from Tim Gill's donor universe and creating an online presence for the grass-roots rage that still smoldered two months after the failed Senate vote. The website, in English and Spanish, branded Monserrate a "criminal" and "incompetent."

Fight Back used strategic campaign approaches that weren't dissimilar from those we'd deployed in Massachusetts except that this effort was focused on going negative on our opponents. In his apprenticeship working for Karl Rove, Bill took away three lessons: focus, discipline, and repetition. They identified the residents most likely to vote in what they knew would be a low-turnout special election, and they hit their houses with at least eight pieces of direct mail, flooding them with messages in Spanish and English. The goal was not just to be a presence but to be an overwhelming force to block Monserrate's reelection. The pieces were tough, using images from the chilling black-and-white surveillance video that showed Monserrate dragging his girlfriend in the hallway. "He brutally assaulted a woman and tried to cover up his crime," one said. "Now he has the nerve to run again. Many of us have voted for Hiram before. But we cannot vote for him again."

In the end, Peralta won the contest by thirty-nine percentage points and became the next senator from the district, his victory raising the number of proven yes votes on the freedom to marry from twenty-four to twenty-five. Peralta gave Fight Back New York a huge shout-out at his victory party in Queens.

Word spread quickly about Fight Back in tight-knit New York political circles. Gay advocates were on the rampage, the buzz went, and they'd scored their first win, spending about 40 percent of the total that was invested into electing Peralta. Yet most everyone had assumed that, because of Monserrate's criminal behavior, he would lose. The next act would be a much heavier lift.

Some wanted Fight Back to target some of the highest-profile law-makers who opposed the freedom to marry, particularly Democratic senator Ruben Diaz, the Pentecostal minister and unapologetic leader of the opposition. But the group was relentlessly focused on races that, in their analysis, showed there was a clear path to victory. Diaz's primary challenger didn't appear to pose a serious enough threat. Fight Back also looked at Democratic senator Shirley Huntley in Queens but decided against it both because she didn't appear vulnerable and because she was especially close to John Sampson, the Democratic Conference leader. It was still important to stay on good terms with leadership.

On the other hand, Bill Stachowski, a thirty-year Democratic incumbent from Buffalo, appeared to be an attractive target. He barely defeated his Republican opponent in 2008, 53 to 47 percent. Gay advocates felt especially angry toward him, as Senate Democrats had diverted some of their campaign war chest stocked with gay dollars to save him at the last minute in 2008, and still he voted the wrong way.

"Stach," as he was known, was obstinate in his opposition. Kitty Lambert, a Western New York lesbian advocate, had met him at a cocktail party in Buffalo prior to the vote in the Senate. She and her partner told him that he really needed to reconsider his stance against marriage equality. "No I don't," he said. "I'm against it now. I'll be against it forever."

Before Fight Back could go on the offensive against Stachowski, they needed to make sure a strong pro-equality Democrat would challenge him in the September primary. Emily Giske, the Albany lobbyist, had deep connections in Buffalo, and a colleague suggested that she meet with Erie County lawmaker Tim Kennedy. He had answered several questionnaires the right way on marriage, but he was pro-life and had support from his county's Conservative Party (In addition to the Democratic and Republican parties, New York has several nonaligned third parties, and candidates can run on multiple tickets.) Those credentials don't usually go along with support for the freedom to marry, so Fight Back wanted to verify.

Emily met Kennedy for dinner in Buffalo where he looked her in the eye and promised her that he would vote for the freedom to marry bill if he won. She went back and told Bill Smith and Val Berlin that she was sure Kennedy would be for marriage. That was enough for Bill; Stachowski became the next target for Fight Back New York.

As the team polled in the district, it became clear that Stachowski suffered from serious vulnerabilities. Constituents identified the three-decade incumbent with the problems endemic to Albany. Fight Back

New York gathered intelligence on his votes and his financial dealings and started to pepper the district with messages that spoke to the anti-incumbent mood.

More than 137,000 pieces of mail were sent to 22,000 voters in the district. The campaign ran a radio spot called "The Big Stachowski," a play on the Coen brothers' film *The Big Lebowski* about an unemployed slacker, to remind voters that even though lawmakers aren't supposed to be paid when the budget is late, Stachowski used a loophole to get paid with per diems.

Stachowski desperately tried to stir up resentment toward the outside interference. He produced an automated call to more conservative voters. "Special interest money from leading gay organizations is lining up behind Kennedy right now, and Kennedy has promised his vote for that campaign cash," went the script.

Meanwhile, John Sampson, the leader of the Senate Democrats, was not pleased. It was one thing to go after Monserrate and support the chosen Democratic candidate, but it was another thing entirely to go after an incumbent in good standing with leadership. It was part of the leader's job to protect all incumbent Democrats in good standing. Moreover, if gay donors were giving money to Fight Back New York, an independent PAC, that meant their dollars were not flowing to his official Democratic campaign committee for the Senate.

Bill and Patrick Guerriero, the former Massachusetts lawmaker who was Bill's boss as the executive director of Gill Action Fund, sat down with Sampson. The Brooklyn lawmaker argued that Democrats were the only hope for a marriage victory. He was angry that they were going after Stachowski, who was well known in the district and had been reelected multiple times, potentially leaving the seat vulnerable to Republican takeover. "We have to be in control. If the Republicans are in control, this isn't going to happen," he said.

"You're not going to love us in August," Bill said. "But you're going to love us in September," referring to when they'd turn to the general election.

Kennedy defeated Stachowski in the primary election on September 13 by a whopping thirty-seven percentage points. In this case, though, winning the primary was only half the battle. An ambitious Republican member of the Assembly, Jack Quinn, who had voted against the marriage bill, was the Republican nominee for the Senate seat. Quinn hinted that he would be open to a yes vote on the freedom to marry in the Senate, but when Fight Back met with him in New York City, he would not agree to come out publicly for it. That sealed it; they went all in for Kennedy to see his campaign through to a successful conclusion.

Just as Bill and Patrick had promised Sampson, when August turned to September, Fight Back moved away from Democratic primary challenges to taking on anti-equality Republicans. They looked closely at one of the longest-serving incumbents, Frank Padavan, who seemed ripe to be targeted in the general election. The seventy-five-year-old senator, who had been in office since 1973, no longer fit the demographics of his increasingly Democratic district in Bayside, Queens, near the border with Long Island. Where marriage equality was concerned, advocates had long found the nature of his opposition deeply offensive. Padavan had been one of the sponsors of the so-called Defense of Marriage Act in New York, even opposing civil unions.

As in the Monserrate and Stachowski contests, Fight Back New York first did extensive polling in Padavan's district. The data showed that although constituents knew and liked their senator, his thirty-seven-year career made him vulnerable to anti-incumbent messages about the corrupt culture of Albany.

Through intermediaries, Bill got word to Senate Republican Leader Dean Skelos that theirs wasn't an anti-Republican campaign. It was an effort to go after vulnerable opponents of the freedom to marry who were being challenged by a viable candidate, Democrat or Republican. And they would leave alone the few like Alesi who, under the right conditions, would vote for the bill. The Republican leadership wasn't pleased, but they understood and even felt some grudging respect.

In the Padavan race, Fight Back sent 275,000 pieces of mail to 35,000 voters. They criticized Padavan for $3 million in office expenses over recent years ("Frank Padavan's paper clips must be made of gold," said one mailer); his opposition to funding for mammograms for women; and his decision to give his staff raises in the middle of the recession. The mailers compared that move to tactics at Goldman Sachs, which was then a radioactive name at the height of the financial crisis. Automated calls to more than 22,000 voters reinforced the messages.

Padavan lost 47 to 53 percent to Tony Avella, a charismatic Democratic City Council member from Queens and stalwart supporter of the freedom to marry. The close margin suggested that the investment of Fight Back New York made a crucial difference. In an interview with *Politico*, Padavan attributed his loss to the group, calling Fight Back "insidious" for never mentioning marriage in the campaign. That's exactly how the team intended it.

Nearly 400 miles to the northwest in Buffalo, Tim Kennedy was taking a beating from Jack Quinn's negative TV ads. Based on the polling, Fight Back New York knew that voters in the economically struggling district cared about changing the political culture of Albany. Voters wanted fresh representation. The team decided to go all in with radio and TV ads, committing more than $200,000 to reinforce the message that Quinn, a veteran lawmaker, was part of the capitol's "revolving door," as their TV ad said. The radio ad focused on the "circus of Albany," saying, "Every year we send the same people, like Jack Quinn, back to Albany, and every year we get the same results: higher taxes, more debt, and late budgets."

Kennedy eked out a victory by a margin of 43 to 40 percent, with 17 percent of the vote going to other candidates. The close margin allowed Fight Back New York to make a strong case that it made the difference in this race.

In the end, Fight Back replaced three anti-equality Senate incumbents —two Democrats and one Republican—with senators who had committed to vote yes on marriage. And if they broke that promise? Well, the buzz in Albany was clear: Democrat or Republican, the gays will not only stick by their friends but also take out vulnerable legislators who vote against equality. Fight Back New York spent almost $800,000, making it the largest independent-expenditure campaign in the state focused on the Senate.

Around the country, another dynamic was at play: the Tea Party "wave" elections were sweeping across the nation. It began when Massachusetts State Senator Scott Brown won the open US Senate seat in Massachusetts in January 2010, vacated by the death of Ted Kennedy. The wave continued into November, when the US House of Representatives shifted to GOP control. The impact on state legislatures was even more profound. In Minnesota, where advocates had been preparing to move a freedom to marry bill in 2011, the GOP swept out 2–1 Democratic majorities in both branches of the Legislature to take control. So instead of working to pass marriage legislation, local advocates would have to work to fight off a Prop 8–style constitutional amendment from reaching the ballot. In New Hampshire, solidly Democratic majorities in both branches became GOP majorities of 75 percent in the House and more than 80 percent in the Senate, and the new Republican leadership prioritized repealing that state's marriage law. In Massachusetts, our allies who'd represented politically conservative districts and won re-election during the marriage battles—including Paul Kujawski, Barbara L'Italien, and Matt Patrick—were swept out in this antitax, Tea Party wave. And in New York, three Senate races were so close that they required recounts. After weeks of ballot counting and court wrangling, it was the Republicans who came out on top by a margin of 32–30, putting the fate of the marriage bill in their hands and leaving most advocates deflated, sure that the bill would die once again.

But something else was on the horizon in the Empire State. A new governor had been elected with a mandate to shake up Albany and get big things done, and that mission included passing a freedom to marry bill.

Andrew Cuomo was an unlikely hero of the gay community. The former attorney general didn't occupy the same soft spot in the community's heart enjoyed by outgoing governor David Paterson, the state's first African American governor who traced his LGBT rights commitment to close family friends he knew as Uncle Stanley and Uncle Ronald. Cuomo, on the other hand, brought a reputation as a tough guy from Queens with a penchant for hot rods and Harleys. He offered none of the familiar anecdotes about gay family members, friends, or associates, and suspicions lingered about his level of commitment, fueled by a story in the *New York Times* the previous year.

The article told about Attorney General Cuomo's role in the 2009 marriage vote, saying that as the vote neared in the Senate, Cuomo made phone calls to lawmakers when requested, but his office viewed the campaign as Paterson's show. Cuomo played a less prominent role than some other elected officials, and the *Times* explored that role in the context of what it called the long-running "fraught relationship" between the attorney general and the gay community. The story revisited homophobic tactics employed in his father's race against Ed Koch in the New York City Democratic mayoral primary in 1977. The younger Cuomo, then nineteen, served as a campaign aide for his father, his first formal political role. Mario Cuomo was promoted as a "family man" from Queens, in contrast to Koch, a single man who lived in Greenwich Village and never spoke about his personal life. Posters appeared in Italian sections of Queens and Brooklyn saying, "Vote for Cuomo, Not the Homo." Both father and son denied any involvement with the posters, but Koch—who went on to win—wasn't so sure.

For some in the gay community who were well acquainted with the attorney general, however, that reputation was undeserved. Rob Coburn, a forty-seven-year-old investment executive, had become friendly with Andrew Cuomo several years before, first getting to know him at a dinner party for prospective donors. Since then, Rob had become an admirer of Cuomo's work and donor to his campaigns and the two scheduled occasional one-on-one visits just to stay in touch.

During one of their get-togethers in August 2007, they discussed the latest developments in their work and personal lives. The new attorney general was doing well and riding high in the polls on popular initiatives like his investigation into corruption within the student loan industry. Rob told Cuomo about his recent separation from his partner of seventeen years. Their conversation seemed to be winding down, when Cuomo threw Rob a curveball.

"Almost everyone in my political life right now," Cuomo said, "has come to me at some point and said, 'Here is an issue or two that is really important to me, this is my view on it, and I would like you to shepherd it.' You haven't done that, and I feel like I need to ask you. I don't shape my policies toward individuals, but as someone who has given me the time and support you have, and to the extent I believe in the issue, it may energize me that much more."

Rob initially demurred at the suggestion.

"That's one of the reasons I took such a liking to you at that dinner a while back," Rob replied. "I felt like I could trust your instincts and I sensed a real combination of principle and pragmatism. There's not anything I would say right now to change your agenda."

Cuomo would have none of it. "That's a really nice thing to hear," he responded. "Let me rephrase the question. Say, God forbid, that you were diagnosed with a horrible disease and you knew this was the last time we were ever going to see each other, and you had one last chance to tell me, 'Make sure you do X; it's the right thing to do.' What would that be?"

To his own surprise, Rob blurted out, "Marriage equality."

The attorney general smiled, as if he had known there was something inside, and he was glad Rob was not holding back.

"Tell me why," he said.

Rob proceeded to review some of the standard reasons. For starters, he did not understand the compelling government interest in preventing gay couples from marrying. When he asked Cuomo how he saw the issue, the AG—who had first voiced support when he ran for the office in 2006—responded, "It's a difficult thing for me."

"There is no doubt," Cuomo continued. "It's as plain as the nose on my face; it's an issue of abject injustice. There's no question about it, and it pains me, like any injustice done on the basis of some kind of classification and labeling. It's just unfair and it pains me."

"I suppose on this issue overall," Cuomo continued, "I have been focused on the symptoms of not only marriage equality but also other LGBT issues in terms of the effects on employment, housing, access to services, adoption, or whatever else it might be. The focus has been, can we find ways to try to address some of the specific unfairness?"

"I think it's deeper than that," Rob replied. "I would ask that you think of this really as a matter of civil rights, which I know you are a big believer in."

Rob told Cuomo about his coming out at the age of twenty-eight and how, during that time and afterward, he had never felt ashamed of his revelation or questioned himself. He talked about his upbringing in a very supportive family outside Boston, the youngest of five children raised by liberal Unitarian parents. Even with that background, being gay had still been a heavy burden for him. So he couldn't imagine how some people justified their opposition by arguing that being gay was simply a lifestyle choice. If sexuality were a choice, said Rob, there's still about a thousand reasons why he logically would have chosen to be straight. It's the expected path, the easy way. And since being gay is the way people are, it had to be considered a civil rights issue.

He also explained how, during the time his partner and he were together, they were good citizens: good to their families, civically active, and generous supporters of causes. But, he said, if one of us would have been hit by a bus, or died in some other accident, the other would have been left without any presumptive rights, a diminished person trapped in contractual and legal defenses unlike anything a straight married couple would have faced. "And yet," he said, "Britney Spears can go to Las Vegas, drink an extra cocktail, chat up the busboy she met that night, get married, and wake up the next morning with all of those rights we didn't have. I don't understand how that reflects the values I believe exist in America and that the government wants to encourage in people."

When Rob finished, Cuomo sat at his desk in his typical casual posture, with his hands clasped behind his head. He rubbed his eyes and nodded. Seconds passed with no words. In the few years Rob had known him, Cuomo had increasingly impressed him as a genuine, world-class listener. He looked Rob in the eyes and tapped on his desk. More time passed.

"Let me make a promise to you," Cuomo finally said. "It's not because of what you said, and I'm not making this promise just to you. We're going to change this. I'm still wrestling with how to address the inertia that many people—respectable people whom I like, whom a lot of people know and like, smart people—have on the word marriage. Their concept of what marriage is has its own inertia, and I'm not saying, let's wait until it plays out. I'm willing to help change it, but I haven't figured it out yet. I'm spending a lot of time on this issue."

After some reflection, Rob imagined the attorney general had been having this conversation with others in his life and was grappling with how to put together the right rhetoric at the right time to help get the job done. Rob had no doubt that he was genuinely on board. Cuomo seemed to be waiting for a moment that made sense, an opportunity such as a case with an example of a clear harm that his office could join and he could use as a teachable moment.

—

By the time Cuomo neared the launch of his gubernatorial campaign in 2010, he had a record that interested gay donors. Bill Smith and Patrick Guerriero went to Manhattan to visit the attorney general in March of that year, one of many such meetings they commonly arranged to evaluate a politician for Tim Gill's network of donors. In this instance, the circumstances were especially delicate because Governor Paterson, who had assumed office after Eliot Spitzer resigned in a prostitution scandal, had not yet announced whether he would seek a full term. His ethical troubles were mounting, though, over incidents including interference in a domestic violence case against a top aide. It looked likely that Cuomo would be the next governor, and Bill and Patrick needed to feel him out without broadcasting a lack of faith in Paterson.

They met up at an office in Midtown Manhattan. Only the three of them were in the room, Patrick and Bill on a couch and the attorney general in a chair across from them. The three spent the first part of the meeting gabbing about political news in general, as if they were old friends on a front porch. They discussed political developments in New York and talked baseball. To Bill, it seemed like a very old-school Italian approach, a heritage that Cuomo and Patrick shared, spending some time getting comfortable with one another before they switched to business. When they finally did, Cuomo grew serious and started to speak about his commitment to equality.

Bill had never met with Cuomo before, but he immediately noticed that something about the attorney general was different from other politicians. When elected officials spoke about the freedom to marry, they often talked about someone in their life who was gay and how the issue mattered to them, seeking to make an emotional connection. Sometimes, their vocabulary was awkward and they would flub the words, even if their heart was in the right place. Cuomo was not warm and fuzzy like that. He spoke about it as a matter of fundamental equality and as a matter on which New York should lead. To Bill, he had the vocabulary down that would enable him to make a powerful public case, and he did not blink or flinch.

Patrick and Bill said that, after the previous year's debacle, the donors they represented needed a real leader on marriage equality.

New York is behind on this, Cuomo said. I'll get it done.

Cuomo did not say when it would happen, but Patrick and Bill were not looking for an exact timeframe. The point of this meeting was to do a gut check, and they were satisfied. Cuomo was a formidable politician who was clearly serious about this cause. He had their seal of approval.

=

Cuomo's opponent in the race was Buffalo businessman and Tea Party favorite Carl Paladino. With Cuomo running twenty points ahead,

Paladino dropped his version of an October surprise while speaking to a group of Orthodox Jewish leaders in Brooklyn.

"I just think my children and your children would be much better off and much more successful getting married and raising a family," he said. "I don't want them brainwashed into thinking that homosexuality is an equally valid and successful option. It isn't."

Local reporters tweeted his remarks, and the backlash was swift and furious. Paladino put up an awkward defense. He argued that he'd been handed a script by his hosts and that at least he had crossed out an even more egregious passage, which read, "There is nothing to be proud of in being a dysfunctional homosexual. That is not how G-d created us."

Following two months of high-profile tragedies in the area that had included a vicious antigay gang assault in the Bronx, an attack at the Stonewall Inn, and the suicide of gay Rutgers University freshman Tyler Clementi after his roommate secretly broadcast him having sex with another man, the words from Paladino sparked national outrage. The next morning, he found himself seated opposite Matt Lauer, cohost of *The Today Show* on NBC. While trying to contain the damage, he made it much worse.

"Mr. Cuomo took his daughters to a gay pride parade," said Paladino to an incredulous Lauer. "Is that normal? Would you do it? Would you take your children to a gay pride parade?" "I don't think it's proper for them to go there and watch a couple of grown men grind against each other," he continued. "I don't think that's proper. I think it's disgusting."

=

The Empire State Pride Agenda (ESPA) had been trying everything to get Cuomo to speak at their fall dinner. It was a highlight of the New York political calendar and generally a mandatory stop for Democratic hopefuls, but ESPA's invitation had gone unheeded.

Cuomo had included marriage equality in the "five-point plan" he was running on. However, the race had largely focused on economic issues. Voters were anxious about the budget, taxes, and job creation, and the ever-disciplined Cuomo was staying on message.

Just hours before the event, Cuomo's people called ESPA to ask if he could speak during the cocktail hour. So on Wednesday, October 14, two days after the Paladino attack, Cuomo addressed the packed room of about 1,000 at the Sheraton Hotel in Midtown Manhattan.

"I don't want to be the governor who just proposes marriage equality," he said, as attendees stopped their mingling at the cocktail hour to listen. "I don't want to be the governor who lobbies for marriage equality. I don't want to be the governor who fights for marriage equality. I want to be the governor who signs the law that makes equality a reality in the state of New York."

=

By the fall of 2010, it was clear to me that my work in California to build a campaign to win back marriage at the ballot had been overtaken by events. In May of 2009, soon after I arrived, a new group called American Foundation for Equal Rights (AFER) filed a lawsuit in federal court challenging the constitutionality of Prop 8. Gay campaign strategist Chad Griffin, with support from Hollywood producer Rob Reiner, had formed AFER and brought together former George W. Bush Solicitor General Ted Olson and Democratic attorney extraordinaire David Boies—the two lawyers who had faced off against one another in *Bush v. Gore*—to serve as lead attorneys.

My initial thinking was that we could work on two concurrent pathways—litigation and organizing for a ballot initiative—to restore the freedom to marry. So with Amy Mello, who had joined me in California, we hired seventeen field organizers and opened seven offices in key parts of the state, working to build and grow support.

Once the judge in the case ordered a trial—the first full-on trial on marriage since Hawaii in the 1990s—the attention of the LGBT community and our allies shifted pretty dramatically to the courtroom and away from our campaign efforts. And when the judge issued his ruling striking down Prop 8 on August 4, 2010, I knew that all the energy for a ballot fight would evaporate. My emotions were mixed. I certainly felt elation that we'd won, that a judge had found Prop 8 as illegitimate as we all knew it was. And having been in California for more than a year, I knew the LGBT community in the state had been deeply hurt by

Prop 8 and that if we could win back marriage without a ballot fight, that would be best. On the other hand, the path ahead for the lawsuit was a long one, with the court of appeals and then potentially the US Supreme Court to come. So marriage wouldn't be restored any time soon. We could also lose in court, and we'd have to go back to the ballot anyway. And for me personally, the idea of having moved across the country to build a campaign, and then having to dismantle it before it really got going, was frustrating. I wanted to keep driving and overturn Prop 8. But that wasn't going to happen, so Amy and I closed the field offices and let our staff go.

Over the summer of 2010, Evan Wolfson, whom I'd known since the early days in Massachusetts, and I began talking about my joining him at Freedom to Marry.

At the time, Freedom to Marry was a less than $2 million a year organization with a handful of staff and no political advocacy arm. With limited resources and constant juggling to shore up movement buy-in and bring people along, Evan had primarily focused on enunciating a powerful call to action and keeping the marriage movement moving on its strategy to get to a national victory, what Freedom to Marry called the "Roadmap to Victory": win a critical mass of states, achieve a critical mass of support, and then bring a case to the Supreme Court to finish the job. However, Evan largely relied on local groups to build and drive the campaigns that would achieve the wins. He was finding that that approach led to mixed results.

Having seen California repeat the Hawaii experience—a victory in court snatched away at the ballot box—and also seeing opportunity in the tremendous wake-up call from the Prop 8 loss as well as the advent of a new political era with Barack Obama as president, Evan determined that Freedom to Marry seize the moment and step up the work. He talked to me about building an in-house campaign center with the strategic political know-how to drive forward on the roadmap aggressively.

From my experience in Massachusetts and elsewhere, I knew that was exactly what our movement needed. Tim Gill's political shop, the Gill Action Fund, had stepped up and deployed a top-notch crew of operatives who were doing a good job on state legislative battles. We needed more of that skill, and we needed an effort that focused on every aspect of winning marriage systematically, from long-term public education and messaging work, to assessing the political landscape in the states and determining which were most winnable, and then putting together campaigns to win in the legislature and at the ballot. We needed to win over more Republicans and expand the geographic reach of our campaign nationally. We needed to grow support on Capitol Hill and within the Beltway. In short, we needed to leverage power our way using every means at our disposal, building momentum and putting points on the board every single day.

To turn Freedom to Marry into the kind of national campaign organization we both felt was required to do the job—one with a top-notch team of operatives with expertise in campaign management, communications, organizing, messaging, new media, federal lobbying, and public education—we'd have to grow our budget and staffing massively (by 2014, we were at more than 30 staff and a budget well north of $10 million, by far the leading funder and driver of marriage work in the country). We would serve as a central resource and a swat team, helping build strong state campaigns and ensure they were operating strategically and driving toward victory. We'd launch a federal effort in Washington, DC, focused on marriage: building support for repealing DOMA while making the case to influential audiences—members of Congress, the press, political consultants, pundits, and indirectly the Supreme Court—that support for the freedom to marry was a winner. Too many were still stuck with the disproven narrative that nevertheless took hold after John Kerry's loss in 2004, that gay equality, and marriage especially, was a dangerous subject for Democrats and toxic for Republicans.

For me, it was the perfect opportunity. Building campaigns was what I loved doing the most and was best at. I viewed campaign terrain as a blank canvas on which I could be as creative as possible to mobilize people, build power, and win. Now, instead of focusing on one state at a time, I'd have the whole country.

It was also exciting to join up with Evan. Evan had always challenged me to think big, boldly, and courageously in my years of working on the cause. He'd also always been a great support, whether things were going well or poorly at the moment, because he had a confident, long-term vision of how we would win. I felt like together—with Evan's ability to inspire a vision, lay out and drive a national strategy, and frame our campaign to the media and public, and my ability to conceive of and build campaigns that could achieve tangible victories and grow momentum and support—we could build a powerful organization that would hasten the day we'd get to our goal—the freedom to marry nationwide.

I was in, enthusiastically. I'd start my work as Freedom to Marry's national campaign director from California in November, and then move to New York, where Freedom to Marry was headquartered, in April of 2011.

Back in New York that November, Andrew Cuomo pummeled his opponent 62 to 34 percent. And once elected, he didn't let up on his commitment to marriage. In his January state of the state address, Cuomo said, "Let's pass marriage equality this year once and for all."

Two months later, Cuomo had gotten a budget passed, on time for the first time since 2006, and his political capital was sky-high among both Democrats and Republicans. Yet he felt something was missing. Speaking with his father, who rose to national prominence as the conscience of the Democratic Party, Cuomo told him that his budget accomplishments were "operational." He didn't want them to define his first year in office. According to the *New York Times*, he told his father that "at the heart of leadership and progressive government" lay marriage equality. "I have to do this."

On Tuesday, March 8, 2011, Cuomo's office called Evan to invite him to a meeting in Albany with the governor and other advocates to discuss advancing a marriage bill. We hadn't had a state win in more than a year, and the other two states in play—Maryland and Rhode Island—looked as if they weren't going to pan out in 2011. New York was crucial.

The next afternoon, as he entered the ornate Red Room in the capitol building for the gathering, the fifty-four-year-old Evan was impressed by its majesty. Chandeliers hung from the high, intricately designed oak ceiling, and a bronze leaf band covered the upper half of the walls. The room had been carefully prepared for the day's meeting, with place cards around a large table and an empty space at its head for the governor. Snacks were set up on a side table, and there were seats assembled behind the large table for staff. The press had been tipped off to the meeting, and they were gathered in the hallway outside.

Evan took his seat across the table from Danny O'Donnell, the openly gay assemblyman representing Manhattan's Upper West Side who was the lead Assembly sponsor of the marriage bill. As Evan looked around, he saw many familiar faces, people with whom he'd been fighting the New York marriage fight for many years. Among those in attendance were the lead Senate sponsor of the bill Tom Duane; new Pride Agenda Executive Director Ross Levi; New York lead for the Human Rights Campaign Brian Ellner; and uber-lobbyist Emily Giske, whom Evan had known since they went to Yiddish summer camp together as kids in upstate New York.

Evan had no idea what to expect of the governor. Cuomo had said the right things on the campaign trail, but Evan was used to politicians pandering to the gay community for votes and money, only to see marriage downplayed when they were forced to prioritize.

The governor entered through a side door, accompanied by New York City Council Speaker Chris Quinn. He took his seat at the head of the table and welcomed everyone.

This is the room where Franklin Delano Roosevelt had his office, Cuomo began. The desk he used is over there, he said, pointing to the desk on a platform. He pointed out a portrait of Alfred Smith, the four-term governor of New York who was a progressive reformer during the 1920s and the Democratic nominee for president in 1928. He explained that he had had the portrait of Smith installed on the wall because Smith was a man who did big things. New York is a leader, Cuomo told the group. It has a profound history of national leadership. We used to do big things, and now we've somehow lost our ability to do them.

Marriage equality, he continued, is something New York needs to get ahead on. Being a leader means that we cannot be behind on issues of fundamental equality. That's what this is all about. Cuomo spoke about gay people in his life, friends that he had. But the primary focus was on New York's leadership on civil rights. We were behind here, and we need to rectify that.

"I will be personally involved," he told the group.

I'm prepared to lead. I want to get this done and am prepared to play a strong role if that's what you think makes sense. I'm going to put my top staff on it full time, and I'm going to make it a personal top priority.

But, he continued, I can't do it on my own. I need all of you to work together, to do all the things that need to happen to create the best, most conducive environment to win.

Cuomo told the advocates that from what he'd observed, there was a real lack of coordination in 2009 and that was part of what contributed to the loss. He'd seen it firsthand as attorney general, when he was getting uncoordinated and sometimes conflicting asks for him to reach out to members of the Senate. That would need to change this time.

Cuomo gave those assembled a chance to speak and many praised the governor for stepping up and leading. Evan stayed quiet until Cuomo turned to him. It was clear Cuomo had been briefed on who everyone in the room was. Tell us what you're thinking, Cuomo said.

"I really appreciate how you've connected the freedom to marry to the larger dynamic of New York, its history and its role as a leader," Evan said. I also think you're right on target that this is bigger than a cause for the gay community, that the values of freedom and equality are American values, and that's the way to lift people and get them behind it." He then committed Freedom to Marry to doing all it could to help.

Ross Levi, who succeeded Alan Van Capelle at the Pride Agenda, was listening carefully. An Albany veteran, Ross heard a couple of things that impressed him a great deal. He heard Cuomo say that he'd be transactional, that he'd make deals if he had to in order to bring about a win. In Albany, the deal is the way business gets done. And he heard Cuomo say he'd play a hands-on role and be a closer—that he'd seal the deal. Threading the needle with a Republican Senate to get this done would take strong leadership from the governor.

At the same time, Ross didn't think Cuomo sounded arrogant or un-realistic. Cuomo was well aware he wasn't king, recognized that he had assets including the bully pulpit and the power of persuasion, but also saw the limits and knew that all the groups, as well as legislative leaders, needed to be pushing hard together to have a real shot at pulling this off.

Cuomo wanted to make sure there was full agreement not to go for a vote unless we had the votes lined up to win. On his watch, he didn't want a repeat of 2009. Do we all agree?

There was no disagreement.

After forty-five minutes, Cuomo told the group that his top staffer, Steve Cohen, would be his lead strategist on the effort and turned the meeting over to him.

Cohen was a former federal prosecutor who had built a reputation for cracking down on violent criminals at the height of New York City's gang epidemic in the 1990s. He joined the Cuomo orbit his junior year of college, when he interned for Governor Mario Cuomo and then was hired by the governor as a junior staffer immediately after graduating. He had served as the junior Cuomo's chief of staff in the attorney general's office, was a top adviser during his campaign for governor, and was, more than anyone else, the new governor's alter ego.

Cohen felt a great deal of pressure with this assignment. Over the course of their years together, he'd learned that what Cuomo cared about was putting points on the board, not intentions. They had to get this done; failure was not an option. The governor knew that Cohen planned to leave the administration in the fall. Cuomo also knew that Cohen would do whatever he could to avoid leaving on a loss and so would be driven to get the job done.

Cohen felt his job was to ensure that the coalition of advocacy groups followed a single plan and supported the governor's efforts to nail down the necessary votes. He was confident that if they could get things to the right place, in the right way, then marriage equality would get passed, because he knew Governor Cuomo could get it done. But everything had to be arranged just so, and to Cohen, that meant Team Cuomo needed to be in control. He knew the job would require that he not always be the nicest guy in the room.

Cohen explained to the group that he'd begin holding regular meetings with the advocates in the governor's New York City office to drive the strategy forward.

⁂

I arrived in New York on April 7, 2011, and jumped right into the New York fight. As I looked at the different pieces of the campaign, I could see we were in good shape in some and deficient in others. We had great lobbyists—the 2009 team of Mike Avella and Jeff Cook on the GOP side and Emily Giske, who'd worked with Bill Smith on Fight Back New York, leading the Democratic work—all under the supervision of Bill at Gill Action and Ross Levi of the Pride Agenda. The field program, too, was well run. Marty Rouse, my predecessor in Massachusetts and now national field director for the Human Rights Campaign (HRC), had put a strong program in place, with organizers stationed throughout the state focused on priority districts. On the "grasstops" front—activating influentials—New York City Council Speaker Chris Quinn had gotten a Who's Who of Wall Street CEOs to sign onto a letter in support of moving the marriage bill. And HRC's lead in New York, Brian Ellner, had enlisted famous New Yorkers from the sports, political, and entertainment worlds to do a series of short public service announcements.

We had two major weaknesses. We didn't have anyone driving the press effort. We needed a constant drumbeat of news stories making the case for marriage and demonstrating momentum—poignant stories about same-sex couples, positive editorials, endorsements, unusual spokespeople such as Republicans and business leaders speaking out, and the like.

Second, our campaign wasn't nearly as coordinated as it needed to be. Thanks to the insistence of Freedom to Marry's political director Sean Eldridge, Freedom to Marry, the Pride Agenda, and HRC were now having weekly phone calls, yet the Pride Agenda and HRC were essentially running separate campaigns, which was a recipe for disaster. What we really needed was one singular campaign that was as integrated as we could make it. We needed the lobbyists and field organizers to be in sync on which lawmakers were our targets and what kind of pressure would be most effective for each. We needed the field team to be talking to the media team to help identify couples who would make powerful media stories and to put together events in the field that were most compelling to the media. We needed to be in sync with the governor's time line, and we needed to balance a governor who was relentlessly determined and who wanted to drive the process with our need to make sure the Republican Senate was being tended to carefully.

I shared my observations with Bill Smith, and he asked me to try to pull the effort together. And so I went to work. I had longstanding relationships with the Pride Agenda and HRC, as well as with Gill Action, and could make a strong case about the level of coordination that was required to pull off a victory in a challenging marriage campaign. Over the course of my first week in New York, I had multiple conversations with both the Pride Agenda and HRC, working to pull together a unified campaign with those two organizations and Freedom to Marry as its anchors. Gill Action would be a critical player but preferred working behind the scenes.

We discussed bringing to the table Albany power broker Jennifer Cunningham, a managing director at top public affairs firm SKD Knickerbocker, to guide the media efforts. I'd never met Cunningham, but her reputation preceded her. She was a close confidant to Governor Cuomo, had been married to New York attorney general Eric Schneiderman, and had served as political director to the most powerful union in the state, SEIU 1199. The *New York Post* described her as the "most powerful woman in Albany."

By the end of the week, after a series of late-night calls and my word to be an honest broker and hold us all accountable to working together, we agreed to come together under one campaign and hire SKD Knickerbocker to manage all communications. We inked the agreement in a memorandum of understanding, with each of our three organizations committing $250,000, all in time for a Friday, April 15, 3:30 p.m. meeting with Cuomo point man Steve Cohen at Governor Cuomo's Manhattan office on Madison Avenue.

I took the elevator to the thirty-eighth floor, was whisked through security, and joined this room of New York political players. Brian Ellner and Ross Levi were there, as well as Emily Giske and several of Cuomo's top aides. We waited for Cohen to join us, and he entered the room with Jennifer Cunningham, both of whom I'd spoken to on the phone but never met in person.

"The team is now complete," Cohen said, as he sat down, referring to Cunningham.

I'd known she was close with Cuomo, but at that moment it dawned on me just how close.

Cohen was a former high-profile prosecutor who was raised in Chicago, and now served as the head staffer for the notoriously demanding Cuomo. I'd expected a frenetically intense guy in the mold of Eliot Spitzer or Rahm Emanuel. Instead, Cohen seemed relaxed and self-effacing yet confident and commanding respect when he spoke.

Cohen's main subject for this meeting was paid media. It was clear he'd been talking with Cunningham beforehand about what Cuomo was looking for. "I understand you are going to be working with Jennifer to figure out television," he said. I was taken aback because our plan was to work with Cunningham on placing newspaper and television news stories, not on a major ad buy. "I have a couple of principles I want to share with you."

"First, more is better." He talked of their desire to have wind behind the sails of Cuomo's effort, to buttress the case the governor would be making with lawmakers and demonstrate our strength in a tangible way.

Second, he said, "I want to know how much is in the tank before we get started." He didn't want to move with a plan relying on a certain amount of TV only to see it fall off halfway through.

From my vantage point, TV was not a high priority. We were trying to make the case to about a dozen lawmakers, and we really needed to focus dollars on an aggressive field effort, with a barrage of quality and quantity constituent contacts into target lawmakers. Support for marriage was already at 58 percent in New York; we didn't need to grow public support in order to win. And New York's tremendously expensive media market would make it exorbitant to make a real dent. I had been talking to the Pride Agenda's Ross Levi about a small amount of television, a couple hundred thousand dollars' worth, to make a splash in a few key districts. But this sounded like a lot more. I took what Cohen said seriously, though. Cuomo was by far our most potent weapon. If this is what he required, I figured we'd have to figure out a way to do at least the minimum amount for him to feel as if we had his back as he made the case.

After about an hour of conversation, Cohen left and we had our first meeting of just us with Cunningham. Despite her tough reputation, Cunningham was soft spoken and had a gentle demeanor. Our first order of business was what to name our coalition. Cunningham handed out a sheet of paper with three proposed names on it. We quickly settled on New Yorkers United for Marriage.

We then talked about our press strategy. Cunningham proposed getting at least one story of one sort or another placed every day between now and when the Legislature would vote. It could be an endorsement from a union, a positive editorial, business leaders who came out in support, a human-interest story of a couple who wanted to marry, or an article about all the field organizing taking place. But one a day.

I loved the relentlessness of that approach and was all in for that.

She distributed a sheet that had several tiers of approaches for paid media: combinations of television, newspaper ads, and direct mail. There was a "bare-bones" approach for $602,000, a middle range of $914,000, and a higher range of $1.5 to $2 million.

As you've heard, Cunningham said, the governor's office is very interested in paid media. So I prepared some options.

I asked her what she thought the governor's team wanted to see, and she replied that it was at least the $1.5 million option. I didn't know where we'd get that kind of money—we all agreed we needed a few days to discuss paid media.

As I left the governor's office, I was impressed with Team Cuomo. From just one meeting, I could tell this operation was smart, disciplined, aggressive, and relentlessly dedicated to winning. I'd never been part of an operation like this one, where the lead elected official wanted to drive the process. Usually, I was spending much of my time trying to convince top electeds to invest political capital into our cause, knowing that the number of "asks" we could make was limited. This time, it was Cuomo who wanted to drive and was asking us to help navigate.

There were some red flags. In the end, an elected's interest is in protecting his image, while ours was passing a marriage bill at pretty much whatever cost. I knew we'd need to be careful and potentially assert our independence, depending on how things unfolded. I knew that we had to be especially careful with the GOP-led Senate, ensuring their needs were taken care of, as we couldn't win without them. Nevertheless, given Cuomo's apparent relentlessness to get this done and his clout with both Republicans and Democrats in the state, having him drive and New Yorkers United for Marriage help navigate was a no-brainer.

The next Wednesday, we had Cunningham and her team pitch a story to the *New York Times* announcing New Yorkers United for Marriage. We also invited Log Cabin Republicans of New York and the grassroots group Marriage Equality New York to join us. Titled "Cuomo Helping Rights Groups on Gay Marriage," it explained that in contrast to 2009, we were working together and were prepared to do what it took to win. It went beyond what we'd agreed to, stating that we'd intended to raise "more than $1 million for a media blitz." More troubling was that it made it sound as if Cuomo was going to have to drive Republicans to do something they didn't want to do—the truth but much better left unsaid—and then called out several potential GOP targets by name. I knew that would be a problem for our GOP team. At the same time, Cuomo's message couldn't have been clearer: he was in 100 percent. And that was more important than anything.

Bill Smith saw the story in the *New York Times*. He was pissed and immediately shot me an e-mail.

"It's bad," Bill wrote me. "We're going to have clean up to do."

Ever since it was clear the Republicans would assume control over the Senate, Bill had built a GOP effort with excruciating care. And yet here was a story all about Andrew Cuomo being the hero, dragging along recalcitrant Republicans, while also calling out individual Republican senators. He thought it was sloppy and unnecessary, and given how challenging it would be to get the Republican Senate to agree to move a marriage bill, he knew we couldn't afford unforced errors.

I knew Bill figured that, as a fellow operative and former Republican, I'd get it. I told him I'd keep a careful eye on the campaign messaging to make sure it wouldn't cause heartburn with Republicans.

New York's unique electoral system presented the most serious challenge to getting Republican support. New York is one of a small number of states that uses "fusion voting," whereby multiple political parties on a ballot can list the same endorsed candidate. In many instances, the Conservative Party of New York endorsed the Republican Party's candidate, but that was not a given. In some contests the Conservative Party ran their own candidate and, in rare occasions, even endorsed the Democrat. While enrollment in the party statewide was less than 2 percent of voters, in certain Senate races, 10 percent or more voted Conservative Party. And given how close many elections were, Conservative Party votes could make the difference between a win and a loss. We knew that party Chair Mike Long was a strong opponent of ours, but we didn't know how he'd enter the conversation.

The day after the *New York Times* article ran, Long issued a statement. "The intensity is rising," it said. "So we are making our plans to do everything we can to make sure that the bill that would destroy marriage does not pass." He continued, "We're not a single issue party, but there are a few issues where the line in the sand is drawn. Changing the sanctimony [*sic*] of marriage is one of them."

This gave me serious heartburn. Republican senators feared this guy and having him weigh in so assertively would make it hard on our GOP team to secure the votes.

To date, the GOP cultivation work had been going very well. Just before the 2010 elections, GOP lobbyist Jeff Cook had gotten Senate Republican Leader Dean Skelos to attend a Log Cabin Republicans fundraiser in Manhattan. Speaking to reporters, Skelos went beyond what most advocates had even hoped for, saying that he would recommend that his conference let the marriage equality bill come to the floor for a vote if they recaptured the majority. "I've always said that it will be a vote of conscience with our members, and subject to speaking to my conference, I would put the bill out for a vote," he said.

Early in the 2011 session, lobbyist Mike Avella circled back with Skelos to see where he stood. Skelos's position hadn't changed, but he had a lot of questions. Cuomo was saying that he was making this a priority, but could he deliver the handful of Democrats who had voted no last time (there were four who remained)? Would they declare their stance in advance? How many Republican votes would be needed? The Republican leader told Mike he would not recommend that his members take a vote unless he was sure the Democrats delivered new votes. The fiasco of two years ago remained fresh in his mind, and there was zero incentive for Skelos to preside over the same kind of mess that happened on his predecessor's watch. If he was going to take the political hit from the right for moving a bill, he wanted to be sure it passed and they got it over with. And that meant Cuomo delivering the Democrats—at least two or three—and the Republicans supplying three or four votes to finish the job.

Bill Smith thought Skelos was being honest about putting the bill on the floor for a vote, but he knew he'd be under immense pressure not to—from the Conservative Party; from religious groups such as the Catholic hierarchy and Orthodox Jews, who were a power in New York politics; and from some of his own Republican members. After all, Republican Legislatures were known for moving anti-marriage constitutional amendments not marriage equality bills. Bill wanted to take nothing for granted. So he turned to a new, powerful Republican living in New York who had recently come out of the closet as gay, former chairman of the Republican National Committee (RNC) and campaign manager of the 2004 Bush-Cheney reelection campaign, Ken Mehlman.

Bill had been introduced to Ken by Kelley Robertson, a fellow Alabaman with whom he'd worked on judicial elections and who had gone on to become Ken's chief of staff at the RNC. The two smart operatives who now straddled LGBT and Republican worlds became close friends and confidants.

Ken had jumped into the national freedom to marry efforts with a bang, joining the board of and co-chairing a Manhattan fundraiser for the American Foundation for Equal Rights, the group sponsoring the Ted Olson and David Boies–led lawsuit challenging the constitutionality of Proposition 8. The event raised $1.4 million, much of which came from fellow event chair and Republican comrade-in-arms, billionaire hedge fund investor Paul Singer. That event was a coming out of sorts for Ken as well as for Singer, who had for years invested in LGBT causes, including ours in Massachusetts, but had never spoken out personally about them.

At the fundraiser, Singer shared a different side of himself, telling the crowd about leafing through the wedding album of his son and son-in-law. "At the moment they are pioneers," he said. "Although I felt like a loving father and father-in-law, not a pioneer, as we were looking at the pictures."

When I read of Singer's words, which were covered in the press, I e-mailed Andrew and Corey Morris-Singer, with whom I had maintained a relationship ever since their crucial contribution in the final days in Massachusetts, congratulating them for their dad's loving words.

Ken was living in Chelsea and working as the global head of public affairs for the private equity firm Kohlberg Kravis Roberts. Bill thought the New York battle was the perfect project for Ken to take on: a GOP-controlled branch of a Legislature that stood between gay and lesbian

New Yorkers and their freedom to marry. Bill pitched it to Ken, who was sold immediately.

Ken, in turn, thought Singer would be the perfect partner—for financial support, to enlist other Wall Street investors to the cause, and to make the case to Skelos. Singer was such a big player in national Republican politics that that would be a game changer.

Ken reached out to Singer's team of advisers, all of whom he'd worked with. Annie Dickerson and Margaret Hoover had both worked on the Bush '04 campaign, and Dan Senor had served in the Bush administration as a foreign policy operative. Singer's team had questions. Singer had certainly supported gay causes before, largely at the behest of his son, but had never gotten involved personally in a gay political fight. Wasn't that all about supporting Democrats? Paul would never go for that. Ken vouched for Bill Smith and the rest of Tim Gill's political operation, urging Singer's folks to meet with Bill.

In several meetings, Bill laid out the strategy for victory to Singer's team and how they could help. It was all about two things. First, Cuomo was driving, and they had to provide the governor with the media campaign he asked for so he'd have some wind at his back as he made the case. Second, they had to reassure Republican Senate leadership that allowing the vote and freeing up a few Republicans to vote for marriage wouldn't hurt the party's electoral standing. Bill told Singer's people he would be adding two key people to the GOP campaign team: John McArdle, the former top aide to Skelos who was now a communications consultant, and Claude LaVigna, the Senate Republicans' trusted pollster. Bill explained that they'd have LaVigna poll in the districts of GOP senators and then sit down with leadership and explain for whom yes votes would be least risky.

In a subsequent meeting, this time with Paul Singer himself joining his team and Patrick Guerriero joining Bill, they closed a deal. Bill immediately called me and told me that $425,000 was being wired from Singer to Freedom to Marry for the GOP polling and communications work and to support the TV buy. We were off to the races.

The next play was for Team Singer to reach out to other Wall Street heavyweights to join the fight. Margaret Hoover took the lead in pulling a meeting together. A thirty-three-year-old sharp and stunning blonde who was a regular on Fox TV's *O'Reilly Factor*, she was also the great-granddaughter of President Herbert Hoover and on the boards of the Herbert Hoover Presidential Library Association and the Hoover Institution at Stanford.

Being part of this effort meant more to Margaret than anyone knew. As a twenty-five-year-old, she had joined the 2004 Bush reelection campaign and learned from an equally appalled colleague how the campaign was actively working to get anti-marriage constitutional amendments on the ballot in targeted states to rally the socially conservative base and drive up turnout. It disturbed her to her core. She thought about leaving and decided to stay, but only after promising herself that she would dedicate herself to playing whatever part she could in shifting the GOP position on gay rights. And now, here she was, staffing Singer—one of the largest Republican donors in the country—on this New York marriage effort, while also writing a book on modernizing the GOP, with a major focus on the need for the party to change its tune on gay rights.

Margaret and Annie Dickerson, who prior to joining Singer had served as director of major donors for Bush-Cheney '04, went over lists of Wall Street execs with Singer. They settled on thirty-two to invite to a briefing on the New York campaign: CEOs of top firms such as Goldman Sachs and Morgan Stanley, as well as top leaders in the hedge fund world, including Cliff Asness, Dan Loeb, and others.

Margaret prepared invitations for Singer, and from his own computer, Singer sent them individually to each person on the list. Some would be interested, and most wouldn't be, but Singer never minded making the ask.

Bill Smith arranged for Cuomo Chief of Staff Steve Cohen and our communications consultant Jennifer Cunningham to attend the meeting and provide a briefing on the plan to win, Cuomo's commitment, and how much it would cost.

On Thursday, April 28, about a dozen people gathered around a conference table at Singer's Elliott Management offices on Fifty-Seventh Street. Of the thirty-two executives Singer had reached out to, three joined personally: hedge fund leaders Cliff Asness and Dan Loeb, and

Jay Sammons, a younger openly gay principal at the Carlyle Group asset management firm. There were also top advisers from two other hedge fund investors.

Bill took a seat at one end of the conference table, next to Cohen and Cunningham. He was fascinated by the dynamic in the room. This was the first time many in the crowd had interacted with Cuomo's team. As attorney general, Cuomo had investigated the Carlyle Group for its involvement in a state pension fund scandal. The mood toward the new governor was cautious. Bill knew that if it weren't for their mutual interest in the marriage cause, they wouldn't be in the same room together.

Bill set out to demonstrate that the lead advocates and team of consultants were pros coming from both sides of the aisle who were focused only on winning and had a plan to do so. He explained that he worked for Tim Gill and gave political advice to a network of major donors about how their investments could bring about policy advances for the gay and lesbian community. He spoke of how New York was ripe for a win: the advocacy groups had come together to form New Yorkers United for Marriage, and that would be the vehicle for a paid media campaign that would provide support to Governor Cuomo to get the job done. He laid out the GOP strategy: the active engagement of Ken Mehlman and the Republican dream team of consultants they had hired.

Cohen spoke up next, addressing the governor's commitment to the issue. He explained that he and Cuomo had worked together for years, and like many of those gathered in the room, they were middle-aged straight men who had seen gay rights issues go from marginal to mainstream in their lifetimes. Now was the time for New York to step up and get the marriage equality bill passed. He explained that the governor was fully in but that it was a difficult challenge and they needed partners in the work.

Cunningham then detailed the media buy she thought was advisable. She talked about television, direct mail, and newspaper spots, and put a dollar figure on a robust campaign at more than $1.5 million.

After they finished, Cohen and Cunningham waited for questions. But there were none. So they went on their way, really unsure of how the whole thing had gone.

Singer's team inferred that the mere fact that those heavy hitters attended the meeting meant they were in for big checks, barring a poor performance; people at this level of high finance don't waste their time. Soon after, Margaret and Annie, the Bush campaign veterans, did a job they knew well: following up and collecting the checks. But this time, instead of collecting for Republican candidates or PACs, they were asking the hedge fund leaders to invest in the New York freedom to marry effort.

One week later, on May 4, Margaret e-mailed Cunningham to let her know that the spoils from the lunch, combined with what Singer had put in, would amount to nearly one million dollars. That, combined with the $250,000 each that Freedom to Marry, HRC, and the Pride Agenda had agreed to raise, meant that we'd be able to exceed the fully loaded paid media program that Cuomo thought was sufficient.

Soon after, the *New York Times* ran a prominently featured story entitled, "Donors to G.O.P. Are Backing Gay Marriage Push." Pitched by Singer's staff and Bill Smith, it said, "As gay rights advocates intensify their campaign to legalize same-sex marriage in New York, the bulk of their money is coming from an unexpected source: a group of conservative financiers and wealthy donors to the Republican Party, most of whom are known for bankrolling right-leaning candidates and causes." It spoke of Singer's role, contributing $425,000 and raising another $500,000. And it talked of Ken's role in recruiting donors.

"F'ing awesome!" I texted Bill, as soon as I read it.

That would show Albany this was a different kind of campaign.

=

The next step in the Team Singer engagement strategy was for Singer to host Senate Majority Leader Dean Skelos and Deputy Majority Leader Tom Libous.

For Bill Smith, the goal of this meeting was to introduce Skelos and Libous to a universe of prominent Republicans who supported the freedom to marry and believed it was consistent with Republican values. It was unstated, but the fact that some of the most powerful Republican donors in the country—donors who were used to meeting with presidential hopefuls not state legislators—cared enough about this issue to make the case to two New York Senate leaders signaled that they'd be in this fight for the long haul.

On Friday, May 6, Skelos and Libous arrived at Singer's Midtown Manhattan office. They sat next to each other facing windows overlooking the city, with a glass wall behind them that separated the room from the hallway. Singer sat directly in front of them. Ken Mehlman, Patrick Guerriero, Bill Smith, Margaret Hoover, and the GOP pollster Claude LaVigna joined, as did hedge fund titan Dan Loeb who had become a strong advocate, and Jay Sammons, the younger, openly gay finance executive. At just after 8:00 a.m., Singer began: "I'm happy to host this discussion on the critical importance of the marriage issue to our families and our state." He told Skelos and Libous that he wanted to introduce them to a group of influential Republicans strongly committed to making marriage equality a reality.

"This issue is especially important to me," Singer continued. "We're pleased that in the past two weeks we've raised $1 million for the media campaign from Republican donors, some in this room and many others outside this room. We are here today because we want to help you and your conference navigate the issue successfully."

After a round of introductions and brief comments by Bill, Patrick, and the GOP pollster, Ken took the floor. I'm not here simply as a businessman in New York who believes this is the right thing to do, he said. I'm also here as someone who spent a number of years working to build the party that you serve in, and I believe this is right for the party. This is important because it's consistent with the principles of our party: the values of liberty and freedom, he said. And it's consistent with where the majority of the people in this state are, and that number is only going to increase in the coming years. Support for marriage equality among young New Yorkers was off the charts.

He also spoke of how, when he was chair of the RNC, the party had made mistakes around race and gender and that they were hitting one of those periods now with gays and lesbians. He wanted to help the party avoid making the same mistake.

Dan Loeb, the outspoken hedge fund leader, chimed in and spoke up about how he'd been a big Obama backer four years before but had been sorely disappointed and now was backing Romney. On this issue, though, he said it was a no-brainer. "We're in favor of individual freedom," Loeb said, referring to Republicans. "We have to be in favor of this."

Skelos and Libous were listening but said little.

Jay Sammons spoke up. He talked of his staunch Republican background and then told the leaders about his family. He was married to his partner, and they were raising a two-year-old child. "I'm a big boy and I can understand a lot of things and I can understand politics," he said. "But it is different for kids," Sammons explained. He wanted his children to see that there were others who had married dads and for them to see that those marriages were the same as anybody else's marriage.

The two leaders remained silent. Finally, Skelos spoke up: "If we are contemplating doing this, this could wreak havoc on our conference politically, so we need to understand the playing field."

There were countervailing political calculations Skelos was considering. First and foremost, voting for the marriage bill could pose a serious risk to his members. They could lose in a low-turnout primary to a socially conservative Republican, who then might be too conservative to win in a general election. And even if the incumbent made it through the primary, without the support of the Conservative Party, a win would be that much more difficult. On the flip side, if the Republican-led Senate blocked consideration of the bill, or if it couldn't produce a few votes in favor, Fight Back New York or something similar would be back, and this time the Republicans would have a bull's-eye on their backs.

Libous, the deputy majority leader, spoke up about the politics, and a conversation ensued about the political calculus. Now the legislative leaders were engaged. If they sent the bill to the Senate floor, could they retain their Republican majority?

For their part, Skelos and Libous knew this group was serious, but they had been burned before. People often talk about how serious they are about an issue and say that they'll be there for support, but then they fail to follow up and stand by the lawmakers in the aftermath. What would happen when the extremists come, as they inevitably would, and try to drive out the Republicans who voted for the marriage bill?

Bill had an answer at the ready. Based on his and Patrick's years of work, not a single Republican across the country who voted for marriage equality had ever been defeated because of that vote.

"We've always been there for people who've been there for us in the community," Bill said. "We will continue to have peoples' backs."

Bill left the meeting with the feeling that Skelos wanted to find a way to move the bill. The polling from the Senate Republicans' own pollster showed that it wouldn't be a dangerous vote for certain members. Also, the level of sophistication of the advocates, the A-crowd of GOP donors who cared about this, and the unspoken threat of what would happen if they didn't do it seemed to offset the concerns about losing backing from the Conservative Party.

Later in May, Dan Loeb hosted a final round of meetings at his hedge fund office on Park Avenue, this time with rank-and-file Republican senators who were the most likely—based on all the intelligence—to come our way. They were short, thirty-minute meetings, with some but not all of the participants from the meeting with Skelos and Libous. Again, the goal was to impress upon the senators that a vote for marriage equality was consistent with Republican values and that there was a strong network of Republican leaders who were backing the marriage campaign.

New York City Mayor Michael Bloomberg swung into action as well. On Tuesday, May 17, Bloomberg—who had donated nearly a million dollars to the Senate Republicans in the last election cycle—spent the day in Albany making the rounds, visiting with Skelos and with senators who were on the target list. He pledged publicly to support lawmakers financially who voted for the marriage bill, "no matter where they stand on any other issue."

The next week, I attended a spectacular fundraiser hosted by the mayor for New Yorkers United for Marriage at the Bloomberg Foundation. Actor Sarah Jessica Parker spoke, and musician Rufus Wainwright performed. It raised another $250,000 for the media campaign. The following day, May 26, Bloomberg gave a powerful public address on the cause at Cooper Union in the East Village.

"We are the freest city in the freest country in the world," he said. But "freedom is not frozen in time." He warned those who were putting up roadblocks. "On matters of freedom and equality, history has not remembered obstructionists kindly," he said. "Not on abolition. Not on women's suffrage. Not on workers' rights. Not on civil rights. And it will be no different on marriage rights."

By the end of May, New Yorkers United for Marriage was firing on all cylinders. We'd launched the paid media campaign with an ad entitled "Vows," highlighting a New York lesbian couple who had been together for twenty-nine years speaking of their desire to marry in their home state. Human Rights Campaign (HRC) now had more than a dozen organizers in the field, collecting postcards and getting phone calls into lawmakers. I was focused on making sure that meetings between same-sex couples and target lawmakers were happening, so I turned our Freedom to Marry organizing staff to that endeavor and got reports back on how those meetings were proceeding. Jennifer Cunningham and her team at SKD were getting quality stories placed nearly every day in newspapers around the state, sometimes more than one a day. We were meeting with Cuomo's team at least weekly and were having coordination and strategy calls of New Yorkers United for Marriage nearly every other morning.

Yet as we entered the first week of June, we still hadn't gotten any public commitments that anyone would change their vote. We knew we wouldn't get any Republicans until two or three of the four holdout Democrats came around; Skelos had been very clear about that. And yet none of the Democrats had announced a change in position. Some Republican senators had told the press that they hadn't heard from Cuomo, even though Cuomo's staff was telling us the calls and meetings were happening. Cuomo continued to say that he didn't want a vote until we knew we were going to win. With the apparent lack of progress, some in our community began to accuse Cuomo of using that as an excuse. The *New York Times* editorial board jumped in, calling Cuomo's position on waiting for a vote until he was sure the bill would pass "the wrong decision" and arguing that only a vote would require lawmakers to take a public position. Without it, lawmakers would keep their positions to themselves.

Most nerve-racking was that time was running out, as the session was scheduled to end in less than three weeks, on June 20.

On the evening of Friday June 10, I got a call from Andrew Cuomo's office. The governor wanted to meet with a small group of advocates on Monday afternoon in Albany. Could I make it? I said I'd be there.

=

While I was en route to Albany Monday morning, Governor Cuomo and Steve Cohen huddled up. The marriage bill was stuck, with only ten days to go in the legislative session. On one hand, the Senate Republicans would love to have any reason to not have a vote on the bill, as long as they could blame it on the Democrats and not take the heat or the retribution for killing it. Dean Skelos had made it clear up front that if Cuomo didn't deliver two or three of the four Democrats who were still in office and had voted against the bill last time, the bill wouldn't pass and so he wouldn't send it to the floor. So far, no new Democrats had announced, and so Skelos had an out.

On the other hand, for many Democrats, their ideal scenario was to support the bill but not have it pass, as long as they could blame the Republicans for not moving the bill. This was a great election issue for them, especially for raising money from national gay donors. They weren't even being terribly subtle, with Minority Leader John Sampson publicly predicting the Republicans would never bring it up. If they could pin inaction or defeat on the Republicans, they knew gay donors would pummel the Republicans and bankroll the Democrats to flip the Senate back to Democratic control.

=

Cuomo had spent weeks thinking about how to break the logjam. That day it was time to advance his plan. In addition to Cohen, Cuomo pulled together senior adviser Larry Schwartz who oversaw Cuomo's relationships with the Legislature and his counsel Mylan Denerstein.

"I want you to go on Fred Dicker," Cuomo said to Cohen, referring to the legendary *New York Post* political columnist who also had a radio show. "You go on the show and say that, if the Senate leadership lets the legislation go to the floor of the Senate and they let their members vote their conscience, then it will pass."

Both Cohen and Schwartz responded with quizzical looks. Schwartz noted that while the Democrats were tentatively committed, they didn't want their commitment discussed publicly. Cohen asked whether this would make it easier or harder to lock in the needed Republican votes.

"Life is options, and this is our best one," Cuomo responded.

"We really will have the votes," Cuomo said. The three Democrats he needed had privately committed to support the bill if it went to a vote. The fact that they didn't want to say so publicly was merely an effort to hedge their bets. Then they'd need just three Republicans, and based on his conversations and his gut, he knew they had at least that.

"So you go onto Dicker and you say, 'If the Republicans let it go to the floor, if the leadership lets their members vote their conscience, it will pass.' No qualifications and say it with confidence."

"What do I do about particulars?" Cohen asked, knowing that Dicker would immediately ask for names.

"You tell Fred that we're not in the business of revealing how legislators will vote. That's up to them." Cuomo said, waving the question off. "You know how to handle this."

A little after ten, Cohen walked upstairs to the third floor of the Capitol to Fred Dicker's tiny radio studio.

Anything new with the gay marriage bill? Dicker asked Cohen on the air.

"The only issue is whether the Republicans will allow it to go to the floor and whether senators will be allowed to vote their conscience. If that is allowed, the votes are there to get this passed."

"My expectation is this will go to a vote, but it's up to the Senate leadership," Cohen concluded.

As Cohen left the studio, a scrum of ten or so reporters huddled around him. There were other big issues in Albany but none that attracted anywhere near the attention of the marriage bill. He repeated that if Skelos allowed it to come up and allowed members to vote their conscience, they had the votes.

Cohen walked back downstairs to his office. He was immediately met by Schwartz who told him he had just kicked a hornet's nest. Rob Mujica, Skelos's chief of staff, had called and he was furious. Skelos had been consistent for months that, once Cuomo had lined up the three other Democrats—everyone but the virulently opposed Senator Ruben Diaz—and a bill had been introduced, the Senate Republicans would allow the bill to be considered. But unless and until it was clear those Democrats would support the measure, Skelos felt no obligation to let the bill go to the floor. Nothing had changed. As far as Skelos knew, there had been no movement on the Democratic side.

On Skelos's behalf, Mujica told the press corps that Cuomo and his team were playing games. He then reiterated the Republican position. The problem remained where it always had been: with the Democrats.

Back in the governor's office, Cuomo had his press shop schedule a media availability for the afternoon. He deployed Joe Percoco, the brusque forty-two-year-old aide who'd been Cuomo's confidant and enforcer since the 1990s, to ensure that the recalcitrant Senate Democrats were at that press conference and ready to publicly announce their support. Cuomo then called John Sampson, the Democratic leader of the Senate, and told him what he wanted.

"I want your members to announce publicly today," Cuomo told Sampson. "I want them to come, and I want them to say publicly that they're a yes."

Cuomo wanted Sampson to deliver the three Democrats who were hedging—Joe Addabbo, Shirley Huntley, and Carl Krueger—for the media availability. Sampson restated their view, that they were all there, ready to vote yes, but they wanted to keep their options open in case the bill never got to the floor.

Cuomo made the case to Sampson. "You want to wait for the vote? I understand you want to wait for the vote. That's a cautious thing to do. That's politically maybe a smart thing to do. But that's not an option.

Haven't you heard what Dean Skelos said? Unless we are prepared to publicly commit, he's not letting it go. Don't you understand? He will blame us. And we will be to blame. You are out of options. Either you're going to come, you're going to stand with me. You're going to do the right thing and we're going to get this passed, and you will make history. Or it's going to fail, and the problem is going to be on you because you've been set up by the Republicans."

Sampson and the three recalcitrant Democrats agreed to stand with the governor at a news conference, which was set for 3:00 p.m.

Once I arrived in Albany, I dropped my bags at the Pride Agenda's Albany office and walked up the hill on State Street to the spectacular Romanesque capitol building. It was my first time there; all the meetings I'd been part of were at the governor's New York City office. I passed through security and took the elevator to the governor's office on the second floor. I gave my name to the security guard standing outside the executive corridor and was escorted into a small waiting room where I met up with the governor's staff working on marriage, along with several of the other advocates I usually met with in New York City—about ten of us in all.

We had been scheduled to meet with the governor at 3:00 p.m., but instead, we were all ushered into the Blue Room, where the governor conducts press conferences, for the announcement with the Democrats. Many of the Democratic senators were gathered, and I sat there and marveled at the political skill of the governor who had orchestrated this event.

Senator Sampson began. "For every setback there's a comeback," he said, introducing the three Democratic senators who were changing their positions. Senators Addabbo and Huntley, both of Queens, each took the microphone and talked about how they'd heard from many more constituents on our side of the issue and that that was the reason they'd be voting our way.

"For me," Addabbo said, "my vote was about one thing: my people and my district." He continued, "6,015 people have weighed in, and 4,839 wanted me to vote yes. So in the end, that is my vote." It wasn't terribly inspirational, except to the field organizers who'd worked tirelessly to get them huge numbers of postcards. But by then, I'd already learned Albany wasn't about inspiration. It was about transactions and results.

The last of the three, Senator Carl Kruger, had more to say. Recently indicted for bribery and corruption, the Brooklyn lawmaker spoke fondly of his colleague, Tom Duane, the openly gay Chelsea Democrat who was the lead Senate sponsor of the marriage bill. "He pointed out for me the difference between right and wrong," Kruger said, "and so we go forward with an agenda of rights and equality."

Duane then took the microphone. "I am very touched and moved and gratified," he said about his Democratic colleagues. To have twenty-nine out of thirty Democrats voting his way was both a great milestone and demonstration of personal support. The remaining Democrat, Ruben Diaz of the Bronx, had long made it known that he was virulently opposed.

Governor Cuomo then took the podium. "I'm very proud to be a Democrat right now," he said, standing with the Senate Democrats with whom it was widely known he had a rocky relationship. "This is an issue of social justice, an issue of social progress," he said. "We're not home yet, but this is a very significant development that will generate a lot of momentum."

He took several questions.

Do you have the votes?

"I believe the votes are there if a vote happens," he answered, putting the pressure squarely back on Skelos.

What would you say to Republican lawmakers who are getting pressure on this issue?

"Vote your conscience, not your fears," Cuomo replied. "Represent the people of this state," referring to the 58 percent of New Yorkers who supported the freedom to marry.

He repeated, "Vote your conscience, not your fears."

"Are you now going to advance a marriage bill?" a reporter asked.

"I am not going to make that decision on my own. First I need to consult with the advocates," he said.

Following the media event, we were escorted back into the waiting room. The governor's lead civil rights staffer, Alphonso David, then briefed us on what was coming next.

"The governor is going to ask you if you're ready to support moving the bill," he said. "If you have any concerns, let me know now."

Basically, it was speak now or forever hold your peace.

No one spoke up.

We were then ushered into the governor's conference room, where we took seats around a large dark-wood conference table. The governor's staff sat in chairs along the wall. Joining the Pride Agenda's Ross Levi, HRC's Brian Ellner, and me were our two lobbyists, Democrat Emily Giske and Republican Mike Avella, along with New York City Council Speaker Christine Quinn and the lead sponsors of the marriage bills in the Assembly and Senate, Danny O'Donnell and Tom Duane. Governor Cuomo sat at the head of the table. "Now's the moment of truth," he told us. We need to decide if we're going to introduce a bill or not, and I want your counsel.

The stagecraft was impressive; I was sure the governor wanted to hear from each of us directly that we were in so there could be no finger-pointing later. But after that press conference, there was no question we were going.

Bill Smith couldn't make it up from DC that day. He and I talked in advance, and we both agreed we had to pull the trigger now. He was concerned that some in our group might not be enthusiastic enough and encouraged me to do all I could to set an atmosphere where people would say yes, it's time to go. So I spoke up early: "I've been working on this issue for nearly ten years—in Massachusetts, Connecticut, Vermont, California, and now here in New York. There is never a slam-dunk on this issue. It's never easy. But never before have we been in a better position to win. There's no question in my mind that it's time to go."

Christine Quinn thanked the governor for his amazing leadership in advancing the freedom to marry, something no governor had ever done before with the tenacity and effectiveness of Cuomo. She too urged him to go. And so it went, as Cuomo went around the room. Until he got to Senator Duane, the lead sponsor of the bill in the Senate.

Governor, I want to back you, and I don't want to be pessimistic, Duane said, but I've got to tell you I'm concerned.

I winced. He was clearly still reeling from the 2009 defeat. Would this lack of enthusiasm from our lead senator unnerve Cuomo? But the governor very coolly sought to reassure Duane. We have twenty-nine votes lined up on the Democratic side, and I've been talking to some Republicans who I think are ready to vote with us. And besides, it's a win either way, Cuomo said. If we lose, you'll win back the majority. The Republicans had only a two-vote margin for their majority. The gay community had proven its ferocity in the elections. If the Republicans killed the bill after the Democrats lived up to their part of the deal, it would almost assuredly lead to a Democratic takeover of the Senate.

Duane was in.

Cuomo wanted everyone to commit that they were in and supported moving forward. So he went around the room and asked us to each raise our hands if we were. The count was unanimous.

Okay, let's go, Cuomo said.

Emily Giske, a close confidant of the governor's, thanked Cuomo for his strong leadership on the issue, and we gave him a rousing round of applause.

"If the governor's been the coach, then Steve's been the quarterback," I said. And we all applauded the self-effacing Cohen loudly as well.

A slew of press had camped outside the governor's office, awaiting our decision. We needed a spokesperson, and I nominated the Pride Agenda's Ross Levi to announce the decision. I stood by his side as he told the press that we'd unanimously recommended to the governor that he move forward with introducing a bill and that he agreed to do so.

Then Ross and I walked next door to Cohen's office. We discussed preparations for introducing the bill for a few minutes until the governor's assistant came down to tell us that the governor would like us to come back in.

What had we done wrong? I wondered. Did we say something wrong in the press announcement?

We sat back down in the conference room along with everyone else who had been there before. Then the governor emerged from his inner office and took his seat at the head of the table.

I want to tell you about a courageous man, he said, a senator who is doing something brave and to whom we all owe a great debt of gratitude. I just met with Senator Jim Alesi, and he wants to be the first Republican to come out publicly in support. He also wants to say a few words to you. The governor then got up, opened the door to his private office, and welcomed in Senator Alesi.

Alesi entered the room, and we all cheered loudly. One by one, we grabbed his hand and shook it. Alesi told us that he would be voting from his heart, that this is a simple matter of freedom and equality for people. He then turned to Duane and apologized to him. "I feel terrible about the 2009 vote. It was a political vote. And I apologize to you, Tom, for that vote." All eyes were on Duane. I had a noticeable lump in my throat.

For months, we'd been working to get six senators to move our way. We'd felt as if we'd been making headway but still hadn't gotten one public commitment. Today we had four. Pretty amazing.

We were told by the governor's office to stay within fifteen minutes of the Capitol, indefinitely. That meant I wasn't going home. So I booked a room at Seventy-Four State Street in desolate downtown Albany, just down the hill from the Capitol. I went out for a big steak dinner with a couple of lobbyists and then went to bed to rest up for what I hoped to be another productive day.

The next morning, Tuesday, June 14, I was working in my hotel room when we were called back to the governor's office. We gathered around the conference table, and the governor walked in with two of his three teenage daughters. He asked us, tongue in check, if we minded if his two closest advisers joined us. It was clear he was very conscious of the history he was helping make. Cuomo was divorced from Kerry Kennedy, the seventh child of Bobby and Ethel Kennedy, and it was especially poignant to me that Cuomo was showing his daughters—the granddaughters of Mario Cuomo and Bobby Kennedy—how their father was leading in advancing one of the crucial civil rights issues of the day.

At this meeting, we had a better idea of what to expect. Cuomo was once again masterful with the theatrics of the moment. Another brave Republican senator was ready to make a public announcement, this time Senator Roy McDonald from Saratoga. McDonald had been saying publicly for some time that he was undecided, and we'd heard positive reports from the meetings he'd held with constituents.

McDonald entered the room to a round of handshakes and thanks. He told us that he was a Vietnam vet and the first in his family to go to college. His father, a laborer in the local steel mill, was a religious man and had a pretty simple view of religion. "Jesus taught one thing," he told us, recalling his father's teaching. "He taught us to be nice." As he spoke, I noticed Cuomo holding the hand of one of his daughters.

McDonald had two grandsons who had been diagnosed with autism, and we'd heard from people close to him that had sensitized him to all kinds of difference. Now he was ready to stand with us.

After McDonald left the room, Bill Smith, who'd arrived that day, turned to the governor. "How many more rabbits are you going to pull out of the hat?" he asked. Cuomo responded, "You never start the train unless you know how you're going to get to the station." I loved that answer.

That afternoon, Cuomo submitted the bill, named the Marriage Equality Act, to the Legislature. In his public statement, the governor referred to New York's history in leading the fight for civil rights. "From the fight for women's suffrage to the struggle for civil rights, New Yorkers have been on the right side of history," it said. "When it comes to fighting for what's right, New Yorkers wrote the book, and Marriage Equality is the next chapter of our civil rights story."

We were asked by Cuomo's people to continue to stay close to the Capitol for the rest of the day, ostensibly for the next announcement. We'd heard that it would be Senator Mark Grisanti, the first-term senator from Buffalo. He hadn't even been on our target list, but we were told the governor had been working him hard. For all practical purposes, that would have done it; we'd then have the six votes we needed to pass the bill. And that would seemingly put such enormous pressure on the Republican leadership in the Senate that it would be nearly impossible for them to justify bottling up the bill and denying a vote.

But the announcement didn't come that day, and the process turned out to be much more difficult and drawn out than we thought.

The next day, Wednesday, June 15, the Senate Republicans met together in what's known as conference to discuss how they'd handle the marriage bill. With the momentum of the previous two days and only five days left in the session, we thought they'd resolve to move the bill and make an announcement. Instead, after four hours, they decided they wanted to try to secure changes in the bill to provide additional protections to religiously affiliated institutions to ensure they wouldn't have to host celebrations of same-sex couples' weddings. They assigned a group of three senators to negotiate so-called religious-exemption language with Cuomo and then adjourned to meet again on Thursday.

Late that afternoon, I headed over to the Assembly to watch that body debate and vote on the legislation. It was a foregone conclusion that they'd pass it; they'd done so twice before. This time, after several hours of debate, it passed by a vote of 80–63. Everything was teed up and ready for the Senate to act.

The next morning, Thursday, Mayor Michael Bloomberg returned to Albany and met with the Republican conference, pushing them hard to do the right thing. But still, there were no decisions. Governor Cuomo had us in again to give us an update. He told us that the challenge was getting two more Republican votes because no one wanted to be the deciding thirty-second vote. He joked it was like the thirteenth floor of a building: you could have a twelfth and a fourteenth but not a thirteenth. So he was working to find two more Republican votes. He didn't seem particularly worried since he'd been in meaningful talks with a handful of Republicans, but this time he didn't have any rabbits in his hat—at least not any he was willing to show us.

Bill Smith wanted to believe it was done, but he knew better. On the one hand, they were so close and Cuomo had so much political capital that it was hard to imagine they wouldn't pull it out. Plus there were now two Republicans who had gone public with their support. They were flapping out in the wind, and it seemed really unlikely the GOP leadership would hang them out to dry without calling for a vote. On the other hand, this was Albany, and in Albany bad shit happened all the time.

Unbeknownst to us, Cuomo would soon get commitments from two Republicans. Freshman Senator Mark Grisanti, from Buffalo, was elected in an overwhelmingly Democratic district. Cuomo knew the politics were favorable for Grisanti, and after engaging him on the issue,

Grisanti had seemed very amenable. So Cuomo had continued to work on him. Grisanti had gotten enormous pressure back home to vote for the bill. The local marriage advocacy group had met with him several times, and they'd had couples bear their souls to him. Grisanti told the governor that he would be one of the two thirty-third votes. Cuomo thanked Grisanti and told him that if he didn't have the second vote, Grisanti was off the hook.

Senator Steve Saland, an erudite lawyer from Poughkeepsie, was one of the senators whom our GOP team had identified in 2009 as a likely yes vote had things unfolded differently. Over the past few months, the organizers in his district had arranged several constituent meetings with him, and he would routinely tell his constituents that his wife pushed him every day to vote for gay marriage. Saland was heading up the GOP group negotiating the religious-exemption language. If they reached a reasonable accommodation on that—which it appeared they would—Saland told the governor he would be the other thirty-third vote.

So Cuomo knew we were there, as long as Skelos lived up to his word and the Democrats didn't do anything to screw it up.

As Thursday turned to Friday, it became clear that this wasn't going to be resolved before the weekend. We'd need to stay vigilant, organize at progressive churches in our target districts to control the narrative and demonstrate momentum, and gear up for what was supposed to be the last day of session, Monday, the twentieth, though the session was likely to be extended given the amount of work that had to be done, on marriage and several other issues.

Over the weekend, we won the media wars, out-organizing our opponents. But we lost a vote. Grisanti came back to Albany on Monday and asked to speak to the governor. He explained to the governor that he was no longer sure he could vote for the marriage bill.

In the Cuomo code of ethics, breaking your word was among the worst things you could do.

"You shook my hand," Cuomo said to Grisanti. "You looked me in the eye. We had an understanding. What kind of person are you? It doesn't work that way."

That meant we were back down to thirty-one, and we needed to find our other thirty-third vote.

=

Even as things were deadlocked in the Capitol, New Yorkers United for Marriage was moving at a frenetic pace. Field organizers were focused relentlessly on getting phone calls from constituents to a small number of target lawmakers, adjusted by the day at the direction of our lobbyists. They stood out at grocery stores, shopping centers, and train stations—wherever people congregated—and asked them to "stop and dial," which meant taking the organizer's cell phone and calling the lawmaker right then and there. Each day we extended our television buy for one more day. Our lobbyists also thought it was important to keep the buzz going in the Capitol. So over the course of this period, Brian Ellner arranged for New York Rangers star Sean Avery, Tony award-winning actor Audra McDonald, and famed New York City chef Mario Batali to make the rounds. I found it hard to believe these would make a difference, but Albany was a world I didn't pretend to fully understand.

The Senate turned its attention to rent control and property taxes, deciding to put all the large remaining items other than the marriage bill together in a legislative package that quickly got the nickname "the Big Ugly." The other advocates and I would spend our days sitting in the hot Capitol building, waiting, usually on the couches and chairs outside the Senate chambers. We'd huddle nervously with our lobbyists for updates, wait for the governor's office to call us in, watch the Twitter feed from the most reliable Capitol reporters to see if they picked up anything new, and listen to the increasingly intense chanting from protesters on both sides of the debate.

Bill Smith was staying in close touch with the Wall Street crowd. At the direction of GOP lobbyist Mike Avella, he would have Paul Singer, Dan Loeb, or Ken Mehlman make phone calls to Skelos and Tom Libous. The message was that we're still watching, we know the session is still going on, and this still matters to us.

And we knew Cuomo was doing everything he possibly could. Publicly, he was meeting with Saland and the other Republican negotiators on the religious language. But by that point, he and Cohen knew they were just polishing pebbles; the language was done, and it wasn't the real issue.

Privately, Cuomo was hunting for votes. But he wasn't having much luck, and he was growing increasingly frustrated. He thought Skelos really did want to get the marriage issue over with, but he wasn't an old-school boss who could simply deliver votes. The governor knew not to try to make Skelos do something that simply wasn't part of his makeup.

On the other hand, Cuomo said to us, if Skelos really wanted to get this done, why couldn't he deliver OJ? He was referring to Owen Johnson, the thirty-nine-year veteran of the Senate who was a sickly octogenarian, and who owed his position in leadership to Skelos. "Give us OJ," the governor said with frustration.

"I think the Republicans' strategy is to hope a tornado hits the Capitol," Cuomo said to us. They had no plan and were stuck, hoping for some way out.

A week before, I'd presumed that the governor had everything under control. But it was increasingly clear that it wasn't at all a done deal. Jennifer Cunningham, our communications lead and an Albany hand for decades, felt we were in a real danger zone. The Republicans had met two times in conference, and still the bill was stuck. The session was supposed to conclude any day, and the Senate and Assembly still had to reach agreement on big, contentious items. Things fell apart all the time in Albany, particularly at the end of sessions. Legislators grew tired; lobbyists were crawling up and down the walls; and the two houses of the Legislature grew testy with one another. And there were plenty of reasons the Senate Republicans wouldn't want to move the marriage bill, the Conservative Party chief among them. On multiple occasions, Cunningham had seen the Republican Senate simply complete work on what it wanted to and adjourn. If that happened here, it wouldn't shock her.

=

Once Team Cuomo and the three Republicans reached agreement on tighter religious-exemption language, the governor called Poughkeepsie Senator Steve Saland and asked him to come by his office.

"I don't know if I'm going to have that extra vote," Cuomo said to him.

"We had a deal," he continued, referring to his promise not to make Saland be the deciding vote. "We shook on it. I'm a man of my word. I believe in what I said."

Cuomo went on, "You have all the respect in the world for your commitment. I will always be your friend. I will always appreciate what you did. But if you feel, given your politics, that you can't vote yes at this point, you have no problem with me."

Saland said to the governor, "I'll be there for you."

The two shook hands.

So now Cuomo knew we had the votes. We just needed the Republicans to bring it to a vote.

=

Thursday evening, Emily Giske and Bill Smith stopped by the Senate Democrats' office on the third floor of the Capitol to check in. They knew that the Democrats felt—with some justification—that they were being taken for granted with all the focus on the Republicans. Democratic leader John Sampson entered the room and told Bill in an annoyed tone, "We're not going to have all our people here tomorrow. There's five of them that have to go." He proceeded to list the absentees. Carl Kruger, who'd been indicted, needed to be in court on Friday, he told them.

Bill couldn't believe it. After all of this, the Democrats weren't going to show up? "Let me tell you what we're going to do," Bill yelled, in his Alabama twang. "If you have five people who aren't going to show up tomorrow, we're going to know exactly who killed marriage equality. And you've seen what we've done campaign-wise. And we're going to do it again. Cause I think we know and you know that the votes are there to pass marriage equality. And it will be the Democrats who killed marriage equality."

Bill had never raised his voice at an elected official before. He felt as if he'd crossed some kind of invisible boundary. But he didn't care. "Senator, I don't think you want to tell the story of how when marriage equality came for a vote, it didn't pass because Democrats wouldn't show up for their jobs," he said. "We have to be able to work this out. We've come too far. There's no way you cannot be there."

"I'm just telling you," Sampson said, and he left the room.

Emily and Bill stormed out and went down to the governor's office to fill in Steve Cohen. Cohen had been hearing rumors from the Senate Democrats that there could be issues with attendance, and he knew there continued to be a not-so-small contingent of Democrats who wanted nothing more than for things to run aground at the feet of the Republicans. That would mean another electoral cycle where gay dollars could bankroll the Democrats. Cohen couldn't believe senators would miss the most historic vote of their careers because they had to give a high school graduation speech or something like that. But the Kruger thing seemed problematic. They had to have every Democratic vote there for the bill to pass.

At about 7:30 p.m., Cohen told the governor, who asked Cohen to find out if Kruger actually had to be in court. Cohen had spent seven years as a prosecutor in the US Attorney's Office in Manhattan, which was prosecuting the case against Kruger. During that time, he was teamed with Richard Zabel, now the chief of the criminal division. Cohen rang him up.

"You know anything about Kruger having a court appearance tomorrow?" Cohen asked Zabel.

"I don't know," Zabel responded. "But I'll find out."

At about ten, Zabel called Cohen back.

"Perhaps Kruger is going to court for the waters," Zabel said.

Cohen had no idea what he was talking about.

Zabel then added, "There are no waters in the courthouse, so I assume you have been misinformed."

Zabel told Cohen that he was riffing on a famous exchange from *Casablanca*. What it meant, he told Cohen, is there's no court appearance.

"Not only is there no court appearance," Zabel continued. "His appearance is waived. He doesn't even need to show up when there is a court appearance."

Thank you, Cohen said, and he hung up the phone and reported to the governor.

"Are you sure?" asked the governor.

"100 percent."

"Get Sampson and his crew up here."

Sampson and a few other members of Democratic leadership came over and gathered around a small table in Cohen's office. Cuomo walked in.

"You guys want to tell me what's going on?" Cuomo said, asking about Kruger.

Sampson responded, "Well he's got to be in court. His lawyers can't get him out of it."

Cuomo responded, "There is no court appearance."

Sampson stammered that he understood Kruger needed to be in court. Cuomo cut him off.

"The games have to end," Cuomo said. "You want to have a future? You want to be respected? You want to be viewed as legitimate? Stop playing games."

"We've had some troubles this session," Cuomo continued, speaking of his frosty relationship with the Senate Democrats. "We're not going to have troubles on this. The games end now. This matters too much, and I've worked too hard on this to have you mess this up by playing games. There are going to be no more games. Your entire conference is going to be there tomorrow. They're going to vote. It's either going to pass or it's not going to pass. But it's not going to fail because you have members who suddenly have commitments or other places they have to be. It's not true. It's not right. And it's not going to happen. Do we understand each other?"

"We understand," Sampson said.

And Cuomo walked out.

First thing Friday morning, the governor called us in. He'd just gotten off the phone with Dean Skelos, and the Republican leader told Cuomo that he wanted the Assembly to pass the marriage bill again, this time with the new religious-exemption language included in it. Then the Senate would consider taking that up.

It was an unreasonable demand, Cuomo told us. Assembly Speaker

Sheldon Silver had been accommodating throughout the process, waiting for the Senate to get its act together. He wasn't going to make that demand of Silver, in part because there was simply no reason for it as a matter of procedure. The Assembly could pass the religious-exemption bill on its own and the Senate could approve both, or the Senate could combine them into one bill, pass it, and send the bill back to the Assembly. The Republicans were making unreasonable demands, demands that showed Cuomo that they were looking desperately for an excuse to avoid taking action and pin the blame back on the Democrats. The governor told us he'd told Skelos that he was ten minutes away from calling a press conference with the advocates blasting the Republicans' obstructionism.

Don't do it, Mike Avella, our Republican lobbyist, e-mailed urgently. We'll get this worked out, he promised, but not if you blow it up.

Bill Smith chimed in. "We trust you," he said to Cuomo. "We know you're going to get this into the end zone. We're behind you 100 percent of the way." Bill was nervous, but he knew his job right now was to buck up the governor.

Cohen asked to see us in his office. He told us the day was going to be bumpy. It's going to look as if the deal is going to fall apart, he said. Probably several times. But he likened the situation we were in to negotiating for the purchase of a car. At some point, if they refuse your best offer, you have to walk away.

"You cannot panic. You cannot blink," Cohen said.

We've given as much as we can give, he continued, and we need to keep our resolve and make sure that everyone knows this is the deal or we're walking out.

I'd seen my father negotiate for a car in this exact manner. The stakes here were a hell of a lot higher, but I agreed with Cohen's analysis. We needed to call the Republicans' bluff and hold tight. But it sure was nauseating thinking that things could fall apart.

=

Inside the dense walls of the oak-paneled Republican conference room, Cuomo could not lobby the senators, nor could the advocates or the protesters, whose presence had gotten increasingly larger over the course of the week but still nowhere near what the scene was like in Massachusetts. The conference was engaged in a members-only, marathon conversation over what to do about the marriage bill. Senior staffers had long since been dismissed from the room. Members were sitting in their usual spots. Some sat on couches around the wall; others sat in antique leather chairs. Skelos sat at the end of a long table. The mood was intense. For months, the senators had sensed the day would arrive when they'd have to make a decision on the marriage equality bill. Skelos had tried to prepare them with gentle mentions now and then, but most refused to acknowledge it. There was always some reason they could avoid thinking about it. Too much time still remained in the session. Other big business needed to be tackled. On this final day of session, the conference had run out of excuses.

Inside the conference, some of the senators dished it out to Jim Alesi. Not only was he the first Republican to declare his support, the one to breach the dam, but also, even more galling, he seemed to be reveling in the spotlight. Earlier that week, he had attended a rally on the Capitol lawn organized by New Yorkers United for Marriage, and there was even chatter that he might become a "national marriage ambassador" for the gay marriage cause. Didn't he care that his loud mouth and showmanship could hurt the conference in the next election?

Alesi pushed back hard. He reminded his colleagues that he had swallowed hard in 2009 and voted against the marriage equality bill, which he supported back then, for the political sake of the conference. At the time, he reminded them, he swore he would never betray his principles like that again.

As the conference wore on, the thirty-two senators, all white, overwhelmingly male, and older, exposed their raw feelings. Most of the time, the conference discussed dry issues such as tax cuts and transit allocations. They gave a level of deference to the in-house expert, oftentimes a committee chair. People would ask questions of that member, and the conversation was intellectual, philosophical, and political.

Marriage was a searing departure, one of those issues that, like abortion or the death penalty, come along every few decades or so. Remarks swung from emotional to highly analytical. Alesi played the lead role in challenging the arguments of the opponents.

Some members talked about their own experience having raised children with a mother and father, just as their parents had before them. This is what's right, and this is what we should be promoting, they'd say.

"I can't make that statement," Alesi said. "As much as it's nice that you have that wonderful life, you can't impose that on anybody. There's another side of life that is just as real. Do you understand that there are people who are raising children in same-sex households now? It's legal. It's okay."

Alesi was listening carefully to the arguments and watching people's body language for clues as to who was leaning which way. Some look exasperated, while others leaned in and listened quietly or nodded their head. Based on Alesi's assessment, about eight to ten members could easily have voted yes.

For us outside the room, the wait was excruciating. Several hours in, rumors began circulating that there had been a coup attempt against Skelos.

Mike Avella, the former lawyer to Senate Republicans, was getting e-mail and text updates from some inside the conference, and after a few hours, he told us that progress was being made and that he was confident there'd be a vote.

—

Skelos counsel Diane Burman reached out to Steve Cohen, Cuomo's legislative liaison Larry Schwartz, and counsel Mylan Denerstein to prepare for the debate and vote if that's where they ended up.

"If we let this go to the floor, we don't want to have long, haranguing speeches," Burman told the Cuomo staffers. "If that happens we will pull the bill. You're not there to embarrass us. You're not there to beat us up. It's going to pass. You can do whatever you want after it passes. But you're going to make it very difficult for us to keep our conference together in agreement that this should go forward and allow the vote if this becomes a session where we are beaten up on."

Cuomo's team swung into action again, facilitating several meetings with the Senate Democrats and Republicans to work out the speaking program. They agreed that Saland would go first to explain the religious-exemption provision. Then Tom Duane would introduce the bill and speak about its merits on behalf of the Democrats. Ruben Diaz, the antigay Democrat, would then do what he felt he needed to do. As the day went on, they learned that Senator Grisanti, from Buffalo, the one who had gone back and forth, had in the end decided to vote yes and wanted to give a speech. Both sides agreed that would be it.

Cohen and Denerstein went over that program several times with Democratic leadership and Republican senior staff. The Democrats didn't like it, and Cuomo warned Cohen that some would still like nothing better than to give long speeches about how they'd been there for years on this issue, how they were providing nearly all the votes, to tempt the Republicans to pull the bill and kill it. The threat was still so real that Cuomo joined in a couple of the meetings to make sure the Democratic leaders knew he was listening and would hold people accountable.

=

As the marathon session continued, Republican lobbyist Jeff Cook spotted Linda Saland, the senator's wife, all dressed up. We'd heard that she was a passionate advocate for us, and she clearly didn't show up to watch her husband vote no or see the bill fail. Jeff told Bill Smith, who immediately contacted Steve Cohen. "Steve, how about we get Mrs. Saland in to see the governor right now, and pin roses all over her?" Before long, Linda Saland was visiting with the governor, who was praising her husband for his courage and the seriousness he'd brought to the issue.

Back inside the conference, Skelos was letting his members get everything they needed to say out of their system, even as he prepared them for the fact that there would be a vote that day. When things seemed to reach a natural break, Skelos asked, "Okay, is there anybody else? Because we have these bills and we're ready to go out and do them." The

Democrats had been conferencing the other remaining items and they were ready. "We've got other work to do. Let's go do it," said Skelos.

Alesi guessed that, were they to take a vote of the conference about whether or not to have a vote on the marriage bill, by more than two to one, they would have voted it down. But Skelos never offered up that choice.

Finally, at close to 6:00 p.m., after a seven-hour marathon session, Skelos emerged from the conference room and announced to the scrum of reporters waiting outside the door that there would be an up-or-down vote on the marriage bill. It was going to happen.

After two weeks straight in Albany, I was ecstatic, relieved, and nervous all at once. I knew that, in a place like Albany, you couldn't celebrate until the bill was inked into law.

The Senate first turned to the other remaining business it had, passing "the Big Ugly" omnibus bill. After a couple of hours, they took a short break. They would reconvene at 9:30 p.m. to consider the marriage bill.

I was sitting in the gallery above the Senate floor along with Jeff Cook, Bill Smith, Brian Ellner, and Ross Levi. The governor was in his second-floor office getting ready to watch the proceedings on television with his daughters, who had joined him once again. Cohen walked upstairs to watch the historic vote take place on the Senate floor. It was unusual for him to be up there, but this was no ordinary night. Dozens of Assembly members had packed the Senate floor to watch, along with other of the governor's top aides. You could feel the emotion and the solemnity. It was clear they were about to debate a historic bill.

Saland rose first and gave a dry speech recounting the religious exemptions that he had helped negotiate. As he neared the conclusion of his remarks, still without stating his position, he said, "My intellectual and emotional journey has ended here today, and I have to define doing the right thing as treating all persons with equality, and that equality includes within the definition of marriage. I fear that to do otherwise would fly in the face of my upbringing." As he concluded his words, a tremendous round of applause went up from both the floor and the gallery.

With his colleagues standing for him out of respect, Tom Duane took the floor. He thanked Governor Cuomo for his "truthful and strong leadership." Choking up, he thanked his partner of nineteen years, Louis Webre. "Marriage says that we are a family. Louis and I are a family. And marriage strengthens all families."

Next, Ruben Diaz launched into a rant that seemed to have no end. The presiding officer, Lieutenant Governor Bob Duffy, banged the gavel several times to try to limit Diaz's speech, asserting Diaz had only five minutes. Finally, Duffy said, "Senator you've really got to cut it short. You're bound by your five minutes and we have twenty-three other people who want to be heard on the bill."

Twenty-three people? Cohen's heart almost fell out of his chest. He asked a Duffy staffer what he meant. "Twenty-three people indicated they want to speak on the bill," she confirmed. By now, everyone was focused on Duffy as he tried to curtail Diaz and shut him down. A Democratic colleague of Diaz's came to the floor to confront the lieutenant governor and defend Diaz's right to speak. All the cameras were focused on that skirmish.

Meanwhile, Skelos counsel Diane Burman approached Denerstein delivering the same news that Cohen had just learned. Cohen joined Denerstein as Berman was stressing her point. "Twenty-three people are not going to speak on this bill," she said. "That wasn't the deal. We're going to pull the legislation. I just want you to know. If you can get this fixed in five minutes, fine. But if you can't, there's going to be no vote and the session's going to end."

Cohen and Denerstein rushed to confront Sampson: "John, I thought we had an understanding."

"We had no understanding," said the Brooklyn lawmaker. "For a lot of members, this is the only time anyone is ever going to be covering them. This is an important vote for them. They have a right to explain it. I can't control them. We live by our rules here. They're going to do what they want to do and I'm not going to stand in their way," he said.

Albany wasn't exactly known for decorum, but having staffers like Cohen challenge lawmakers on the Senate floor was highly unusual. Yet Cohen's whole life was flashing before his eyes at this point. This can't happen on my watch, he thought. Burman could hear Cohen's voice getting louder as he confronted Sampson. She walked over to him and said, "You're about to become the news story. You are really loud. Take it off the floor."

Up in the gallery, I could tell something was amiss. Debate had stopped; the lieutenant governor had left his spot as the presiding officer. And there were a couple of centers of activity. But I had no idea what was going on or how serious it all was.

Cohen left the floor, huddled up with Denerstein, and then called the governor. "You're up there; I'm not," Cuomo said. "Just get it fixed."

Cohen looked to Denerstein, who shrugged and said, "Let's find Sampson."

It took a minute or two to track him down, but those minutes felt like an eternity to Cohen. At first, Denerstein tried to reason with Sampson. That didn't seem to be working so Cohen, drawing on lessons learned from many years working for Cuomo, broke in.

"John, you know the rumors are that I am leaving. They are true. I'm not working here much longer. Which means, nobody can control me. And if this goes down this way and this vote fails, I know what you're thinking. You're going to blame the Republicans. But it's not going to happen that way. Because I'm going to tell every reporter that it failed because of you. And that this was your fault. And John, I'm going to keep doing it. And I'm going to do it forever, until your political career is over. So the choice is yours. I don't care how you do it. You want to let your members speak. You want to have the bill pulled, fine. I can't control that. But you know what I'm going to do. You understand?"

Denerstein then looked at Sampson and said, "John, he's not joking. He can be a world-class asshole."

"This conversation's over," Sampson said.

Cohen and Denerstein didn't know what to think.

Sampson went back to the floor and told the Democratic senators that there would be no more speeches.

The lieutenant governor recognized Senator Grisanti. He acknowledged that he had struggled mightily with the issue and held a different position when he ran for office in 2010. "As a Catholic," he said, "I was raised to believe that marriage was between a man and a woman." But, he said, "I would not respect myself if I didn't do the research, have an open mind, and make a decision." He concluded his talk: "Who am I to say that someone does not have the same rights that I have with my wife that I love? I vote in the affirmative, Mr. President."

Another huge cheer broke out from the gallery.

Immediately after, the Senate moved to a vote. Saland and Grisanti, along with Alesi and McDonald, were the only four Republican votes, and the bill passed by a vote of 33–29. There were roars in the gallery, people chanting USA, USA. I couldn't keep my eyes off a gay male couple sitting near me in the gallery, rejoicing with their two young daughters. Jeff Cook, the openly gay GOP lobbyist who had worked nonstop lobbying senators since 2008, was weeping. On the floor of the Senate, there were hugs everywhere. Governor Cuomo came up to the Senate floor to ecstatic applause.

Cohen caught my eye, and he e-mailed me to come to his office immediately and to help gather my colleagues. I did so, and at 11:55 p.m. that night, we were ushered into the governor's office where—along with Bill Smith, Jeff Cook, Brian Ellner, Ross Levi, and Emily Giske—I stood behind Governor Cuomo as he signed the bill into law. The governor shook my hand, thanked me, and handed me one of the several pens he used to ink his name. We then adjourned to the Governor's Mansion for a late night of celebrating. Later we had an after-party with about twenty of us who made up the core of the effort at the bar at Seventy-Four State where we had retreated nearly every night over the past two weeks. Danny O'Donnell, the lead assemblyman, was buying champagne, and we were toasting and hugging one another, while keeping an eye on the TV. CNN was showing clips of the vote, the signing ceremony, and the massive celebration that was taking place at the Stonewall Inn in New York City.

After celebrating with us at the governor's mansion, Jim Alesi headed over to the Hill Street Café, a popular watering hole. There, he found an unbelievable scene. The bar was packed with loads of young people whom he knew from the Capitol. It seemed as if employees from every

Republican Senate office were there, marking the passage of the marriage equality bill with a party. When he entered, the crowd erupted in cheers.

The sixty-two-year-old Alesi was overjoyed, but he felt as if he wanted to cry, too. Why couldn't more of his colleagues see the world the way these young people saw it? One thing was for sure: change was in the air, and the country was heading in only one direction.

=

After joining us at Seventy-Four State, Cohen retreated to his family's country house about forty minutes from Albany, arriving at about 4:00 a.m. After a few hours of sleep, he headed out to the local store in Spencertown, picked up all the newspapers, and got a table at Dan's Diner, a beautifully restored diner next to the volunteer fire department in the idyllic town just across the state line from Massachusetts's Berkshire Mountains.

He was eating his eggs and staring at the papers, looking with disbelief at the giant headlines and photos capturing joy and celebration, when he got a call. It was Cuomo.

"Have you seen the papers?" Cuomo asked.

"I'm looking at them right now," he responded.

"I can't believe this," Cuomo said. "I can't believe the coverage. Did you understand how big this was going to be?"

"No," Cohen said. "I'm stunned."

And so Cohen sat there talking with Cuomo for about forty-five minutes, reflecting on what an incredible moment this was, one of the great moments in their lives. They talked about Mario Cuomo and Cohen's father Herb Cohen and how making a difference in the lives of so many people was the fulfillment of the best lessons that they had learned from their fathers. They talked about how fleeting life was and how they needed to savor moments like this because they'd soon wake up and be onto the next thing, this powerful moment rapidly receding into the past.

I awoke that morning and settled in on the Empire Service 12:05 p.m. Amtrak train back to Manhattan, my one-day trip having turned into a thirteen-day stay. I read over the news clips on my computer and saw that pundits were talking about how Cuomo's leadership on this issue would position him well for a 2016 run for the White House. I could only sit back and think with wonder about how far we'd come in the seven years since pundits argued that the issue had sunk John Kerry and had helped the GOP capture the White House. Now, it was a Republican state senate that had allowed the legislation to move and people were talking of how after Obama, all Democratic contenders for the White House would have to support our cause to be considered a serious candidate.

That weekend couldn't have been any more magical. Sunday was the forty-second annual New York City LGBT Pride March. A couple of days before, Democratic lobbyist Emily Giske had convinced the coalition to buy $15,000 worth of swag for the parade: a giant New Yorkers United for Marriage banner as well as thousands of signs that said, "Thank You Governor Cuomo" and "Promise Made, Promise Kept." I'd been reluctant to place the order before the vote, not wanting to pop the cork on the champagne before we'd won. But I figured by then we were all in, so we might as well go for it.

Jennifer Cunningham, who led our communications effort from her office in New York City for the whole two weeks, joined the governor near the front of the parade route. When Cuomo saw Cunningham, he gave her a giant hug. "We'll never do anything as good as this in our lifetime," he said.

I tried to say hello to the governor, but he was mobbed. So I walked back to the next cluster of people, where New Yorkers United for Marriage was meeting up. Holding onto our brand new banner that spanned much of the block, I marched next to Evan for the triumphant parade through the city. The crowd was electric, an estimated two million people cheering ecstatically as we walked by, many holding the signs we'd had made.

Toward the end, as we traversed the narrow streets of Greenwich Village and approached the Stonewall Inn, the roars of the crowd and waving of signs and rainbow flags reached an incredible intensity that took my breath away.

Cohen brought his two sons with him to walk in the Pride celebration, while his daughter and wife watched from the sidelines. He simply wanted to walk in the crowd and take it all in, staying away from the scrum around the governor. The outpouring of gratitude and joy was one of the most exceptional things he'd ever experienced. Over the course of his political work with Cuomo, he'd marched in many parades and attended many rallies. Never before had he experienced such a sense of joy and accomplishment. From afar, Cohen watched as the crowd erupted when they caught a glimpse of the governor. He was sad to be leaving, heading back to the private sector after a great ride with Cuomo. But he knew he was leaving at a moment that could never be topped.

Lead civil rights lawyer for Gay & Lesbian Advocates & Defenders, Mary Bonauto, reading the Massachusetts marriage ruling outside the courthouse in Boston on November 18, 2003. She first thought it was a loss and then realized it was a full win! Photo by Marilyn Humphries.

Rep. Carl Sciortino ran as a twenty-five-year-old openly gay candidate against a homophobic incumbent and defeated him by ninety-three votes in the ugliest campaign I've ever seen. He embodied the indefatigable spirit of our movement. Here he is pictured with Rep. Byron Rushing, another of our most powerful champions in the State House. Photo by Marilyn Humphries.

Marty Rouse, MassEquality's first campaign leader who went on to become national field director for the Human Rights Campaign, was a great mentor, showing me how to be strategic and relentless in field and state electoral work. Photo by Marilyn Humphries.

Ralph Hodgdon (right) and Paul McMahon showed up every-where with their simple yet powerful sign—which they up-dated every year—that said so much about the integrity of their relationship and the potential of all of our relationships. Photo by Marilyn Humphries.

Gov. Mitt Romney flanked by Kris Mineau (right), the head of the religious right Massachusetts Family Institute and Rep. Phil Travis (left), the lead sponsor of the anti-marriage amendment. As soon as Romney decided he was running for president, he began running his hardest against the freedom to marry in Massachusetts. Photo by Marilyn Humphries.

Deb Grzyb (left) and Sharon Murphy on their back porch in rural Charlton, Massachusetts. Together twenty-four years when they were married in 2004, the two were reluctant advocates who became instrumental in moving two key lawmakers our way.

On the day of the final vote in Massachusetts, clergy from twenty-three denominations marched across the Boston Common to join marriage advocates in front of the State House while singing a South African freedom song. The march was organized by the Religious Coalition for the Freedom to Marry. Photo by Marilyn Humphries.

Our opponents, with their "Let the People Vote" signs, were at every legislative vote, lining the street across from our supporters, with police guarding the neutral territory in between. Photo by Marilyn Humphries.

Freedom to marry advocates standing in front of the State House greeting openly gay senator Jarrett Barrios. Nothing buttressed me more than seeing these sign-holding activists every time I'd walk near the State House the day of a vote. Photo by Marilyn Humphries.

Watching the final vote in Massachusetts on a small television in the State House. I am in front wearing glasses, lobbyist Norma Shapiro is to my right. Behind Norma is lobbyist Arline Isaacson, and to her left is Patrick Guerriero. Photo by Marilyn Humphries.

At an ebullient rally right after the final victory in Massachusetts. I'm clasping hands with Governor Deval Patrick, a true champion. House Speaker Salvatore F. DiMasi, another great champion, and Rep. Kathi-Anne Reinstein look on. Photo by Marilyn Humphries.

One of the marriage movement's secret weapons, MassEquality field director Amy Mello (who went on to work with me in California, Maine, and at Freedom to Marry). A straight, Catholic school–educated activist, Mello is the best organizer I've ever known. The mobilizing in the marriage campaigns hasn't happened on its own; it's talented organizers who have made it so. Photo by Marilyn Humphries.

Victory! All smiles at Boston gay bar Club Café right after the final vote in Massachusetts. I'm in the middle. My best friend and soul mate, Alex Hivoltze-Jimenez, is on my left, and Marty Rouse, now with the Human Rights Campaign, is on my right. Devastatingly, Alex died less than a year later. Photo by Marilyn Humphries.

Evan Wolfson, founder and president of Freedom to Marry (described by the *Daily Beast* as "The Godfather of Gay Marriage"), making the case for the cause as he's been doing powerfully for more than thirty years.

New York Governor Andrew Cuomo signing the marriage bill into law just before midnight on Friday, June 24, 2011. There are smiles all around as Cuomo hands a pen to Gill Action's Bill Smith, the strategist who was especially crucial to bringing about the win. Also pictured, left to right: Jeff Cook, me, Ross Levi, Brian Ellner, Lieutenant Governor Robert Duffy, and Emily Giske.

Marching through Greenwich Village with Evan Wolfson on my left in an ecstatic NYC Pride celebration the Sunday after victory in Albany.

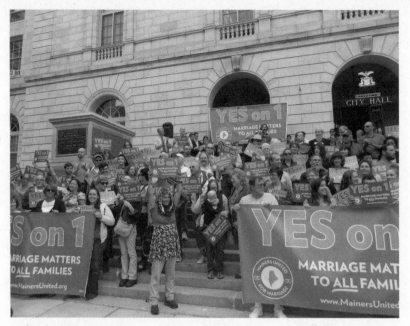

Launch of the Maine Yes on One campaign in front of Portland City Hall. This was the first time our community had ever proactively gone to the ballot on marriage. And we won. Photo by Meagan Dobson.

Mainers United for Marriage campaign manager Matt McTighe, who was also my political director at MassEquality, announcing victory for the first time ever on a ballot fight on marriage! Photo by W. Jo Moser.

Senator Al Franken (D-MN) outside the Minnesotans United for All Families campaign booth at the state fair. The booth attracted bigger crowds than any other for a political cause in the history of the fair. Photo by Jake Loesch.

Ecstatic campaign staff in Minnesota the moment the AP called the election and knew we'd defeated the anti-marriage amendment to the Minnesota Constitution. Photo courtesy of Rebecca Jean Lawrence Photography, © 2012.

Victory moment in Washington State. For this couple, and for so many, this election was personal. Photo courtesy of Sorella Photos.

Then-candidate for the US Senate Barack Obama with Chicagoans Lauren Verdich (left), Obama's LGBT co-chair in the campaign, and her partner Gail Morse. Over the years, Verdich and Morse worked hard to push Obama to come out in support of marriage.

Joyfully entering the county clerk's office in Salt Lake County, Utah, on Monday, December 23, 2013, are Amanda Lee Brock, thirty (left), and Andrea Olsen, thirty-one, of Vernal, Utah, as an employee points them in the right direction to apply for a marriage license. There's no stopping love! Photo courtesy of David Newkirk Photography.

WINNING AT THE BALLOT

November 5, 2008. It was close to midnight, and I was in an up-stairs suite of the Westin St. Francis on Union Square in San Francisco. The room was being used as the No on Proposition 8 campaign's "Boiler Room," where results were being tallied and analyzed in real time. A couple of electoral data gurus had come in from Washington, DC, to lend a hand. "That's not good," one of the data guys said to me as we looked together at the maps of Southern California counties whose results were now coming in rapidly. "That's really not good."

He left the room, as had the others who had gathered to analyze the returns. I was the only person there, and for that moment I felt really alone. Outside the hotel, there was a raucous scene. People were going crazy, whooping it up to celebrate the Obama victory that had been called several hours before. It sounded as though the Giants had just won the World Series. I shared in that happiness. The Bush reign had finally come to an end, and we'd now have a president whose values I shared and who was a much closer ally on the freedom to marry.

Yet even in Harvey Milk's San Francisco, we were left out of the cele-bration. Obama was winning California overwhelmingly, but Califor-nians were voting at the same time to take away the freedom to marry from same-sex couples who had been enjoying that right for five and a half months.

I went downstairs to the ballroom where the thinned-out crowd, still a few hundred strong, was watching the returns on giant television monitors. The numbers on the screens were showing about a 52 to 48 percent win for Prop 8. While the Northern California counties around San Francisco were all favorable for our side, the five largest counties in the state—all in Southern California—looked as though they would all go against us. That included Los Angeles County, the state's largest.

Geoff Kors, the executive director of Equality California, looked exhausted. He was one of the movement's most talented strategists, the first to convince a Legislature to approve a marriage bill without a court mandate. He did so twice, only to see them vetoed both times by Governor Arnold Schwarzenegger. Geoff hadn't run the No on 8 campaign. The campaign board had brought in an outside consultant with a strong track record winning California ballot fights to do so. But he had served as a key fundraiser and spokesperson and more than anyone else was associated with LGBT politics in California. He was trying to keep his chin up and stay hopeful. There are still millions of absentee votes to count, he told me. But I could tell his heart wasn't in what he was saying. At 12:35 a.m., the Yes on 8 campaign declared victory, while the No on 8 leaders vowed to wait until more of the votes had been counted. I packed up and got in a taxi to return to my friends' house where I'd been staying for the last two weeks, having come there from Massachusetts to lend a hand to the campaign.

Throughout the year, I'd been in Boston watching the goings on in California from afar with great interest. I didn't pretend to be an expert in running a ballot campaign. But I did know something about how to persuade people on marriage, and as I watched the television spots coming out of the No on 8 campaign in the fall of 2008, I grew concerned. Most of our side's ads looked like typical political spots, using a voice-over that told about how politicians such as Barack Obama, Dianne Feinstein, and now even Arnold Schwarzenegger were against the proposition as were the major newspapers from throughout the state. The ads said the amendment "changes our Constitution," "eliminates fundamental rights," and "treats people differently under the law." They closed with some variation on, "Regardless of how you feel about marriage, it's wrong to treat people differently under the law."

I understood what the campaign was trying to do, but I didn't think it would work. I thought there were a few flaws. First, the conventional wisdom on ballot measures—one that the No on 8 campaign seemed to be following—was that getting voters to vote no was much easier than getting them to vote yes. A campaign simply needed to poke holes in a proposed amendment and voters would choose the status quo. But I didn't think that would work here. Marriage for gay couples was what was new to voters in California. We needed to make our strongest case in favor of marriage equality, essentially running a "yes" campaign. Our opponents were the ones who could work to poke a few holes to try to get people to vote against marriage for same-sex couples.

Given that the burden of proof was on us, our side needed to make the most emotionally compelling case we could. However, that's not what I thought we were doing. The arguments we were using in the ads appealed to the head: protecting the Constitution, highlighting the support of key electeds, and protecting fundamental rights in the abstract. They didn't elicit emotions. Our opponents were masterful at conjuring up fear about what would happen to society, to the institution of marriage, and to the family if gays were allowed to marry. The only antidote to fear was love, empathy, connection, and an appeal to people's better angels. That required using real people talking poignantly about why marriage was important to their family—their parents, their children, and themselves. If we didn't evoke those emotions in a powerful way, I felt we'd be in serious trouble.

Moreover, our side was trying to skirt marriage in the campaign. I understood why. Support for marriage was less than 50 percent, so what the campaign tried to do was to focus on concepts that did have solid majority support: protecting the Constitution, not infringing on fundamental rights, and so forth.

However, in California, gay couples were already marrying. It wasn't credible to make the case that this vote was anything other than a referendum on marriage equality. Even if we didn't emphasize it, our opponents would, and in the worst light possible. Every time I heard the line in one of our side's ads "Regardless of how you feel about marriage," I got a bad feeling in the pit of my stomach. We needed to invest our dollars into persuading people to support marriage, rather than trying to change the subject. I didn't know if we could grow support sufficiently to win, but it seemed clear to me we had to try.

I voiced my concerns to a few people I knew who were in leadership roles in the campaign. But I was also cognizant of the fact that I'd never before run a ballot campaign and that the consultants who were leading it had multiple victories on thorny social issues in California. Also as someone who had run marriage campaigns myself, I was wary of "armchair quarterbacking"—asserting based on my own different experiences that I knew what to do to win and that those in charge were getting it wrong.

We faced a strong adversary. Our opponents hired Frank Schubert, a top Sacramento-based Republican campaign consultant who had a successful history of defending corporations in ballot fights. He'd protected tobacco companies from having to pay higher taxes and restaurants from having to provide health insurance to their employees. By his own admission, he hadn't given much thought to the marriage issue when he was hired. This was in spite of the fact that his sister was a lesbian with a partner and two kids. I imagine that, with the commitment of the religious right—and particularly the Mormon hierarchy—to invest significantly, it must have seemed to him to be a very lucrative, high-profile opportunity.

=

On October 7, 2008, one month from Election Day, the situation at the No on 8 campaign was dire. The campaign's internal polling showed that our side was losing, and we were nearly out of money. Our opponents had far outraised us, thanks in part to massive infusions from Mormon donors who were pressured by the church hierarchy to give.

Part of the reason for the lackadaisical fundraising on our side was that the public polls—those reported in the newspapers—showed our side leading by as much as 55 to 38 percent, so our community and our progressive allies thought we were winning. Those numbers aligned with what our supporters saw in the places where the vast majority of them lived: the Bay Area, Silicon Valley, the west side of Los Angeles, and so on.

The No on 8 campaign decided it needed to shock our side out of its complacency. So it sent an emergency e-mail under Geoff Kors's name to its e-mail list of hundreds of thousands to set the record straight. "Our worst nightmares are coming true," Geoff wrote. He warned of the more than $25 million the Yes on 8 side had reported raising compared to only $16 million for the No on 8 side. Even worse, Geoff wrote, the campaign's internal polls told a completely different story than the public polls that ran in the newspapers, showing that our side was losing 47 to 43 percent.

"This is crunch time," Geoff implored. "With less than a month before the election, we must get on the air now to answer these lies and swing votes back to our side."

The e-mail had the intended effect, as contributions immediately picked up. However, Frank Schubert had an October surprise waiting. The Yes on 8 campaign immediately began airing a devastatingly effective television ad.

Called "It's Already Happened," the ad depicted a young Latina girl enthusiastically approaching her mom and asking, "Guess what I learned in school today?"

"What, sweetie?" the mother replied.

Handing her mother the children's book *King and King*, she said with a big smile, "I learned that a prince can marry a prince and I can marry a princess."

The mother opened the book and looked at it with horror.

A Pepperdine University law professor then appeared on the screen and said, "Think it can't happen? It's already happened. When Massachusetts legalized gay marriage, schools began teaching second graders that boys can marry boys. The courts ruled parents had no right to object." A voice-over then finished the spot. "Under California law, public schools instruct kids about marriage. Teaching children about gay marriage will happen here unless we pass Proposition 8."

The spot was diabolically brilliant. Schubert had given people who really didn't care much about the issue and who supported gay rights generally, particularly young parents, a reason to vote no. It would harm their own young children. The ad buy was massive, blanketing the state from the Bay Area to San Diego.

Our side wasn't prepared for this spot, and it didn't have the resources to fight back quickly. Two weeks later, No on 8 aired a spot featuring the California superintendent of public instruction stating that Prop 8 had nothing to do with education and that using schoolchildren like this was "shameful." It was an effective spot and appeared to stem the tide. But shortly after it went up, San Francisco media reported on a kindergarten class that was taken by their school to witness their teacher marry her partner; the media was invited along for the event. It directly undercut what the superintendent had said. Our opponents exploited it to no end, in television spots as well as newspaper articles and TV stories. For the rest of the campaign, our side never escaped the kids/schools issue. Even our affirmative spots said that "Proposition 8 is not about schools or kids."

Over the final two weeks, as the LGBT community and our allies realized that we really might lose, the dollars flowed like crazy. On one day toward the end, the campaign took in more than $1 million in online contributions. Even though our opponents vastly outraised and outspent us for much of the campaign, by the end we'd surpassed their contributions, $44 million to $39 million. But unpredictable late money is difficult to put to good use; television buys need to be placed at least a few days in advance, ideally as part of a well-thought-out sequencing plan. So the No on 8 campaign was scurrying to put in place last-minute, paid phone-calling programs until the night before the vote, trying desperately to spend as much as they were taking in.

The morning after the vote, I descended the steep hill from where I was staying and walked into the heart of the Castro, the famous gay neighborhood where Harvey Milk, my longtime hero, had run for office and began harnessing political power for the gay community. The enormous rainbow flag that flew over the Castro—the one that had provided me with strength and a sense of belonging when I was coming out of the closet—was hanging at half-mast. I was devastated and knew the spirit of the gay community—in California and nationally—would be broken until Prop 8 was lifted. That meant we had to figure out how to win at the ballot.

n Portland, Oregon, fifty-four-year-old Thalia Zepatos, a longtime strategist in progressive politics and the marriage movement and new director of public engagement for Freedom to Marry, spent much of 2010 culling through literally hundreds of polls and focus group reports from multiple marriage campaigns. In her second-floor home office, Thalia had stacks of yellow legal pads with her notes, the pages folded back on the sheets that had the most interesting tidbits. "I know this sounds silly," a middle-aged woman in Northern California had said, "but I never thought about it—that gay people could get *old*!" Another, a man from Oregon, said, "I just don't get it—why would a *gay* person want to get *married*?"

A straight ally who had been drawn to fight for LGBT equality in part because of multiple antigay ballot fights in Oregon, Thalia's background was in organizing. She helped guide field strategy on the No on 8 campaign and, before that, on the unsuccessful 2004 campaign to defeat an anti-marriage ballot measure in Oregon. From her vantage point, field organizing wasn't the issue on these campaigns. We could run the best field campaign ever, but if we weren't making a persuasive enough case, we'd lose.

In the 2004 Oregon campaign, Thalia recalled organizers going door to door with a piece of literature listing the rights and benefits that came with marriage and arguing that it was wrong to deny same-sex couples those rights. The reports back from the organizers were that voters seemed really uninterested. Instead, they wanted to talk about the lesbian physician on the popular television show *ER*. The character's partner—a fire fighter—died in the line of duty, and the physician faced a painful custody battle with the deceased partner's parents. To Thalia, it was as if the campaign and voters were speaking two different languages: one, a list of benefits, and the other, a powerful human story about a committed couple and their family.

From her vantage point, the messaging hadn't gotten any better on the No on 8 campaign. Frustrated, she left California and returned to Oregon prepared to take on a different cause. But then she decided to make the case to Evan to join Freedom to Marry and head up a comprehensive effort to retool the marriage movement's messaging. Evan agreed and Thalia went to it.

Before engaging in any new research, Thalia had gotten dumps of dozens of focus group reports and polls from multiple state and national marriage efforts. To her knowledge, this was the first time anyone had looked at the research across campaigns, to see if patterns emerged. As Thalia analyzed it, she did find some common themes, but it was the response to one question in an Oregon poll that made her stop and take notice. The question asked Oregon voters, "Why do couples like me get married?" An overwhelming majority of 72 percent responded, "for love and commitment," with 18 percent responding "for rights and benefits." They were then asked, "Why do same-sex couples get married?" The answers were remarkably different: 42 percent responded, "rights and benefits," with 36 percent saying, "love and commitment." A full 22 percent didn't know why gay couples wanted to marry.

What a huge disconnect this was. Straight people thought gay couples had completely different reasons for wanting to get married than they did. They themselves wanted to get married out of a sense of love and commitment, yet they were unsure why gay couples wanted to marry, with most thinking it was about wanting to access rights and benefits.

No wonder we weren't doing well on ballot fights, Thalia observed. She recognized this was in no small part because our marriage campaigns had focused far too much on tangible harms, such as the woman who couldn't make medical decisions for her partner; the elderly man who had to move out of his home after his longtime partner had passed away because he was ineligible for social security survivor benefits; and couples who had to pay extra taxes.

Yet for the vast majority of both straight and gay people, rights and benefits weren't why they got married. It was out of deep and abiding love and commitment and a desire to profess that love and commitment in front of family and friends and have it respected by their state. It wasn't that our efforts had monolithically focused on rights and benefits; in Massachusetts and elsewhere, we emphasized human stories of love and family. But this research showed us that we had a movement-wide imperative to be much more disciplined in our messaging. Overall, we'd effectively made the case for a full set of benefits, or civil unions, but not yet for marriage.

After more analysis and research, Thalia felt as though she'd cracked the code on how to make the most compelling case.

First, we needed to explain why same-sex couples wanted to marry. The answer was, for the same reasons as straight couples, to make a lifetime commitment to the person they love. Our opponents' best message point had long been that gays wanted to "redefine" marriage. But we didn't want to "redefine" it; we wanted to join it. The core of marriage is love and commitment, and that applies to both gay and straight couples.

Second, we needed to be real, and that meant respectfully acknowledging that many straight people were conflicted on the issue. After all, pretty much everyone had been raised in a society where they learned that marriage was between a man and a woman and that there was something wrong with being gay. Many religions still taught that. So it was perfectly understandable that many people were conflicted. It didn't mean they were bad people. If we forced people who were conflicted to pretend they weren't by shaming them, we wouldn't be able to engage them honestly and probably wouldn't be able to persuade them.

Third, we needed to model for them the journey to support that other conflicted people had taken. This journey would be guided by their core values. More often than not, it was the value of the Golden Rule— treating others the way you want to be treated—that led people to support the freedom to marry. Another value that we found over time to be very strong and persuasive—particularly with men and Republicans— was freedom: the right of everyone to choose with whom they spend their life without interference from the government.

Richard Carlbom, whom I hired to run Freedom to Marry's state campaigns after he successfully managed the Minnesota marriage effort, described the messaging challenge in an especially effective way. He spoke of three concentric circles. In the center was the individual; in the next circle out were those closest to the individual—immediate family especially; and in the last circle were those with whom the individual came in contact but weren't especially close, like those who live in the same community. The least effective form of persuasion was to show the impact of the freedom to marry on those in the outer circle: generic people in one's community, including generic gay and lesbian couples. A more persuasive approach was to show that those in the next circle would be affected. That's what our opponents did by making the case that marriage equality would hurt one's own children. What was most persuasive was to demonstrate to the individual that the position they hold affects how they think of themselves. We needed to make the case to people that, in order for them to live up to their own value system, they needed to support the freedom to marry.

As important as the message was, the messenger was at least as important. What Thalia found was that our best messengers were straight people who were close to same-sex couples—parents, grandparents, clergy, and neighbors—who had once been conflicted but then, after really getting to know the couple and recognizing that their relationship was very similar to their own, journeyed to a place of acceptance and support. These were the messengers with whom the voters in the middle—those we needed to persuade—could best identify.

By the end of 2010, Freedom to Marry was putting this modified messaging frame to work in a nationwide public education campaign Thalia was leading called Why Marriage Matters. She'd enlisted dozens of national and statewide organizational partners and done endless trainings to change the way people spoke about the cause: away from highlighting the rights and benefits that accompanied a marriage license to speaking about the love and commitment that same-sex couples who wish to marry share.

Later, when Thalia heard President Obama talk about "loving, committed gay and lesbian couples" who had been harmed by the Defense of

Marriage Act, she knew the frame was getting through. And she really knew it was working when the Minnesota Catholic Conference began talking of how marriage was about "more than love and commitment."

With our core messaging challenge largely solved, Thalia then turned to developing responses to our opponents' most effective attacks, particularly the "harms kids" line of attack that proved so viciously effective in California.

=

There was no higher priority for me when joining Freedom to Marry than reversing our streak of losses at the polls. It was the one talking point our opponents had that we couldn't rebut: that every time this issue went to a popular vote, our side lost. And after shuttering the California ballot effort, I was doubly hungry to help bring about a win at the ballot. The best chance, it seemed to me, was in Maine, where advocates from GLAD and Equality Maine had gone right back to work following a ballot loss in 2009 by a margin of 47 to 53 percent. Maine was a small, manageable state. Our side had lost by only 33,000 votes out of 570,000 votes cast. That meant that, with the same level of turnout, we'd need to convince only 16,500 voters to change their position on the issue in order to prevail. That seemed manageable, certainly when compared to the millions of voters we'd begun working on in California. Moreover, we knew that in a presidential election year, more like 725,000 people would come to the polls, and the voter pool would be younger than the pool that had gone to the polls in 2009.

Heading up the Maine campaign was my former MassEquality political director, Matt McTighe. Matt hired Amy Mello, my field director in Massachusetts who had joined me in California, to serve as his field director in Maine. I had huge confidence that if anyone could figure out how to win a marriage ballot fight, it was Matt and Amy. GLAD Executive Director Lee Swislow and Civil Rights Project Director Mary Bonauto, a denizen of Maine, were both on the executive committee. It almost felt like a MassEquality family reunion, so I was thrilled to join the executive committee when Matt asked me.

By December 2011, the campaign had collected more than 100,000 signatures, nearly double the number required to get a measure placed on the ballot. It was now decision time for the executive committee: should the campaign turn in the signatures and go to the ballot, or should we wait? We'd never before gone to the ballot on our own volition. We had only tried to fight off measures advanced by our opponents. So if we were going to do it, we wanted to make sure we were ready. On Tuesday, December 20, I met up with my old comrades-in-arms, as well as other Maine advocates, about twenty in total, in a large, airy room at the University of Southern Maine in Portland, to make a decision.

California-based pollster Amy Simon, whom I'd recommended to the campaign, first took us through the numbers. She explained that Maine was in a solid and steady position, with 54 percent support today and the opportunity to grow our support over the next eight months, before the back-and-forth of television wars would begin after Labor Day.

Next, Matt described the extensive messaging research they'd taken on, hundreds of thousands of dollars worth over the past year. He'd taken the messaging frames that Freedom to Marry had developed, on love, commitment, and freedom, and filmed a wide variety of messengers making the case: male and female same-sex couples, brothers where one is gay and the other is straight, veterans, blue-collar guys, parents with gay and straight kids, clergy, Catholic grandparents, Republicans, firefighters—you name it. He'd also shot spots that he imagined our opponents would use—one making the case that civil unions were sufficient and others using different versions of the "harms kids" argument—in order to simulate an actual campaign environment as much as possible to see if our responses worked.

Through extensive testing, Matt confirmed Thalia's findings. The love and commitment messaging frame, combined with appeals to the universal values of the Golden Rule and freedom, was effective. Matt also tried out and refined approaches Freedom to Marry and some of our partners had developed to respond to the "harms kids" attack.

What didn't work, Matt found, was one of the approaches that appealed most to our base of activists. Criticizing our opponents didn't work. Calling them extremists, pointing out how homophobic they were, and even highlighting their distortions all caused those in the middle to tune out and think of this fight as just another political battle. It definitely didn't move people our way on marriage.

In sum, Matt told us he felt very confident that they had powerful approaches to proactively make the case and to respond to our opponents' most effective attacks.

Next up was Amy Mello, who described the field campaign she was creating. The effort built on what she'd been developing in California. Canvassers would make the case for marriage to undecided voters in one-on-one conversations at their door and over the telephone, engaging them personally and addressing their concerns, with the goal of guiding them through their discomfort to a place of support. Amy had already hired and trained dozens of paid canvassers to have conversations at the door. She was carefully tracking success rates, making tweaks to the approach every week to improve outcomes. Over the year, they'd already had 30,000 persuasion conversations, and their yield was a "persuasion rate" of 22 percent, meaning that 22 percent of those who were undecided or opposed moved to a place of greater support.

Amy spoke of the campaign's plan to have one-on-one conversations with 200,000 voters, which according to their estimates would amount to most of the "swing voters"—neither strong supporters nor strong opponents of the freedom to marry. Everyone was wowed.

We turned to the finance plan. Matt explained that what was included in the $5 million budget was primarily paid media and field organizing. The pollster Amy Simon had insisted that the budget include two tracks of paid television: one that she described as the "empathy track" where we put forward our core messages regardless of what our opponents were doing, and a second track to respond to our opponents' inevitable attacks. Without the two-track approach, she told us very bluntly, we'd lose. She thought one of the fatal flaws of the No on 8 campaign was getting stuck responding to our opponents' attacks—playing on their turf—without pivoting back sufficiently to our core messages.

Another staffer walked us through the fundraising plan: we'd raise at least $5 million from major donors both inside and outside of Maine, as well as from house parties, online contributions, and the like. Nothing in it seemed insurmountable or unrealistic.

Finally, we'd reached the moment of truth; we had to make a decision. I spoke up near the beginning, wanting to make sure the conversation got going on a positive note. There was no question in my mind that to continue to grow momentum, we needed to win at the ballot.

"Never before have we had an opportunity like this to win," I told them. "Based on my assessment of the national landscape, Maine is the best opportunity to break our opponents' streak and put to rest their talking point that we can never win at the ballot."

I said that with marriage cases headed toward the US Supreme Court, winning at the ballot and undermining our opponents' last, best talking point would be powerful.

"It's not a sure thing, and it never will be," I said. "But this is a better than fifty-fifty proposition, our best shot ever, and we should go for it." I promised them that Freedom to Marry was 100 percent in and that I personally would be very involved in the campaign.

Lee Swislow, the GLAD executive director who was my great friend and partner in the trenches from the Massachusetts battles, chimed in. "If we think we don't have a strong chance of winning," she said, "we have a responsibility to stop now. At the same time, if we do think we have a real chance to win, we have a responsibility to move forward—a responsibility to the couples in Maine that have been waiting, and to the national marriage efforts where winning at the ballot will be a huge boost." She thought the evidence pointed clearly to the fact that we had a solid chance to win, and so she urged the group to move forward.

In the end, everyone was in; we were going.

One month later, on January 26, 2012, teams of volunteers from throughout the state gathered in Augusta, the State Capitol, to deliver box upon box of petitions, assorted by town, 105,000 in all, to the secretary of state's office. This far exceeded the minimum of 57,277 signatures required. On February 23, the secretary of state verified the signatures, qualifying the petition for the November 2012 ballot.

Maine wouldn't be the only ballot measure we'd be fighting in 2012. In North Carolina and Minnesota, legislatures moved anti-marriage constitutional amendments to the ballot to permanently ban the freedom to marry. North Carolina's would be on the ballot in May and Minnesota's in November. In Maryland and Washington, building on years of work, lawmakers advanced freedom to marry bills to the governor, and they were signed into law. However, our opponents took advantage of "people's veto" laws in both states and collected the requisite number of signatures to put the measures on the November ballot before the laws would take effect.

Five ballot measures was a huge amount of work—more work than I thought we could do well, particularly given that our movement had never won one of these before. We needed to focus on taking away our opponents' last, best talking point—that we'd never won one of these. That meant being all in to win, not simply "showing the flag." Ballot campaigns were also massive expenses, and following Prop 8, our movement's leading funders were very wary about investing in ballot fights, particularly in a crucial election year with so many other demands. So we'd have to carefully evaluate which campaigns we'd engage in and then do all we could to ensure the campaigns were strong: that they had the funds they needed, had a strong campaign manager, had a solid governance structure, used research-tested messaging, and operated well on all cylinders with all the elements a campaign required. This would require active, daily engagement.

Thalia and I developed three criteria for deciding which campaigns Freedom to Marry would take on. First, we needed to see a realistic pathway to victory based on polling. Second, each state campaign needed a serious fundraising plan that was not over-reliant on out-of-state funding. And third, the state campaign needed to be well structured with a strong campaign manager and board managing the effort. We would help make all of these happen, but it also would take solid local leadership and, ideally, many months if not years of work in advance to ensure sufficient public support, engaged donors and allies, and the like.

Evan agreed. I told him that I thought we could go all in on two ballot fights; he was pushing for three. Using our criteria, we finally settled on three campaigns that Freedom to Marry go all in on—Maine, Minnesota, and Washington—but only after hiring another top operative based in the Northwest who would focus on Washington. That meant that we had to leave two—Maryland and North Carolina—for others to push, even as we'd make available messaging, opposition research, and everything else we were already doing or had available. Several of the major funders I spoke to thought we were spreading ourselves far too thin by taking on three. They thought that one, or at most two, might make sense but no more. So Freedom to Marry took heat from some for being too aggressive and from others for not being aggressive enough. But that was okay—I felt like we'd set our movement up well to give us a solid chance to prevail in each of our three priority campaigns. By the end, Freedom to Marry supported all four November campaigns, and became the largest out-of-state funder of three of them.

A few months later, on May 8, our opponents prevailed at the ballot in North Carolina by a vote of 61 percent to 39 percent. Based on polling, I knew North Carolina offered us next-to-no chance of winning. Once the legislature chose a low-turnout election day, when voters would skew much older than they would in November, we knew we were doomed. That didn't mean it didn't hurt badly.

===

On March 22, Freedom to Marry announced a Win More States Fund to invest in these fights, with a lead gift of $100,000 from Facebook cofounder Chris Hughes and his fiancé Sean Eldridge, who had stepped back from a day-to-day role with Freedom to Marry. The biggest challenge would be funding these campaigns to scale, with enough early money to lay the groundwork appropriately. In total, the three ballot fights to which we'd committed would cost about $30 million, with at least $10 million needing to come from major out-of-state donors. We committed to raising and investing at least $3 million into our priority campaigns. Now we had to find the money.

I reached out to hedge fund titan Paul Singer's team. Since New York, I'd worked closely with them to build a campaign to protect the freedom to marry law in New Hampshire. Singer had been the lead investor in that effort, at $250,000. I got in touch with his advisers Margaret Hoover and Annie Dickerson, as well as with Paul's son and son-in-law Andrew and Corey Morris-Singer.

On April 23, Evan and I took the train to Boston to meet with Corey and Andrew. Over sushi at their Cambridge home, we talked about the historic opportunity to win at the ballot and how Freedom to Marry had for the last two years been methodically preparing for this moment. Now was the time to kick it into high gear.

As we finished dinner, Corey asked directly, "How can we help?"

"We'd like to ask you for a million dollars to catalyze this work," I said, stuttering just a bit because it was the largest request I'd ever made.

They didn't blink. "We want to help," Corey said. They would talk to their father and his team and would get back to us.

On a late Friday afternoon in May, Corey told us that they'd do the full million and that Paul would also make the case to some of the donors who had given to the New York campaign.

I was full of thanks and Evan and I were both ecstatic. We were well on our way.

Evan reached out to Jon Stryker, the openly gay billionaire heir to a medical supply company and one of the largest and most important funders of gay causes in the country. He also agreed to invest a million dollars in the Win More States Fund. Paul Singer followed through with his outreach and raised another $700,000 from some of the hedge fund titans who'd played a lead role in New York. So by midsummer, we'd already hit our $3 million goal and were working to raise more.

＝

In Seattle, Jennifer Cast, the finance co-chair for the Washington marriage campaign, was tapping her deep social network and reaching out to literally hundreds of friends and family members for dollars. A fifty-year-old Yale and Stanford Business School grad from an upper-crust

Indiana family, Jennifer was finding it harder than she'd imagined. The campaign had an $8 million budget—which it considered bare bones—but in late July it had only raised just over $2 million, and getting to the full $8 million seemed like a real stretch. Jennifer knew there was one ask she still had to make, and it was the one that could make the biggest difference. Jennifer had been among the first employees at Amazon. She needed to reach out to its billionaire founder, Jeff Bezos.

Jennifer put the finishing touches on a seven-page e-mail to Bezos she'd been working on for a long time. She shared her own journey: her serious contemplation of suicide at Yale as she struggled coming to terms with her sexuality; the pain and indignity of "passing" as straight; and the importance of her own family, especially the love of her life, Liffy, to whom she'd been engaged for twenty years.

At the end of her e-mail, she made her ask. In bold, she typed, "I'm writing to ask you to make a donation. To consider making a $100,000– $200,000 donation. A big/generous/hmmm-I-surprised-myself donation." She knew he could give a lot more if he wanted, but this felt to her like the right number to ask for, and he could decide if he wanted to give more. "I beg you not to sit on the sidelines and hope the vote goes our way," she concluded. "Help us make it so." She read it through one last time, took a deep breath, and at 5:10 p.m. on Sunday, July 22, hit send.

The following Tuesday morning, Jennifer was driving with her partner, two kids, and their cancer-stricken Portuguese water dog to a photographer to have some pictures taken to remember their beloved pet. Just as they pulled up, she looked at her phone and there was an e-mail from Jeff and McKenzie Bezos. She opened it immediately.

"Jen, this is right for so many reasons. We're in for $2.5 million."

Here was a thirteen-word reply to her nearly three-thousand-word e-mail, but it couldn't have been any better. She was filled with gratitude and, as finance co-chair of the campaign, great relief.

When the campaign announced the gift, it made big news nationally and raised the bar for leadership gifts to the marriage fight. Most importantly, it catapulted the Washington campaign toward its fundraising needs.

=

On July 24, I walked into the campaign headquarters of Mainers United for Marriage, a large, old two-story building filled with asbestos on the edge of downtown Portland. It was humming with organizers and volunteers, reminding me of the MassEquality office during some of the most intense periods but with many more people.

I sat down with field director Amy Mello and was blown away by what she'd put together. She now had more than 100 staffers working out of four regional field offices around the state, all focused on persuading conflicted voters to vote our way. She'd developed sophisticated models to identify the characteristics of voters who were most likely to be conflicted and had canvassers and volunteers going to their doors or phoning them to make the case.

Amy's persuasion effort was built on three principles: be authentic, be personal, and always meet voters where they are. That meant that her canvassers didn't memorize a pitch but instead asked questions to get voters to open up about their concerns and then engaged them authentically, weaving in personal reasons they felt so strongly about the cause. The goal was to get voters to understand why gay couples wanted to marry and then help them see how it's in sync with their own values to support extending that opportunity to them.

Amy told me about one canvasser named Jenn Grant who she thought wasn't being personal enough on the phone as she conveyed her reasoning for why marriage was important to her. Amy pulled Jenn aside and gave her some homework. "You have to go home and write a Hallmark card. You're going to give it to your girlfriend. It's going to be everything that you love about her and why you love her," Amy said. The next day, Jenn came back. "Oh my God," she said to Amy. "I feel like I've been in couples therapy." From then on, as Amy listened in on Jenn's phone calls, she would hear these beautiful conversations about why Jenn loved Stephanie, her partner, often concluding by saying, "When you go into that voting booth, I want you to think of the two of us."

By this point in the summer, the canvassers and volunteers had had more than 150,000 in-depth conversations and had reached more than half of the people who their models told them were conflicted about the issue. They were getting more than 20 percent to move to a position closer to full support.

The hardest conversations for the staff were with those who focused on their faith as the reason for not being supportive. Canvassers and volunteers just didn't like to engage here. Most weren't especially religious, and they preferred to pivot and talk about separation of church and state. But Amy, who'd gone to Catholic school from when she was a young child until she graduated from Providence College, knew we had to meet voters where they were if we had a hope of helping them change their perspective. Faith was by far the most common reason people would give for being opposed or conflicted, so it wasn't an area that could be avoided.

Amy and her leadership team divided the staff into those who had some level of Christian belief and those who didn't. For those who did, she explained that if voters bring up their Christian faith, they needed to engage directly, by talking about Jesus. Not "be good to other people" or "the Golden Rule" in the abstract, but "Jesus." "We can say this word," Amy told them.

So she sat them in a circle on the floor and had everyone go around and say Jesus, one by one. "Jesus." "Jesus." "Jesus." Around they went. Then she had them practice how to talk about their own faith and what Jesus meant to them. Amy would share her own story as an example: when a voter would talk about being Catholic as the reason for being opposed, she'd say that she was raised Catholic too and had gone to Catholic school from when she was a child through college. "What I learned was that Jesus was about bringing people into the church," she'd say. "Jesus is about inclusion not leaving anyone out." And she'd talk about how supporting marriage for gay couples was, for her, in sync with Jesus's teachings about not leaving anyone out, what she imagined he'd want. The canvassers came up with their own versions, based on what resonated with them, and they tested it out on one another before trying it at the doors.

Amy liked to rib me that I never went out door to door myself. She wanted me to see in action what they were doing. I was definitely game, so she paired me up with a twenty-nine-year-old gay actor named Michael Wood who grew up on a farm in rural Maine. I met up with him in a middle-class residential neighborhood in Scarborough, just a few miles outside of Portland, where he was in the middle of a shift. He told me he'd been going door to door nonstop for three months now.

He showed me his iPod Touch and explained that every canvasser had one, programmed daily with the voters they would talk to based on targeting information. He showed me how it had basic information: age, party affiliation, and who else lived in the household.

We approached the first house, and the guy we were supposed to talk to was out by his garage. "Hi, I'm Michael Wood with Mainers United for Marriage," he said. He reminded the man there would be a vote on marriage in November. "Generally, how do you feel about marriage for same-sex couples? Would you say you strongly support it, somewhat support it, somewhat oppose, or strongly oppose marriage for same-sex couples."

The guy said he strongly supported it.

Michael probed more deeply. "Okay, then which of the following is closer to your point of view: same-sex couples should be allowed to get married, or they should be allowed legal recognition, like a civil union." The research had shown that those who were open to civil unions could be swayed away from marriage later in the campaign, so if they opted for civil unions, the canvasser would stay and make the case about why civil unions were deficient compared to marriage.

This guy was solid, though. "I don't have any problem with gay people marrying," he said. "If they want it to be marriage, why would I want it to be something else?"

Michael then explained that they were talking to hundreds of thousands of voters and asked the guy if he'd consider a contribution. But he wasn't interested in that either. So Michael thanked the guy for his time and entered a "1" on his iPod, indicating strong support.

My own reaction was one of relief; we'd found a supporter. But that wasn't what the canvass was about. It was about finding people who weren't firm in their support—who maybe would go for civil unions or who were leaning against—and moving them toward full support of marriage.

I continued with Michael for another hour or so, but we only hit supporters or people who weren't home. So I asked him to tell me about someone whose mind he'd changed recently. He proceeded to tell me of a woman in her eighties to whom he'd spoken who was in the strongly opposed camp, someone who preferred no legal recognition to civil unions.

For voters in that category, the instructions were to move on. But it was a really hot day, and he was in a rural town where the houses were ten minutes apart, so he gave it a shot anyway. "What is your marriage like?" he asked, using one of the questions that often provoked an in-depth discussion.

She told him that she'd been married for more than forty years until her husband passed away a couple of years before. Now her children helped take care of her.

"Wow, that's a really long time," Michael said. "You must have really loved him." He continued, "I have no idea what that's like. I'm still young and figuring that out." Michael then probed more deeply about what her marriage meant to her.

The woman suddenly began to cry. Michael wasn't ready for that, and he expected her to excuse herself and go back inside. But she just stood there, crying, for what seemed a really long time.

He finally broke the silence. "It sounds like you really loved your husband," Michael finally said, tears welling up in his own eyes.

The woman nodded.

"Your family is really important to you," he said.

The woman nodded again.

"All I can ever hope for in the world," Michael said, "is to feel as strongly as you feel about your husband and your family."

After another few minutes, the woman stopped crying, and Michael followed up with his closing question, asking her again how she felt about marriage for same-sex couples. Did she strongly support it, somewhat support it, somewhat oppose, or strongly oppose?

"Strongly support," she said.

Michael knew he had forged a connection with the woman, but he was surprised by her about-face. He figured she'd be conflicted at best. He asked her what changed her mind.

As soon as you got me thinking about my family, you got me thinking about how important they are. Why wouldn't I want you to have that?

Michael gave her a hug goodbye, recorded her as a 1, and then headed off to the next home on his list. To be sure, this was more dramatic and intense than most conversations, Michael told me, but this was his job, to open himself up and get people to open up and really reconsider their position.

As I headed back to Portland for the evening, I thought to myself how emotionally taxing that job was—how draining it would be to have these personal conversations day after day, opening oneself up to rejection and painful comments. Courageous work, indeed.

The next day, I sat down with Matt McTighe and reviewed the campaign's media plan. Matt showed me some of the television spots, and they were perfect. My favorite, set to air the next day during the opening ceremonies of the Summer Olympics, featured ninety-year-old World War II Marine veteran Harlan Gardner, along with four generations of his family, including Harlan's lesbian granddaughter and her partner, from the town of Machias on Maine's northernmost coast. On Mother's Day, Matt had gone up with a crew to film the family. As soon as he met and heard Harlan, he knew he had to be the feature of the spot.

"We have four generations of our family sitting around this table," Harlan began in the ad. "I flew in the last battle of World War II."

He spoke in his classic Maine accent of his fifty-nine-year marriage to Dottie. With his lesbian granddaughter and her partner sitting next to him he continued, "It takes a great deal of bravery to be a lesbian. I'm so proud of Kate and Alex."

His wife Dottie then said, "I would in my lifetime really like to be able to see Katie and Alex get married legally."

The camera then faded out to show the entire table, with nine people from four generations sitting around it. "This isn't about politics," Harlan concludes. "It's about family and how we as people treat one another."

It was a home run.

Matt showed me about a dozen other spots: Republicans, firefighters, parents talking about their gay son or daughter, a college kid with lesbian moms, and clergy—all Mainers. They all hit the love and commitment or freedom theme, many featuring straight people who spoke of their journey to marriage. Some combatted our opponents' arguments but in a way that conveyed their values of the Golden Rule and freedom, and put a human face on why our opponents' arguments didn't convince them.

Then we turned to money. Matt told me there was new urgency: the pro-Romney super PACs were gobbling up network television in Maine, as it reached into sections of the swing state of New Hampshire. As a result, prices were going up quickly, particularly for ad reservations for the last couple of weeks before Election Day. Prior to Labor Day, Matt wanted to lock in as much television as possible for the final weeks of the campaign. I promised him we'd prioritize this.

Pleased with where the Maine campaign was, I made similar trips to Minnesota and Washington to "kick the tires" a bit, see how things were going firsthand, and get some one-on-one time with the campaign managers to develop a more personal rapport. I wanted them to feel 100 percent comfortable calling me any time about anything.

The campaign managers in Minnesota and Washington told me that they too were seeing television time bought up much earlier than expected. When I returned to New York, I met with Evan and we moved large amounts from our Win More States Fund to our priority campaigns. We encouraged others to do the same so the campaigns could lock in television as early as possible. In the end, that turned out to be a huge advantage, as our campaigns paid as little as half of what our opponents paid for the equivalent amount of air time.

We knew we were going to need to bring our best game to these fights. We learned that Frank Schubert, the mastermind behind Prop 8, would be running each of these ballot initiatives simultaneously for our opponents. Not that I needed much more incentive than I already had, but I really wanted to pummel this guy.

n late August, Minnesotans United for All Families was preparing for the biggest public event of the campaign so far, the Minnesota State Fair. It was America's second largest, drawing nearly two million people between late August and Labor Day. Undeterred by poll numbers that said opposition to the antigay amendment lingered slightly under 50 percent, the campaign was knocking out of the park every benchmark they'd set out: 830 house parties and $8.5 million raised, including contributions from many of the leading civic players in Minnesota. Mainstream Minnesota-based companies like General Mills were speaking out against the amendment.

The fair was best known for its deep-fried apple pie and Twinkies, beer gardens, and award-winning grains and animals, but Minnesotans United was determined to get fairgoers to consider the freedom to marry. They built a booth using the bright orange of the campaign and painted "Vote No" in white lettering on the roof. They had thousands of T-shirts for sale, as well as lawn signs, bumper stickers, and buttons, and they created miniature lawn signs on a stick that doubled as fans they could hand out for free.

As soon as the fair began, campaign manager Richard Carlbom was overwhelmed. Tens of thousands of people mobbed the booth, clamoring to buy campaign merchandise and sign up to help. The very first day, they sold out of all 12,000 T-shirts they'd ordered at $30 a shirt.

A few days in, the fair director and police chief asked to meet with Richard. They had a complaint: volunteers were leaving their posts at the Minnesotans United booth and canvassing in other parts of the fair, which was against the rules. Richard explained that that might be what it looked like, but in fact, there were just so many people mobbing their booth that the lines stretched out forty or fifty people deep in every direction.

"We've never seen something like this," the fair director said when he heard Richard's explanation.

To the thirty-one-year-old openly gay Richard who hailed from the small city of St. Joseph, seventy-five miles northwest of the Twin Cities, the response of Minnesotans of all stripes to their cause was affirming and gave him tremendous confidence. He realized that the people of Minnesota would take ownership of the campaign if the campaign gave them the tools to do so. With this kind of energy, Richard was more convinced than ever that moving the needle to a majority was attainable.

By Labor Day, Freedom to Marry had transformed itself into a central hub to support the ballot campaigns. We had one operative focused on each of our priority ballot fights, and I was overseeing the effort, with a focus on working with Evan to raise funds, as well as troubleshooting and carefully watching the internal tracking polling across the campaigns. In addition to serving as our lead on Minnesota, Thalia Zepatos was heading up our rapid response to our opponents' attacks.

We'd organized biweekly calls of all the campaign managers to compare notes, troubleshoot, and share research and messaging. Together with the Human Rights Campaign, we hired Andrew Cuomo's opposition research guy to help the campaigns respond to our opponents' attacks in real time.

All the campaigns had ads ready to go: the proactive "empathy-track" spots highlighting love, commitment, and freedom, as well as the response ads to the "harms kids" and "civil unions are sufficient" lines of attack.

On the money front, there was a huge imbalance. To date, according to campaign disclosure reports, our campaigns had outraised our opponents $19 million to $3 million. But I didn't expect that to last. Our opponents at the National Organization for Marriage and the Catholic fraternal organization Knights of Columbus might be trying to woo us into complacency, only to surprise us by moving huge amounts of money in one fell swoop to each of the campaigns. And, of course, we were sure Frank Schubert would start using his diabolical tricks to convince voters that marriage for gay couples was harmful to them. However, the opposition's dollars hadn't yet come in, and television prices were going up every day.

=

By the first week of October in Maine, Matt McTighe knew his campaign's unopposed run on television—which had begun in July with the ad featuring the ninety-year-old World War II Marine veteran and his lesbian granddaughter—was about to end. Protect Marriage Maine had purchased TV time beginning Monday, October 8. Matt waited with nervous anticipation, knowing he'd prepared for every contingency he could imagine.

On the 8th, the opposition went up with two spots at once. The first was one we expected—a "civil unions are enough" spot. It used soft music with photos and images of opposite-sex couples, many with children, and a voice-over saying that "marriage as between a man and a woman has served Maine for hundreds of years." It claimed, falsely, that "same-sex couples already have the protection of marriage in virtually all matters" and that protections that aren't provided can be made available by changing laws. "Every Mainer has a right to love who they choose," it concluded. "But nobody has a right to redefine marriage." That had always been our opponents' bread-and-butter line. Would it continue to work this time?

The second spot was much more ominous. "If Question 1 passes redefining marriage, we can expect consequences for Mainers," the voice-over said, with dark music playing in the background. It then featured a bearded man named Don Mandell, with images of kids in school behind him.

"I was a successful school counselor in Maine for over twenty years, once nominated as teacher of the year," Mandell said. "Yet, when I supported traditional marriage, they tried to get me fired. They went after my state license, claiming that supporting marriage as between one man and one woman is discriminatory."

"When gay marriage has become law elsewhere," the voice-over said. "People who disagree with it have been fired, sued, fined and punished. Don't redefine marriage. Vote no on Question 1."

Schubert was again peddling "consequences," yet this time, it wasn't harm to kids but alleged harm to regular people who oppose marriage equality. The fact was that Mandell was a school counselor who had been an outspoken opponent of marriage for gay couples during the 2009 ballot fight, calling it "inherently evil" and opposing the freedom to marry on television. Some of his school counselor colleagues were concerned about how his public virulence would affect his ability to counsel gay students effectively, so they filed a complaint challenging his license with the state regulatory authority. The ad conveniently omitted the fact that the complaint was dismissed.

Matt and team immediately sprung into action, circulating fact-checks about both spots to the media that highlighted the omissions in Mandell's story and called out the lie in the first spot, which claimed that same-sex couples in Maine already had nearly all the benefits of marriage when in fact they had next to none. The *Portland Press-Herald* subsequently ran two "Truth Tests" on the ads and labeled both of them "mostly false."

The Maine campaign went up with two new spots of its own. The first featured Stacey Fitts, a middle-aged man and self-described lifelong Republican who talked of how he voted the other way last time but, after talking it over with his family, decided that "voting yes protects religious freedom and it protects individual freedom. To me that's what our country is all about." It wasn't a direct response to Mandell's attack, and that was by design. Instead it was a regular Mainer addressing the charge that people's freedoms would be taken away if gays were allowed to marry.

A second spot hit the civil union argument head on. It featured an elderly couple, Cathy and Phil Curtis, who spoke of their fifty-two-year marriage and of their three daughters, one of whom was a lesbian. "People will ask," Cathy said, "Why wouldn't a civil union be enough for her. When we were young, we never dreamed about having a civil union or signing a piece of paper. We wanted to be married." The camera showed the two of them looking through family albums. "I want our Katie to have what we have through the joy and security of marriage," Phil said.

The minute the Maine opposition spots went up, we at our virtual campaign war room at Freedom to Marry transcribed them and sent them to the other ballot campaigns and, working with the opposition research firm, distributed facts about our opponents' allegations. Not surprisingly, Schubert, trying to manage four campaigns at once, was running a cookie-cutter operation. While he didn't use the Maine-specific Mandell spot in other states, he did run very similar ones with the same theme of "consequences." For example, he showed Vermont innkeepers who were sued because they refused to host a wedding of a same-sex couple (a violation of nondiscrimination laws not the marriage law) as well as a Canadian sportscaster who was allegedly fired for publicly stating that he backed "traditional marriage" and more. This was a line of attack for which we were prepared.

On October 24, the "harms kids" attack finally hit, first in Minnesota. "If gay marriage happens here, schools could teach that boys can marry boys," the voice-over said, showing the book *King & King* used in the California spot with ominous-sounding music in the background. The ad then focused on David and Tonia Parker, parents from Massachusetts. "After Massachusetts redefined marriage," David said, "local schools taught it to children in second grade, including the school our son attended. Courts ruled parents had no right to take their children out of class or to even be informed when this instruction was going to take place." Tonia then implored, "If marriage is redefined in Minnesota, same-sex marriage could be taught in local schools, just as it was in Massachusetts." The camera then did a close-up of Tonia's face: "Don't make the same mistake and think that gay marriage won't affect you." This exact ad was aired in the other ballot states soon after.

Within twenty-four hours, our response ads went up. Parents of older kids from Maine, Minnesota, and Washington talked about how values are taught at home and that the values they wanted their kids to have are those of the Golden Rule, treating others the way they wanted to be treated. This wasn't a head-on response, but it was what tested as most effective. It reminded parents that they don't have to worry about the schools because they, the parents, are the ones who impart values to their children.

I thought our spots were great: upbeat, honest, featuring local families, and with hundreds of thousands of dollars of research behind them. But would they work in a real campaign?

We also finally saw an infusion of cash into our opponents' campaigns, largely from Catholic organizations: about $3 million to Minnesota, $2 million to Washington, and $1 million to Maine. But our campaigns were still vastly better funded than theirs.

Every morning, I'd wait anxiously for the daily tracking polls to come in. But once the "harms kids" spots came on the air, I was especially nervous. In Maine, there was no immediate drop in the polls; we were still consistently above 56 percent. In Washington, where everyone voted by mail, more than a third of respondents said they'd already voted, and of those, 55 percent said they had voted yes. In Minnesota, the "harms kids" ads did appear to have an effect, as support for our side dropped from 50 to 47 percent. Yet, soon after, it crept back up to 50 percent, considerably better than it had been when the campaign began.

=

The final week leading up to Election Day turned out to be a very difficult one for us to do our work. Hurricane Sandy pounded New York and left our office—and my apartment—without power. After a couple of days, I packed a bag and walked over the Brooklyn Bridge to my sister's place, where I could better monitor the races.

Friday, November 2, was the final day for tracking polls before Election Day, and the Maine numbers were cause for some concern. They had held steady between 56 and 58 percent for months, but the final track showed that we'd declined over the last few days, to 53 percent support. The same day, a Maine newspaper reported that its polling showed we were at 52 percent support. On Sunday, a final public survey came out showing us at 50.5 percent, the worst poll I'd seen in Maine over the entire campaign. Intellectually, I knew that I shouldn't compare one poll to another, since they all made different assumptions about the electorate. But the fact that the numbers seemed to be getting tighter and tighter made me very nervous.

Amy Mello could see some decline in support over the past week in calls they were making to voters. She noticed a measurable shift in people they'd identified as "soft" supporters; they were moving the other way. She knew the Catholic churches had turned up the pressure at services and that Mainers, who were the oldest voters in the country, were susceptible to that pitch.

On Saturday, November 3, when the New York airports finally opened back up, I took one of the first flights to Portland, Maine. I was too antsy not to be on the ground with one of the campaigns, and I wanted to join Matt and Amy and team to offer any support I could.

As soon as I walked into the campaign office, Matt asked me into his office and closed the door. Grim faced, he told me about an incident that had taken place the previous week at a middle school in Gorham, eleven miles west of Portland. For its Diversity Day, the school had invited a group called PRYSM (Proud Rainbow Youth of Southern Maine) to talk to the students about homophobia. During the question-and-answer period with eighth graders, one of the presenters asked the students if, in sex education courses, they'd been taught about safe gay sex. According to the mother of one of the students, the presenter went on to speak about gay foreplay and suggested the use of plastic wrap if condoms weren't available. The parent had gone to the local television station to complain, and on Friday evening—the night before—a segment aired on Portland TV news about it. "I don't want my child taught heterosexual foreplay let alone homosexual foreplay in school," she said. "I don't think it's the place."

That Saturday, our opponents seized on it with a vengeance. Protect Marriage Maine issued a release saying, "If (Maine schools) are willing to teach our kids how to engage in foreplay, do you really think they won't force gay marriage instruction of young children when it is the law of the land?"

It seemed like a well-scripted nightmare. It reminded me of the kindergartners in San Francisco who'd been taken by their school to see their teacher marry her female partner right after the No on 8 campaign ran an ad saying that marriage was never taught in schools. This incident had nothing to do with marriage, but I was worried that would be lost on parents, who might retrench in fear if our opponents could get this story out widely and tie it in to the narrative about consequences. From the huge amounts of message research we'd done with social psychologists, I'd learned that the fearful brain is neither logical nor rational.

The good news was that it was too late for our opponents to get a new television spot up publicizing it. At worst, they could hand deliver a last-minute flier, or run radio spots, and it could be covered in Maine newspapers, but it would be hard to broadcast this incident broadly.

To be extra cautious earlier on Saturday, Matt called his data firm— the firm that sliced and diced Maine voters into different categories based on issues of concern—and asked them to pull lists of mothers who were most susceptible to the "harms kids" messaging. He reached out to the teacher who was also the mother of teenagers whom they'd used in their response ad to the "harms kids" charge and asked her to record an automated call, which they delivered to that list of voters.

Matt told me there wasn't much more he could do other than hope the story didn't catch on. I sat with him in his office and tossed a ball back and forth, keeping him company as we passed the time. The communications team, next door to Matt's office, was high strung, overloaded with caffeine, and giddy with exhaustion and nervousness, bantering back and forth. I chatted with them for a bit. After a while, I took Matt out for dinner. We had a couple of martinis to take some of the edge off, and then I headed to my hotel.

=

The next day, Sunday, across the country in Seattle, Zach Silk—the campaign manager of Washington United for Marriage—had reason to feel good. The volunteer numbers for the weekend were off the charts, and the final tracking poll showed that, with more than half the votes already cast by mail, 53 percent of those who voted said they'd voted our way. Historically, older voters were the ones who sent their ballots in first so if that were the case this time, we'd be in good shape. This was especially great news because, for most of the fall, the tracking polls showed support hovering barely above the 50 percent mark—enough to give us all heartburn and provoke intense debates about which ads to run and where. Zach had handled the tension with calmness and confidence, and things were now looking very good.

Yet Zach was still worried. He knew well what the LGBT community's track record on marriage ballot measures was. Movement veterans had told Zach, a gregarious, married straight campaign veteran in his mid-thirties, not to believe the polls, that people would lie on the phone, saying they were in favor because they knew that was the politically correct answer but secretly being—and voting—against. That day, Zach was downtown near CenturyLink Field, where the Seattle Seahawks were playing a home game. A huge fan and frequent attendee, Zach saw a big contingent of our opponents standing outside the stadium holding "Vote No" signs. He knew who typical Seahawks fans were: beer-drinking guys who'd set records for being the loudest in the National Football League. He was concerned about how they would respond. And yet the Seahawks fans were booing our opponents relentlessly. Zach was amazed. The polling made Zach feel hopeful, but this was visceral confirmation that something really different was going on in Washington State.

=

Back in Maine on Monday, the *Portland Press Herald*, the state's largest newspaper, called the campaign and explained they were working on a story on the Gorham Middle School incident and its connection to the marriage fight. It would run the next day, Election Day. Matt thought they'd made it through without any more attention other than the TV news, but clearly they hadn't.

David Farmer, the campaign's communications director, did everything he could to kill the story. I could hear him on the phone, making the case to the editors. This incident was wrong and inappropriate, he said. But it has nothing to do with marriage. What's more, this was now old news. It happened more than a week ago. To run this old story on

Election Day when it could impact the election, repeating our opponents' assertion that this was a consequence of gay marriage, was complete bullshit, and totally unfair. "You're going to fuck us," Farmer said.

Matt pulled Amy aside and told her what was going on. She in turn notified her team of more than 150 organizers statewide. "This is really serious," she told them. "This can cost us tomorrow." She handed out a script that she'd just pulled together. They would shift from get-out-the-vote calls to making calls to soft supporters for whom, according to their database, the kids/schools argument was most persuasive. Amy was impressed with how her staff simply rolled with it. They were ready for anything. She wished she could have been as calm and collected; she thought that with the falling polling numbers and this story hitting, they really might lose.

The first version of the story appeared online at 11:00 p.m. I saw it on my phone while I was driving back to my hotel, and it was pretty bad. It was the lead story online, the headline in large letters, and it talked of the graphic details of the incident, quoting our opponents that it was a precursor of things to come if there was gay marriage. I thought it didn't include a strong enough counterargument about how one stupid and unfortunate incident had zero to do with whether or not gay couples should be able to marry.

At campaign headquarters, Matt was heartbroken. Two years could come down to this, he felt. It was unbelievable. Farmer called the paper and pushed back on key parts of the story, trying to get them to revise it and perhaps undo some of the damage. After midnight, a second version came out. It was considerably better but still bad. And of course, no one knew what the print version would say, or what the placement would be. Judging from the prominence of the online story, we had to assume above the fold, front page.

I shot an e-mail to Bill Smith, the operative who'd worked for Tim Gill, to get a one-step-removed read on this second version of the story. His response was, "Not horrible and well handled. Will take a lot more than this to blow things up on actual Election Day." That gave me a sense of relief. I was thinking we might be getting overly caught up in this story. We were all so concerned about the pernicious narrative that our opponents had peddled, that gay men posed a threat to children, going back to fights like the 1978 Briggs Initiative in California to ban gays from teaching in the classroom and of course the Prop 8 fight four years before. It was hard to look at things objectively. But still, with the polls tightening and our history at the ballot, I was nervous.

Matt had been sleeping about two hours a night for the past two weeks, sometimes crashing on a cot in the office. That night, though, he didn't sleep at all. In the wee hours of the morning, he left the office and drove over to the parking lot of a Mobil gas station where he waited for the first newspaper delivery. When the delivery truck dumped the bound papers outside, Matt grabbed one and left a dollar.

The story wasn't on the front page. He turned to the second section, and there it was, the front of that section. "Gorham Incident Used against Maine Same-Sex Marriage Effort" was the headline. The subheadline read, "But Supporters Say an Inappropriate Discussion at Gorham Middle School Has Nothing to Do with Marriage." It was the better version of the story, focusing on how the incident was being used by our opponents rather than simply the incident and our opponents' allegations. It could have been a lot worse.

=

When I woke up the next morning, there was an e-mail from Matt that he'd sent to his entire staff.

Date: Tue, 6 Nov 2012
Subject: Good sign

Team,

I know most of us are running on fumes, fighting off colds (with varying success) or both. But as a follow up to my message the other night, I just wanted to pass on a good omen:

While out making rounds to the headquarters and a couple of staging locations this morning, I decided to drive by the Holiday Inn, the site of tonight's election night party in Portland. Just as I was pulling up to the stoplight on the corner of High Street & Spring, with the Holiday Inn directly in front of me, I flipped stations on the radio. The Muse song "Uprising" was playing, and—I'm not exaggerating when I say this—it was RIGHT at the point in the song with the following lyric: "They will not control us . . . we will be victorious."

Normally I'm not superstitious, but that has to be a sign, right? No matter what level our opponents stoop to, no matter what news stories happen to break, and no matter how sick and tired we all are, we still have the plan and the team to make history. We built something amazing over the last two and a half years and changed a lot of hearts and minds. If you can hang in there a few more hours and continue to give it your all as I know you will, we WILL be victorious.

Now get to work!

Matt

Amy hadn't slept that night either, but that morning, the last thing she wanted to do was to see the newspaper. She had 150 staffers and 3,500 volunteer shifts she was responsible for statewide. She needed to keep it together. There were two major elements of the day's plan. First, volunteers were to call and knock on the doors of everyone in the state who had told canvassers and phoners they were a supporter to make sure they went to the polls. Second, they would do "blind pulls" at college campuses and throughout most of the city of Portland, which meant talking to any voters without knowing if they were supporters and asking them to go to the polls. Support was so strong in those two groups that it was highly likely that the voters would be supporters.

Amy and her team had scoped out and made a plan for every college and university in the state, focusing on gaining access to dorms. For the major apartment complexes in Portland, they'd arranged for supporters who lived in the buildings to let canvassers in so they could knock on doors and urge people to go to the polls.

As Amy got reports from the field throughout the day, it was clear that the 3,500 volunteer shift number was being blown out of the water. They had enough volunteers to call and knock on the doors of identified supporters over and over. In Portland, some doors were being hit eight or nine times.

At 5:00 p.m., as the final shift of volunteers came to the campaign offices around the state, Amy decided she had to get out of the office. She was spent and needed some fresh air. So she got in her car with her boyfriend, sister, and niece to "blind knock" her Portland neighborhood. Soon after leaving the office, though, one of her organizers called urgently. "They're out of ballots," the organizer said.

Where? Amy wanted to know.

At polling places around Portland, the organizer responded. Several staffers had called and said they'd run out of ballots.

Amy freaked. To win, they had to maximize the vote in Portland, by far Maine's largest city and their most favorable area. What's more, the voters who would go to the polls in the evening were overwhelmingly younger voters on their way home from work—*their* voters.

Find out where the biggest lines are and just make sure people stay, Amy instructed her staff. Get pizza, get coffee. Whatever it takes. They can't leave.

Amy checked on a polling place in her neighborhood, and sure enough, it was out of ballots.

"How many people have left?" Amy asked the warden.

He said that nine people left but not to worry; they all said they were coming back.

"They're not coming back!" Amy barked. "How the hell do you run out of ballots?"

The warden explained that turnout was extremely high in Portland and that they'd been out of ballots for thirty-five minutes but should have them in about another twenty minutes.

Amy went to two other polling locations, and they were both out. But soon after arriving at the second location, a church right next to her house, they brought in new ballots. The line was snaking all through the building and around the outside. She sent her sister to Dunkin' Donuts to buy coffee. Then she found a campaign volunteer who had just voted and asked her to help give out coffee to everyone. "Tell them to wait," Amy said. "Beg them not to leave the line." Within the hour, all the polling sites had ballots again.

When the clock hit 8:00 p.m. and the polls began shutting down, Amy knew there was nothing more to do. She was worried, prepared to hear that they'd lost. Sitting in the backseat of her sister's car with her niece, on the way to the Holiday Inn where the election night party would take place, Amy cried. She thought back to the meeting at the University of Southern Maine nearly a year before when we'd made the decision to go to the ballot. She'd wanted that decision badly, and she'd presented all the field data about why she thought they could win. But now all she could think about were the thousands of volunteers: the young people who came to spend a week with the campaign and ended up spending more than a month, working hard and sleeping in substandard housing; the summer volunteers who decided not to go back to college and instead took the semester off to see the campaign through; and the mom with her nine-year-old daughter who was so devastated after the 2009 loss that she vowed she wouldn't volunteer again yet ended up running canvass trainings. Amy also thought about the staff members who were working double time and triple time to hit their goals for conversations and persuasions. If they'd lost, after all she'd asked people to do and after they'd delivered in such incredible fashion—it was too unbearable to think about. Amy's young niece kept trying to hug Amy and console her.

"Don't talk to me, Anna," Amy said. She was inconsolable.

Earlier in the afternoon, I'd stolen away from the campaign office and headed out for some fresh air. I'd driven out to Portland Light, a quintessentially picturesque Maine lighthouse a few miles from the campaign headquarters. It was crisp and cold, but the New England salty air felt restorative. It was hard to believe that the big day was here—not just in Maine but around the country. Months and years of preparation all came down to this one day.

I headed back to my hotel to shower and dress for what I knew would be a very long night, arriving at the Holiday Inn at about 8:30. As I entered the ballroom full of hundreds of volunteers and staff, I wanted so badly for this to be a night of celebration.

There was a speaking program of campaign executive committee members, and I had the final slot. But all I wanted to do was get upstairs to the "Boiler Room" and get the results in real time.

"Are you ready to win?" I shouted to the crowd when it was finally my turn. Many cheered. "I said, are you ready to win?" A lot more cheers that time. I told them that we had a lot to be proud of—all the incredible work the campaign had pulled off—and that by the end of the evening, I hoped we'd have some great news to celebrate, our first ballot win ever. But my heart wasn't fully in it—I wanted to know what was happening.

I exited quickly and headed to the second floor, to the restricted area where campaign operatives were tallying results. In one room, about twenty volunteers were taking phone calls from staff and volunteers throughout the state who were at city and town halls collecting official tallies as they came in. Across the hall, Amy Mello was huddled on the floor with Ryan Brown, another MassEquality alum. Ryan was being given the numbers as they came in, town by town, and Amy was entering them into a spreadsheet that had the percentages for each town from the ballot campaign in 2009, when our side had lost 53 to 47 percent. They were looking for more than a three-point swing in support in our favor, on average, compared to the 2009 numbers. That would put us above the 50 percent threshold.

I chatted for a bit with the others on the executive committee who had gathered, including Lee Swislow and Mary Bonauto from GLAD. Many were watching the presidential results coming in on television. By that point, I was trusting *New York Times* guru Nate Silver's projections and was confident the president would win. For me, it was all about these ballot fights. I got down on the floor where Amy and Ryan were tallying results.

"Amy, how are we really doing?" I asked.

"It looks close," Amy said, but they didn't have enough information yet. Results were coming in in no particular order. We were consistently ahead of where we were in 2009 but by just a few points—four points in Bangor, three and a half in Augusta. In Auburn, the fifth-largest city in the state, the numbers were right at where they'd been the last time. I had a sick feeling in the pit of my stomach.

Still huddling with Amy and Ryan, the numbers started looking up. Lewiston, Maine's second-largest city, which we'd lost 41 to 59 percent in 2009, we lost again but by a much smaller margin: 47 to 53 percent.

The last time we'd lost Biddeford, Maine's sixth-largest city, 47 to 53 percent, but this time we'd actually won, 57 to 43 percent—a ten-point turnaround. The numbers from Maine's largest city, Portland, which was our stronghold, were coming in very slowly—not surprising because of the ballot debacle.

Finally, the results began coming in quickly, and things were definitely looking up. City by city, the numbers were now coming in five, six, and more points ahead of last time. It was looking good.

Mary Bonauto came over to me. "Tell me that we're going to win," she said.

"It's going to happen," I told her. We hugged, and Mary got teary eyed. We'd been battling together now for more than a decade. Finally the freedom to marry would be coming to her state and through our first win at the ballot.

Matt McTighe came into the room. Never one to be risk averse, Matt asked, "Guys, is there any reason not to call it?" He wanted to declare victory. Some were ambivalent; neither the AP nor anyone else had called the race, and most of the results from Portland were still not in.

All of a sudden, a huge roar came in from the next room. CNN had just called Ohio—and the presidential election—for President Obama. So we decided to wait until the media storm from the presidential race announcement died down a bit. I took the opportunity to check with our operatives who were focused on the other ballot states. In Maryland, we were clinging to a small lead. What was especially promising was that some key counties that were primarily African American were running strong, reflecting the surge in black support following President Obama's announcement of his support for the freedom to marry in May. In Minnesota, the early returns were in line with what the campaign's modeling said we'd need for a win, but there was still a lot more counting to do.

At 11:50 p.m., Matt conferred with pollster Amy Simon and communications director David Farmer and decided to pull the trigger. "Let's go," he said. Matt led a procession of thirty or so of us down to the ballroom, where hundreds of people were waiting with anticipation.

Matt took the microphone, and we all stood behind him along with dozens of campaign staffers. His voice quivering with emotion and exhaustion and cameras flashing in his face, he said, "It has been a long time in coming. And that just makes what I'm about to say all the more sweet. Tonight, because of the work of everyone in this room and so many staff and volunteers and supporters all over the country, we have finally won the freedom to marry."

The room erupted. People were jumping up and down. A young man standing to my right who I guessed was a field organizer burst into tears. People were hugging and jumping for joy. Michael Wood, the canvasser I'd gone door to door with, was crying, hugging the people with whom he'd done this excruciatingly difficult work. For me, I was so proud—of Matt, of Amy, of the campaign they'd run, and of how far we'd come. We'd finally broken the streak at the ballot, with a 53 to 47 percent victory.

After more hugs and celebrating, I headed back upstairs, where I learned that Maryland had also pulled out a victory and was heading to a 52 to 48 percent win. I stuck around upstairs gabbing, celebrating, and drinking.

At three in the morning, Thalia called me from Minnesota. Richard Carlbom, the campaign manager, had just declared victory there as well, with numbers showing a 53 to 47 percent victory. A little later, I spoke with Zach Silk in Washington, who he told me that even though they weren't calling it because ballots would still be arriving in the mail over the next couple of days, it was looking very good—so good that Governor Christine Gregoire had all but called it when she spoke at the campaign's party. The final tally in Washington ended up being 54 to 46 percent.

At close to 4:00 a.m., I joined Matt, pollster Amy Simon, campaign Communications Director David Farmer, and a few others in polishing off a bottle of bourbon. We toasted to our win in Maine, to President Obama's win, and to all four marriage victories. I had been thinking that two ballot victories would allow us to make the case that we'd transformed the dynamic of ballot fights. I had barely allowed myself to dream that we'd win all four, and yet here we were. I knew this would be a transformative momentum boost in our drive to make the case that American was ready for the freedom to marry.

I thought back to four years before, when election night was so bittersweet: the Obama victory accompanied by the brutal Prop 8 loss. And four years before that, we'd swept our Massachusetts legislative races yet were crushed in marriage ballot fights in state after state, and John Kerry lost the presidency to George W. Bush, with our community being used as a scapegoat. Tonight, there was nothing bittersweet at all—just the sweetness of victory.

A PRESIDENTIAL JOURNEY

L ate during the 2008 presidential campaign, I, along with Massachusetts State Representative Carl Sciortino, who was now one of
my closest friends, organized a bus trip from Boston to Columbus, Ohio, to campaign for Barack Obama.

While I, like most in our community, had supported Hillary Clinton
in the primary, I was now focused 100 percent on electing Obama—
both because I shared his values and vision for the country and because
that would be the only way we would get any help in advancing the
freedom to marry.

Like Clinton, Obama said he didn't support marriage for gay and
lesbian couples. But he did support repeal of the so-called Defense of
Marriage Act (DOMA), the law that barred the federal government from
respecting the marriages of same-sex couples performed in a state like
Massachusetts. My strong hunch was that he was really with us. In fact,
in 1996 when running for the Illinois State Senate, he'd filled out a survey for a Chicago LGBT newspaper expressing his support. And yet I understood that, in order to be seen as a viable presidential candidate, there
was a modest range of positions on any given subject that candidates
felt they could enunciate. Supporting the freedom to marry wasn't yet
considered in the "acceptable" range. If Obama were elected, it would be
our job to advance the cause nationally to the point where a sympathetic
president believed that support for the freedom to marry was politically
viable, while simultaneously pushing him hard to take the leap.

Senator John McCain, Obama's opponent, was not at all supportive.
He had roamed the country in a bus called the "Straight Talk Express."
So Carl and I loaded up our bus, which we had named the "Not So
Straight Talk Express," and headed with friends and supporters from
Boston to Columbus.

The Obama campaign had arranged for some of Barack and Michelle Obama's gay and lesbian friends from Chicago to meet us in Columbus, campaign with us, and do some interviews with the gay press to shore up support from our community. It was great to get to meet some of the gay folks who'd known Obama for a long time. Obama had surged onto the political scene, so I just didn't know all that much about him. Among the people I met was Kevin Thompson, who was one of the Obamas' oldest gay friends, someone who'd been very influential back when Barack Obama was first running for the US Senate.

≡

Kevin Thompson first got to know Michelle Obama (then Michelle Robinson) when both worked in the policy shop of Chicago Mayor Richard Daley in the early 1990s. Over the years, the two stayed close, working together again at the University of Chicago Hospitals and swapping home improvement and gardening ideas over meals. When Barack Obama first began his run for an open US Senate seat in late 2002, Michelle asked Kevin if he would play an active role in the campaign. Obama was the kind of candidate that Kevin usually gravitated toward—an underdog and a progressive. The two had something else in common as well: both were biracial, with a white mother and black father, though Kevin was very light skinned and many assumed he was white. Kevin was all in.

Then a state senator, Obama would be facing off in the Democratic primary against businessman Blair Hull and State Comptroller Dan Hynes, both of whom were much better known and resourced. It was well known that to win a Democratic primary, you had to do well on the liberal Lakefront on the North Side of Chicago. So Kevin dedicated all of his spare time to the effort, helping open up a Lakefront office and mapping out a strategy to get Obama known on the North Side, where Kevin himself lived.

Obama had very little gay support to speak of. He wasn't familiar with the social or political scene in Boystown, the uber-gay neighborhood on the North Side centered on North Halsted Avenue. Kevin

knew that had to be fixed. So in early 2003, he organized a Sunday afternoon meet-and-greet event at a small bar called Cocktail.

Though he was new to this scene, Obama was calm and cool as usual.
He strode in wearing his shades, signature white shirt with sleeves rolled
up, and khaki pants. He drank beer, smoked cigarettes, and chatted
with the crowd of a few dozen for a couple hours. Kevin stood up on
the bar and introduced Obama, who focused his talk on prospects for
passing an Illinois state law that would add sexual orientation and gender identity to the state's nondiscrimination statute, a measure of which
he'd been a longtime cosponsor. He spoke of the politics and how they'd
be able to get it done now that the Democrats had taken the majority in
the State Senate after ten years of GOP control.

After Obama cruised to victory in the March 2004 primary, the race
shifted from urban Cook County to the entire state. Kevin joined the
campaign full time to become Obama's "body man," which meant he'd
be with the candidate from morning to night, making sure he was prepared for every event, briefing him in advance on who was who and
what the politics of the event were.

One day they were driving to a Democratic Party event in Schuyler
County, known in the Illinois political world as Forgottonia, in the very
rural west-central part of the state. Cell coverage was fading in and out
as they drove the four hours to the gathering. Kevin was worried they
might be late, so he called ahead to the host of the event from the road.

"Well we're so excited," the host said. "We've never had a colored man
speak down here before." Kevin was incredulous. After he hung up, he
looked at Obama and said, "They've never had a colored man speak
here before." Obama just died laughing and said in a whisper, "You're
kidding. He did not say that."

"He did say that," Kevin responded. "So when you get there, you better do a good job."

As they cruised along the two-lane highways, Obama took the opportunity to ask Kevin some questions about the gay community that
had been percolating as they'd been out on the campaign trail. One
question on his mind was why it was so important that he explicitly

name the community by saying, "the gay community." To be sure, gay people were part of the Illinois, and the America, he cared about. But it seemed so important to the community to be consistently mentioned by name. Why was that?

Kevin explained that, unlike other communities, the gay community needed legitimizing from allies in power because there were still plenty of people who thought legal rights for the gay and lesbian community wasn't a legitimate conversation. That was no longer the case for African Americans or women, but for the gay community, it remained true, at least in certain segments of society. Candidate Obama simply talking about the LGBT community signaled to them that they were on his agenda, that they had a seat at the table, and that they were being heard. He analogized it to Ralph Ellison's *Invisible Man*, about an African American who thought of himself as invisible to the white society around him. As Kevin made the parallels to other civil rights efforts, he could see that Obama was getting it.

Kevin talked about the history of the modern gay rights movement in the country, beginning with Stonewall.

"Well, what's Stonewall?" Obama asked.

"You've never heard of it?" Kevin asked.

"No," Obama responded.

Kevin was surprised. This was a sophisticated Columbia- and Harvard-educated scholar and political organizer. He needed to know. So Kevin gave him a primer, explaining that the riots that took place at the Stonewall Inn in Greenwich Village in 1969 represented a demarcation for when the gay community fought back against police intimidation and arrest and demanded their legal equality.

Kevin was glad he was able to be a safe person for Obama to ask questions of, with no judgment, and just have an honest back-and-forth.

The two had several in-depth conversations about gay rights. During one of them, they spoke a little bit about marriage, which had emerged in the news after the Massachusetts court ruling just a few months before. Obama said that, as a legislator, he had to think strategically about how to pass a law. The law before him at that time was nondiscrimination in the workplace, in housing, and in public accommodations—pretty basic and crucial things. Marriage just wasn't on the radar. Obama compared it to the African American civil rights movement. "During the civil rights era, folks weren't protesting over something much larger," he said. "They were talking about basic stuff, like, we want to sit at the same lunch counter that you're sitting at." Obama contrasted that with *Loving v. Virginia*, the aptly named Supreme Court case that ended the ban on interracial marriage, which wasn't until 1967, when some of the more basic issues were already dealt with.

On this, Kevin didn't disagree with Obama. From his perspective, marriage sort of emerged as an issue out of nowhere, and it just wasn't where they were in Illinois right now.

In the election, Obama caught an extremely lucky break. The formidable GOP nominee Jack Ryan dropped out in June after news surfaced of a sex scandal he'd been involved in. The GOP was in complete disarray. It cynically nominated the extreme right-wing political gadfly Alan Keyes, an African American former Reagan administration official who'd run twice for president and twice for the US Senate and who had no ties to Illinois. At the same time, Obama's stock was soaring after he gave his tremendously well-received speech at the Democratic National Convention in Boston nominating John Kerry for the Democratic nomination for president. I watched it live and thought it was the most powerful speech I'd ever seen.

In the aftermath of marriages beginning in Massachusetts, the virulently antigay extremist Keyes kept trying to bait Obama into talking about the subject. He finally succeeded, when Obama was grilled by a moderator in a 2004 television debate with Keyes on Chicago's public television station.

"What I believe is that marriage is between a man and a woman," Obama said to the moderator. "What I believe, in my faith, is that a man and a woman, when they get married, are performing something before God, and it's not simply the two persons who are meeting."

When lesbian realtor Lauren Verdich heard what Obama said, she couldn't believe it. An early supporter from Chicago, Lauren co-chaired LGBT for Obama. She had organized a huge LGBT fundraiser for him, with more than 400 RSVPs, and it was only a few days away. She immediately began getting phone calls. Many of the politically sophisticated people were okay with Obama taking a "safe" position on marriage. But the fact that he brought God into his response—that God favored heterosexual marriage and that's what determined his position on civil marriage for same-sex couples—went way overboard. It felt to some loyal supporters as though he'd just tossed the community under the bus.

Lauren dialed Obama's cell phone, and he picked up.

"How can you do this?" she asked him.

"You have to understand that I'm a Christian," he responded.

"This community is expecting you to stand beside them," she answered.

But he wasn't budging, arguing that that was his position, and he'd be sticking with it.

It dawned on Lauren that as progressive as Obama was, it came down to the fact that African American churches were a key part of Obama's base, and they didn't want him to be for gay marriage. The biracial Kevin Thompson later agreed that Obama's language about God and marriage was meant for his African American base.

Lauren expected people to bow out of the event, but they didn't. A large crowd stood on the dance floor of the Green Dolphin Street nightclub and restaurant as Obama took the stage. "I know that you're not too happy with my recent remarks," he said. "And I'm working through it." He explained that marriage was an issue that he was thinking about and getting his head around, even as he didn't change his position.

Lauren could tell that those assembled were willing to give him a chance. Marriage wasn't on many gay people's agenda yet in Illinois. And he was running against a rabid homophobe.

Lauren's partner Gail Morse, a politically active, high-powered attorney at a major downtown firm, thought that in spite of Obama's protestations, his position was purely political. Here was a progressive guy and a constitutional law scholar who was the product of an interracial marriage that would have been illegal in many states at one point in the country's history. She didn't believe he had a discriminatory bone in his body. But she knew she had to take what he'd said at face value, and she would make it her job to try to move him along.

After Obama won his election to the Senate, he called a meeting with some of his LGBT supporters to discuss his federal agenda. Gail couldn't make the meeting, but Lauren could. Gail wanted the educating on marriage to begin. So she called Evan Wolfson, who wasn't just the national guru on the issue but also a lawyer who had argued before the US Supreme Court and could perhaps help break through to Obama using constitutional arguments. She asked Evan to sign a copy of his book, *Why Marriage Matters: America, Equality, and Gay People's Right to Marry*, to Obama. Evan obliged and mailed her the book. Gail asked Lauren to hand the book to the senator-elect at the meeting. She didn't know if he would read it or not, but Gail was determined to do everything in her power to make the case.

Nearly four years later, Obama was in the fight of his life to be president, facing off in the primaries against Hillary Clinton. In the first week of March 2008, Jonathan Pizer and his partner of twenty-two years, Brad Lippitz, got a request from a friend of theirs asking if they'd be willing to host a fundraiser for the Obama campaign at their large North Shore home. They agreed since they were both big fans. Because they were active in both the gay and Jewish communities, they had strong social networks they could reach out to. In a week, they'd lined up more than 300 people to come to their home, with commitments of more than $350,000.

The day of the event, they waited at the agreed-upon location in the back of their house for Obama's motorcade to pull up. As he got out of the car, Jon and Brad greeted him and introduced him to Max and Jack, their two children, aged seven and five. Obama lit up when he saw the kids. He shook their hands, chatted with them, and posed with them for some photos.

Entering the house, Obama was escorted to the third floor for a small, high-donor VIP reception. After some intensive schmoozing and signing of autographs, Obama excused himself to use the couple's office to take care of some pressing work while the VIP guests went downstairs to the larger reception where the other guests were gathered. When Obama finished, Brad offered to escort him downstairs. He knew this would be his one chance to be alone with the candidate.

As they headed down the narrow staircase in the back of the house, Obama greeted and shook hands with the catering staff and then complimented Brad on the beautiful home.

"I'm glad you like the house," Brad said.

But he told Obama there was something more important on his mind: "If you win the nomination and get to the White House, please don't forget my family."

Obama looked Brad in the eyes. "I won't," he said.

Obama paused on the stairs with Brad and looked closely at the wall with dozens of pictures of Brad and Jonathan's family. It seemed to Brad as though in that moment Obama was really taking in what he said.

As the program began, Jonathan and Brad had seven-year-old Max within eyesight, but they couldn't find Jack anywhere. After Jonathan introduced the candidate, Obama began to speak. But then he stopped, looked behind him, and said, "Who's pinching my butt?" It was five-year-old Jack, who was poking Obama in the rear to let him know he was there.

"First of all," he continued, "I want to just thank our hosts. Not just Jonathan and Brad who I appreciate, but especially Max and Jack." There was lots of laughter and some applause. "We are so grateful to you guys. I know that you cleaned up and we appreciate it."

The event went perfectly. Jon and Brad just hoped that their senator, who seemed so at ease with their family, would be elected president and that they'd made an impact on him by showing him what their family was really like.

=

Obama's November 2008 victory against Senator John McCain was exactly what Evan had been waiting for. Having a sympathetic president offered up multiple opportunities to advance the national marriage strategy that he'd been shepherding. It was welcome, indeed, after two terms of George W. Bush and, before him, Bill Clinton, who had signed the Defense of Marriage Act into law.

Evan had two priorities. First, he was looking for help to get rid of the Defense of Marriage Act, which required the federal government to treat married same-sex couples as legal strangers and deny them more than 1,000 protections. This help would come in two ways: (1) responding to lawsuits challenging the constitutionality of DOMA in a way that would be most helpful to the cause; and (2) supporting legislation repealing DOMA. Through the courts or by Congress, Evan wanted to see DOMA eliminated under this president. Second, he wanted to see the president use his bully pulpit to advocate for the freedom to marry—sooner rather than later.

Evan knew that progress on marriage wasn't going to be the most immediate LGBT priority of the new administration. Under Bush, every priority of our community had been opposed and stifled, and we had to fight against retrograde measures used to placate the religious right, including the so-called Federal Marriage Amendment, a federal constitutional amendment that would have barred the freedom to marry nationwide. So there was a long list of basic protections for which our community was clamoring.

But that didn't mean Evan wasn't going to push hard to make sure marriage was on the agenda.

One approach that he thought would make a real difference in getting DOMA overturned, and would be less difficult for the administration to get behind, had to do with how the administration defended the law in court. For laws that classified people based on race or gender, judges were required to give extra scrutiny. For laws that classified based on sexual orientation, however, no such review applied.

Evan believed that if the new administration would argue in court that a "heightened scrutiny" standard of review should be required for laws that classified based on sexual orientation, it would have a very difficult time justifying the constitutionality of DOMA, or any other law that singled out gay or lesbian people for that matter. Evan ran the idea by Barney Frank, who agreed that persuading the administration to apply "heightened scrutiny" would be a game changer.

Evan had his first chance to engage the administration early in 2009, when Tina Tchen, director of the White House Office of Public Engagement—the office that did outreach to constituency groups— organized an initial conference call with LGBT leaders. Evan laid out the argument for applying heightened scrutiny, and then turned to marriage.

"You will never get full credit for anything you do, and you will never be in a satisfactory stance," Evan said, "until you support the freedom to marry. You will always find yourself being criticized for not having done more. It's better to do it and let us help you do it."

=

At the time, I had just moved from Massachusetts to California. Given the backlog of priorities for our community along with the severe economic challenges, I didn't expect much on the marriage front in the short term from Obama. But at the least, I expected him to do no harm, which would be a vast improvement from the last administration.

On June 11, 2009, the administration weighed in for the first time: the Justice Department issued a memo to dismiss a lawsuit challenging DOMA, a lawsuit that our community's leading legal groups didn't think was well constructed. I printed out the memo to read at home that night. Lying in bed, I began to read and was floored. The lengthy document made an elaborate case that DOMA was fully constitutional and "entirely rational," a "cautiously limited response to society's still-evolving understanding of the institution of marriage." It argued that DOMA doesn't "distinguish among persons of different sexual orientations" but instead "limits federal benefits to those who have entered into the traditional form of marriage." That seemed like an argument the religious right used to use: that "homosexuals" weren't being barred from marrying. They could marry someone of the opposite sex just like anyone else.

For me, this was a big "strike two" for this president. In December 2009, Obama had declared himself a "fierce defender" of the LGBT community, and yet he infuriated the community by having Rick Warren—the evangelical megachurch pastor from Southern California who had been an outspoken supporter of Proposition 8—give the invocation at his inauguration. Two months after the devastation of Prop 8, that felt like a slap in the face. Now the administration was advancing a particularly robust, full-throated defense of DOMA's constitutionality, in a memo that looked as though it were written by the Bush administration Justice Department on a particularly antigay day. I was so infuriated, I lay in bed unable to sleep.

The reaction in the community to the memo was fast and furious. The Human Rights Campaign ripped the brief in an open letter to the president. *AMERICAblog*, a gay-focused progressive blog, called it a "hate brief." And community leaders like Mary Bonauto pulled out of a Democratic National Committee fundraiser later that month.

Within the White House, the memo created a firestorm. The president made clear to his staff that he didn't want something like this ever happening again. The Justice Department should not be making legal arguments that were at odds with his own values. From then on, every Justice Department brief related to anything LGBT was scrutinized by the White House Counsel's office before it was filed. And at an LGBT Pride Month celebration at the White House, the president subtly acknowledged the screw up with the memo, saying about DOMA that "we have a duty to uphold existing law, but I believe we must do so in a way that does not exacerbate old divides."

President Obama called a high-level meeting in the Roosevelt Room in the West Wing of the White House to address the administration's approach to DOMA as well as to LGBT equality more generally. In attendance were nearly all of the major players: Vice President Joe Biden; senior advisers David Axelrod and Valerie Jarrett; Deputy Chief of Staff Jim Messina; Vice President Biden's Chief of Staff Ron Klain;

White House Counsel Greg Craig; Director of the Office of Public Engagement Tina Tchen; Tchen's deputy and lead liaison to the LGBT community Brian Bond; and several senior attorneys from the Justice Department.

From the outset, it was clear that the president wasn't happy with how they'd begun with the LGBT community. He wanted his team to get things in order.

There were legislative priorities: a hate crimes law, repealing the ban on open service in the military, protection from employment discrimination, and repeal of the Defense of Marriage Act. Driving those forward in a systematic way wouldn't be easy, but at least his position was clear on each of these.

What was more difficult was how to approach lawsuits challenging DOMA. They now had a strong suit meticulously crafted by Mary Bonauto and her colleagues at GLAD on behalf of multiple married same-sex couples from Massachusetts. In his role as leader of the executive branch of government, the president was responsible for faithfully executing laws on the books, and that meant defending them in court, whether or not he agreed with them. And yet he also swore an oath to "preserve, protect, and defend the Constitution." The question they were potentially grappling with was what to do when the two obligations came into conflict. This was a big and important question, and the constitutional law scholar president wanted to make sure his administration got it right. That meant a serious analysis of what the precedent was. He'd withstand the pressure from the LGBT community about his continuing to defend DOMA in court, while the Justice Department and White House lawyers undertook the legal analysis.

In the meantime, he instructed his staff to do two things. First, until the analysis was complete, they'd use much less objectionable arguments in defending the law. And secondly, knowing that this would be unsatisfying to the LGBT community and that progress on legislation would take time, he instructed his staff to proceed with administrative fixes that they could make without congressional approval.

The White House lawyers proceeded with the analysis with the seriousness the president expected. This wasn't to be a political effort to satisfy an important constituency, nor was it to be a policy analysis about how to repeal DOMA. They used what the lawyers nicknamed the "Sarah Palin Test": if Sarah Palin became president, they wouldn't want to have created any precedent that she could use to stop defending laws on the books like the Affordable Care Act. The standard they gravitated toward was whether there were any reasonable legal arguments that could be made in court for the constitutionality of an existing law. If there were, it was their duty to defend—or else they'd fail the "Sarah Palin Test."

They also began a weekly White House meeting of key aides with expertise in different areas of policy to identify and implement regulatory changes that would improve the lives of LGBT people, first taking on discrimination in housing policy. They had another such priority dropped on their desk as well, in fact literally. Chief of Staff Rahm Emanuel handed the lawyers an article he'd cut out of the newspaper about a woman who was kept from her partner's bedside in a Florida hospital as she died from an aneurysm. "Fix this," Emanuel barked. And so they solved hospital visitation for partners as well.

n late October 2010, longtime gay blogger Joe Sudbay received a call from White House Online Programs Director Jesse Lee.

Would you be interested in sitting down and talking with the president?

"Sure," a shocked Sudbay responded.

The meeting would be on the record, Lee explained. The only condition was to not get the word out in advance or else they'd be barraged by others who wanted to participate. Lee asked Sudbay to send in the required information—full name and social security number—and to show up at 2:30 p.m. on October 27. He'd be joined by several other progressive bloggers.

Sudbay had no idea why he'd been chosen. As deputy editor at the progressive, LGBT-focused *AMERICAblog*, he had been especially critical of what he saw as the bungling, slowness, and indifference of the Obama administration on policies affecting the community.

At that time in late October, there was a lot for the gay community to be upset about. The Matthew Shepard and James Byrd Jr. Hate Crimes Prevention Act, which expanded hate crimes law to cover those motivated by bias against LGBT people, had become law, yet eleven years after Matthew Shepard had been brutally murdered, the law felt like cleanup work. The community wanted three crucial pieces of legislation: the Employment Non-Discrimination Act; a repeal of the Don't Ask, Don't Tell law banning gays from serving openly in the military; and a repeal of the Defense of Marriage Act. In addition, the community badly wanted the president to come out in support of the freedom to marry.

Yet things were going terribly on all fronts. The Nancy Pelosi–led House had approved a repeal of Don't Ask, Don't Tell in May, only to see John McCain successfully filibuster the bill in the Senate, holding proponents to fifty-six votes, short of the sixty required to advance the bill. Pelosi wouldn't move the Employment Non-Discrimination Act until after the military ban repeal was complete, arguing that the community needed to stay focused on getting it done and not spread itself too thin. So both were stalled. And DOMA-repeal legislation was in its infancy, a long way from advancing.

Even worse, following the passage of the Affordable Care Act in March of that year, the Tea Party revolt was well underway. Democratic control of the House of Representatives had seemed assured for the foreseeable future, with seventy-seven more Democrats than Republicans. However, polling was increasingly showing that the GOP was almost sure to capture control of the House and maybe even the Senate that November. That would mean no more legislative advances whatsoever on matters LGBT; John Boehner, who was positioned to replace Nancy Pelosi as speaker, would simply bottle them all up. The community was beginning to despair that, after surviving eight years of George W. Bush, we might not accomplish any of our top legislative priorities under President Obama. A new direct-action group called GetEQUAL began organizing protests, interrupting the president at fundraisers and other events to demand swifter action.

Sudbay felt an enormous responsibility on his shoulders. In the past, he had been tough on LGBT people and groups that had had an audience with the president but didn't push him or hold him accountable. He wanted to make sure that he didn't do the same. By the day of the interview, Sudbay had prepped and rehearsed exhaustively. He would hit two subjects, Don't Ask, Don't Tell and marriage, and would make it as difficult as he could for the president to evade.

At about 2:15 the afternoon of October 27, Sudbay met up with another invitee, John Amato from the progressive political blog *Crooks and Liars*, at the Washington Hilton around the corner from his place. The two walked over to the White House, passed through security, and were escorted to the Jim Brady Briefing Room, where the White House press secretary did the daily briefings. A short time later, he and the four others were brought into the Roosevelt Room, near the center of the

West Wing. There were nameplates in front of the seats, and Sudbay sat down at his seat at the end of the row. Across from him and the other bloggers were five chairs, the one in the middle elevated just a bit.

Sudbay rehearsed in his mind the questions he'd be asking. He'd read that the president had a new rug in the Oval Office on which the famous Martin Luther King Jr. quote had been written, "The arc of the moral universe is long, but it bends toward justice." Sudbay wanted to somehow incorporate that quote into his questioning.

At 3:15, the president came in with several of his staff and took his seat.

For his first question, Sudbay asked about Don't Ask, Don't Tell, speaking of "disillusionment and disappointment in our community."

After answering the substance of the question, Obama argued that he understood impatience but that disillusionment wasn't justified. "It's not my place to counsel patience," the president said. "One of my favorite pieces of literature is *Letter from Birmingham Jail*, and Dr. King had to battle people counseling patience and time. And he rightly said that time is neutral. And things don't automatically get better unless people push to try to get things better. So I don't begrudge the LGBT community pushing, but the flip side of it is that this notion somehow that this administration has been a source of disappointment to the LGBT community, as opposed to a stalwart ally of the LGBT community, I think is wrong."

For his second question, Sudbay turned to marriage.

"Since you've become president, a lot has changed. More states have passed marriage equality laws. This summer a federal judge declared DOMA unconstitutional in two different cases. A judge in San Francisco declared Prop 8 was unconstitutional. And I know during the campaign you often said you thought marriage was the union between a man and a woman, and there—like I said, when you look at public opinion polling, it's heading in the right direction. We've actually got Republicans like Ted Olson and even Ken Mehlman on our side now. So I just really want to know what is your position on same-sex marriage?"

"Joe," Obama responded, "I do not intend to make big news sitting here with the five of you, as wonderful as you guys are."

Sudbay replied, "I would be remiss if I didn't ask you this question."

"Of course," Obama said.

"People in our community are really desperate to know."

"I think it's a fair question to ask," the president said. "I think that—I am a strong supporter of civil unions. As you say, I have been to this point unwilling to sign on to same-sex marriage primarily because of my understandings of the traditional definitions of marriage. But I also think you're right that attitudes evolve, including mine. And I think that it is an issue that I wrestle with and think about because I have a whole host of friends who are in gay partnerships. I have staff members who are in committed, monogamous relationships, who are raising children, who are wonderful parents. And I care about them deeply. And so while I'm not prepared to reverse myself here, sitting in the Roosevelt Room at 3:30 in the afternoon, I think it's fair to say that it's something that I think a lot about. That's probably the best you'll do out of me today."

Sudbay wanted to give it one more push. "Part of it is," Sudbay said, "that you can't be equal in this country if the very core of who you are as a person and the love—the person you love is not—if that relationship isn't the same as everybody else's, then we're not equal. And I think that a lot of—particularly in the wake of the California election on Prop 8, a lot of gay people realized we're not equal. And I think that that's—that's been part of the change in the—"

The president interjected, "Prop 8, which I opposed."

"Right. I remember you did. You sent the letter and that was great. I think that the level of intensity in the LGBT community changed after we lost rights in that election. And I think that's a lot of where the community is right now."

"The one thing I will say today," Obama replied, "is I think it's pretty clear where the trendlines are going."

"The arc of history," Sudbay said.

"The arc of history," President Obama repeated.

Sudbay was exhausted. That exchange had been really intense. It seemed significant that the president had used the word "evolve" when talking about his position, but it had gone by so quickly he wasn't sure.

He felt really good that he'd pushed, and he was happy that he'd weaved in the reference to the MLK line. As he left the room, one of his fellow bloggers told Joe that it had been quite an experience watching him and the president go back and forth.

Sudbay's instincts were right about the evolving line. National news outlets featured it prominently, as the main piece of news coming out of the blogger discussion.

=

At the time of the interview, I was just about to start at Freedom to Marry and to me, President Obama's pronouncement about evolving was an almost explicit invitation to put pressure on him to complete his evolution as quickly as possible. He'd even invited the pressure with his reference to King's *Letter from Birmingham Jail* about challenging calls for patience. So from my vantage point, it was game on!

This was a campaign we had a good chance of winning. After all, there was only one place the evolution could end up. But the deadline that felt important to me was for him to pronounce his support prior to the 2012 presidential election. If we could demonstrate that having a president supporting the freedom to marry would not hurt, and ideally would help, his reelection chances, we'd have transformed the politics of our cause in a monumental way.

It would be transformative in other ways as well. It would tell so many other conflicted Americans that it was okay to complete their own journey in favor of the freedom to marry, shifting the center of gravity on the issue. It would also give hope to LGBT people throughout the country that they truly were equal citizens worthy of the American dream. The president could propel our cause forward in a way that no other person in the country could, so I felt strongly that it was our responsibility to try to bring it about as swiftly as possible.

Practically, I knew that if it didn't happen by early summer 2012, it would be unlikely to come about prior to Election Day. It would look crass and political to come out for marriage right before the election, and his political advisers would probably tell him it wasn't worth whatever risk it entailed. And after Election Day? He could lose. He would surely have other priorities. And his advisers would likely tell him that it wouldn't be smart to "evolve" too soon after the election, as it would look as if he waited until right after he won to do so. That could cost us at least another year.

This meant we had about a year and a half to put smart, effective pressure on the president and to show his political team that this would be a politically wise position to take. In short, we needed to create an environment where the president and his advisers would consider it wiser and more comfortable to come out in support rather than to wait.

=

On November 9, 2010, lesbian New York attorney Roberta Kaplan filed a lawsuit in federal court on behalf of her client, eighty-one-year-old Edie Windsor, challenging the constitutionality of the Defense of Marriage Act. Windsor and her life partner Thea Spyer had been together for forty-four years, marrying in Canada in 2007. Thea had suffered from multiple sclerosis for much of her adult life and passed away in 2009 at the age of seventy-seven. New York State respected Edie and Thea's marriage, but because of DOMA, the federal government had treated the two as legal strangers. In practical terms, that meant that on top of grieving the loss of the love of her life, Windsor was forced to pay an estate tax bill of $363,053 to the federal government for property that they had owned. Had Spyer's name been Theo instead of Thea, Windsor wouldn't have had to pay any tax at all.

There was now real urgency on the "heightened scrutiny" question. In the court where the Windsor case would be heard, there was no precedent on the level of scrutiny applied to sexual orientation discrimination. That offered the Justice Department an opportunity to change its approach. And it had until only February to respond to Edie Windsor's complaint.

Evan reached out to Brian Bond, the deputy director of the Office of Public Liaison at the White House and lead liaison to the gay community, and reminded him of its importance.

=

On December 22, 2010, Freedom to Marry's political director, twenty-four-year-old Sean Eldridge, was returning from the White House where he'd been invited to the signing ceremony of the bill to repeal Don't Ask, Don't Tell. After the elections—when the Republicans did take control of the House—everyone had gone into overdrive to get this one done, knowing the chance to repeal the law would die once the new Congress was sworn in.

In addition to being a savvy strategist wise beyond his years, Sean was dating Facebook cofounder Chris Hughes, who had left Facebook to work as Obama's social media guru on the campaign. The two were fixtures on White House and Democratic VIP lists.

Sean boarded the Amtrak Acela for the return trip to New York City. Just before the train pulled away, several secret service agents boarded, with Vice President Joe Biden in tow, en route home to Delaware. As the train approached Wilmington and Biden got up to depart, Sean thanked him for the bill signing that morning.

"Next is DOMA, right?" Sean asked the vice president.

"Yep, we're on it!" Biden responded confidently.

Two days later, on Christmas Eve morning, Biden appeared on *Good Morning America* with George Stephanopoulos. The host asked Biden about the next frontier on gay rights—marriage. "There is an inevitability for a national consensus on gay marriage," Biden responded. "I think the country's evolving. And I think you're going to see, you know, the next effort is probably going to be to deal with so-called DOMA."

=

Early in the new year, Brian Bond arranged for Evan and Sean to meet with Valerie Jarrett, Obama's senior adviser and trusted confidant. On February 16, 2011, the two headed over to Jarrett's office in the West Wing of the White House to make their case.

Evan did most of the talking. First he laid out the argument for using heightened scrutiny in its filing on the Windsor DOMA case. Gays were a discriminated-against minority, he explained, and clearly met every legal test for heightened scrutiny. If the administration made the case for that standard of review, it would make a powerful difference.

After some back-and-forth, Evan turned away from DOMA and focused more directly on getting the president to support marriage. Sean updated Jarrett on the states Freedom to Marry was working on to advance marriage legislation—New York, Maryland, and Rhode Island—and made the case for the president to use his bully pulpit to help get marriage laws passed in those states. Evan followed up by arguing that the president needed to come out for the freedom to marry.

With all respect, he said, until you do it, you're not going to get the credit you deserve.

Evan could tell that Jarrett didn't particularly like hearing that.

If he's on the right side, she asked, and doing positive things around DOMA, why wouldn't that do the job?

"I know you think it's unfair," Evan said. But, he explained, until the president says he believes in our fundamental right to marry, there will be a disconnect and gays and lesbians won't feel that he's fully with us.

Evan handed Jarrett a copy of Freedom to Marry's *Moving Marriage Forward*, the messaging manual that Thalia Zepatos had developed on how to talk about marriage most compellingly. Now that the president was talking of evolving, Evan explained, he could be extremely powerful in modeling the journey to support that so many Americans are on.

Jarrett was a staunch defender of the president, and yet she also listened carefully, asked lots of follow-up questions, and seemingly enjoyed engaging with Evan. Evan knew that if she agreed, she would be a strong advocate inside the White House. He left the meeting feeling hopeful, but he had no idea what they'd decide to do.

By now, the lawyers at Justice and the White House were far along in their analysis, and they had concluded that using heightened scrutiny for laws classifying based on sexual orientation was absolutely appropriate. LGBT people were a small, discriminated-against group. Laws that classify people based on sexual orientation need to be evaluated extra carefully because of the history of discrimination. And in applying heightened scrutiny to DOMA, they found there were no justifiable arguments they could make for the law that would pass constitutional muster. Not defending the law would in fact pass what they continued to term the "Sarah Palin Test"—it wouldn't give any new license to a future president to refuse to defend laws on the books. The president reviewed the multiple analyses conducted on the question and concurred. DOMA was unconstitutional, and he was ready to say so.

One week later, the morning of February 23, Jarrett called Evan back to share the news. He was thrilled. He knew how unique it was for an administration to refuse to defend a law that was on the books. This was a bold and powerful step. He could also tell Jarrett was thrilled as well.

Later that morning, Attorney General Eric Holder released a statement on DOMA: "The President has concluded that given a number of factors, including a documented history of discrimination, classifications based on sexual orientation should be subject to a more heightened standard of scrutiny. The President has also concluded that section 3 of DOMA, as applied to legally married same-sex couples, fails to meet that standard and is therefore unconstitutional. Given that conclusion, the President has instructed the Department not to defend the statute in such cases."

As the law required, the attorney general sent a formal letter to House Speaker John Boehner informing him of the decision and inviting Congress to defend the law. In striking contrast to the 2009 memo, this letter declared that DOMA was rooted in "precisely the kind of stereotype-based thinking and animus the Equal Protection Clause is designed to guard against."

On March 9, 2011, the Republican-led House formally decided to mount a defense of DOMA, hiring Paul Clement, George W. Bush's former solicitor general, to defend the law in court.

=

By early 2011, the Obama campaign operation was gearing up for reelection. In Chicago, longtime Obama backer Lauren Verdich—who had co-chaired Obama's LGBT committee when he was running for US Senate—and her partner Gail Morse were being asked to engage with the campaign. But this time, they weren't having any of it. Gail in particular was pissed off. She felt as if they'd been taken for granted after the 2008 campaign. More importantly, she had become something of an absolutist on marriage. She now asked candidates for their position on marriage, and before she'd agree to make a contribution, she wanted to see something public and in writing indicating support. She'd altogether stopped giving money to the Democratic National Committee (DNC), which supported Democrats no matter their position. And she just couldn't believe Obama still wasn't on board. She told other people in the Obama inner circle in Chicago that she simply wasn't interested in reengaging.

One day in April, her secretary got a call from an Obama staffer. Where would Gail be at a specific time because the president would be calling. The secretary relayed the message to Gail with some trepidation, fearing it was a prank.

But at the appointed hour, the phone rang.

"This is Air Force One," the operator said. "Is Gail Morse available?"

"Yes, I'm here," Gail responded.

She waited a moment until she heard a familiar voice.

"Hi Gail."

It was the president calling, and she was floored.

"Do you even remember who Lauren and I are?" she asked.

"Of course I do," the president said. He explained that he was reaching out to old friends from Chicago.

"How about marriage equality?" she asked the president.

"We're going to get it done," he responded succinctly.

She told the president that she and Lauren were having a civil union, which as of January was legal in Illinois. "What are you doing on June 2?" she asked, inviting the president and Michelle to attend.

"It's kind of hard for me to travel these days," he said.

She laughed. She'd be back in the fold. But she was still really impatient about the president's reluctance to support marriage equality.

=

By the spring, Sean Eldridge was playing an active role in the Obama campaign. He and Chris had agreed to chair the New York City LGBT Leadership Council Gala, a major Democratic fundraiser that the president would headline. As the event approached, Sean saw a potential train wreck in the making, as the New York state marriage debate was heating up, and it looked as though the crucial vote in the Senate would take place at about the same time as the fundraiser. Sean reached out to Obama Campaign Manager Jim Messina and told him they needed to prepare the president and ideally have him say something positive about marriage, as everyone in attendance would be focusing on Albany with rapt attention.

On June 23, the day of the Obama fundraiser, Sean's prediction about Albany seemed prescient, as things were coming to a head. It looked as though the vote would be that night. The plan was for me to text Sean from the capitol as soon as something happened so he could give the president the news personally. But the State Senate recessed to the following day, the final day of session, and the outcome still wasn't certain. The donors who would be attending would be on edge. Many of them had invested huge amounts of time and money into the New York battle and had been on an emotional roller coaster since the 2009 defeat.

Walking past LGBT protesters gathered outside the Sheraton, Sean attended the VIP reception with Chris. As the two of them got their picture taken with the president, Sean told Obama that they had some good news of their own. "We're engaged. We're going to get married."

"That's great," the president said, with a huge grin on his face.

It was clear to Sean that the president was genuinely happy for them, but the whole thing was still uncomfortable. He had told the president he was engaged not simply to share the good news but to apply subtle pressure to get him to evolve by personalizing the cause, particularly on this eve before what he hoped would be the vote in Albany that would allow him and Chris to marry in their home state.

After an opening bit by the emcee for the event, Neal Patrick Harris, and an introduction by New York City Council Speaker Christine Quinn, Obama offered remarks. A couple of minutes into his speech, a woman in attendance interrupted the president and began shouting, "marriage, marriage."

"I heard you guys," the president said. "Believe it or not, I anticipated that somebody might," he joked, referring to the now frequent interruptions from protesters from GetEQUAL, the direct action group. But the crowd wasn't in the mood for jokes.

"Traditionally, marriage has been decided by the states," he said. "And right now, I understand there is a little debate going on here in New York about whether to join five other states and DC in allowing civil marriage for gay couples. And I want to say that under the leadership of Governor Cuomo, with the support of Democrats and Republicans, New York is doing exactly what democracies are supposed to do. There is a debate, there is a deliberation about what it means here in New York to treat people fairly in the eyes of the law and that is—look, that's the power of our democratic system."

The response to the president was the most tepid Sean had ever observed from an LGBT crowd. Everyone left deflated, including Sean. That night Obama could have helped the fight in New York State in a big way. State lawmakers were watching. Governor Cuomo was watching. And in that moment, the president chose not to.

On Sunday, the day of New York City Pride, when Cuomo and all of New York were celebrating, the *New York Times* editorial page took the president to task. Titled "Gay Marriage: Where's Mr. Obama?" the editorial said that the Thursday speech offered "a perfect opportunity to show the results of his supposed evolution on gay marriage." Instead, "the next night the Republican-led New York State Senate, of all places, proved itself more forward-thinking than the president on one of the last great civil-rights debates in this nation's history."

=

One of the biggest challenges we were up against in getting the president to move was the conventional wisdom that coming out in support was still politically perilous. For some time now, national polls were showing support for the freedom to marry at greater than 50 percent. Yet shifting the conventional wisdom in DC is hard.

To help us with this task, we sought to line up a bipartisan dream team of pollsters. We needed validators who were respected enough by those on both sides of the aisle that they would draw the attention of political journalists, pundits, and ultimately the Obama campaign. We reached out to Joel Benenson, the Obama campaign's lead pollster, and Jan van Lohuizen, the lead pollster for George W. Bush, asking them to analyze trends on the freedom to marry and write a joint memo that we'd release to the press. I honestly didn't think either would say yes, given the public role we were asking them to play. But they both agreed. They'd evaluate publicly available polling since the late 1990s and write a memo on their findings.

On Wednesday, July 27, Benenson and van Lohuizen presented their findings to assembled media at the National Press Club, with Evan Wolfson providing context and talking about the path forward. The pollsters highlighted the fact that growth in support of this cause was historically remarkable; neither had seen support grow like this, from 27 percent in 1996 to a solid majority in 2011, on any other social issue. And, they argued, this wasn't just a phenomenon of younger voters overwhelmingly supporting the freedom to marry. It also reflected a reevaluation by voters in nearly every cross-section of society they'd looked at: Democrats, Independents, and Republicans; people at all age levels; people in most religions; and so on.

They debunked the idea that our opponents would be more motivated to go to the polls because they cared much more, highlighting that "supporters of marriage for gay couples feel as strongly about the issue as opponents do, something that was not the case in the recent past."

Finally, they emphasized that given the demographics, support would move in only one direction. "As Americans currently under the age of forty make up a greater percentage of the electorate, their views will come to dominate."

The effect was exactly what we'd hoped. *Politico* ran a story titled "Bush, Obama Pollsters See 'Dramatic' Shift toward Same-Sex Marriage." It began, "In a new polling memo intended to shape politicians' decisions on the question of same-sex marriage, the top pollsters for Presidents George W. Bush and Barack Obama jointly argue that support for same-sex marriage is increasingly safe political ground and will in future years begin to 'dominate' the political landscape."

We followed up with an off-the-record media salon hosted by lesbian political commentator Hilary Rosen, featuring Joel Benenson and Evan, and attended by some of the top DC political reporters and columnists: *Washington Post*'s Ruth Marcus, *National Journal*'s Ron Brownstein, and a host of others. In a subsequent column entitled "The Good Politics of Gay Marriage," Marcus wrote that "the data ought to give comfort that Obama would not commit political suicide were he to complete the evolution he clearly knows is inevitable. In the politics of 2011, survival of the fittest does not compel opposition to marriage equality."

=

On December 14, Evan went to the White House for a second meeting with Valerie Jarrett. This time, he was full of thanks, for the administration's embrace of heightened scrutiny and strong stand on the unconstitutionality of DOMA, and for backing the Respect for Marriage Act—the bill to repeal DOMA—when it was introduced earlier in the year. But Evan wasn't there simply to congratulate. He was there to make the case that the president needed to finish the job and come out for marriage.

"With all respect, until you do it, you're not going to get credit," Evan told Jarrett.

She continued to push back, highlighting the president's record on matters LGBT, including the bold actions on DOMA.

"You're going to stop here?" Evan asked. "You won't even get full credit for this amazingly wonderful thing."

Evan shared the Benenson–van Lohuizen analysis and said that he believed strongly that supporting marriage would be to the president's electoral advantage. He'd motivate younger voters who wanted to be with him but had become disillusioned over the last four years. And he was already too pro-gay to get the votes of those for whom opposition to marriage was a deciding issue.

He also said that, more than a year after the president said he was evolving, he was now coming across as inauthentic. That couldn't be politically smart during the election season.

Jarrett bristled at the characterization of inauthenticity.

Evan then shifted to a hypothetical of how the president could come out for marriage if he decided to. "Would I love you to have the president come to some kind of Freedom to Marry event? Absolutely," Evan said. "Or have me into the Oval Office and come out with a joint statement? Of course. But that's not what you should do." "What the president should do," Evan asserted, "is sit down in an interview, in a conversational tone, with a reassuring message, and explain to the American people."

Talk about the gay and lesbian couples in his life and the love and commitment they share, Evan suggested. And talk of the journey the president and first lady have taken and why they've resolved their own inner conflict in favor of the freedom to marry. This would be authentic, and it would model for the American people the journey that so many of them are on.

Jarrett listened carefully and engaged with Evan. Yet she didn't show her cards on what she'd be encouraging the president to do.

The pollster memo and subsequent press made a splash, but as fall turned to winter in 2011 and the election grew closer, it still wasn't at all clear if the president would come out in support prior to the election. The Democratic operatives I knew thought the president wouldn't do it. After all, he was cautious by nature. And the word I got from one insider was that the campaign was most concerned about courting blue-collar white Democrats in rust belt states such as Ohio, Michigan, and Pennsylvania—not exactly our best demographic.

I, on the other hand, could not imagine how the president could go into the election still "evolving" on the issue. During a campaign, he wouldn't be able to escape media interviews, debates, and the like. Would he really say, in a presidential debate with the Republican nominee, that nineteen months later he was still evolving? That would come off as not at all credible. Also, another powerful narrative was taking hold: that younger voters who were crucial to the 2008 victory and whom Obama needed in 2012 were disillusioned and might stay home rather than vote at all. Unlike any other issue, marriage equality appeared to inspire younger voters. So if the president enunciated a position of support before the election, it would help counter the cynicism that was seemingly at the heart of younger voters' reticence to go to the polls. I believed he would move our way. I even wagered cocktails with a *Huffington Post* reporter that he would announce his support by the spring.

It seemed to me we needed another major public push. So I came up with an idea that wouldn't target the president directly but would put pressure on him nonetheless: a freedom to marry plank in the platform ratified at the Democratic National Convention. I knew that most leading Democrats—including those in the LGBT community—would not want to put direct pressure on the president. Now was the time to rally around him and get him reelected, not push him to do more. But the platform was an indirect target; we were pushing the party, not the president. Of course, since the Clinton years, the party platform for the Democrats had been largely under the control of the Democratic nominee. The campaign would want to ensure it was in sync with the candidate's position, at least on a high-profile issue such as this. So I knew it would be a pressure point.

I also knew that we could wage a serious, robust campaign that could make things difficult for the Obama campaign and the Democratic National Committee (DNC). There would be an official process for approving a platform. It would likely include field hearings around the country, and then a Platform Drafting Committee would make recommendations to a full Platform Committee, which in turn would recommend a platform for ratification to the 5,556 delegates. Polling showed that 70 percent of Democrats were with us, and I figured that, of the active Democrats who would be delegates to the convention, that number would be closer to 90 percent. Stopping an aggressive effort for a plank would come at real political cost; the Obama folks would really have to put their foot down on something the vast majority of delegates would want and something that younger voters overwhelmingly supported.

It was also the case that the Democratic National Convention was looking to be a real yawner. The press would be searching for any kind of controversy or drama. This could be it, and the press would eat it up.

My main hesitation was that it could hurt the president, whom I supported and who had done so much good for our cause. Freedom to Marry had done our own polling and electoral analysis, even using Obama's lead pollster, but if the Obama campaign's much more intricate

research showed it would be harmful for him to come out in support—
an argument that many people, including many in the gay community, were making—we'd be boxing him into an uncomfortable place.
He'd have to either reject something that much of his base—gay and
straight—cared a great deal about or do something that could hurt him
electorally. Also, I'd lived through the 2004 presidential election, when
the marriage movement was scapegoated for John Kerry's loss. If Obama
were to lose by a small margin to our Massachusetts nemesis, Mitt Romney, soon after Obama had endorsed marriage equality, I could see the
finger-pointing coming at us again. That was nerve-racking.

I thought long and hard about it, I spoke with a few confidants, and
Evan and I batted it around. I concluded that, based on everything I
knew, it was politically smart, even necessary, for him to come out in
support. During the campaign, he couldn't hide from the question.
And the evolving line was simply untenable. What's more, he'd already
taken so many proactive steps on LGBT equality that anyone who would
say they were voting against him because he supported the freedom to
marry would almost assuredly already be against him. And finally, my
mission was to drive the cause forward; the president and his team
would have enough firepower to push back if they wanted to. Evan concurred, and so we moved.

I figured this idea would be controversial enough that we wouldn't
be able to get elected national Democrats to sign up right away. So our
plan was to create momentum for the plank on social media with online
petitions, Facebook ads, and the like. We'd then go to elected Democrats beginning with our closest allies to sign them up as well as enlist
couples, parents, clergy, and other good spokespeople to testify at field
hearings throughout the country and talk to the media closer to the
summer's official platform meetings. We'd use multiple pressure points
on those serving on the committees working on the platform, and then
target individual delegates through a variety of means, building a drumbeat up to the convention.

Evan gave Valerie Jarrett and Brian Bond a simple heads-up that we
were launching this effort. These were our friends whom we wanted to
push, not our antagonists.

On February 13, we launched the campaign, which we called "Democrats: Say I Do!" We released specific platform language that we hoped to see adopted and got a few news stories, mainly in the LGBT press, about the effort.

Our slow-build plan was immediately overtaken by events. That night, Chris Geidner, a reporter with *MetroWeekly*, a DC LGBT newspaper, reached out to House Democratic Leader Nancy Pelosi's office and asked if the leader supported the initiative. Her staffer contacted us to learn more and let us know that the leader did support it and was likely to say so publicly. The next evening, Geidner ran a short piece that quoted her spokesman as saying, "Leader Pelosi supports this language." This was huge: Pelosi was disciplined and took seriously her role as a party leader. To have her on board would signal to others that this was an acceptable position to take.

The following week, the Obama campaign announced a list of thirty-five co-chairs of the campaign. Nearly everyone on the list—from Massachusetts Governor Deval Patrick to Los Angeles Mayor Antonio Villaraigosa, California Attorney General Kamala Harris, and New Hampshire Senator Jeanne Shaheen—was an outspoken supporter of the freedom to marry. This was a perfect list to mine and get as many as possible to take a stand in support of the marriage plank and then release that to the press.

I reached out to Senator Shaheen's staff, whom I'd gotten to know well through the marriage campaign in New Hampshire. I knew they'd felt as though she'd never gotten the kind of recognition she deserved for her leadership on marriage. That, combined with her importance as a senior lawmaker from a swing state, made her an attractive and potentially motivated first senator to embrace the platform initiative. She was in, enthusiastically.

"If we look historically at the Democratic platform," Shaheen told *Huffington Post* after we announced her support, "it has really been a vision document for where we'd like to go in the Democratic Party. Certainly I think this is a place where most of us believe we need to encourage the Democratic Party to go." There was no question that now this was going to turn up the heat on the White House and the campaign.

Chris Johnson, a reporter with the LGBT publication the *Washington Blade*, saw the power of this story and reached out to all of Shaheen's Democratic colleagues in the Senate to ask them if they, like Shaheen, supported the marriage plank. The subtext was, do you want to be left off a list when it goes public?

We piggybacked onto the *Blade* effort, making the case to senators, sharing the plank language, and telling them that the *Blade* would soon be calling and writing a story listing senators in support.

On Friday, March 2, the *Blade* ran its story. Titled "22 U.S. Senators Call for Marriage Equality Plank in Dem Platform," the *Blade* explained that it had solicited written statements from all fifty-three Democratic senators and had received twenty-two in support. It quoted from each. John Kerry wrote, "I think this is an historic moment for the Democratic Party in our commitment to equal opportunity and our opposition to discrimination." Senator Chris Coons of Delaware said simply, "Of course marriage equality should be a part of the Democratic Party platform."

Los Angeles Mayor Antonio Villaraigosa had been appointed the chair of the Democratic National Convention. One of the first questions he was asked was whether he supported the plank initiative. A stalwart support, his answer was that he did.

The week of March 5, both Obama campaign manager Jim Messina and White House Press Secretary Jay Carney were asked at press briefings about the initiative. Neither had much to say, but I loved it. There was no way the White House and Obama campaign weren't paying attention now. We needed to keep the pressure and momentum going.

The following week, *Huffington Post* ran a long feature article on its home page about the pickle the Obama campaign was in with the platform initiative. Titled "Barack Obama, Gay Rights Groups Struggle over Democratic Platform," the article spoke of conversations with "more than a dozen party officials and activists." It said, "The wave of support to make it a component of his convention has both surprised aides and set off a private push to keep emotions and expectations in check." It spoke of the campaign and the DNC "searching for ways to split the difference: showing support for equality but stopping short of a full-fledged endorsement." The article cited sources who said "that the DNC has been asking advocates for patience, worried that more sweeping platform language would put the president in an awkward bind."

We'd created a legitimate controversy, and the White House and campaign were coming to know that there would be a cost for the party—and the president—to not embrace the freedom to marry.

On March 25, 2012, I was watching the Sunday morning talk shows, and my ears perked up when I saw George Stephanopoulos turn to the platform initiative as he interviewed Obama senior advisor David Plouffe. Several months before, I had heard Stephanopoulos give a talk, and in response to a question, he'd said he seriously doubted that the president would come out in support of marriage prior to the election.

"I want to show the first sentence right there," Stephanopoulos said to Plouffe, showing him the language we'd developed. "It says 'the Democratic Party supports the full inclusion of all families in the life of our nation, with equal respect, responsibility, and protection under the law, including the freedom to marry.' Now, the president has said he's evolving on the issue of gay marriage, but he's still opposed. Does that mean that he's going to fight the inclusion of this plank in the Democratic platform?"

Plouffe was extraordinarily astute at staying on message and avoiding questions he didn't want to answer. "We don't even have a platform committee yet, much less a platform," he responded. He then went on to focus on the differences between the president's record and the Republicans' on all matters of equality for the LGBT community.

Stephanopoulos kept pushing. "Why can't he say what he believes on this issue?"

"He has said what he believed," Plouffe responded, in a very unconvincing way. "As he said, it's a very—this is a very important issue. It's a profound issue. He's spoken to this, you know, at—with great detail. I don't have anything to add to that."

This exchange only confirmed this story had serious legs. We needed to keep pushing.

I reached out to Steve Grossman, who was the chair of the DNC under Bill Clinton and was now the elected treasurer of Massachusetts. Steve had been a tireless supporter during the Massachusetts marriage campaign, and now I asked him to sign on to our effort and to enlist other former DNC chairs.

Steve knew the campaign wouldn't be crazy about it, but he said, "This is the right thing to do." He'd be happy to help and agreed to reach out to a list of former chairs. By April 4, we'd lined up four of them: recently retired chair Howard Dean as well as Clinton DNC chairs Don Fowler and David Wilhelm joined Steve in calling for a marriage plank. Steve penned an op-ed in the Capitol Hill newspaper, *The Hill*, explaining his reasoning. "From my vantage point," Steve wrote, "today's most crucial civil and human rights battle is how we treat our gay, lesbian, bisexual and transgender citizens. Doing the right thing here is at the core of what our Party should stand for. That's why I am joining Freedom to Marry, 22 Democratic senators, Leader Nancy Pelosi, and more than 35,000 Americans in urging the Party to include a freedom-to-marry plank in the platform that will be ratified at the Democratic National Convention in Charlotte this September."

I n early April 2012, HBO executive Michael Lombardo and his husband, architect Sonny Ward, agreed to host Vice President Joseph Biden at their home in the tony Hancock Park section of Los Angeles. The campaign had another event in the neighborhood, and it wanted a meet and greet for LGBT leaders and donors nearby to lay out their case for reelection, give people the chance to ask questions, and ultimately enlist them to help organize a major LGBT fundraiser headlined by the president.

Together for twelve years, Michael and Sonny were one of the 18,000 couples who married in California during the five and a half months it was legal in 2008. They were raising two children, seven-year-old Josie and four-year-old Johnny.

Without much time, they reached out to a group of connected gay and lesbian folks they knew, people they thought would be interested in hearing from the vice president and would potentially want to help raise significant money for the campaign. Together with Chad Griffin, the strategist who'd pulled together the Prop 8 lawsuit who was also a lead fundraiser for the president's reelection efforts, they'd lined up a crowd of about fifty representing a who's who of gay LA.

They'd made plans for their kids to be out of the house for the event, but the night before they had second thoughts. The vice president was coming to their home. This was a really big deal. They were a politically active family; the kids had even been to the White House for the annual family Easter Egg Roll. They wanted them to share in this experience too.

Michael and Sonny explained to the kids what was going on and told them they'd be staying home from school the next day to meet the vice president. At first, they had zero interest, but after awhile, they started getting excited. Johnny went up to his room and picked out a shirt and tie, and Michael and Sonny got flowers for him to give to Biden. Josie wrote a short letter to Biden on her stationery to hand to him. "Dear Mr. Vice President," it said. "We are so proud of you."

By 3:00 p.m., the time the event was scheduled to begin, a good-sized crowd had gathered in the living room. The plan was for Biden to come in through the kitchen door, chat briefly with the family, take a few pictures, and then meet with the rest of the invitees. Michael, Sonny, and the kids were in the kitchen waiting to greet the vice president, who was running late.

Finally, the electric gate to their driveway swung open, and official-looking cars pulled up. Biden came in through the screen door, holding two stuffed-animal German Shepherds. He'd owned German Shepherds since he was a child, and that was his usual shtick when he was going to a house with kids.

He said a quick, gracious hello and thank you to Michael and Sonny, and then completely lit up when he greeted Josie and Johnny. Josie gave him the letter she'd written, and Johnny handed him the bunch of yellow daisies they'd gotten for him. Biden gave the kids the stuffed dogs and sat down on the couch with the kids right next to him. I have grandchildren, he told them. You want to see them? He took out his iPhone and showed them pictures of his grandchildren and his dog Champ. He bantered back and forth with them. Josie asked him if he wanted to play freeze tag in the backyard, and the vice president just giggled.

After a while, Michael and Sonny started getting uncomfortable. Biden had arrived late, and they had fifty guests waiting who knew Biden was with them in the kitchen. They didn't want to seem as if they were hogging him to themselves. But there was no rushing Biden. He was having a great time. After about fifteen minutes, he finally said goodbye to the kids and went into the other room. There, he gave what Michael and Sonny thought was very much a stump speech. He talked about how the Obama administration certainly hadn't been perfect, but the comparison with Governor Romney couldn't be more stark. To many of the guests, it sounded like the same old BS—safe, reserved, and guarded. And he seemed to go on forever, almost as if he was filibustering, trying to run out the clock and avoid questions.

When he finally got to questions, Chad Griffin raised his hand.

You're at the home of a gay couple with two kids, Griffin said. What did you think when you came into this house? And what's your position on gay marriage?

Biden looked over at Michael. "I came in. I saw these two kids. I saw this family," Biden said. He talked more about the kids and said that it's hard to be against gay marriage. "But," he continued, "I don't make policy. The president makes policy." Biden then pivoted to a personal story. He talked of how, when he was young, he'd never known black people and he'd held some stereotypes that he'd been raised with. But then when he played sports in school, he'd gotten to know a bunch of African American kids and they became friends, and he learned the stereotypes weren't true. "It's about changing hearts and minds," Biden said. "It's about people meeting. It's undeniable. It's going to happen. How could it not happen?"

Biden gave a shout-out to *Will and Grace* creator and producer Max Mutchnick who was in attendance.

That show introduced millions of people to gay people and who gay people are, Biden said.

To Sonny, it felt as if Biden really wanted to say that he was for gay marriage, but he couldn't, so he didn't. The implication, however, was certainly clear. It was refreshing, given the constraints, to hear someone sound so genuine.

Biden took several more questions and then wrapped up and went on his way.

On Sunday morning, May 6, the phone at Michael Lombardo and Sonny Ward's home rang very early. Sonny turned over in bed and saw that it was his mother calling from Mississippi. She must have forgotten that Los Angeles is two hours earlier, Sonny thought. So he let it ring. When he saw the voice mail hit, he picked it up to listen.

"Your aunt Linda just called," Sonny's mother said excitedly. Linda had told her she'd been watching *Meet the Press* and Joe Biden had been on. The vice president had been talking about Mike and Sonny, Linda had said.

Sonny was sure it was a mix-up, a classic crazy story that seemed to happen often in his home state of Mississippi, where his mother and aunt lived. His mother knew they had hosted the vice president, and she'd shared the news with the family. Through some version of the telephone game, word must have come back that Biden had talked about them on national TV.

After listening to the message, Sonny couldn't fall back to sleep so he got out of bed, went online, and found the *Meet the Press* transcript. He scrolled through the conversation to a part about marriage equality.

DAVID GREGORY: You know, the president has said that his views on gay marriage, on same-sex marriage, have evolved. But he's opposed to it. You're opposed to it. Have your views evolved?

VICE PRESIDENT BIDEN: Look—I just think—that—the good news is that as more and more Americans come to understand what this is all about is a simple proposition. Who do you love? Who do you love? And will you be loyal to the person you love? And that's what people are finding out is what—what all marriages, at their root, are about. Whe—whether they're—marriages of lesbians or gay men or heterosexuals.

DAVID GREGORY: Is that what you believe now? Are you—

VICE PRESIDENT BIDEN: That's what I believe.

DAVID GREGORY: And you're comfortable with same-sex marriage

VICE PRESIDENT BIDEN: I—I—look, I am vice president of the United States of America. The president sets the policy. I am absolutely comfortable with the fact that men marrying men, women marrying women, and heterosexual men and women marrying one another are entitled to the same exact rights, all the civil rights, all the civil liberties. And quite frankly, I don't see much of a distinction—beyond that.

To Sonny, it sounded so much like what Biden had said at their home a couple weeks before. Biden even gave the same shout-out to *Will and Grace*, saying that it "probably did more to educate the American public than almost anything anybody's ever done so far." Sonny kept reading.

VICE PRESIDENT BIDEN: I—I was with—speaking to a group of gay leaders in—in Los Angeles—LA—two, two weeks ago. And one gentleman looked at me in the question period and said, "Let me ask you, how do you feel about us?" And I had just walked into the back door of this gay couple and they're with their two adopted children. And I turned to the man who owned the house. I said, "What did I do when I walked in?" He said, "You walked right to my children. They were seven and five, giving you flowers." And I said, "I wish every American could see the look of love those kids had in their eyes for you guys. And they wouldn't have any doubt about what this is about."

Sonny was shaking and had goose bumps. Aunt Linda was right; the vice president was talking about their family on national TV.

Biden had seemed so real, so genuine with them. He had mailed photos to them after the event and signed the one to Josie, "Next time we'll play out in the back yard," referring to her offer of playing tag. The fact that they'd really had this big impact and he was talking about their family was one of the craziest and most powerful things he'd ever experienced in his life. Tears flooded his eyes.

I hadn't watched *Meet the Press* that morning, but as soon as the Biden interview aired, I was barraged with e-mails about what Biden had said. I read the transcript carefully, and while Biden hadn't said explicitly that he supported marriage for same-sex couples, the meaning was clear and it was certainly far closer than the careful words the president had always used. I talked with Evan Wolfson about what to say, and not surprisingly to me, he wanted to be assertive, thanking Biden for his support. So we quickly put out a statement from Evan: "The personal and thoughtful way [Biden] has spoken about his coming to support the freedom to marry reflects the same journey that a majority of Americans have now made as they've gotten to know gay families, opened their hearts and changed their minds. President Obama should join the Vice President, former Presidents Clinton and Carter, former Vice Presidents Gore and Cheney, Laura Bush, and so many others in forthright support for the freedom to marry."

The White House immediately went into full damage control. "The vice president was saying what the president has said previously—that committed and loving same-sex couples deserve the same rights and protections enjoyed by all Americans, and that we oppose any effort to roll back those rights." But in fact, everyone knew he'd gone further.

Later that day, the *New York Times* decided it. Its headline was "A Scramble as Biden Backs Same-Sex Marriage." This was huge; it wasn't just Freedom to Marry asserting that the VP backed marriage. It was now the *New York Times*.

At the White House daily press briefing on Monday, spokesman Jay Carney was bombarded with questions. Carney's position was firm; Biden had said nothing new, and the president didn't have anything new to say. Adding to the White House challenge was Education Secretary Arne Duncan's definitive statement in response to a question on the MSNBC morning show *Morning Joe* that he supported the freedom to marry. *ABC News*'s Jake Tapper questioned Carney especially aggressively, stating that he didn't "want to hear the same talking points 15 times in a row" about the president's record on gay rights. After the briefing, Tapper said on the air, "Probably his mind has been made up, [so] why not just come out and say it and let voters decide? It seems—it seems cynical to hide this until after the election."

That same day, we announced that Caroline Kennedy—one of the crucial early supporters of President Obama's campaign in 2008 and co-chair of Obama's search committee for vice president—had joined the campaign to call on a marriage plank in the Democratic Party platform. Sean Eldridge had reached out to her, and she was proud to stand with us.

=

On Wednesday morning, May 9, Evan called me and told me that he'd gotten a call from Brian Bond at the White House. The president would be making an announcement that day, Brian had told Evan. He wouldn't tell Evan what it was, but it had to be about marriage. We immediately prepped a statement to release if the president did what we hoped, and we flipped on the television in our conference room in the office. In the early afternoon, I joined Evan and others on our staff in front of the TV as Diane Sawyer and George Stephanopoulos interrupted the scheduled show for an *ABC News* Special Report.

"This is an historic political and cultural moment in this country," Sawyer said.

They went to *Good Morning America* anchor Robin Roberts, showing an excerpt from a longer taped interview that would be running later that night. Roberts was seated with the president face to face in the White House as the president spoke:

> Well you know, I have to tell you, as I've said, I've—I've been going through an evolution on this issue. I've always been adamant that gay and lesbian Americans should be treated fairly and equally. And that's why in addition to everything we've done in this administration, rolling back Don't Ask, Don't Tell so that you know, outstanding Americans can serve our country. Whether it's no longer defending the Defense Against Marriage Act, which tried to federalize what has historically been state law.
>
> I've stood on the side of broader equality for the LGBT community. And I had hesitated on gay marriage—in part, because I thought civil unions would be sufficient. That was something that would give people hospital visitation rights and other elements that we take for granted. And I was sensitive to the fact that for a lot of people, you know, the—the word marriage was something that evokes very powerful traditions, religious beliefs, and so forth.
>
> But I have to tell you that over the course of several years, as I talk to friends and family and neighbors. When I think about members of my own staff who are incredibly committed, in monogamous relationships, same-sex relationships, who are raising kids together. When I think about those soldiers or airmen or marines or sailors who are out there fighting on my behalf and yet, feel constrained, even now that Don't Ask, Don't Tell is gone, because they're not able to commit themselves in a marriage.
>
> At a certain point, I've just concluded that for me personally, it is important for me to go ahead and affirm that I think same-sex couples should be able to get married.

I looked over at Evan and for the first time since I'd worked for Freedom to Marry, I could tell he was deeply, profoundly touched.

For me, I had several reactions. On a tactical, professional level as an advocate, I felt really great about the effort we'd waged to get the president on board before Election Day. There were many naysayers; nearly everyone I spoke to told me they thought he'd never come around before the election. Others were angry that we were even trying, concerned that we were hurting the president's chances for reelection. So I felt vindicated in taking this risk and driving hard. I also felt that, with the platform initiative in particular, we'd run a really great campaign.

I also was gratified to see the president talk about the freedom to marry using the messaging frame that we had developed and that Evan had, in one of his meetings with Valerie Jarrett, recommended the president use when this time came. In a relaxed, one-on-one conversation, Obama spoke of the gay and lesbian couples in his life and of their love and commitment. He talked of how he wanted to be a good role model for his children. He spoke of Christ and the lessons of his faith, talking of how it comes down to the Golden Rule for him. This would reverberate around the country in a big way.

On a deeper and more personal level, I had an abiding feeling of peace, this feeling deep inside of myself that I as a gay man was okay, was a full citizen and a full human being in this country. The president is one man, but the presidency represents more than anything else the official voice of the nation, and I felt, in a profound way, as a gay man living in America, that all was all right.

ABC News went back to Sawyer and Stephanopoulos. Stephanopoulos talked of how there were many people within the White House who didn't want to see this happen before the election. "But," he continued, "he was forced into a bit of a corner." He talked of Biden's comments and the fact that the president would be getting questioned until the election. "And probably the big key," Stephanopoulos concluded, was that "already his convention chairman, the Democratic leader in the House Nancy Pelosi, [and] a majority of Democrats were trying to put into the platform at the Democratic convention support for gay marriage. So the president [was] also facing a big fight at his convention that he did not want to have."

At the time, many pundits spoke of how Biden's comments forced the president to complete his evolution before he was ready. But later accounts show that wasn't the case. According to Mark Halperin and John Heilemann's *Double Down*, Obama had decided well before then, in 2011, that he would speak publicly of his support prior to the election. Some of his advisers were antsy about it (not Valerie Jarrett—she wanted the president to be true to himself and enunciate his values) and it dragged on, but the looming plank debate at the September Democratic convention was among the things that served as a deadline. "I'm not going to have a convention where I am taking a different position on this than my party," Halperin and Heilemann paraphrased the president as saying to senior adviser David Plouffe.

For his part, Plouffe wanted enough time before the September convention so that it didn't appear the president's hand was being forced by it. According to Plouffe in an interview with *The Dish*'s Andrew Sullivan, the deadline was set for June. He also knew that the president was inevitably going to be asked about his position as the campaign heated up so it couldn't keep dragging on. But it's clear that Obama himself had made the decision, it was a decision he believed in, and he wasn't forced by his vice president into anything other than accelerating the announcement by a couple weeks or so.

"I feel so good about that," Obama said to Plouffe right after the interview back in the Oval Office, according to *Double Down*.

Chicagoans Lauren Verdich and Gail Morse weren't moved when Obama announced his support. About damn time, they both thought. It was two weeks later that Gail had something of an epiphany. It happened when she learned that on May 19, the NAACP board of directors approved a resolution supporting the freedom to marry. Of the sixty-four board members, only two voted against the resolution, even with many older religious leaders on the board. Gail had always wanted Obama to be a chest-thumping, flame-throwing leader who would assert his support for gay marriage and demand that it happen. But that wasn't who he was, she'd come to understand. He was a consensus builder whose gentle leadership helped guide the country to resolution. The fact that the NAACP followed the president's lead showed her the value of that approach. She concluded that on marriage, Obama's invitation of a national conversation and his help in building to an emergent consensus made a big difference and was in fact the correct approach.

Some of the earliest news coverage focused on the negative reactions of a few especially vocal African American clergy, and pundits began asking if Obama's support for marriage would cause him to lose some of his African American base, or at least cause them to stay home.

Jamie Citron, the head LGBT staffer for the Obama campaign, immediately reached out to me. Could we line up clergy who would speak out in support, particularly African American clergy? I went right to work; we wanted to make this as easy as possible for the president and show Team Obama that they'd done the right thing.

In actuality, African Americans stayed with Obama, with more than 90 percent of the vote going the president's way. And turnout in November was historically high. A full 65 percent of African Americans voted, about the same as the numbers that voted in 2008, even as turnout overall declined from 62 percent in 2008 to 58 percent in 2012. What's more, support among African Americans for the freedom to marry grew massively, almost overnight, as a result of the president's announcement. A *Washington Post*–ABC poll taken two weeks after Obama's announcement found 59 percent of African Americans in support nationwide, up from 41 percent before the announcement. In the crucial state of Maryland, where the African American vote would play a major role in determining whether or not we'd win at the ballot, Public Policy Polling (PPP) in March showed that 56 percent of African Americans would vote against the law. After the president's announcement in May, PPP found that number was nearly reversed, with 55 percent backing the law. This support was a critical factor in our side prevailing in Maryland.

=

On July 28, I headed to Minneapolis for the DNC's platform-writing committee meeting to testify in support of the freedom to marry plank. By then, I assumed it was a done deal that it would happen. The DNC had not only embraced our cause but also offered to work with us to get wavering Democrats on board, as it was now in both of our interests to have as much consensus as possible on support for marriage. I sat down next to Brian Bond, who had moved from the White House to the DNC until Election Day. Brian told me that some within the party were still trying to screw around with the platform language even after the president's announcement. He gave me the best compliment a campaign guy can get. "I told them, if we didn't do it now, we wouldn't know what hit us from Freedom to Marry." And he was right. We had a delegate targeting strategy mapped out. I knew that Brian, who was partnered, soon to be married, and had worked for many years on LGBT advocacy, wanted to see this job finished. So the threat of our continued pressure had given him the cover to insist upon finishing the job.

In Minneapolis, I met up with a couple with a powerful story whom we'd flown out to testify in support of the marriage plank. Chief Warrant Officer Charlie Morgan, who served in the New Hampshire National Guard for more than seventeen years, was married to her partner of fourteen years, Karen, and together they were raising their daughter, five-year-old Casey Elena. Charlie had terminal breast cancer, and yet because of the Defense of Marriage Act, Karen and their daughter were ineligible for survivor benefits from the military.

When it was their turn, Charlie introduced herself to the committee, which included Congressman Barney Frank. She congratulated Frank on his recent marriage. Then she said in a quiet, high-pitched voice that Karen would have to do most of the talking because a tumor was pushing against her vocal chord and she was having trouble speaking.

Karen spoke of their commitment to care for one another in sickness and in health. She told the panel that she didn't have health insurance because she'd left her job to care for Charlie and their daughter and, because of DOMA, couldn't be covered under Charlie's plan.

At the end of Karen's prepared remarks, Charlie took the microphone back and extemporized.

"Ladies and gentlemen," she said in her raspy voice. "I'm not afraid to die. As a soldier, I'd accepted that possibility when I deployed. But I am afraid that Karen will not receive the benefits that we have earned as a family to take care of Casey Elena when I am gone. Thank you for the opportunity to share our story."

Barney Frank immediately chimed in. "There's no greater service people can perform than to share their personal pain in the service of trying to help other people avoid it, so we're deeply grateful."

As he wrapped up and the Morgans were about to return to their seats, Frank's cell phone rang. "Excuse me, it's my husband," he said to laughter.

Afterward, I took them out for lunch and thanked them for what they had done. I was grateful that, on what might be one of the remaining weekends of her life, Morgan was willing to fly to Minneapolis and share her story.

"Thank you," she said to me, emphatically. She told me it was an honor and that as long as she was able to speak out, she wanted to do so. It gave her final days meaning and purpose.

The committee voted unanimously to include the freedom to marry plank in the platform.

Charlie passed away nine months later, on February 10, 2013.

=

While it had been a real challenge to get the president and the party to embrace the freedom to marry, once they had, the Democratic Convention became a celebration of that embrace. That might have been a surprise to some, but it wasn't to me. My experience was that once electeds got over their caution and fear and came on board, they recognized the fact that their support represented the best of who they were and the best of what the country is. For Democrats in particular, it embodies the aspirational call for justice and equality, and the expansion of civil rights, which is the party at its best.

At the convention, speaker after speaker elevated the party's position as a point of pride. In his keynote, San Antonio Mayor Julian Castro used it to differentiate Obama from Romney, saying that "when it comes to letting people marry whomever they love, Mitt Romney says, 'No.'"

Most moving was Michelle Obama, who situated our cause squarely into the American struggle for civil rights and the American Dream.

If farmers and blacksmiths could win independence from an empire . . . if immigrants could leave behind everything they knew for a better life on our shores ... if women could be dragged to jail for seeking the vote ... if a generation could defeat a depression, and define greatness for all time ... if a young preacher could lift us to the mountaintop with his righteous dream ... and if proud Americans can be who they are and boldly stand at the altar with who they love ... then surely, surely we can give everyone in this country a fair chance at that great American Dream. Because in the end, more than anything else, that is the story of this country—the story of unwavering hope grounded in unyielding struggle.

With the president on board, Freedom to Marry asked the Obama campaign if it would urge voters in Maine, Maryland, Minnesota, and Washington to vote our way on the marriage ballot measures. I worked with the campaign on language, and on October 25, just over a week before Election Day, the campaign issued four clear and strong statements from the president, one for each state.

My favorite sign of how much the Obama campaign was embracing the president's support was when the campaign began running a get-out-the-vote radio spot targeting young voters, using marriage as a key motivator. "What are you going to tell them?" a young woman said in the spot. "You were just too busy? You didn't think it mattered? Is that what you're going to tell your friends who can't get married?" It contrasted Obama's position with Romney's on marriage, open service in the military, and abortion, and urged people to get out to vote.

And younger voters responded. In 2012, in spite of predictions of younger voters staying home because they were disillusioned, a greater percentage of the national electorate was made up of younger voters than in 2008.

—

On a chilly, sunny January 21, 2013—Martin Luther King Day and Inauguration Day—I stood on the mall with my friend, Andrew Cuomo's LGBT adviser Erik Bottcher, waiting for the president to offer his second inaugural address. About two-thirds of the way through, the president proclaimed, "We, the people, declare today that the most evident of truths—that all of us are created equal—is the star that guides us still, just as it guided our forebears through Seneca Falls, and Selma, and Stonewall." Erik and I looked at one another with our mouths agape, and I had to pinch myself. Just like the day the president had announced his support for the freedom to marry, I felt as though I was floating. For this president—in his inaugural address, on Martin Luther King Day—to speak of our struggle for equality as central to the great American trajectory of civil rights struggles was extraordinary.

Kevin Thompson, Obama's former body man for his Senate campaign whom I'd met in Ohio during the 2008 presidential campaign, was on the mall watching with his partner Greg Ratliff. He harkened back to the day in 2004 when they were driving across Illinois and Obama said he didn't know about Stonewall.

"Well, he knows what it is now," Kevin said to Greg.

Obama continued, "It is now our generation's task to carry on what those pioneers began. For our journey is not complete until our wives, our mothers, and daughters can earn a living equal to their efforts. Our journey is not complete until our gay brothers and sisters are treated like anyone else under the law—for if we are truly created equal, then surely the love we commit to one another must be equal as well."

I was still on a complete high from the Stonewall line. And here the president was talking about the equality of our love and commitment in his inaugural address. It was clear the president was talking of the freedom to marry. I was speechless.

As I went to inaugural parties afterward, the president's words were still sinking in. It dawned on me that no longer was this simply an issue for the president. His full-throated embrace of the freedom to marry, combined with the progress we were making—with his help—during his presidency, meant that gains on the cause would be a key part of the legacy he'd leave behind, perhaps one of the two most significant accomplishments along with the Affordable Care Act. I imagined a section of his presidential library dedicated to the cause of equality for LGBT people, with marriage at the center of it. And with the power of the presidency now so strongly behind us, we were considerably closer to the critical mass of support and momentum that we would need to make a successful case for marriage nationwide.

Mission accomplished.

COURTING JUSTICE

On Wednesday morning, March 27, 2013, I woke up at 7:00 a.m. in my Capitol Hill hotel room after only three and a half hours of sleep. Late the night before, I'd driven down to DC after going to a Passover Seder at my sister's place in Brooklyn, arriving at the hotel after 2:00 a.m. I showered, dressed, had a continental breakfast at the hotel, and quickly walked over to the Supreme Court. This was the day the court would hear *United States v. Edie Windsor*, the case challenging the Defense of Marriage Act.

I met up with Evan Wolfson on the large plaza in front of the court, just beyond a row of gray protective barricades. I'd been able to score two of the coveted seats that justices give to visitors. I was really happy to be able to watch these proceedings with Evan, who had been at the oral arguments for every one of the major LGBT cases that had come before the Supreme Court. That included his own oral argument before the court challenging the Boy Scouts' exclusion of gay scouts and leaders, in which unfortunately the Boy Scouts prevailed, five to four.

We ascended the first set of white marble stairs and waited in line outside, greeting others we each knew through our work in the movement. As we got closer to the front, I gazed up above the massive Corinthian columns at the simple inscription etched into the front of the building. "Equal Justice Under Law," it said.

Would it be our turn this time? I wondered.

=

In December 2012, the court announced that it would take up two marriage cases: Edie Windsor's challenge to the Defense of Marriage Act and *Hollingsworth v. Perry*, the challenge to California's Proposition 8.

The court had four DOMA challenges to choose from. It seemed unfair that the court didn't choose the case painstakingly assembled by

Mary Bonauto and the team at GLAD. Mary had begun mentally preparing for a DOMA challenge the day the Massachusetts court ruled in our favor nine years before, and she'd begun identifying couples for that challenge soon thereafter. I knew because, when I was at MassEquality, she asked me to reach out to our database of married couples for prospective plaintiffs. Mary had filed the case more than a year and a half prior to the filing of Windsor. While the court doesn't provide justification for the cases it selects, most assumed that it skipped over the GLAD case because Justice Elena Kagan had worked on it in her previous job as Obama's solicitor general and would have had to recuse herself.

That's not to say the case they did choose wasn't extraordinarily powerful. It was. Eighty-three-year-old Edie Windsor made for a compelling plaintiff. The injustice of her story—having been hit with a huge inheritance tax bill after Thea passed away—was unambiguous. And her commitment to Thea was unwavering. For more than thirty of their forty-four years together, Thea had been afflicted with multiple sclerosis and Edie had taken care of her as the disease grew progressively worse.

Arguing her case was Roberta Kaplan—better known as Robbie—a married lesbian with a young son who was a partner at top New York corporate law firm Paul, Weiss, Rifkind, Wharton & Garrison. Robbie wasn't new to high-profile cases—she had argued for the freedom to marry before the high court in New York State. The ACLU had teamed up with Robbie as co-counsel, and Robbie asked Mary Bonauto to lead the effort to assemble friend of the court briefs in support of the case.

In the Proposition 8 case, Ted Olson and David Boies sued on behalf of two California couples, Kristin Perry and Sandra Stier of Berkeley and Paul Katami and Jeffrey Zarrillo of Burbank, who were denied marriage licenses in the aftermath of Prop 8. These two lawyers teaming up had the feel of a big-screen movie: the two powerful adversaries coming together to tackle this injustice.

In fact, the case had its origins in Hollywood. Actor and producer Rob Reiner introduced Ted Olson to political strategist Chad Griffin, who pulled the case together and created a not-for-profit, American Foundation for Equal Rights, to sponsor the case.

Enlisting Ted Olson was tremendous for our side. He could argue with great credibility that support for the freedom to marry was a conservative value. His conservative Republican credentials were impeccable: He was a founding member of the conservative legal group the Federalist Society, part of the Reagan administration Justice Department, solicitor general in the George W. Bush administration, and even debate-prep coach to 2012 vice presidential nominee Paul Ryan. His treatise "The Conservative Case for Gay Marriage," which appeared on the front cover of *Newsweek*, made an especially powerful argument. "Many of my fellow conservatives," he wrote, "have an almost knee-jerk hostility toward gay marriage. This does not make sense, because same-sex unions promote the values conservatives prize." Among those he pointed to were "a stable bond between two individuals who work to create a loving household and a social and economic partnership ... thinking beyond one's own needs ... establish[ing] a formal investment in the well-being of society."

While the DOMA and Prop 8 cases had certain things in common —both were about marriage for gay couples and relied on arguments about the Constitution's Equal Protection Clause—the scope of the outcomes they sought were vastly different. The DOMA case sought to require the federal government to recognize and respect the marriages of same-sex couples granted marriage licenses in one of the nine states where it was already legal, but not to make marriage legal in states where it wasn't already. The Prop 8 case, in contrast, was go big or go home, asking the court for a national resolution whereby the court would require that every state's constitutional amendment from Alabama to Texas was invalid.

The idea of a case asking the US Supreme Court to rule for marriage nationwide wasn't new. It was the end game of the Roadmap to Victory strategy Evan had been advancing for many years. However, nearly every group working on the cause—Freedom to Marry, GLAD, the ACLU, HRC, and others—thought we hadn't yet built the critical mass of state wins or public support to think we would get a win out of the Supreme Court. As a result, they believed it was too early to bring a case like this given the risk that it could force a right-leaning court to take a position on marriage for the whole country before it was ready to take the right one. If the high court ruled that there was no constitutional right to marriage for same-sex couples, it would be a huge legal and moral defeat and momentum setback. In a legislature, you could go back year after year to pursue a victory. However, once the Supreme Court rules, the justices are loath to reconsider the ruling for some time.

Freedom to Marry's Roadmap to Victory called for first winning a critical mass of states and building and diversifying a national majority. Then we could make the case that marriage equality was the norm and it was up to the Supreme Court to finish the job. Evan liked to point to *Loving v. Virginia*, the case that found all state bans on interracial marriage unconstitutional. At the time of *Loving,* thirty-four states had already gotten rid of their bans even though public support for eliminating such bans was at only 30 percent.

At the time that the Prop 8 case was brought in May 2009, marriage for gay couples was legal in four states—Massachusetts, Connecticut, Iowa, and Vermont—and support nationwide was in the mid-40s. That clearly wasn't a critical mass of either. I too thought we had a lot more work to do—more states to win, more unexpected allies to surface, more support to grow—before the Supreme Court would rule our way on a national freedom to marry ruling.

By December of 2012, when the court announced that it was taking the *Perry* case, we had now won nine states plus the District of Columbia and had grown public support to greater than 50 percent. That still seemed insufficient for the court to decide to finish the job.

Thankfully, a full national win (or loss) wasn't the only option before the court in the Prop 8 case. Another option gave the court an "out" if it didn't want to take a position on the constitutionality of every state ban. The court could rule that our opponents didn't have the "standing" to bring the case to the Supreme Court in the first place. Since Olson and Boies had won in district court, the state of California—in the persons of the governor and attorney general—had to decide whether or not to appeal the ruling. They elected not to. So the supporters of Prop 8—the advocates who had collected signatures and launched the ballot campaign—brought the appeal. But there were serious legal questions about whether they could do so.

To have "standing," a party has to demonstrate "personal and tangible harm," not simply a "generalized grievance." Whether they could show personal, actual harm from gay couples' marrying was questionable at best. And if the Supreme Court found that the proponents didn't have standing, then it could punt. The district court order would stand and nothing more. That would mean the restoration of marriage in California while leaving the national question for another case in the future.

Now that these two cases were in front of the Supreme Court, all of the previous debates about timing and strategy were only distractions. We had one imperative: to make a public case over the next six months that the country was ready for the broadest rulings possible.

=

The conventional wisdom was that, on both cases, the four reliably liberal justices would be sympathetic and at least three of the four reliably conservative justices would be hostile.

The key to both cases looked to be seventy-six-year-old Justice Anthony Kennedy, the Reagan appointee from Northern California who was often the swing vote on the court. On economic matters, Kennedy was a consistently conservative vote. However, on gay rights, Kennedy had written the two landmark Supreme Court opinions, one striking down a Colorado constitutional amendment that prohibited all laws protecting gays from discrimination and the second striking down all state laws banning sodomy. In the latter opinion, Kennedy spoke poignantly of "homosexual persons" as a class of people who are "entitled to respect for their private lives." He wrote of how the drafters of the Fifth and Fourteenth Amendments to the Constitution "knew times can blind us to certain truths and later generations can see that laws once thought necessary and proper in fact serve only to oppress." He continued, "As the Constitution endures, persons in every generation can invoke its principles in their own search for greater freedom." That was certainly an invitation to return to the court as we battled for respect for our relationships.

Some court watchers predicted that Chief Justice John Roberts also might be sympathetic. They pointed to his time in private practice, when Roberts's firm represented those challenging the antigay Colorado constitutional amendment and Roberts had been especially helpful in preparing for court. In addition, his monumental opinion in 2012 upholding the Affordable Care Act gave some hope that he was tacking toward the center.

It's impossible—and inappropriate—to directly "lobby" the court. However, knowing that justices live in the real world, stay apprised of current events, and follow what's going on inside the Beltway with their two sister branches of government meant that it was time to make our best case possible that the country was ready for bold rulings.

The most tangible demonstration of progress and momentum would be to win additional states. Tim Gill's Action Fund, along with local players, had been active in legislative elections in Delaware, Illinois, Minnesota, and Rhode Island to elect pro-equality majorities. We at Freedom to Marry now moved aggressively to build legislative campaigns in each state, working closely with local and national partners. None of these states offered an easy pathway to victory, but we had the opportunity to win each before June.

Separately, Freedom to Marry joined together with the Human Rights Campaign and the groups leading the litigation battles—the ACLU, which had teamed up with Robbie Kaplan on the Windsor case; the American Foundation for Equal Rights, which was leading the Prop 8 case; and GLAD, which was helping on Windsor—on an all-out media campaign to demonstrate that the country was ready. We ran ads during the Sunday morning news shows demonstrating bipartisan support for the cause. My favorite spot used clips of Republicans Laura Bush, Dick Cheney, and Colin Powell each expressing support for the freedom to marry and then concluding with President Obama's powerful words at his inaugural address.

We also worked to secure coverage of stories in newspapers and on television news that would help make our case. Now that gays and lesbians could serve openly in the military, we were able to highlight compelling stories of military families who were sacrificing for their country and yet as a result of DOMA were being denied health care benefits, the ability to live together on a base, and even the ability to be buried together in a military cemetery.

None was more potent than the story of Tracy Dice, a veteran herself who'd been deployed to Iraq and whose wife had been killed in the line of duty in Afghanistan. The Pentagon was required to treat her as a legal stranger, notifying her spouse's parents of the death instead of Tracy, denying Tracy the flag that draped her wife's casket, and even denying her the wedding ring from her spouse's finger. The injustice of this story was palpable. Tracy became an influential spokesperson who was very generous in sharing her heartrending story in the media.

In federal court, including the Supreme Court, independent groups are allowed to file "amicus"—or "friend of the court"—briefs, to add compelling, authoritative voices to the mix to help make the case. These also provided good media opportunities.

Two briefs in particular that the legal teams developed provided excellent opportunities to demonstrate unexpected support. Former RNC Chair Ken Mehlman assembled a brief with an impressive assortment of high-ranking Republicans making the case for a full, national court ruling. It included top officials from the Reagan and both Bush administrations; current and former members of Congress; six former governors, including recent presidential candidate Jon Huntsman of Utah and former Department of Homeland Security Chief Tom Ridge of Pennsylvania; party leaders; and top campaign operatives, more than 100 in all. This brief made a huge splash in the media, with the narrative focused on emerging support in the Republican Party.

The second brief was one that GLAD developed highlighting corporate opposition to DOMA. It featured more than 200 companies, from Alcoa to Xerox, and included a who's who of Wall Street financial firms such as Goldman Sachs, Citigroup, and Morgan Stanley. This too made a splash in the media, and through our media campaign, we amplified the coverage significantly.

On March 15, we received a great gift. Ohio Senator Rob Portman, the respected conservative Republican who had served as George W. Bush's budget chief and had been a lead contender to be Mitt Romney's running mate, spoke publicly about the fact that his son had come out as gay and that he now supported the freedom to marry. "It allowed me to think of [the freedom to marry] from a new perspective," Portman said in a television interview. "And that's of a dad who loves his son a lot and wants him to have the same opportunities that his brother and sister would have—to have a relationship like Jane and I have had for over twenty-six years."

This one was tectonic. Most of those who had signed the GOP amicus brief were appointed officials or former electeds. To have a currently elected, well-respected mainstream conservative Republican from the Midwest, one with rumored ambitions for higher office, talk about his love for his son and resultant support for marriage was a huge momentum boost and another sign of how far the country had come.

By the time of the oral arguments, which would be back to back on March 26 for Prop 8 and March 27 for DOMA, I felt we'd done a very solid job of making our case.

=

On my drive down to DC the night before the DOMA hearing, I listened to the oral arguments in the Prop 8 case that had taken place earlier in the day. I was told by court experts not to make judgments based on questioning in oral arguments; justices could be playing devil's advocate, for instance. But it was impossible not to be disheartened. From across the ideological spectrum, there was little sympathy from the justices for a ruling that would overturn all statewide bans and guarantee the freedom to marry nationwide.

Justice Antonin Scalia wasted no time laying into Ted Olson, who was standing before the justices as he had so many times when he was George W. Bush's solicitor general. "When did it become unconstitutional to exclude homosexual couples from marriage?" Scalia asked. "1791? 1868? . . . When did the law become this?" It was a rhetorical question designed to score points. Scalia knew there was no time and date that you could point to when the claims of discrimination against gays— or women or other disadvantaged groups for that matter—had risen to the level of being deserving of constitutional protection. There certainly was no organized demand for equality for gay people in 1791 or 1868. And if Scalia was applying the standard that gays had to be enumerated as a protected group in the Constitution, that clearly wasn't the case.

"When did it become unconstitutional to prohibit interracial marriages?" Olson responded, asking similarly impossible-to-answer questions. "When did it become unconstitutional to assign children to separate schools?"

After some more back-and-forth, Olson pointed out how bizarre and unfair the question was. "I can't answer that question and I don't think this court has ever phrased the question in that way."

"I can't either," Scalia replied, ignoring the second part of Olson's response. "That's the problem. That's exactly the problem."

Chief Justice Roberts joined in, seemingly showing some of his cards about where he stood. Speaking of marriage for gay couples, Roberts said, "If you tell a child that somebody has to be their friend, I suppose you can force the child to say, this is my friend, but it changes the definition of what it means to be a friend." His point was that you could force people to call a same-sex relationship a marriage, but it still didn't mean that's what it really was.

Didn't sound like an ally to me.

Kennedy raised points that seemed to bolster each side. He spoke of the government interest in protecting children being raised by gay parents but also expressed serious concerns about making a sweeping ruling. "We have five years of information to pose against 2,000 years of history or more," he asserted, even wondering aloud why the court had taken up the case to begin with.

Conservative Justice Samuel Alito raised similar concerns. "Traditional marriage has been around for hundreds of years. Same-sex marriage is very new." He continued, "You want us to step in and render a decision based on an assessment of the effects of this institution which is newer than cell phones or the Internet?"

Even the liberal justice Sonya Sotomayor expressed skepticism about deciding this broad question now. "We let issues perk," she observed. "We let racial segregation perk for fifty years from 1898 to 1954." Perhaps the Supreme Court would be better off sitting this one out, she posited.

That would have the effect of allowing the lower-court ruling to stand and for marriages to resume in California, but it would not overturn the bans in other states.

Even with the negative tenor of the questioning, there were still a couple of things that were very encouraging. First, the question of whether our opponents had standing to bring this case in the first place was being seriously considered, and it seemed, from the very technical questioning on the subject, as though it wouldn't be difficult for the court to conclude that it did not. Given the seeming reluctance to make a broad, sweeping ruling, that would be the next best outcome.

Secondly, it was clear to me how outlandish our opponents' central argument was.

Lawyers for Prop 8 had to come up with some distinction between gay couples and straight couples that didn't appear to be based in prejudice to explain why states should be able to deny marriage to gay couples. In their most important argument ever, the best they could come up with was that marriage is necessary for heterosexuals in order to restrain their urges and ensure they procreate responsibly. By contrast, such restraints weren't necessary for gay couples because they couldn't procreate naturally.

Marriage, our opponent's lead attorney argued, "make[s] it less likely that either party to that marriage will engage in irresponsible procreative conduct outside of that marriage."

This argument was absurd to me. First, while it made a case for why marriage might make sense for straight couples, it didn't provide any rationale about why same-sex couples should be excluded. More fundamentally, if the best our opponents could do, before the US Supreme Court, was to argue that the purpose of marriage is about shackling straight people in order to ensure they didn't have babies out of wedlock, it was clear to me they were really grasping at straws. I knew from intuition, experience, and years of research that the American people believed marriage was about love and commitment, as well as the freedom to enter into a permanent relationship with the person of one's choice. The idea that marriage was really about coercion would never fly. If this was their central argument, I had great confidence we were ultimately going to win national resolution in the courts.

As I went to sleep, I hoped that the tenor of the questioning would be a lot more sympathetic in the next day's case.

=

Evan and I passed through a security checkpoint and entered the Great Hall of the court. Double rows of marble columns rose to the ceiling of the room that was full of busts of former chief justices. We stood in the line for guests of the justices, had our names checked off a list, and then waited in another line, this one to deposit our belongings in lockers. The court was extremely strict about what you could bring into the courtroom—certainly no cell phones, cameras, or recording devices. After emptying our pockets, we passed through another metal detector and then entered the courtroom and were ushered to our seats.

After settling in, I turned to my right, and just a couple of rows up and across the aisle was Edie Windsor. I thought about what must have been going through her head as she got ready to watch the nine justices debate whether her lifelong relationship with the love of her life deserved equal protection under law or whether it was acceptable for the federal government to treat her and Thea as strangers.

As I took in all the activity in the room—lawyers entering and greeting one another and tourists streaming through on guided tours—my attention kept drifting back to Windsor. A who's who of notables came by to wish her well: Ted Olson, Nancy Pelosi, and Valerie Jarrett, who had apparently taken the morning off to observe the proceedings.

At about 9:50 a.m., a stern-looking security guard stepped into the center aisle to give us instructions. Stand when the justices enter, no talking, no noise, and so on. At 10:00 a.m., a buzzer sounded, and we all rose as the justices entered. Chief Justice Roberts, along with the two most senior justices, Scalia and Kennedy, emerged from the center, with two groupings of three emerging from each side. They all took their seats behind the large mahogany bench. Chief Justice Roberts first did pro forma introductions of new members of the Supreme Court bar.

Then, at 10:18 a.m., the clerk called the case, "United States versus Edith Schlain Windsor, in Her Capacity as Executor of the Estate of Thea Clara Spyer, et al."

After in-depth arguments about procedural issues in the case, the court turned to the substance. Paul Clement, the former George W. Bush solicitor general who was representing the House Republicans in defending DOMA, began.

Clement argued that the Defense of Marriage Act was appropriately limited in scope. It didn't tell states how to define marriage. It simply defined marriage for federal purposes, which was the right of the federal government to do.

My attention was squarely on Justice Kennedy, and he jumped in early. He challenged Clement's notion that the federal government was simply allowing the states to define marriage as they want. Marriage "has 1,100 [federal] laws, which in our society means that the federal government is intertwined with the citizens' day-to-day life." By denying all benefits and protections to married gay couples through DOMA, Kennedy argued, the federal government was very much interfering in the state's ability to determine who was married and who was not.

Clement then made the case for "uniformity," that it was appropriate and rational for the federal government to use a single, uniform definition of marriage.

"It's not really uniformity," Kennedy asserted, "because it regulates only one aspect of marriage. It doesn't regulate all of marriage." Kennedy's point was that the federal government wasn't creating a uniform definition of marriage with respect to age, residency requirements, or any other criteria; it was only creating uniformity with respect to the sexual orientation of the couple. And that was problematic.

Clement asserted that, with a stance of uniformity, the federal government was benignly letting "the states develop this and let[ting] the democratic process deal with this."

Kennedy again challenged the assertion, arguing that "Congress doesn't help the states which have come to the conclusion that gay marriage is lawful. . . . We're helping the states if they do what we want them to do."

In short, the federal government was strongly encouraging states to deny the freedom to marry by withholding the federal benefits accompanying marriage from married same-sex couples—and that was an inappropriate use of federal power.

As Clement returned to the argument that DOMA represented a neutral, benign stance, Justice Ruth Bader Ginsburg jumped in, speaking of the myriad ways the federal government explicitly advantages married couples. "Your partner is sick," she said. "Social Security. I mean, it's pervasive. It's not as though, well, there's this little Federal sphere and it's only a tax question. It's, as Justice Kennedy said, 1,100 statutes, and it affects every area of life." She continued, "There's two kinds of marriages. . . . There's full marriage, and then there's sort of skim milk marriage."

I got a big grin on my face. I wrote down "skim milk marriage" on my yellow legal pad, underlined it, and underneath it wrote "line of the day" and showed it to Evan. The analogy was a little awkward, but it made the case in a simple, understandable way that DOMA harmed and disrespected the marriages of gay couples, treating them as second-class marriages. I wondered if I'd ever be able to put skim milk in my coffee again.

Justice Elana Kagan, the newest justice, then went directly after Clement's assertion that it was a desire for "uniformity" that was behind DOMA. She argued that, historically, "the only uniformity that the Federal Government has pursued is that it's uniformly recognized the marriages that are recognized by the State." That is, the federal government had never created its own definition of marriage until it decided to exclude same-sex couples and passed DOMA.

"Maybe Congress had something different in mind than uniformity," she asserted. "Do we think that Congress's judgment was infected by dislike, by fear, by animus, and so forth?"

She then quoted from the House report that accompanied the 1996 DOMA law: "Congress decided to reflect and honor a collective moral judgment and to express moral disapproval of homosexuality."

There were gasps in the courtroom, and Clement appeared a bit shaken as he responded that that was not the only justification for the law and that not all the reasoning behind a law had to be valid in order for it to be constitutional.

Soon Clement's time was up, and it was Robbie Kaplan's turn.

Robbie had prepared for this day for months, participating in moot court after moot court, rehearsing how she'd respond to so many different questions. She'd been intimidated by warnings about how different it would be to argue before the Supreme Court, as opposed to the trial courts where she usually argued for her clients. So she prepared relentlessly. She developed arguments to appeal to Justice Kennedy in particular, even creating a crib sheet of the best quotes from Kennedy's majority opinions in the two major gay rights cases. Over and over, she repeated aloud the phrase "times can blind." That was Kennedy's memorable line from the *Lawrence v. Texas* opinion invalidating antigay sodomy laws, about how people can discover that a law that seemed perfectly appropriate at one time actually served to oppress. Two nights before, while leading a forty-eight-person Passover Seder at the Mandarin Oriental Hotel for her legal team and extended family—of which Edie was now a de facto part—Robbie still couldn't stop repeating the quotes in her mind.

"Times can blind." She must have said it 7,000 times.

That day, as Robbie rose to present her argument, she was feeling focused and at ease.

"Mr. Chief Justice, and may it please the Court," she began.

"Because of DOMA, many thousands of people who are legally married under the laws of nine sovereign States and the District of Columbia are being treated as unmarried by the Federal Government solely because they are gay. These couples are being treated as unmarried with respect to programs that affect family stability, such as the Family Leave Act, referred to by Justice Ginsburg. These couples are being treated as unmarried for purposes of Federal conflict of interest rules, election laws and anti-nepotism and judicial recusal statutes. And my client was treated as unmarried when her spouse passed away, so that she had to pay $363,000 in estate taxes on the property that they had accumulated during their 44 years together."

As with the other attorneys, she was immediately interrupted. Scalia, Alito, and Roberts began peppering her with questions, offering up complicated hypotheticals that were clearly designed to trip her up.

As Roberts began his questioning, Robbie thought he looked angry, his lip appearing to quiver. "So eighty-four senators . . . base their vote on moral disapproval of gay people?" Roberts asked, referring to the 1996 vote on DOMA.

Robbie knew better than to say that eighty-four senators were bigots. She had the perfect retort. "What is true, Mr. Chief Justice," she replied, calmly, "is that times can blind."

"Back in 1996," she continued, "people did not have the understanding that they have today, that there is no distinction, there is no constitutionally permissible distinction—"

Roberts interrupted, "Well, does that mean—times can blind. Does that mean they did not base their votes on moral disapproval?"

Robbie responded, "No. Some clearly did. I think it was based on an incorrect understanding that gay couples were fundamentally different than straight couples, an understanding that I don't think exists today and that's the sense I'm using that times can blind. I think there was— we all can understand that people have moved on this, and now understand that there is no such distinction. So I'm not saying it was animus or bigotry; I think it was based on a misunderstanding of gay people."

The chief justice then turned to the question of why so many people had adjusted their thinking about marriage for same-sex couples. "I suppose," he posited, "the sea change has a lot to do with the political force and effectiveness of people representing, supporting your side of the case?"

"I disagree with that, Mr. Chief Justice," Robbie said. "I think the sea change . . . was an understanding that there is no . . . fundamental difference that could justify this kind of categorical discrimination between gay couples and straight couples."

Roberts wouldn't concede the idea that many Americans had simply evolved and come to believe—through their own lived experience— that loving and committed same-sex couples wanted to marry for the same reasons they themselves did and that they deserved that right.

He grew more provocative: "As far as I can tell, political figures are falling over themselves to endorse your side of the case."

Court gurus had told Robbie to look at Justice Kagan for cues as to how she was doing. Kagan was known to intervene if she thought an

attorney she agreed with was going off course or if one of her conservative colleagues was scoring too many points. Robbie glanced at Kagan,
and she was all smiles. This must be going all right, Robbie thought to
herself. And a new line came to her, one she'd never rehearsed. The opposite of moral disapproval was moral understanding. That's what was
going on in America today.

"I think," Robbie said, "it comes from a moral understanding today
that gay people are no different, and that gay married couples' relationships are not significantly different from the relationships of straight
married people."

Time soon ran out on Robbie's questioning and then, shortly after,
on the oral arguments.

As I exited, I was feeling great. Even taking into account the caveats
about reading too much into oral arguments, Justice Kennedy seemed
to be very uncomfortable with DOMA.

I walked outside and gazed out beyond the barrier that the police had
erected and saw thousands of advocates, many with rainbow flags and
homemade signs. It gave me an even stronger sense of how historic this
day was. I then walked over to the scrum of a couple dozen reporters,
with microphones and cameras all ready for Edie Windsor and Robbie
Kaplan.

As the two walked arm in arm out of the Supreme Court building,
the crowd went crazy, chanting "Edie, Edie." Windsor had a tremendous smile on her face and looked as if she was soaring. She stepped up
to the microphone. "Somebody wrote me a large speech which I'm not
going to make," Windsor said forcefully, holding a crumpled up speech
in her hand.

"I am today an out lesbian," she continued, "who just sued the United
States of America, which is kind of overwhelming for me."

"I wanted to tell you what marriage meant to me," Windsor said.
She explained that, even though she was seventy-seven and Thea was
seventy-five when they married, it made a huge difference. "It's a magic
word. For anyone who doesn't understand why we want it and why we
need it, it is magic."

It seemed to me as though Windsor was responding directly to Roberts, who appeared genuinely perplexed about why so many Americans were coming to the conclusion that gay couples should be able to marry.

With the thousands who had gathered continuing to chant her name, Windsor finally told the reporters, "There are a lot of people who came here to see me, and I'm just going to go see them." She made a beeline right toward the barrier and into the crowd, appearing almost as though she were going to dive in and crowd surf, letting her admirers hold her up. It was beautiful to witness. For so much of her life, Windsor felt as if she had to cloak her relationship in secrecy, wearing a ring-shaped diamond pin to commemorate it instead of a more traditional ring out of concern for being outed at work. Today, she was being celebrated as a lesbian hero who wouldn't accept being wronged by her government without a fight.

=

Each week, justices typically take secret votes on how they are inclined to rule on the cases they heard that week. That vote determines who writes the majority and minority opinions. But that initial vote didn't mean we would stop trying to build and grow momentum. As drafts of opinions were passed back and forth, justices could change their minds. It was widely reported that Chief Justice Roberts had changed his position on the constitutionality of the Affordable Care Act late in the prior session. So we wanted to keep driving hard until the end.

On Capitol Hill, the momentum that took hold before the oral arguments continued. For some time, we'd had success enlisting Democratic senators representing blue states to our side. But red state Democrats were, on the whole, not willing to budge, in spite of persistent lobbying and organizing. However, in a several week period after oral arguments, eleven Democratic senators representing states including North Dakota, South Dakota, Montana, Indiana, and Alaska announced their support. And another Republican, Senator Mark Kirk of Illinois, joined Portman on the GOP side. The power of Edie Windsor's story and the unfairness of the DOMA statute had clearly had an impact. And Portman's announcement had shifted the center of gravity. Democratic lawmakers had to ask themselves: if a conservative Republican from the heartland had the guts to do this, then why can't I? The LGBT blogosphere—with our encouragement—pushed the Democrats hard, asking whether they wanted to be on the right side of history or, conversely, to be the last Democrat left opposing marriage equality. We soon had the backing of fifty-four senators. Only three Democrats— all from the South—remained opposed.

I directed my attention back to state campaigns to pass marriage legislation. As was usually the case, each of the four target states— Delaware, Illinois, Minnesota, and Rhode Island—was a real challenge. Employing all of the tactics we had used in Massachusetts and New York, the state campaigns we were part of were able to drive legislation to the finish line in all but Illinois. On May 2, I traveled to Providence, Rhode Island, as Governor Lincoln Chafee inked that state's marriage bill into law. That was especially sweet, as we were finishing what I'd helped start in Massachusetts with GLAD years before: to win all six New England states by 2012. We were a few months late to do full justice to the plan that GLAD had nicknamed "Six by Twelve," but it was still a great accomplishment. At a reception after the bill signing, Chafee told me that it was his happiest day in office.

Five days later, I was in Dover, Delaware, for the crucial final vote in the State Senate. After a multihour, extremely vitriolic debate, the bill passed by a vote of twelve to nine, and one hour later, Governor Jack Markell signed it into law. We now had an eastern seashore where every state had enacted freedom to marry laws from Maine to Maryland, with the glaring exception of New Jersey. That state's governor, Chris Christie, had vetoed the bill that was approved by the New Jersey Legislature in 2012 and Republican lawmakers were fearful of crossing him and supporting an override, with at least one senator who wanted to vote our way worrying aloud to constituents that Christie would punish the district by removing Hurricane Sandy money if he crossed him on marriage.

On May 14, six days after the Delaware bill was signed into law, the State Senate in Minnesota sent marriage legislation to Governor Mark Dayton, who signed it the next day. With his signature, Minnesota became the first state away from the coasts to approve the freedom to marry legislatively, joining Iowa—which had won through a unanimous court ruling in 2009—as beacons of equality in the heartland.

In less than two weeks, we'd added three new states. It was hard to imagine a more forceful demonstration of momentum than that.

As I was focusing on the state work, Evan took on the crucial task of preparing the administration for a DOMA victory. Even with a win at the Supreme Court, how the administration implemented the opinion would make a profound difference to couples on the ground.

The key issue was how the federal government would treat the marriages of same-sex couples who weren't living in a state that respected the marriage. For example, what would happen if a couple married in Massachusetts and then moved to Ohio? Would the feds still treat the couple as married or not? How about a couple that lived in Alabama, traveled to Washington, DC, to get married, and then returned home? This was an issue the federal government had never looked at in a comprehensive way because it never had to. Until the issue of gay couples marrying came about, states routinely recognized marriages performed in other states.

GLAD's Mary Bonauto took the lead in investigating this question for our side, and it turned out that, on the federal level, there was no standard answer for what constituted a marriage to the federal government. Agencies had their own practices, which in most cases were guided not by law but by regulation or custom.

Evan recognized how crucial this question was. And so, working closely with Mary and other legal groups within the movement, Evan rallied ten organizations behind a simple yet bold proposal to the administration: respect all marriages legally performed, irrespective of where the couple lived, through every part of the federal government.

If the federal government were to do so, it would hasten the day when we'd get to full national resolution. First, it would put the weight of the federal government on the side of equality, which would encourage states that still denied marriage to put an end to their discriminatory laws. Second, because the federal benefits were so important—social security protections, tax benefits, immigration status, and more—committed couples from every part of the country would undoubtedly travel to one of the marriage states, take their vows, get their license, and then return home. That would mean that there would be a significantly greater numbers of married couples whose stories of love and commitment we could amplify through the press in the South, the Mountain West, and elsewhere where the freedom to marry wasn't yet legal. We would also be able to highlight the problems created by the patchwork that currently exists in the country; as Evan liked to put it, marriages shouldn't sputter in and out like cell phone service based on what state a couple happened to be in at the moment.

Most importantly, federal respect for all legal marriages would improve the lives of huge numbers of families in a myriad of ways.

On Friday, May 3, Evan forwarded a confidential memo to the White House on behalf of Freedom to Marry and nine other organizations laying out the case. "As this Administration has poignantly observed, lesbian and gay individuals have long endured a terrible history of government-sanctioned discrimination and deprivations," the memo stated. "This Administration can ensure that, if DOMA is struck down, the federal government is no longer complicit in discriminatorily treating married same-sex couples as unmarried with all the hardship and injustice that would entail." The White House promised to take it seriously, but they didn't want to engage in implementation discussions until after a ruling. They asked Evan and the other advocates who had prepared the memo to plan to talk the afternoon of the ruling.

As May turned to June, I began tuning into *SCOTUSblog*, a website that provided instantaneous updates of the Supreme Court goings-on, every Monday and Thursday, the customary days when the Supreme Court issued decisions. I'd visit the site a little before ten, gaze at the screen as the bloggers told us about each decision that was being announced, and then wait for them to give us the all clear—that there would be no more cases announced that day.

My strong hunch was that the marriage cases would be last. I would often say, only half jokingly, that the justices would rule on them and then go home, lock the doors, and hide. In both Legislatures and courts, it seemed as though marriage decisions came only when decision makers couldn't postpone them any longer. That, plus the flair for the dramatic that the Supreme Court seemed to have, often waiting until the end of the term to announce the most anticipated decisions, made me pretty confident we'd be last. But no one knew, so we had to be ready.

Finally, after a month of that routine, on Tuesday, June 26, the court announced that the next day would be the final day of the session. We'd get our decisions. On Wednesday morning, I was feeling relatively calm. I think it was a combination of having no ability to influence the outcome and a strong feeling that we'd win on DOMA.

The court released decisions by reverse seniority of the justice who wrote the opinion. Since Kennedy was number two in seniority—after the chief justice, who was always first—I crossed my fingers hard that the first opinion announced would be on DOMA written by Kennedy and that the chief justice had written an opinion dismissing the appeal of the Prop 8 challenge on standing. This was the best outcome that seemed possible. I presumed that, if we were to win on DOMA, Kennedy would elect to write the majority opinion, burnishing his place in history as the court's leader on protecting freedoms for LGBT people.

I tuned in to *SCOTUSblog* on my laptop, and at just before ten, the back-and-forth online chatter ceased. The blog reported as follows:

10:01 AMY HOWE: Here's Lyle with the first opinion. It's DOMA.
10:02 AMY HOWE: 5–4 per Kennedy.

"Yes!" I shouted.

Evan texted me from the set of MSNBC, where he was about to offer his reactions live. "DOMA struck down. EP [equal protection]. Great."

At 10:03, *SCOTUSblog* quoted from the decision: "DOMA singles out a class of persons deemed by a State entitled to recognition and protection to enhance their own liberty."

"Woo-hoo," I yelled through our office. This was a full win!

In the courtroom from the bench, Scalia was reading from his dissent, a practice that justices did when they felt especially strongly about the wrongness of an opinion. So we had to wait until he was finished for the Prop 8 ruling to be announced. I paced near our communications director's desk, leaning over her shoulder as she finished up our press statement. Finally, more than twenty minutes later, they were ready to announce the next ruling.

> 10:26 AMY HOWE: We have Perry. By the Chief. The petitioners did not have standing to appeal the district court order.

"Yeah," I shouted again. This meant the district court ruling would stand, and more than four and a half years later, the pernicious Prop 8—the constitutional amendment that had crushed the spirit of our community and had drawn me across the country to try to undo it—was lifted from our shoulders.

I printed out the DOMA opinion and dashed uptown to do an interview with the *Wall Street Journal*. In a taxi on the way, I skimmed Kennedy's opinion. It was poignant and powerful.

> DOMA undermines both the public and private significance of state-sanctioned same-sex marriages; for it tells those couples, and all the world, that their otherwise valid marriages are unworthy of federal recognition. This places same-sex couples in an unstable position of being in a second-tier marriage. The differentiation demeans the couple, whose moral and sexual choices the Constitution protects ... and whose relationship the State has sought to dignify. And it humiliates tens of thousands of children now being raised by same-sex couples. The law in question makes it even more difficult for the children to understand the integrity and closeness of their own family and its concord with other families in their community and in their daily lives.

Later on, I read the dissents. Chief Justice Roberts focused emphatically on the point that this decision didn't point toward future decisions that declared state bans on the freedom to marry unconstitutional.

> While I disagree with the result to which the majority's analysis leads it in this case, I think it more important to point out that its analysis leads no further. The Court does not have before it, and the logic of its opinion does not decide, the distinct question whether the States, in the exercise of their "historic and essential authority to define the

marital relation," . . . may continue to utilize the traditional definition of marriage. The majority goes out of its way to make this explicit.

Roberts was right that the opinion was explicit that the court hadn't opined on whether state bans violated the Constitution. However, Scalia's blistering dissent seemed more prescient to me. Scalia stated that the majority opinion would, undoubtedly, be used at a later date to strike down state bans on marriage for gay couples. "By formally declaring anyone opposed to same-sex marriage an enemy of human decency, the majority arms well every challenger to a state law restricting marriage to its traditional definition." He went so far as to illustrate it, striking and replacing a few key words from Justice Kennedy's opinion and showing how that leads to a ruling for the freedom to marry nationwide. "As far as this Court is concerned," he wrote, "no one should be fooled; it is just a matter of listening and waiting for the other shoe."

Given how quickly momentum was moving in our direction, and how forceful the majority opinion was—it used the term "dignity" nine times as it eviscerated any legitimate justification for denying marriage to same-sex couples—I agreed that, not far down the road, the Supreme Court would be inclined to use the reasoning as the basis for an opinion to strike down all remaining state bans on equal-protection grounds. But we weren't going to wait for anyone's shoe. We were going to do everything we could to create a climate where the court would conclude, sooner rather than later, that the country was ready for the national resolution that the Constitution demanded.

At a little past one, I joined Evan in his office for a confidential call with the White House and a small number of LGBT leaders about DOMA implementation. From Air Force One en route to Africa with the president, Valerie Jarrett congratulated all of us. "This is a truly historic day," she said, "one that's been a long time coming." Someone wants to say a few words, she told us. After about ten seconds, a familiar voice came over the line.

"Hey, everybody," President Obama said to us.

It was thrilling to have the president join us in celebration. He told us that there had been a big cheer on Air Force One as they learned of the ruling.

"This has been a victory long in the making," he said. "We've seen enormous advocacy all across the country, in multiple states." He noted the significance of the ruling coming forty-four years to the week of Stonewall and ten years to the day of the *Lawrence* decision eliminating state bans on sodomy. He also told us that he'd reached out to Edie Windsor and spoken with her. "I've been thinking," the president said, "about the forty years of love and commitment that she had with her partner." The president said that he'd directed his administration to review every single relevant statute and move implementation along quickly and swiftly. But, he explained, not everything would be resolved immediately. There are a lot of federal statutes involved, he told us. But, he promised, they'd work their hardest.

He was true to his word. Two days later, the Office of Personnel Management announced that all legally married federal employees would receive the full array of protections, irrespective of what state the couple lived in. Later that afternoon, the US Citizenship and Immigration Services approved a green card application of a Bulgarian citizen who was married to a man living in Florida, the first time marital status for a gay person qualified that person for a green card. So far, the administration was honoring our request and respecting legal marriages irrespective of where the couple lived.

That evening, I attended services at Congregation Beth Simchat Torah, the LGBT synagogue in New York, for the Shabbat of Pride weekend. The room was packed for special guests Edie Windsor and Robbie Kaplan. When they were introduced and stepped up to the pulpit, people erupted in prolonged cheers.

During services, I glanced at my phone. There was more good news. California Attorney General Kamala Harris had moved swiftly to resume marriages throughout the state and was at that moment presiding at the wedding of plaintiffs Kristin Perry and Sandra Stier.

It had been a long journey to get here, but this was definitely a week for the history books.

Scalia was right.

On Friday, December 20, 2013, a Utah federal district court judge struck down Utah's constitutional amendment barring same-sex couples from marrying, ruling that "the Constitution . . . protects the choice of one's partner for all citizens, regardless of their sexual identity."

In so doing, Judge Robert Shelby, a forty-three year old Obama appointee, relied upon Scalia's scathingly sardonic dissent in the DOMA case. Quoting Scalia that "the view that this Court will take of state prohibition of same-sex marriage is indicated beyond mistaking by today's opinion," Shelby wrote, "the court agrees with Justice Scalia's interpretation of *Windsor.*"

Shelby didn't order a stay of his decision, so marriages would begin right away.

Utah!

This one was about as big a game-changer as I could imagine. Utah was the home of the Mormon Church, which had infamously pressured adherents to contribute the majority of the $39 million that was spent to pass Proposition 8 in California. I thought about the LGBT people throughout the state, particularly those living in smaller cities and towns where the wrongness of being gay had to be drilled into people's beings from birth. How unbelievably affirming this ruling must be. How it will change lives!

=

Thirty-one year old Seth Anderson heard the news and rushed over to the Salt Lake County courthouse with his fiancé, thirty-two year old Michael Ferguson, to get married. Raised in traditional Mormon households and both completing missions, the two were first in line.

Over Twitter, Seth was giving a blow-by-blow account of what was happening. I heard about it and tuned in.

1:17 p.m. Marriage Equality is legal in Utah for about an hour.

1:19 p.m. We are at the office now. DA just walked in. In a meeting now. We were told to hang tight for 20 min.

1:33 p.m. We are not married yet. This is so new. The clerk doesn't have clearance . . . Yet.

1:38 p.m. Application fee is paid for.

1:45 p.m. People are crying. This is happening.

2:12 p.m. Me and my new husband!! My polygamous Mormon great grandparents would be so proud!

This last tweet was accompanied by a picture of Anderson and Ferguson, arms around one another, holding up their signed marriage license. I had goose bumps.

Marriages continued in Utah through January 6, 2014, when the US Supreme Court stayed the ruling pending appeal. By then, 1,362 marriages had been performed in every part of the state. Things had gone exceptionally smoothly. In the first few days, clerks in several counties came up with excuses to avoid issuing marriage licenses, but within a few days, clerks from all 29 Utah counties were issuing them. The Mormon Church expressed opposition but in a moderated tone that was so much different from the virulence of just a few years before. And while politicians like the governor were opposed, the public reaction was pretty quiet except for the celebrations of so many same-sex couples and their loved ones.

Other district court judges followed with similar rulings. By late June 2014, judges had struck down marriage bans in Arkansas, Idaho, Indiana, Michigan, Oklahoma, Texas, Virginia, Wisconsin, Oregon, and Pennsylvania. In the latter two, the states didn't appeal the rulings and the freedom to marry became permanent law. In three other states—Kentucky, Ohio, and Tennessee—judges ruled that states had to respect marriages performed in other states. On June 24, the Tenth Circuit Court of Appeals affirmed the Utah district court ruling. By then, seventy-three cases originating in thirty-one states were pending.

And we were batting a thousand. In twenty-two out of twenty-two rulings since *Windsor*, judges had ruled that state bans were illegitimate, all using the rationale of *Windsor*—as Scalia had predicted they would and as they should have. The constitution's guarantee of equal protection under the law meant that state bans could not stand.

In oral arguments in the Prop 8 case, Justice Sotomayor said that the Supreme Court often preferred letting sweeping issues like marriage "perk" for a while rather than issue decisive rulings before the country had reached resolution. However, given the readiness of judges to apply the rationale of *Windsor* to state bans and the rapidity of cases making their way toward the Supreme Court, it looked increasingly likely that a case could be taken up by the Supreme Court for decision in 2015. Alternatively, the Supreme Court could let appellate court ruling stand and not take up an appeal, thereby letting the issue "perk" for longer.

I believed that now, we could make a truly persuasive case that America was ready for national resolution. By June, we had secured the freedom to marry in nineteen states encompassing 44 percent of the country, overcoming obstacles at every juncture. We were told we'd never be able to defend marriage in Massachusetts and we did. We were told we'd only win on the coasts, and then we prevailed in the heartland. We were told we'd never win in a legislature and we did, over and over. We were told we'd never win with Republicans leading a chamber of the legislature, but then we prevailed in New York. And we were told over and over we'd never win at the ballot, but then we were four for four in 2012.

With respect to public support, a *Washington Post-ABC* poll released the first week of March, 2014 showed that support nationwide was now at 59 percent with only 34 percent opposed. This represented a complete turnaround from 2004, when same-sex couples first began marrying in Massachusetts. Then, a *Washington Post-ABC* poll showed 59 percent opposed with only 38 percent in support. What's more, every region of the country now showed majority support—the South at 50 percent, the West at 59 percent, the Midwest at 66 percent and the Northeast at

68 percent. For the first time, a plurality of seniors was in support: 47 percent to 43 percent opposed for those sixty-five and older. Republican support was growing quickly. A March *New York Times* poll showed that 40 percent of Republicans supported marriage for gay couples, including 56 percent of those who were under the age of forty-five.

The work ahead was to keep driving the narrative in the press that all of America was ready for national resolution. We prioritized two geographic areas where the marriage movement had done little organizing work before—the South and the Mountain West. We launched a fourteen-state public education effort called Southerners for the Freedom to Marry to identify unexpected messengers, including Republicans, business leaders, military, clergy, and electeds whose voices we could amplify through the media. We did the same in the Mountain West, launching local campaign organizations called Freedom Wyoming, Utah Unites for Marriage, Why Marriage Matters Colorado, Freedom Nevada, and Why Marriage Matters Arizona with other local and national partners. Just before appellate court arguments in the Utah case, we released a nationwide television ad featuring retired Republican US Senator Alan Simpson of Wyoming talking about how the freedom to marry is fully in sync with the values of the party that are important to him: "government out of your life and the right to be left alone." Having the eighty-two-year-old iconic GOP senator of the west, who was soon to celebrate his sixtieth wedding anniversary, making the case was powerfully emblematic of how ready our country was.

Even as we drove as hard as we could the narrative that the country is ready, we were also beginning to build out campaigns in the states that offered the best potential for ballot wins in 2016 if we didn't yet have national resolution. Those states included Arizona, Colorado, Michigan, Nevada, and Ohio.

=

On May 17, 2014, we celebrated ten years of the freedom to marry in Massachusetts. I went to a gala sponsored by MassEquality that felt like a family reunion. I sat with Amy Mello who was working for me again, now as Freedom to Marry's field director. Amy had just flown in from a road trip to Wyoming and Oklahoma where she'd been working with our new organizers. Former legislative champions like Jarrett Barrios, Barbara L'Italien, Dianne Wilkerson, and Alice Wolf were there, as was just-retired Mayor Tom Menino and legislators still in office like Byron Rushing and Stan Rosenberg. Carl Sciortino, still a state representative after an unsuccessful run for Congress in 2013, was absent. But he had a good excuse. He was on his honeymoon. I'd had the great honor of officiating at his marriage to Pem Brown in October 2013 at the Old South Meeting House, where we had celebrated the *Goodridge* win ten years before.

A number of the advocates I'd fought with in Massachusetts, as well as some who'd joined the national movement like Marty Rouse, were there too. And dear Ralph Hodgdon, one half of the senior couple who had carried the famous sign showing off the longevity of their relationship, joined up. Sadly, his other half, Paul, had passed away two years before, after nearly fifty-six years together.

After the event, many of us adjourned to Club Café, as we had so many times before.

What a journey!

=

Throughout the journey, I never forgot the words of my friend Eric Garcetti, now the mayor of Los Angeles, from nearly a decade before. "Fight for love," Eric said. Over these years, I had been on my own journey and had come a long, long way in learning to stop fighting against myself and embracing myself as I was.

I thought about the movement I'd joined and then helped build to fight for the integrity of LGBT people's love, as embodied through our desire to marry. To me, it was the essence of what a social movement was all about. There was the determined visionary and strategist, Evan, awakening so many to the prize before us that many of us had been unable to see and laying out a pathway to attain it. There was the equally determined legal strategist, Mary Bonauto, devising and executing a multi-year strategy to secure marriage and knock down discriminatory laws, undeterred by losses or partial-wins. There was the visionary donor, Tim Gill, who began investing to fuel a movement in 1994, sticking with it through victories and losses, enlisting hundreds of other donors to the cause, to the point where by 2014 he'd personally contributed nearly $300 million of his own dollars to advancing equality and helped raise much more. There were the strategic operatives like Patrick Guerriero, Bill Smith, Thalia Zepatos, Marty Rouse, Matt McTighe, Mary Breslauer, and many others who dedicated their skill in winning campaigns to this cause. There were brilliant organizers like Amy Mello who inspired thousands upon thousands of people to take meaningful actions to help bring about the wins. There were the determined electeds, both gay and straight—governors like Deval Patrick and Andrew Cuomo, legislators like Carl Sciortino and Barbara L'Italien—who drove the effort hard. And there were the courageous electeds, people like Paul Kujawski, Richard Ross, and Steve Saland, who were so moved by heartfelt stories of same-sex couples they got to know that they reconsidered their position. They were the journalists and bloggers from Andrew Sullivan in the early days to so many in the present who made the case publicly and held our electeds accountable. And of course, all of this rested on the countless same-sex couples, LGBT individuals, and straight allies who—inspired by the vision and America's promise of equality before the law for everyone—took up the mantle, often going far beyond their comfort zones to make the case, and in many cases coming to recognize their own power to make real change in the process.

All of these actors together had created a movement. And this movement had created an aspirational vision, developed a strategy to accomplish the vision, stuck with it through many tough years, built and relentlessly drove campaigns to put wins on the board, played to win electorally, told the human stories of why marriage matters to committed same-sex couples over and over and over, made the cause a bipartisan and multi-racial one, tapped into the American values of the Golden Rule and freedom, and enlisted new allies every step of the way and welcomed them as though they'd been with us from day one.

This is what a successful social movement looks like. How proud to have been to be a part.

Tuesday, April 28, 2015. This was the day that the Supreme Court would be hearing the case that could very well bring us the freedom to marry throughout the nation. I was staying at the Capitol Hill Hotel adjacent to the Library of Congress in Washington, DC. I woke at 6:30 a.m., eager to hear my dear friend Mary Bonauto present the oral arguments for our side. Mary and I had been fighting this battle together for more than a decade.

Despite the magnitude of the day, I felt oddly calm. I wasn't nervous like I'd been two years before, when the Supreme Court heard Edie Windsor's challenge to the Defense of Marriage Act along with the Prop 8 case. That was the first time the court had heard a challenge to marriage discrimination. Now there were thirty-seven states in the win column, comprising 75 percent of the US population. A February CNN/ORC poll showed that a substantial majority of Americans believed gays and lesbians had "a constitutional right to get married and have their marriage recognized by law as valid"—with 63 percent in favor and 36 percent opposed. Even in the South, 57 percent of respondents supported marriage equality, with 60 percent support or greater in every other region in the country. In addition, we'd been on a tremendous winning streak in court—with more than sixty victories in federal and state courts since DOMA had been struck down, versus only a handful of losses.

Even though I felt confident, however, I still took a few extra precautions for good luck. I wore the same purple tie that I'd worn the day of the *Windsor* oral arguments, and I put whole milk rather than skim in my coffee. That was a nod to the line Ruth Bader Ginsburg had used two years ago, when she said that marriages without federal recognition were "skim milk marriages."

As I walked along the streets of Capitol Hill toward the Supreme Court that sunny morning, the Jewish prayer "Oseh Shalom" (Make Peace) came to mind. After years of fighting for our dignity and equality, I felt like our movement had brought the country to where it needed to be. Now was the time.

=

The federal court victories that had begun in Utah in December 2013 had continued nearly unabated for the next eight months. Oklahoma in January. Virginia and Texas in February. Michigan in March. Idaho, Oregon, and Pennsylvania in May. Indiana, Wisconsin, Kentucky, Colorado, and Florida over the summer. The opinions had been written by judges who had been appointed by both Republican and Democratic presidents, and all relied on the reasoning in the Supreme Court's DOMA decision, which eviscerated any justification for barring same-sex couples from marrying.

Oregon and Pennsylvania didn't file appeals, so those rulings went into effect right away. In the other states, the decisions were "stayed"—in other words, put on hold—while appeals were filed in the circuit courts. Each circuit court controls from three to nine states and—unless the Supreme Court says otherwise—interprets the US Constitution for those states. The outcomes of those appeals were not foregone conclusions. Each case would be heard by a randomly selected panel of three appeals court judges. But the first three panels ruled in our favor, and in time for one of those cases to be taken up by the Supreme Court during the 2014–15 term, which began in October.

=

At the beginning of each term, the Supreme Court's first order of business is to figure out which cases it will consider. Typically, the court takes up less than 1 percent of the cases before it. The nine justices meet in private to vote, with four votes required to hear a case.

On October 6, we received the shocking news that the Supreme Court had declined to hear any of the appeals, which went against all conventional wisdom.

Initially, I was frustrated. Did this mean that we'd have to win in each of the thirteen circuit courts in order to prevail nationwide? How long would that take? And even if we succeeded in that effort, we wouldn't have the finality of a Supreme Court ruling declaring the righteousness of our cause. I wanted to finish with a bang, not a whimper.

There was still the possibility that one of the circuit courts would rule against us, obliging the Supreme Court to arbitrate between competing rulings and clarify what would become the law of the land. Two more circuit court opinions were pending, but we had no idea when those courts would rule. The clock was ticking on this Supreme Court session. I couldn't bring myself to root for a loss, but I knew that a loss would get us to the Supreme Court more quickly.

At the same time, the practical result of the court's action—or non-action—was huge. In the five states that had appealed to the Supreme Court—Indiana, Oklahoma, Utah, Virginia, and Wisconsin— marriages would begin immediately, as the three circuit rulings had rejected those states' bans. What's more, the Supreme Court's refusal to take up those cases meant that the rulings were now law for all the rest of the states in those three circuits. That meant that marriage bans in six additional states—Colorado, Kansas, North Carolina, South Carolina, West Virginia, and Wyoming—also would vanish. So the Supreme Court's non-action would actually end bans in eleven states, increasing the number of freedom-to-marry states from nineteen to thirty.

By rejecting these initial cases, the court had given a strong indicator as to where it would land once it did take up the issue. If the majority of justices ultimately planned to rule against us, it seemed implausible that the court would allow marriage to begin in eleven new states, only to undo that action in the future. On the contrary, it seemed as if the court was laying the groundwork for a positive ruling, helping us out by adding to the number of states with marriage prior to its final ruling.

On October 7, the day after the Supreme Court made its announcement, the Ninth Circuit, covering most of the western states, held unanimously that the Idaho and Nevada marriage bans were unconstitutional. This meant that marriage bans would end in all of the states in that circuit where they remained in place: Idaho, Nevada, Alaska,

Arizona, and Montana. We now had sixteen new states, meaning that 65 percent of the country would soon be living in a state where gay couples could marry.

Based on past experience, we at Freedom to Marry had always argued that there would not be much direct resistance to a favorable ruling. We believed that the fear of a backlash had been overstated. Now, with marriage equality becoming law in a few states in the South, as well as in some of the most conservative states in the country (Utah and Wyoming were Obama's worst-performing states in 2012), we had our sternest test. Overall, we were proven right. Some elected officials took the opportunity to become demagogues but, in the vast majority of cases, clerks did their jobs and provided marriage licenses to same-sex couples. Even where everyone wasn't in agreement, there was very little organized resistance. It appeared that even in conservative states, once marriage became the law, support continued to increase steadily or to actually accelerate.

Once people moved beyond their fears and negativity and saw the love, commitment, and joy of same-sex couples in their own communities, they realized that their concerns had been misplaced.

=

On Thursday, November 6, 2014, our winning streak came to an end. The Sixth Circuit Court of Appeals ruled against us, 2–1, in a decision that covered cases from Kentucky, Michigan, Ohio, and Tennessee. Couples in all four states appealed to the Supreme Court and, on January 16, 2015, we got the news we'd been waiting for. The court would take up these cases, consolidate them all into one, and reach an ultimate decision by the end of the term, in late June or early July 2015. Oral arguments were scheduled for Tuesday, April 28, with briefs due March 6.

Game on!

This case felt like the right one for several reasons. First, each of the four national LGBT legal organizations—the ACLU, GLAD, Lambda Legal, and the National Center for Lesbian Rights—had been involved in at least one of the original cases, before consolidation. This meant they'd all be working together on what had the possibility of becoming the final presentation on marriage to the Supreme Court. Because these organizations had helped guide the legal strategy on marriage equality for many years, it was great news that they'd all get a chance to participate in this historic moment.

Even more thrilling was the fact that the attorney teams had decided to name Mary Bonauto as the lead attorney in making our arguments to the Supreme Court, joined by the solicitor general of the United States, Donald Verrilli, and Supreme Court expert Douglas Hallward-Driemeier. Bonauto had been carefully stewarding the legal strategy on marriage since Vermont in 1998, and it felt like poetic justice that she would argue this one.

Exceedingly modest, Bonauto called Evan Wolfson before agreeing to do the argument. She was especially concerned that she'd only have about a month to prepare.

Evan was thrilled that his comrade-in-arms during all these years had gotten the nod. "You have to do this," he told her. "Nobody could do this better, and you could do it tomorrow if you had to."

Evan had no doubt she'd do it. Mary was steely tough, and she was in.

Bonauto went back to her home in Maine and buried herself in preparations. She, for one, didn't think that a win was a sure thing and was taking nothing for granted. The case would not rest solely on the oral arguments, of course. The briefs of the legal team, along with those of "friends of the court"—interested parties who wanted to weigh in—would lay out the case in powerful terms. And this wasn't new terrain—the justices had heard arguments on marriage just two years earlier. Still, the oral arguments were one of the crucial elements and she felt the weight of the world on her shoulders. She thought about all of the couples and families she'd represented over twenty-five years of heading up GLAD's civil rights practice. As the first attorney to present, she'd be peppered with questions, one after another, and she'd have to be quick on her feet. She wanted to be ready for anything the justices threw at her, so she dove right in to work, determined to squeeze as many minutes of preparation as possible out of each day.

=

While I shared the conventional wisdom that our side would prevail, I wanted our team at Freedom to Marry to uncover every possible person of influence and get them to announce their support before oral arguments. This was our last chance to show both how much momentum we had and how much support we had—in unexpected quarters and from every part of the country. I wanted us to leave no stone unturned.

I asked our team of organizers to enlist signers for friend-of-the-court briefs. In particular, we focused on four briefs—one for major businesses, one for Republican leaders, one for clergy, and one for mayors—that I thought would be most influential among the two Republican-appointed justices that could be in play: Anthony Kennedy and Chief Justice John Roberts.

Two hundred companies had signed onto the business brief for the DOMA case two years before. I wanted us to blow that number out of the water and get an even stronger showing of Fortune 500 companies. The law firm Morgan, Lewis & Bockius led the outreach effort. I pulled in Open Finance, a group of senior LGBT Wall Street execs, as well as several other key individuals and groups with strong ties to the business world. Together, we lined up 379 companies—including 40 from the Fortune 100. The list also included 33 Wall Street and financial firms— more than double what we'd had from high finance the last time out. Knowing the media's interest in anything regarding professional sports, I reached out to old Boston friends who were close with Robert Kraft, the owner of the New England Patriots. Soon we had the Super Bowl champs, along with the World Series champions San Francisco Giants and the Tampa Bay Rays onboard. Our efforts secured the support of many large companies headquartered in the South and Midwest, including American Airlines, Bank of America, Coca Cola, ConAgra Foods, Cummins, General Mills, Nationwide, and Procter & Gamble. We had now grown far beyond such firms as Google and Starbucks, which cater to our community, and become able to reach some of America's most iconic brands.

As for Republicans, Ken Mehlman once again opened his deep Rolodex and worked the phones to compile an A-list group that included twenty-three current and former members of Congress, retired general Stanley McChrystal, and even GOP billionaire David Koch. Freedom to

Marry added multiple young conservative leaders and former state GOP officials, people we'd been cultivating for months.

My personal target was my former long-time boss, US Senator Jack Danforth. I'd stayed in close touch with Danforth over the years, encouraging him to shift his perspective on LGBT equality issues. And he'd done so. His willingness to think independently was something I had always admired deeply. At my request, he'd penned a poignant op-ed in the *St. Louis Post-Dispatch* on why Missouri should pass a strong anti-discrimination law to protect LGBT people. He wasn't quite there on marriage yet, but I thought it was worth one last shot.

I laid out a lengthy case in an e-mail, concluding, "It'd mean a lot to me for you to add your name—and I'll love you whether you do or not!"

Three hours later, I got his answer: "There's time for political debate on values issues and time to bring the debate to a close. It's time to bring it to a close. You can sign me on."

In the end, through the collective effort of many supporters, we were able to enlist more Republican signers to our briefs than our opponents were. Significantly, not one large corporation signed onto a brief against us. We secured nearly 2,000 signers on the clergy brief, with the greatest number from Ohio, where a case was pending before the Supreme Court. And we enlisted more than 200 mayors and 40 cities for the mayoral brief. These were just a few of the many briefs that were filed for our side.

We had one additional burst of momentum in the period before oral arguments. When federal courts in Florida and Alabama ruled our way, the Supreme Court again refused to stay the decisions. So as Mary Bonauto got ready to make our case, Florida—the fourth largest state in the country—and Alabama—the center of many of the civil rights battles of the 1950s and 1960s—had joined as freedom-to-marry states. The subsequent resistance to the federal ruling by the Alabama Supreme Court was a reminder of the importance of US Supreme Court involvement in civil rights cases.

=

On the morning scheduled for oral arguments, Mary Bonauto woke early at the Residence Inn in downtown Washington, DC, after a difficult night of sleep. But that was something she'd grown accustomed to recently. She'd been holed up at the hotel for nine days, and every morning she'd woken at dawn and spent the day reviewing cases and briefs, prepping for potential questions from justices, and practicing the points she wanted to make. She knew that her main job in oral arguments was to drive home the points that would advance the ball while conceding nothing that could harm the case.

Mary had completed several practice or moot courts, including one where five conservatives acted as justices and grilled her for more than an hour. In fact, most of her contact with the outside world was with other attorneys on the case, including her colleagues from LGBT legal organizations (who were in Washington with her), a couple of Supreme Court experts, and Douglas Hallward-Driemeier, who would argue another part of the case. All had helped her hone her arguments.

The night before the big day, Mary did what she had done for every one of her previous oral arguments: she condensed the points she wanted to make in the order in which she wanted to make them, writing them out on two legal-sized pages. She did so knowing that she'd probably only make it through her first couple of sentences before the justices began bombarding her with questions. But now wasn't the time to prepare any differently. This was an approach that had served her well.

＝

That morning, I walked around the front of the Supreme Court building, looking at the signs that thousands upon thousands of our advocates were holding, and greeting people I'd come to know over the past decade of this fight. One woman held a dog on a leash and a sign that read, "Tax-Paying Lesbian With Supportive Black Pug." She told me that she'd officiated at 700 weddings of same-sex couples in Northampton, Massachusetts. We reminisced about the early days in that state, when we went to constitutional conventions and fought back against anti-gay constitutional amendments. We snapped a couple of pictures and I gave her a hug.

I also took in some of our opponents' outrageous signs, including "Homo Sex Is Sin," "Your Sin of Sodomy Is Worthy of Death," and "Homosexuality Is a Threat to National Security." Although this horrific scene was familiar, I now felt almost nostalgic about it. I knew that, if all went as I hoped and expected, this could be my last encounter with such protesters. I also knew that America as a whole had moved far beyond them, that they had become almost a parody of themselves. In fact, one of Jon Stewart's correspondents from *The Daily Show* was standing by, ready to interview some of them for what would clearly be a satiric segment.

I met up with Evan Wolfson at 8:30, between the Russell and Dirksen Senate Office Buildings, a block north of the court. As we walked along First Street, past all those who were rallying on our side, people kept coming up to both of us, especially Evan, with heartfelt thanks. It felt amazing to be walking into the Supreme Court for these arguments with the guy who was responsible—more than anyone else—for driving the movement to this point over the past three decades.

We went up the steps of the court, where I told the guards that we had reserved seats inside the courtroom. I'd secured two of these highly sought-after seats through old Republican connections, and couldn't help but smile at the irony of my own political journey over the years. Evan and I were the special guests of Justice Clarence Thomas. We went through multiple security checks, locked our cellphones in special lockers, then took our places in the ornate courtroom, which was packed for this historic argument.

=

Mary Bonauto had arrived for a 9:00 a.m. briefing in the Supreme Court clerk's office, along with all the other attorneys who'd be arguing that morning. On her way out, she ran into her spouse Jenny and their twin daughters, who were there to watch her argue the case. The past week and a half in Washington was the longest she'd ever been away from her children. They all embraced. "Go get 'em," Jenny told Mary.

What a great omen, Mary thought. She was ready.

=

At 9:55 a.m., Mary walked into the courtroom and took her position at the front of the room.

Five minutes later, the marshal banged his gavel and asked everyone to rise. "God save the United States and this honorable court," he said, as the justices came forward and took their seats.

"Ms. Bonauto," said Chief Justice Roberts.

Mary stepped forward and began: "Mr. Chief Justice and may it please the court. The intimate and committed relationships of same-sex couples, just like those of heterosexual couples, provide mutual support and are the foundation of family life in our society."

She got two more sentences in before the justices began their barrage. I was focused on Justice Kennedy, who spoke up early.

"The word that keeps coming back to me in this case is millennia," he said. "This definition has been with us for eight millennia. And it's very difficult for the court to say, oh, well, we know better."

I'd been told over and over not to read too much into the questioning in oral arguments, but it wasn't comforting to hear our crucial swing vote saying this right off the bat.

Archconservative justice Samuel Alito was clearly prepared to try to knock Mary off her game. He brought up ancient Greece as an example of a place that accepted homosexuality but still didn't allow gays to marry. Trying to show that the notion of gay couples marrying had been a novel one over the course of history, and not as a result of discriminatory treatment per se, he asked, "So their limiting marriage to couples of the opposite sex was not based on prejudice against gay people, was it?"

"I can't speak to what was happening with the ancient philosophers," Mary responded, steering the conversation back to the constitutional issues at hand.

Alito also asked two questions about polygamy. Then fellow archconservative Antonin Scalia chimed in: Would clergy who refused to perform religious marriages for same-sex couples still be authorized by the state to issue marriage licenses? This struck me as an odd line of questioning, since it seemed clear that the First Amendment would protect clergy.

Mary easily shot all of these questions down; for her, they were well-trodden issues.

Chief Justice Roberts raised the most serious question: Wouldn't it be better to continue letting this issue play out in the political arena, in the states, rather than allowing a Supreme Court ruling to resolve the debate, particularly given "how quickly has been the acceptance of your position across broad elements of society"?

"The closing of debate can close minds," Roberts said, "and it will have a consequence on how this new institution is accepted."

Mary Bonauto responded forcefully. Practically speaking, she argued, "there are some serious structural problems," referring to the constitutional amendments barring the freedom to marry in many states. "It is extraordinarily difficult to amend the Constitution."

More fundamentally, though, she spoke of the serious costs of waiting while this debate played out. In many places, there were "virtually no protections for gay and lesbian people in employment, in parenting." She referenced her clients from Michigan, who "are not allowed to be parents of their own children."

When Mary's thirty minutes came to an end, she sat down.

It had been quite a barrage against our position, and the liberal bloc of the court hadn't pushed back very hard, seeming content to let Mary sink or swim on her own. She had weathered the storm well, however, conceding nothing that would hurt the case while also reminding the justices that a drawn-out, state-by-state fight would not be a neutral result, for it would leave many couples and families as second-class citizens for an indefinite future.

Next up was the solicitor general of the United States, Donald Verrilli, arguing on behalf of the Obama administration. The president had been an ally for some time now, but it was still a momentous feeling to have the US government arguing on our side before the Supreme Court.

As Verrilli was about to begin, a religious fanatic a couple of rows behind me started screaming his head off. "If you support gay marriage, you will burn in hell!" he shouted, as security guards rushed over to drag him away. "Homosexuality is an abomination!"

This incident was jarring, but it reinforced Mary's argument that resolving the issue via referendum at the state level would be dangerous for a minority against which there was still so much hostility.

The solicitor general began his argument. Unlike Mary, he was allowed to speak uninterrupted for a while.

At one point, Justice Kennedy spoke of the "tremendous amount" we'd learned as a society about gay people since he'd written the majority opinion in *Lawrence v. Texas*, the case that overturned laws banning consensual gay sex more than a decade ago.

The solicitor general concurred. Those ten years, he said, have "brought us to the point where we understand now, in a way even that we did not fully understand in *Lawrence*, that gay and lesbian people and gay and lesbian couples are full and equal members of the community."

Verrilli closed his argument simply and powerfully. "Gay and lesbian people are equal. They deserve equal protection of the laws, and they deserve it now."

Next up was the attorney for the state of Michigan, John Bursch, a former state solicitor general who was defending the marriage ban.

I presumed he'd rely on the notion that Justice Roberts had raised, that the country would be better off if the issue played out in the states. But instead he focused on the idea that allowing same-sex couples to marry would damage marriage for straight people. His core argument was that the only legitimate purpose of marriage is to bind children with their biological parents. If gay couples can marry, he argued, that would change that definition, which would lead to fewer straight couples marrying. As a result, more children would be born out of wedlock, with resultant harms.

"When you change the definition of marriage to delink the idea that we're binding children with their biological mom and dad," he argued, "that has consequences."

I was floored. Was this the best they could come up with? There were so many ways to poke holes in this argument. None of the conservatives on the court spoke in support of it, while the liberals, along with Justice Kennedy, challenged him aggressively.

What about straight couples who couldn't have children or didn't intend to have children? Should they be blocked from marrying if the only legitimate reason for marriage is to bind kids to their biological parents? How does allowing same-sex couples to marry interfere with the relationship between straight couples and their children? Is there any proof at all—or any logic at all—in the notion that gay couples marrying would lead to a reduction in straight couples marrying? And what about all of the gay parents who have kids and the importance of strengthening those families?

Bursch responded by rejecting "the marriage view on the other side here . . . that marriage is all about love and commitment." He continued: "The state doesn't have any interest in that." And when pushed to offer proof that marriages of heterosexual couples would be diminished if gay couples could marry, he offered none, only the assertion that "it's reasonable to believe that."

Justice Kennedy wasn't buying the limited view of marriage that the Michigan attorney was peddling. He argued that marriage was noble and sacred in its binding of two people together, and that, at its heart, it bestows dignity on committed couples, whether or not they procreated. "Same-sex couples say, of course we understand the nobility and the sacredness of the marriage. We know we can't procreate, but we want the other attributes of it in order to show that we, too, have a dignity that can be fulfilled." At the same time, Kennedy was offended by the implication that gay parents who had adopted children were less well suited as parents because they weren't biologically connected. "You had some premise that only opposite-sex couples can have a bonding with the child. That was very interesting, but it's just a wrong premise."

The four liberal justices also joined in the grilling of the Michigan attorney.

When the oral arguments came to a conclusion, Evan and I quickly exited the courtroom and walked outside, into the sea of our supporters, who were cheering, chanting, and waving flags. I was feeling great. Kennedy hadn't offered up a definitive signal on how he'd vote, but he'd sure sounded unsympathetic to our opponents' limited view of the purpose of marriage. The vapidity of that argument seemed to confirm that we were headed toward a win.

That afternoon, at a reception hosted by Lambda Legal, I got the chance to have a private moment with Mary Bonauto, away from all of the others who wanted to thank her. She and I looked one another in the eyes momentarily, and I could feel the emotion brewing inside of me. I could tell by the way she looked at me that she was feeling it too. We embraced, then I congratulated and thanked her. We'd been fighting on different fronts in the same battle for so many years—and now it seemed we were close to victory.

=

At 9:30 a.m. on Friday, June 26—two months after oral arguments—I was in our New York City office sitting around a large conference table with fifteen staff members, including Evan Wolfson. The walls were adorned with framed front pages of newspapers from the day after victory in each of the first twenty-five marriage states, with another twelve lining the hallway. Nearly everyone's laptop was open, and most of us were typing nervously, finalizing graphics and tweets for social media, organizing press lists, and making other final preparations for a possible decision. A box of Dunkin' Donuts, courtesy of Evan, sat in the middle of the table. The large-screen television at one end of the conference room was streaming *SCOTUSblog*, the best source for up-to-the-minute information on court decisions.

There were only a handful of decisions left for the court to announce that term, so it seemed likely the final decisions would come either on this day or the following Monday. This day was the two-year anniversary of the *Windsor* decision and the twelfth anniversary of *Lawrence v. Texas*, the two most important gay rights decisions by the Supreme Court, both written by Justice Kennedy. If Kennedy were writing for the history books, it made sense that today would be the day.

I'd woken up that morning thinking about two young people. One was a high-school junior, the first cousin of my two nieces, Madeline and Zoe, ages fifteen and twelve, both amazing allies. One of them had recently shown me their cousin's prom picture, with pride. His date had been another boy who looked to be the same age. They were sitting on a swing together, their arms around one another, both wearing black

tuxedos with white boutonnieres, looking happy, adorable, and care-
free. The other young person on my mind was the son of close friends,
a teenager who had just come out of the closet. I'd seen his mother the
night before, and she told me how proud she was of him for telling his
friends and family members. The notion that gay kids in their teens,
along with future generations of LGBT young people, might grow up
in a world where the most important social and cultural institution—
marriage—treated them, their relationships, and their love as worthy of
dignity and respect was profoundly moving to me.

As we waited for news from the court, I showed some of my colleagues the prom photo that my niece had shown me on Facebook and
told them that these teens embodied what I was fighting for.

When the clock hit 10:00 a.m., the room grew completely silent.

I was jittery as I read *SCOTUSblog* aloud for the entire room.

> 10:01 Here's Lyle with the first opinion.

That meant that Lyle Denniston, the octogenarian Supreme Court reporter, had a copy of the first opinion they were releasing that day.

> Marriage.

"Holy shit," I said. *Here it comes.*

About two seconds later, Evan, who was sitting to my left and watching his Twitter feed, said quietly, "We won."

"How do you know?" one of our young staffers asked excitedly.

"Chris Geidner," Evan replied, referring to BuzzFeed's legal editor.

His voice cracking, Evan read the tweet aloud: "The Supreme Court
ends same-sex marriage bans nationwide."

I belted out a loud *woohoo* and joined my colleagues in cheering, applauding, and hugging.

"Well, that only took thirty-two years," Evan said, to lots of laughs.

Then he said, "Oh my God," twice in a row. It was clearly just beginning to sink in.

I just kept letting out hoots and hollers, clapping and asking, to no
one in particular, "Can you believe it?"

I popped open two bottles of champagne and Evan gave a toast.

"We were the campaign working to win marriage nationwide," he said. "Now here's to the campaign that *won* marriage nationwide."

Lots more applause, cheers, and hugs.

=

In Washington, DC, Mary Bonauto was seated in the Supreme Court, waiting for the decision to be announced, just as she had been on three prior decision days since June 15. She'd grown accustomed to taking the 5:50 a.m. flight to Washington from her home in Portland, Maine, getting to the court by 8:00 a.m., then waiting for decisions to be announced at 10:00—only to turn around and go back to Maine each time. This week, she'd come down on Wednesday, preparing to wait until the decision was announced.

Sitting in the majestic courtroom that morning, she noticed a water glass in front of Justice Kennedy's seat. Did that mean today was the day?

After the justices came out, Chief Justice Roberts announced that *Obergefell v. Hodges*, the marriage case, was up first. The room went completely silent as Justice Kennedy began reading a condensed version of his opinion from the bench. Ever cautious, Mary didn't presume victory until Kennedy began talking about the changes in marriage over the millennia. But as she listened intently to Kennedy's words, she began to feel a deep sense of relief. The courtroom was packed with plaintiffs, attorneys, and other onlookers. She could hear sniffles and, in at least one case, sobbing.

When Mary saw that, for the first time in his decade as chief justice, John Roberts would read a summary of his dissent from the bench, she braced herself. Roberts compared Kennedy's majority opinion to the infamous 1905 *Lochner v. New York* decision, which relied on the US Constitution to strike down worker-safety laws. To Mary, the reference couldn't be clearer—he was accusing the majority of inventing a right that didn't exist. As ecstatic as Mary was about the win, this was painful to hear. (In his written dissent, Roberts also compared the court's ruling to the infamous *Dred Scott* decision, which asserted that slaveholding was a property right protected by the Constitution.)

After the justices finished their readings, she strode out of the court-room to the scrum of journalists and cameras waiting outside. Attorneys and plaintiffs stood behind her.

"Today was a momentous decision," Mary said, full of excitement, a smile on her face. "It's going to bring joy to millions of families, gay and straight, around this country," she continued.

But she also wanted to make it clear that this decision was all about the Constitution. "The court stood by a principle in this nation that we do not tolerate laws that disadvantage people because of who they are."

=

In New York, Evan got a call of congratulations from Vice President Joe Biden, whom Evan had worked for when he was a college student. Biden joked about how proud he was of his former intern, then thanked Evan profusely for his vision, his courage, and his willingness to fight so hard for so long.

"You changed the country and we owe you," Biden said. "This makes a big difference because getting this country where we need to be on civil rights will help us lead globally."

"I appreciate that," Evan replied, "and I completely agree with you." Then he thanked the vice president for the administration's leadership. "We wouldn't be here today without your support and the president's support."

Evan shut the door to his office and began reading the 5–4 opinion, authored by Justice Kennedy. Tears rolled down his cheeks. It was almost surreal to read a Supreme Court opinion that contained some of the themes he'd presented in his Harvard Law School thesis thirty-two years earlier. These were ideas that so many people had laughed at or ignored—because they sounded so improbable. Like his thesis, the opinion spoke of the "transcendent importance of marriage," how excluding gay people from marriage exacts a deep and penetrating harm, and how the Constitution's guarantee of liberty and equality meant that participation in such a fundamentally important institution couldn't be denied to same-sex couples.

Evan also realized that an enormous weight had been lifted from his shoulders. For decades, he'd promised that the attainment of marriage for gay couples nationwide was possible if people did the requisite work to bring it about. At so many difficult points along the way—following the passage of DOMA and the numerous state constitutional amendments, during the threat of a federal constitutional amendment, after John Kerry's loss in the presidential election and the resulting blame on the LGBT community—many leaders had wanted to slow down or even stop, and many pundits had called the pursuit either impossible or counterproductive.

All during that time, Evan had been the unflappable, optimistic driving force who argued, persuaded, cajoled, and convinced our community—along with its allied straight leaders, donors, the media, and so many others—that winning marriage was both worth it and could be done. At this moment, he could feel the armor he'd worn as the marriage warrior for so many years falling away. Carrying this burden had taken its toll on him, and now he began to feel a deep sense of relief.

Sitting next door in my office, I felt like I was floating. I too experienced a tremendous sense of relief and unburdening. Ever since we'd won marriage in a Massachusetts court in 2003, I'd had an overwhelming feeling of responsibility. I knew how crucial momentum could be. After that victory, we had to defeat efforts to take it away while continuing to put more wins on the board. That burden had taken a toll on me as well. My neck became so contorted from stress that I suffered permanent nerve damage in the thumb and index finger on my left hand.

After Proposition 8 passed in California, I was driven to relocate there—to build a ballot campaign that would win marriage back. When it became clear that Prop 8 would be handled in court, and Evan described his vision of a campaign operation to fast-track our gains, I made the decision to move to New York and run it. Each time we won a state, my mind would quickly shift to the next battleground—to all the work that wasn't yet far enough along.

But on that day in June, there were suddenly no more states to worry about, no more momentum that needed to be created. It felt amazing.

At that moment, I had a clearer vision of what had been motivating me all this time. It was about much more than marriage. It had to do with my own experience as a gay man, about coming to terms with my sexuality over the past four decades. When I was a child and first began to recognize that I was different, I was sure that there was something terribly wrong with me. Every message I got from the outside world was that homosexuality was a horrible defect, a secret I could never share with anybody else. When I entered my teens, in the 1980s, it also became something that could kill me. And so I stayed firmly in the closet for many years.

On the day we won marriage equality throughout the nation, however, I realized what a powerfully different message young people who were discovering their sexuality would now receive. The Supreme Court decision told the kids of today and the future—as well as the eight-year-old living inside of me—that society accepts and loves you just as you are. That was the transformative power of equality in marriage. For our government and our society to say that same-sex couples could marry sent an unmistakable message that the love of LGBT people was perfect just as it was. I could even imagine that, someday, there might no longer be a closet. Young people would speak about their sexuality once it became apparent to them, free of shame. That felt really, really great.

That evening, I spoke at a massive rally outside the Stonewall Inn in Greenwich Village. Thousands of people were gathered, many holding signs. The atmosphere was electric.

"We did it!" I announced, to great cheers.

"This was the win of a movement," I continued. "Everyone who has had a conversation with a family member or friend about why marriage matters, who has met with a lawmaker, who has volunteered, who has donated—this win is because of you."

I acknowledged that there was still plenty of work to do to advance the cause of LGBT equality, but declared that, "Tonight we get to celebrate. Our work together over these many years has made America better—for LGBT people and straight people alike."

"Let freedom ring!" I concluded.

=

In rereading the decision, what became most powerful for me was its focus on the crucial role of social movements in securing constitutional protections. "The nature of injustice," Kennedy wrote, "is that we may not always see it in our own times." Thankfully, the drafters of the Fourteenth Amendment "entrusted to future generations a charter protecting the right of all persons to enjoy liberty as we learn its meaning."

And how do new groups of people publicize injustice and make claims for their fundamental liberties? "Through perspectives that begin in pleas or protests and then are considered in the political sphere and the judicial process." In other words, through social movements.

In several pages, Kennedy documents the evolution of society's treatment of LGBT people. In the first half of the twentieth century, same-sex intimacy was "condemned as immoral" and criminalized. "Gays and lesbians," he continued, "were prohibited from most government employment, barred from military service, excluded under immigration laws, targeted by police, and burdened in their rights to associate." The consequence was the closet. As Kennedy put it, "a truthful declaration by same-sex couples of what was in their hearts had to remain unspoken."

During the post-Stonewall era, as people began coming out of the closet, agitating for equal treatment, and living more openly, our community was able to make "substantial cultural and political developments," which in turn led to "same-sex couples [beginning] to lead more open and public lives and to establish families."

Kennedy countered the notion that marriage for gay couples was new and untested, pointing directly to the freedom-to-marry movement. He spoke of the "deliberation" that's gone into reaching this "enhanced understanding of the issue," such as "referenda, legislative debates, and grassroots campaigns," along with "extensive litigation in state and federal courts" resulting in judicial opinions "that reflect the more general, societal discussion of same-sex marriage and its meaning that has occurred over the past decades." He also spoke of the amicus briefs supported by "many of the central institutions in American life," including large and small businesses, religious institutions, the military, state and local governments, and others.

So it was the movement for marriage that Kennedy credited with being responsible for making manifestly clear that what "may long have seemed natural and just"—"the limitation of marriage to opposite-sex couples"—is in fact "inconsistent with the central meaning of the fundamental right to marry."

And that led naturally to the opinion's conclusion:

> It would misunderstand these men and women to say they disrespect the idea of marriage. Their plea is that they do respect it, respect it so deeply that they seek to find its fulfillment for themselves. Their hope is not to be condemned to live in loneliness, excluded from one of civilization's oldest institutions. They ask for equal dignity in the eyes of the law. The Constitution grants them that right.

=

The main reason I wrote this book was to show how significant social change can happen in America. It is crucial to recognize that there are no shortcuts: such change requires hard and taxing work, over a long period of time. Also required are a powerful vision and a strategic roadmap for bringing change about, but without hard work the task is impossible. It's not enough to assert that what you want is right. If it were, then Jack Baker and Michael McConnell—who sued the state of Minnesota for the right to marry in 1970—would have prevailed. But their suit lost in the Minnesota Supreme Court, in a decision that quoted from Genesis, and then was summarily dismissed by the US Supreme Court.

In an interview earlier in 2015, Justice Ruth Bader Ginsburg had explained what it actually took to win. "There hasn't been any major change," she said, "in which there wasn't a groundswell among the people before the Supreme Court put its stamp of approval on the inclusion in the equality concept of people who were once left out."

President Obama's words immediately after the decision was announced reflect the same point, reminding me that he is truly a community organizer at heart. Although he acknowledged that our win was the direct result of a Supreme Court ruling, he noted that "it is a consequence of the countless small acts of courage of millions of people across decades who stood up, who came out, talked to parents, parents who loved their children no matter what, folks who were willing to endure bullying and taunts, and stayed strong, and came to believe in themselves and who they were. And slowly made an entire country realize that love is love."

The amount of hard work required to bring about real social change might be frustrating at times, but there are at least three rewards that make such effort so tremendously worthwhile.

First, as President Obama said in those same remarks, "progress on this journey often comes in small increments," but "sometimes there are days like this, when that slow, steady effort is rewarded with justice that arrives like a thunderbolt." Momentum begets momentum, and victories come much more quickly at the end of the larger battle, when that momentum has reached a truly powerful level.

We certainly saw that effect in the marriage movement: although our first victory came in a Hawaii court in the mid-1990s, no state had marriage until our victory in Massachusetts a decade later, and the next victory did not come until California—another four and a half years later. (And that win was subsequently taken away at the ballot.) The New York legislative win, in 2011, gave the movement our sixth state. Then, with public support reaching a majority nationwide, things started moving more quickly. By the end of 2012, we had nine states; by the end of 2013, we had seventeen; and by the end of 2014, we had thirty-five.

The second reward is the deep satisfaction of engaging in the struggle, knowing that you're part of something bigger than yourself, that you're helping move the country in some small way toward a better, freer, more just society. It's impossible to know in advance when the key turning points will come, but the act of working to make progress every day is for me exceedingly satisfying.

So is the act of enlisting others in the work and helping them to find their voices—from couples who discovered the strength to share their lives with lawmakers (and were able to see how their own stories were powerful enough to make a real difference), to business leaders who experienced the satisfaction of lending their power to something so meaningful, to elected officials of both parties who worked through their discomfort, voted our way, then became spokespeople for the cause because they wanted to help bring the country closer to its true values.

For me, it's been especially gratifying to recruit young organizers and campaign staffers into the ranks, something I did along with my partner and field guru Amy Mello for the past eleven years. I'm so proud of having helped hundreds of young organizers and operatives get started in this work, and of seeing so many of them find their voices and blossom. Most went to work in a state marriage campaign, developing strength and courage by sharing their own stories, enlisting others, honing their skills as effective advocates, becoming part of a team. The work they did was challenging physically, emotionally, and financially. I've had organizers who were bitten by dogs, involved in car accidents, chased by cops, and pursued on the street by cursing homophobes. But I cannot think of anyone who's been a part of this work who has regretted having done it.

The third reward is the recognition that, even with difficulties and impediments, America remains a country where profound change can be made by "we the people." The success of the marriage movement should give hope to anyone who doubts that. It certainly gives me the deep and abiding hope that we can create a more perfect union, with liberty and justice—for all!

= = =

Right after the victory, I created a top-ten list of lessons learned that I think are particularly applicable to other social movements.

1. CONVEY A BOLD, INSPIRATIONAL VISION. Identify what you really want to accomplish and communicate that vision early and often. The aspirational possibility of being able to marry spurred hundreds of thousands of regular people to become champions— something a watered-down goal like civil union wouldn't have accomplished. While half-measures along the way are part and parcel of our political system, accepting increments must not preclude reaching the true goal. Remind people and politicians why it matters, and don't settle in the end for anything less.

2. **HAVE AN OVERARCHING STRATEGY.** A strategy maintains focus, provides structure, and is a crucial source of support when the going gets tough. When Evan Wolfson embarked on winning marriage nationwide, he envisioned a pathway to victory that included a national ruling by the US Supreme Court. To get the court to act, however, he knew—based on the lessons of history—that we needed to rack up victories in a critical mass of states and grow public support beyond a majority. That big-picture strategy for marriage was called the "Roadmap to Victory," and it provided a simple (but not easy!) approach that served us well when the going got tough and others questioned whether we were on the right path.

3. **FOCUS ON VALUES AND EMOTIONS.** With a cause that is as fundamentally important to so many people as marriage, it is essential to tap into fundamental values when making your case. We showed straight America that same-sex couples want to marry out of profound love and commitment—which are the same reasons *they* want to! We thus helped them to see that supporting marriage for same-sex couples aligns with their own deep-seated values: respect for the golden rule—treating others the way you'd want to be treated—and for freedom—the right to live the way you want as long as it doesn't hurt anyone else. Tapping into those values was a powerful antidote to the fear-mongering that our opponents employed (that the freedom to marry would harm children, for instance). One mistake that some of our campaigns made along the way was in focusing on messages that polled well but didn't have emotional resonance.

4. **MEET PEOPLE WHERE THEY ARE.** To create lasting change in America, it's crucial to make the case to people who are conflicted about your cause and give them time to really think it through. On marriage, we knew that nearly everyone had grown up in a society where they were taught that marriage was between a man and a woman, and in a faith tradition where they were taught that homosexuality was wrong. Many good people were conflicted, and

we were asking them to take a journey that challenged some of their deepest understandings about marriage, family, and religion. That required engaging with their questions, leaving no question unanswered, and tackling their concerns head-on. To get people to yes, we had to encourage them to open their minds and hearts, to listen, question, and reconsider. That meant starting early, staying with the process, and making the case in multiple ways. A shift like that is much less likely to happen if you write someone off or call someone who isn't with you yet a bigot or bad person.

5. **FIND THE RIGHT MESSENGERS.** The person who delivers the message—and how it is delivered—matter as much as the message itself. The target audience—in this example, conflicted Americans—must identify with and trust the messenger. It was crucial that same-sex couples make their case in person to family members, neighbors, and friends. Over the airwaves, however, it was parents who were most effective. They could speak to their own struggles with accepting a child's sexuality, about their journey to overcome that struggle, and ultimately about wanting their gay kid to have all that they've had, including the right to marry. Straight people could identify and empathize with that story. Unexpected champions—such as Republicans, first responders, service members, and clergy—also were especially effective in explaining and modeling how their own deeply held values of freedom, faith, and service to country fell squarely in line with the freedom to marry.

6. **BUILD STATE CAMPAIGNS DESIGNED TO WIN.** Winning at the state level requires an experienced manager running a professional campaign—with field organizers, communications professionals, and lobbyists—along with a dedicated board helping to raise sufficient resources to carry out the plan. Each campaign must be designed to meet a specific challenge. For example, when we needed to fight against repeal of a freedom-to-marry law in New Hampshire, where the legislature was 80 percent Republican, we built a campaign heavy on GOP operatives and business leaders.

7. **INVEST HEAVILY IN LOCAL ORGANIZING.** Inspiring and mobilizing supporters—then enlisting them to persuade other voters and elected officials—takes a robust organizing campaign. On challenging issues, advocates too often think they can convince a legislature simply by using top-notch lobbyists, or can win at the ballot box merely by deploying good television ads. That's simply not the case. The most effective way to persuade lawmakers and voters is to let them hear from local people—from ordinary citizens to influential leaders—living in their own communities. On marriage, it was especially crucial to show that we were talking about same-sex couples and families who are active participants in their own communities, not "those people out there in the big city."

8. **ACCEPT THIS REALITY: POLITICIANS CARE ABOUT RE-ELECTION ABOVE ALMOST EVERYTHING ELSE.** The most important priority for the vast majority of elected officials is continuing to be an elected official. That means that if elected officials think they're going to lose their seats by supporting your cause, you're going to lose first. So you need to be relentless about engaging electorally. First and foremost, that means helping to ensure that those who vote with you win re-election. In the first marriage state of Massachusetts, we re-elected every incumbent who voted our way—195 out of 195 in both 2004 and 2006—in spite of concerted efforts by Governor Mitt Romney and other social conservatives to defeat some of them. And there's simply no better way to show lawmakers you're serious than by defeating at least a small number who vote against you. That means figuring out who is vulnerable, finding quality candidates to run against them, and using tried-and-true campaign techniques to defeat them. Fight Back New York, a PAC that marriage-equality advocates set up in 2010, did just that. It took out three incumbents who voted against us on marriage and completely changed the political calculus in New York State.

9. **BE SERIOUS ABOUT REACHING ACROSS THE AISLE.** In today's terribly divided political climate, it's extremely helpful—and in

many cases essential—for the cause to be bipartisan. On issues that began as liberal or progressive causes, it's especially important to have Republican voices making the case. Doing so effectively means years of dedicated and serious work, demonstrating to sympathetic Republicans that you're serious about enlisting them, sensitive to their political concerns, and committed to helping them in a way that serves both your needs and theirs. When trying to shift the political center of gravity on marriage, having Rob Portman, Laura Bush, and Dick Cheney speak out was worth its weight in gold.

10. **BUILD MOMENTUM EVERY DAY.** A cause is either moving forward or backward. At the heart of my job as the national campaign director for Freedom to Marry was figuring out how to grow momentum every single day. That meant being consistently creative and nimble in identifying opportunities to move the ball forward, and in building a narrative that our campaign was succeeding. So whether it's enlisting a Fortune 500 company or a new Republican member of Congress, amplifying the results of a public-opinion poll that demonstrates growth in support, focusing attention on a winning streak in court, or going on television with a new ad campaign, connecting real accomplishments to a compelling and cohesive narrative demonstrates that you're continuing to move toward your goals. An especially crucial element of building momentum is conveying optimism—even in the face of defeat. You have to remind your base and opinion leaders that you *can* do this by highlighting the wins, large and small, that the campaign has already secured, while continuing to point toward the end result that you seek.

ACKNOWLEDGMENTS

In writing this book, I'm thankful to my agent, Esmond Harmsworth of Zachary Shuster Harmsworth, a longtime friend and supporter of the cause who put real care into helping me with this project. Thanks to Molly Shapiro, a talented writer and lifelong friend, who gave the book a careful copyedit and provided tremendous feedback when I needed it the most. Thanks to Julie Bolcer, a former reporter for the *Advocate*, who conducted a number of interviews and wrote drafts of the New York section of the book. Thanks to my dear friend Carl Sciortino, with whom I've walked this battle for the freedom to marry for the last decade, for providing such great feedback on the book and especially for his tremendous friendship. I'm thankful to Adam Teicholz for his generosity in giving this a close read, as well as for his friendship and nourishment. Thanks to my lifelong friend Jamie Metzl for his guidance, to Ian Shin for his thoughtful read and constructive ideas, and to Andy Cohen for a careful proofread. Thank you to my editor at University Press of New England, Stephen Hull, for helping give the book focus and shape. Thanks to Marilyn Humphries for allowing me the use of her wonderful photos of the Massachusetts marriage battles.

Thank you to John Henning and Mike Roth, who together directed the terrific 2006 documentary *Saving Marriage* about the battles in Massachusetts. They were extremely generous in sharing transcripts of literally dozens of interviews they did for the film.

Thanks to Governor Deval Patrick for writing such a generous foreword, for championing our cause, and for showing us all that you can lead and govern from the heart.

There are so many amazing colleagues with whom I've worked over thirteen years in this movement to whom I have such deep appreciation. In Massachusetts, I'm thankful to Josh Friedes, Valerie and Jackie Fein-Zachary, Robert Debenedictis, Claire Humphrey and Vickie Henry, Robyn Maguire, Sue Hyde, Robyn Ochs, Jeremy Pittman, Scott Gortikov, Melissa Threadgill, Karen Wheeler, Emily Bruno, Julie Verratti, Matt O'Malley, Ryan Brown, Chris Mason, Jesse Sullivan, Gary Buseck, David Wilson, Julie Goodridge, Hillary Goodridge, Ron Ansin, Steve and Barbara Grossman, Doug Hattaway, Mary Breslauer, Amy Hunt, Sara

Whitman, Peter Hams, John Affuso, Arline Isaacson, Norma Shapiro, and Holly Gunner.

Elsewhere in New England, I'm grateful to Anne Stanback, Beth Robinson, Betsy Smith, Liz Purdy, Craig Stowell, Lew Feldstein, Ray Sullivan, and Brett Smiley.

In California, I want to thank Geoff Kors, who is one of the most creative advocacy minds I know, as well as Jim Carroll, Vaishalee Raja, Shumway Marshall, Joseph Arroyo, Mike Ai, and Suzy Jack.

I want to thank the tremendous team at Freedom to Marry: Thalia Zepatos, Michael Crawford, Jo Deutsch, Richard Carlbom, Thomas Wheatley, Shawn Werner, Scott Davenport, Sean Eldridge, Angela Dallara, Tyler Deaton, Cameron Tolle, Jackie Yodashkin, Nicole Collins Bronzan, Juan Barajas, Kevin Nix, Christian Olveira, Adam Polaski, Michel Dubois, Sarah Moeller, and many more.

I'm also so grateful for these colleagues and partners with whom I've worked so closely: Jamie Citron, Brian Bond, Gautam Raghavan, Ken Mehlman, Margaret Hoover, Jeff Cook, Amy Simon, Joel Benenson, Zach Silk, Annie Dickerson, Lisa Goodman, Mark Purpura, Steven Goldstein, Tom Wilson, Jeanine Larue, Josh Zeitz, Troy Stevenson, Michael Premo, Lynne Bowman, Dave Horwich, Jim Bennett, Bernard Cherkasov, Ross Levi, Mike Avella, Emily Giske, Jennifer Cunningham, Stefan Friedman, Brian Ellner, Josh Meltzer, Sarah Kennedy, Kate Kendell, Shannon Minter, Camilla Taylor, James Esseks, Selene Kaye, Robbie Kaplan, Janson Wu, Kirk Fordham, Sarah Vaughn, Chris Cormier, Michael Fleming, Tim Sweeney, Matt Foreman, Patrick Flaherty, Rea Carey, and Brad Sears.

There are so many lawmakers who have been stalwart champions, in Massachusetts and elsewhere. I wish I could thank them all by name. Unfortunately, that would be impossible. But you know who you are!

I am especially grateful to the many, many couples, families, LGBT individuals, and straight allies who have made the case for marriage to neighbors, family members, friends, and lawmakers, who have put in endless hours of volunteering, and who have contributed dollars until it hurt. You have made this movement!

There are a few extremely close partners in this work who have been key supports over the course of many years. Marty Rouse, who first headed up MassEquality, was a great mentor who taught me so much about the kind of relentlessness and persistence it takes to win these fights. GLAD's Lee Swislow was a great personal support and coach to me when I took the helm of MassEquality, and a trusted and wise partner in the work. Patrick Guerriero has been a mentor, support, and friend every step of the past thirteen years, as well as one of the wisest strategists I know. Amy Mello has been the fiercest, most loyal, and most effective and creative field leader and partner in the work. Matt McTighe is a steely and determined leader, a skilled strategist, and a great friend. And Bill Smith is a friend with integrity whose political judgment I trust and value so much.

There was one experience in my life that truly changed its trajectory and guided me into the marriage struggle: my participation in the Rockefeller Foundation's Next Generation Leadership program. Several from this group are still some of the closest friends and supports I have. Los Angeles Mayor Eric Garcetti has been an anchor, a close friend, and wise counselor. So has Dan Gross, who now runs the Brady Center to Prevent Gun Violence. Same with Otho Kerr, Steven Patrick, Jason Scott, and Omar Wasow. The rest would be if I saw them more often! The late Ingrid Washinawatok, a champion of indigenous people's rights, was always a profound inspiration. And I'm grateful to Jacqueline Novogratz, who directed the Rockefeller program, for selecting me and creating something so powerful.

I am incredibly thankful to my family for their love and support, both in my work and in everything else. My sister Laura is always the first to "like" my Facebook posts and kvell to others about my work. I am so proud of her and lucky to have her in my life. The apples of my eye, my nieces Madeline and Zoe, are simply the greatest, most sensitive, and loving young people I could ever hope to have in my life. My brother-in-law Chuck, the man in their house, puts up with our larger family with grace and tremendous generosity. My father, Mel Solomon, is the kind of Dad who takes pride in calling the Boy Scouts and Chick-fil-A to give them a piece of his mind about their antigay policies. My Mom, the late Linda Zackler Solomon, was super-proud of me and my work and loved volunteering at Pride wearing her "Mom Knows" pin. There's no question that my zeal to fight for justice was sparked and inspired by both my mom and dad and I'm grateful for it.

I also thank my dear friend and soul mate, the late Alex Hivoltze-Jimenez. Alex was a rock and anchor to me, a queer activist who challenged me to my core—and loved me to my core. I will always love him, and he will live within me, and through me, always.

Finally, to the two people to whom I dedicate the book, Mary Bonauto and Evan Wolfson: there are many visionaries out there, but there are very few who keep their eyes on that vision for many years and fight with wisdom, courage, and determination to overcome enormous obstacles and make it happen. What a great lesson. On behalf of us all, thank you.

Lecture Notes in Computer Science

Edited by G. Goos, J. Hartmanis and J.

Advis

Springer
Berlin
Heidelberg
New York
Barcelona
Budapest
Hong Kong
London
Milan
Paris
Santa Clara
Singapore
Tokyo